AF395942

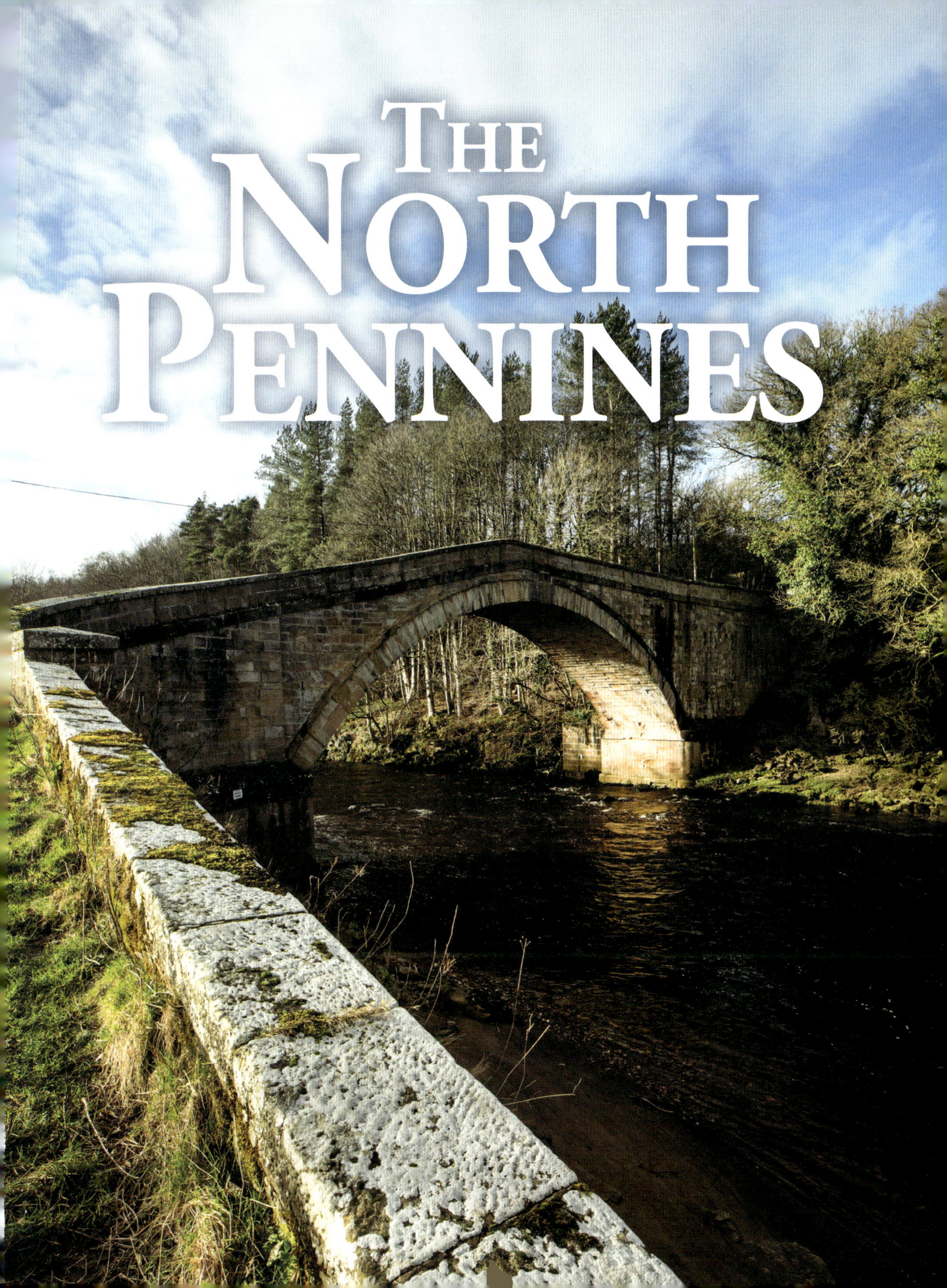

The North Pennines

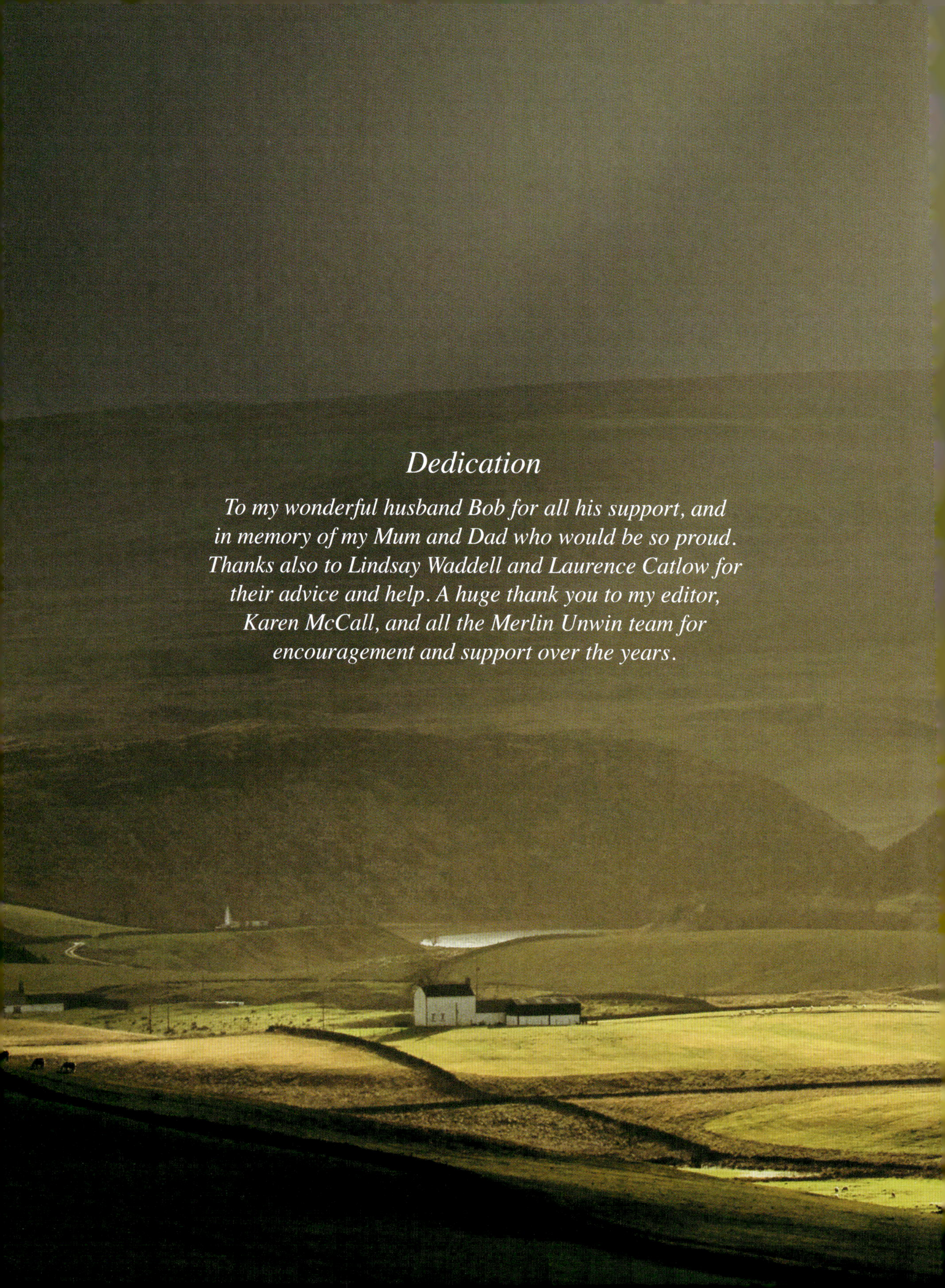

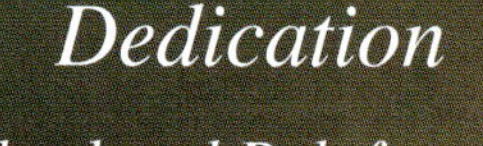

Dedication

*To my wonderful husband Bob for all his support, and
in memory of my Mum and Dad who would be so proud.
Thanks also to Lindsay Waddell and Laurence Catlow for
their advice and help. A huge thank you to my editor,
Karen McCall, and all the Merlin Unwin team for
encouragement and support over the years.*

THE NORTH PENNINES

HELEN SHAW

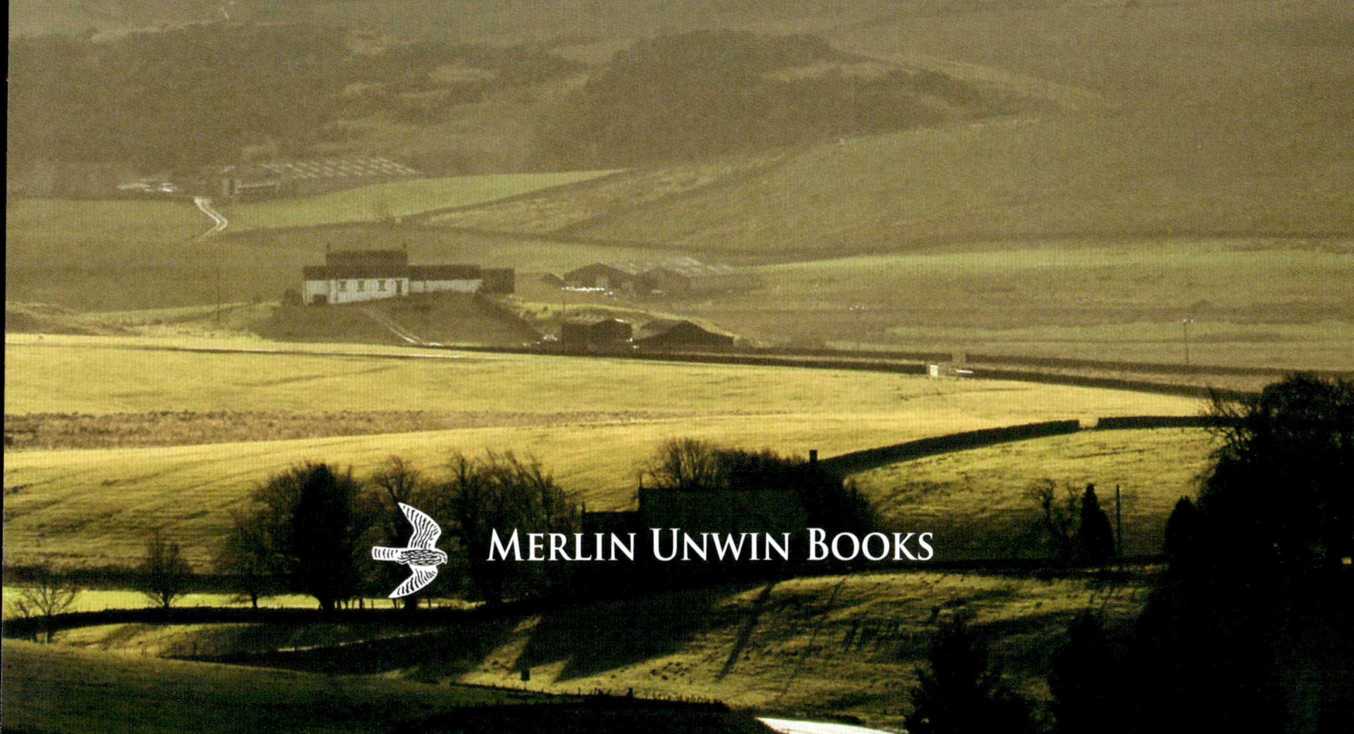

MERLIN UNWIN BOOKS

First published in Great Britain by Merlin Unwin Books Ltd, 2024
Photographs © Helen Shaw 2024
Text © Helen Shaw 2024

Merlin Unwin Books Ltd
Palmers House
Ludlow
Shropshire SY8 1DB
www.merlinunwin.co.uk

The author asserts the moral right to be identified with this work.
ISBN 978-1-913159-69-6
Edited, designed and typeset in Times 12pt by Merlin Unwin Books
Printed by Bell & Bain Ltd, UK

About the photographer

Helen Shaw lives in the North Pennines on a remote hillside south of Garrigill, Cumbria. Her photographs have featured in *The Times*, *Manchester Evening News*, *This England*, *Cumbria Life*, *Westmoreland Gazette*, *The Scots magazine*, *Northern Life*, and countless other magazines and newspapers all across northern England. Her previous photographic books have earned her a strong following: *The Forest of Bowland, Land's End to John O'Groats, The Pennines, String of Pearls (Lake District)*. This is her fifth book of landscape photography and her first one focussing entirely on her home of the North Pennines. A keen walker and lover of wild and lonely places, she is married to Bob Shelmerdine who shares her passion for the outdoors.

Cover photos: Blasted tree, Barhaugh Common, Northumberland
Page 1: Featherstone Bridge over the River South Tyne on the road to Kellah is a Grade II listed structure built in 1775.*
Pages 2-3: Upper Teesdale seen from the road between St John's Chapel in Weardale and Langdon Beck

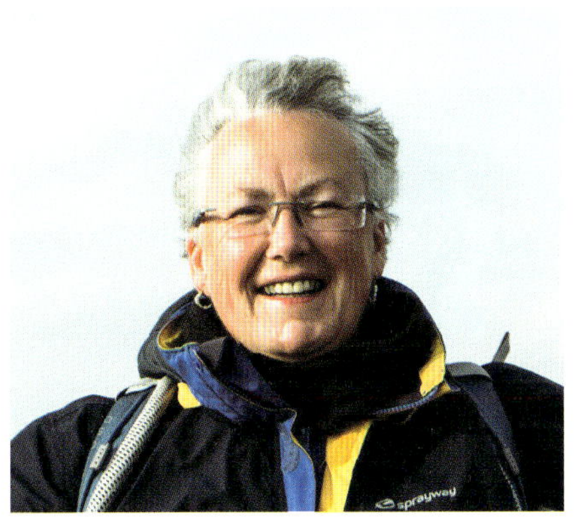

A few weeks ago, I went out for a walk on a sunny Saturday and discovered a part of the North Pennines I knew nothing about. It was quite a shock to find, only a few miles from where I live, an outstanding 14th century castle, the remains of a huge WWII prisoner of war camp, and a quirkily beautiful 18th century bridge over the River South Tyne. And that's my point. Wherever you go in this area, the North Pennines will deliver unexpected delights and landscapes that surprise you. From world class Roman remains, to more recent industrial and mining archaeology, from unspoilt, lonely moors which are home to rare and special flora and fauna, to some of Britain's finest rivers and waterfalls, from beautiful little towns and villages nestled among high fells, to its remarkable geology, this National Landscape (formerly known as an Area of Outstanding Natural Beauty) is waiting to be discovered.

The North Pennines cover some 770 square miles from Mallerstang on the fringes of the Yorkshire Dales, north to Hadrian's Wall on the Whin Sill in Northumberland, west to Cumbria and the Eden Valley and as far east as the outskirts of Consett and Bishop Auckland in County Durham. Cross Fell is the highest point of the entire Pennine range at 2,930 feet, High Force in Teesdale is England's biggest waterfall, the area is home to 80% of England's black grouse population, and more than 35% of the land is designated as Sites of Special Scientific Interest. The North Pennines are an important haven for rare arctic alpine plants, red squirrels, otters and wading birds such as lapwing, curlew, oystercatchers, golden plover and snipe. 40% of Britain's upland hay meadows can be found here, as can 30% of England's upland heathland and 27% of its blanket bog. In these times of serious climate change this area is a vital source of carbon storage in peat bogs.

It has been said that this area is England's last wilderness and no amount of statistics about the importance and diversity of the area can describe the impact that these vast areas of empty and unspoilt land have on our well-being. Breathing clean air, being completely alone, being at one with nature: all this is here in the North Pennines.

This book celebrates in photography everything that is so special about the North Pennines. I live here, and love living here. I hope that my photographs do justice to this amazing and unique place.

Helen Shaw, 2024

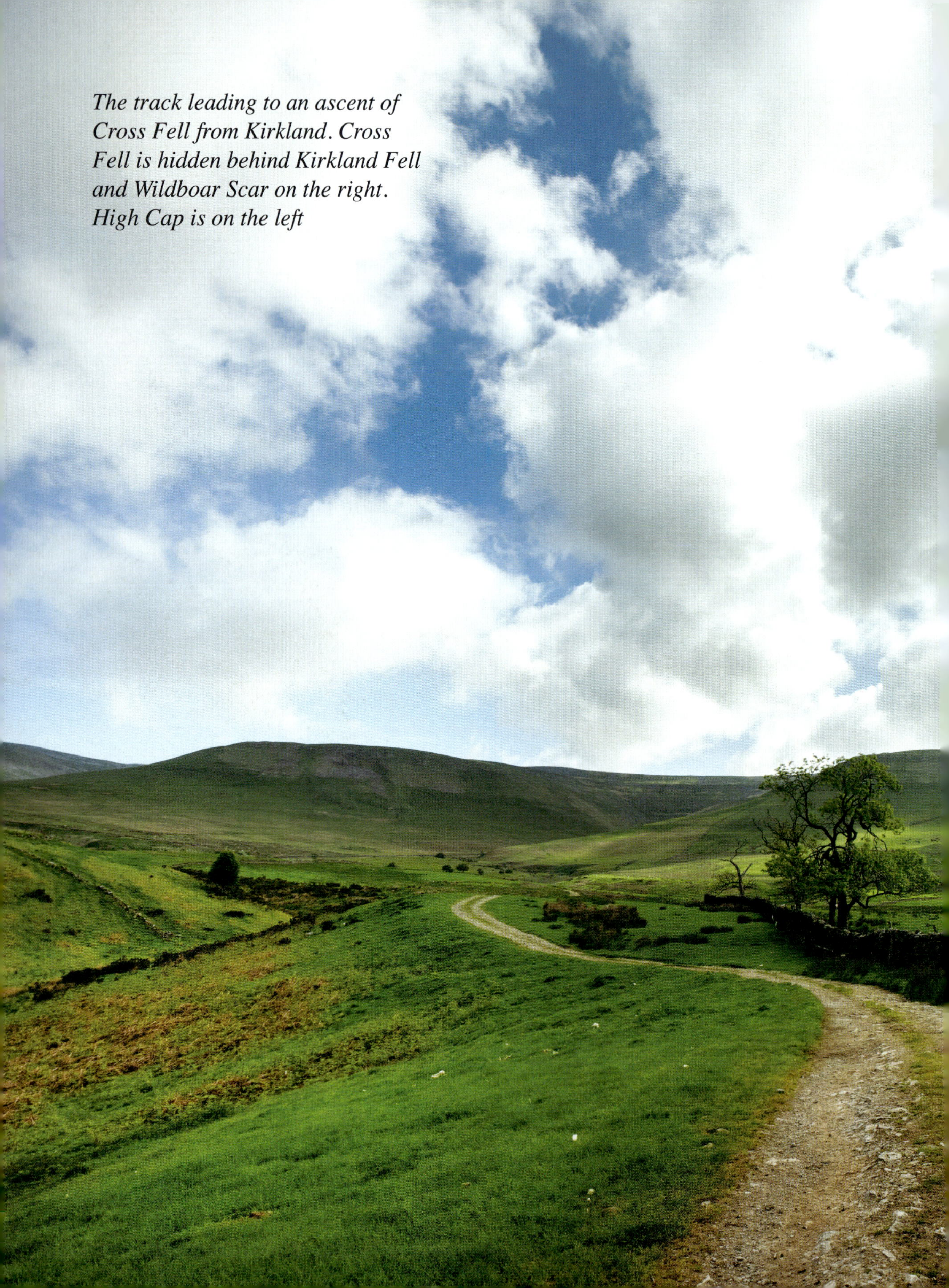

The track leading to an ascent of
Cross Fell from Kirkland. Cross
Fell is hidden behind Kirkland Fell
and Wildboar Scar on the right.
High Cap is on the left

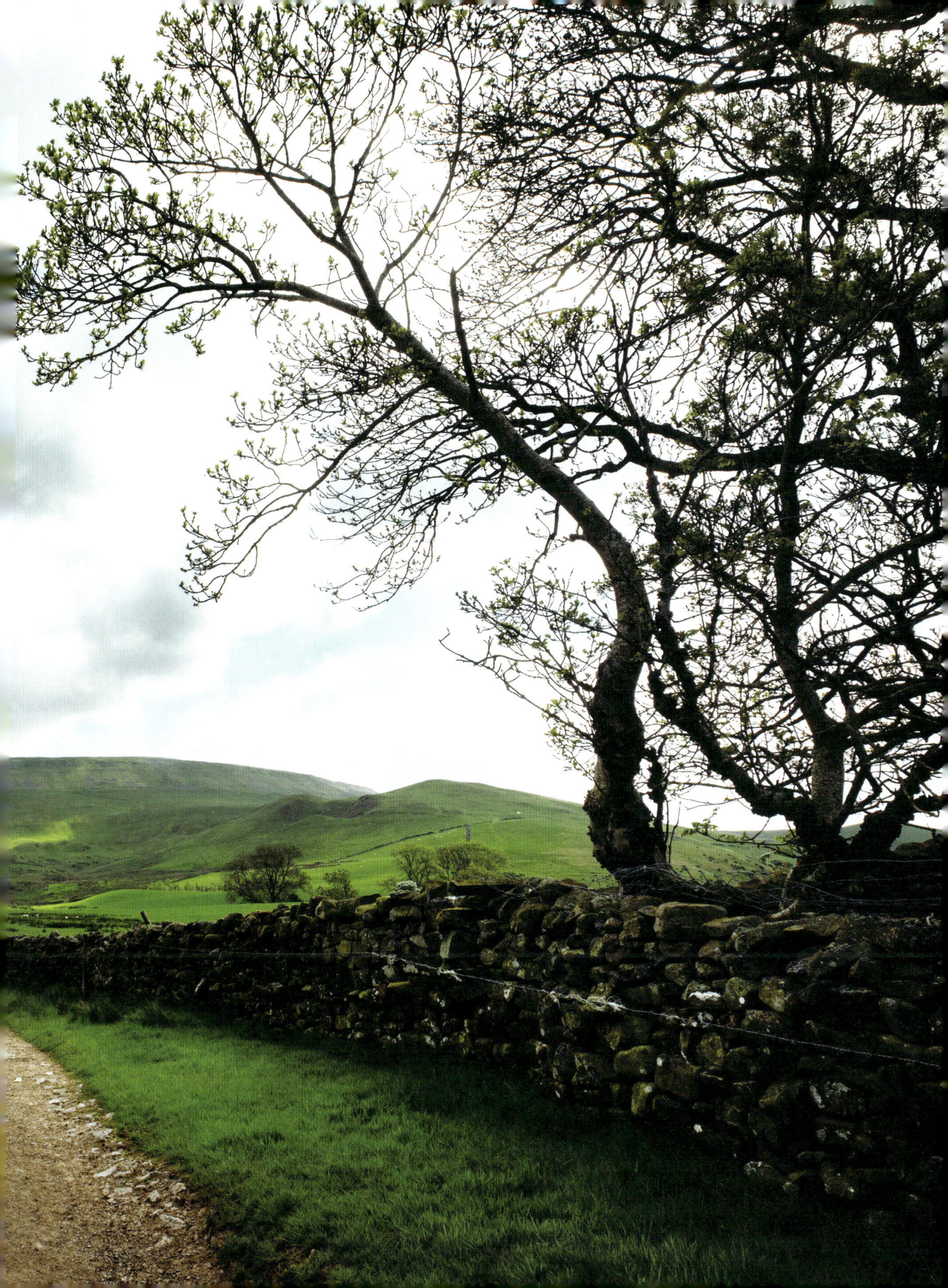

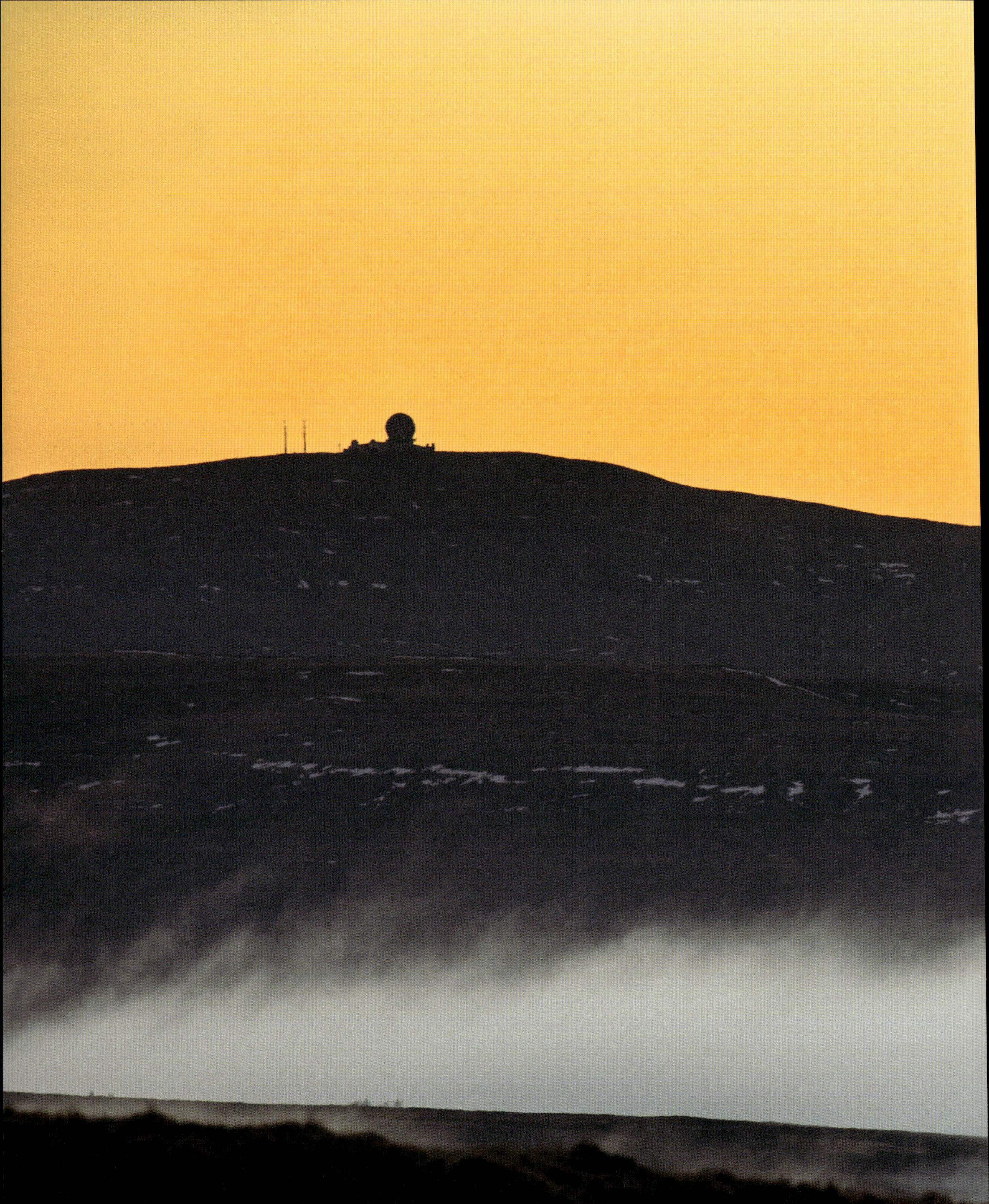

The National Air Traffic Services radar station on
the summit of Great Dun Fell, 2,782 feet, taken
from the watershed between Tynedale and Teesdale

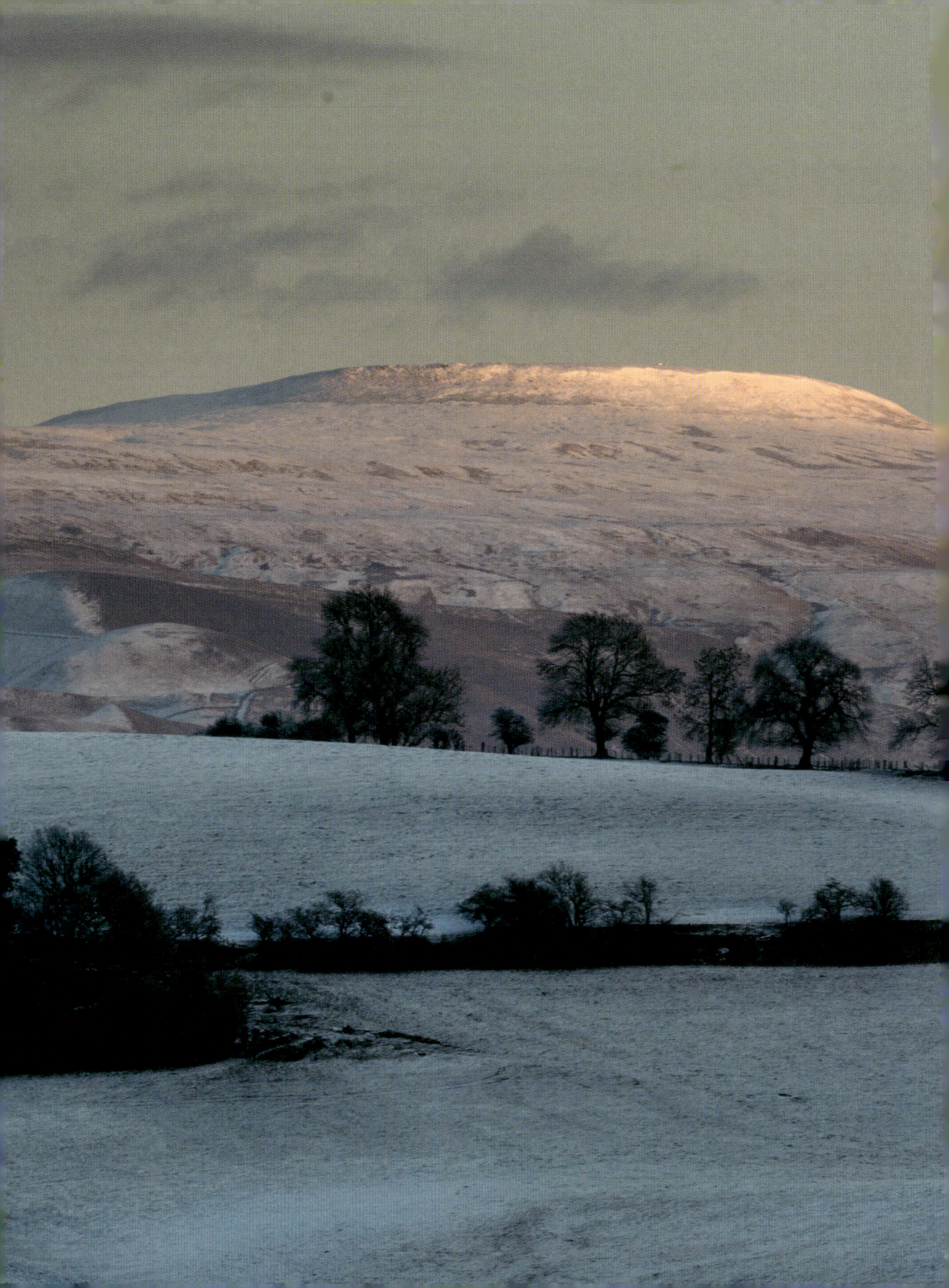

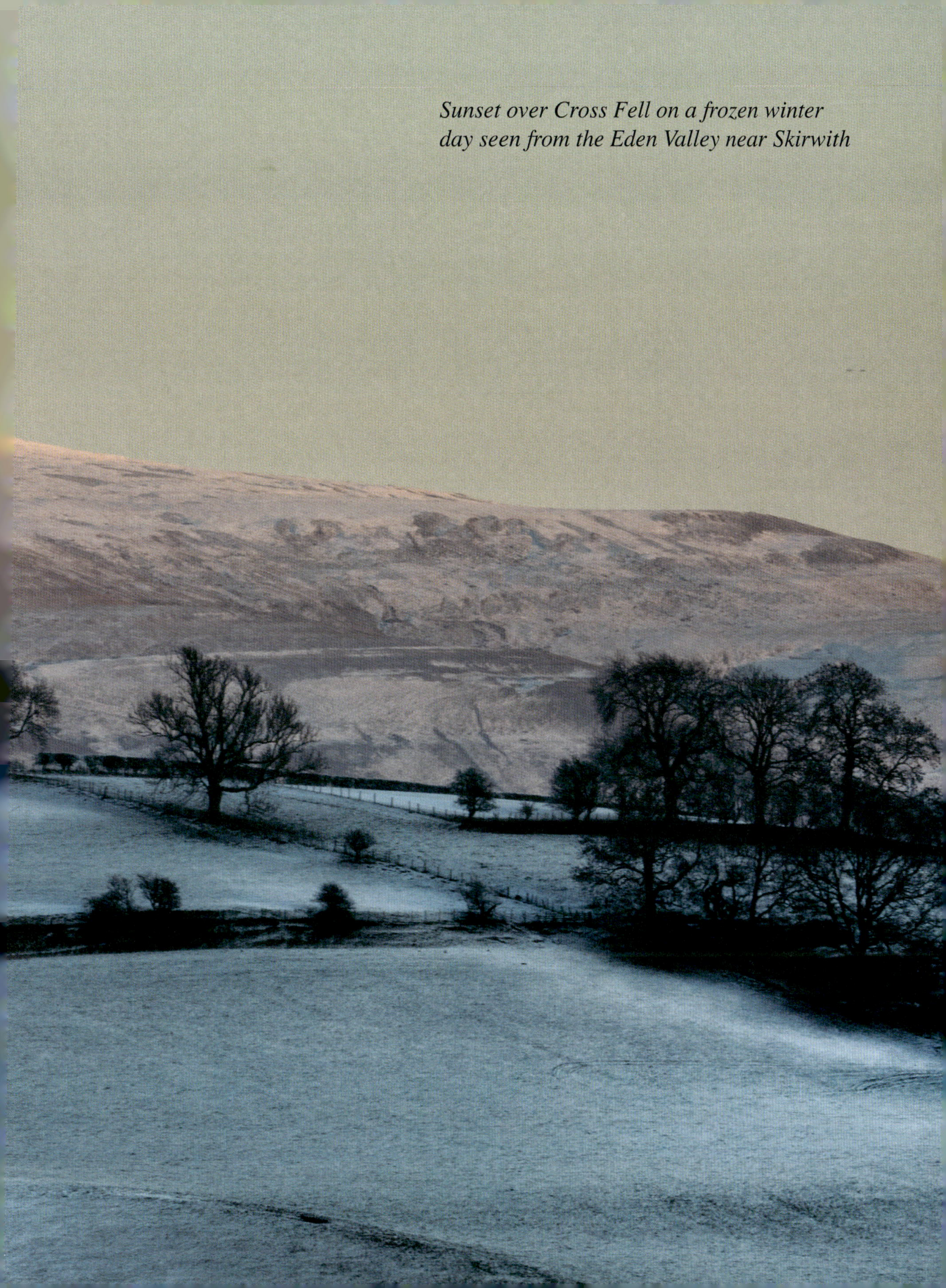

Sunset over Cross Fell on a frozen winter day seen from the Eden Valley near Skirwith

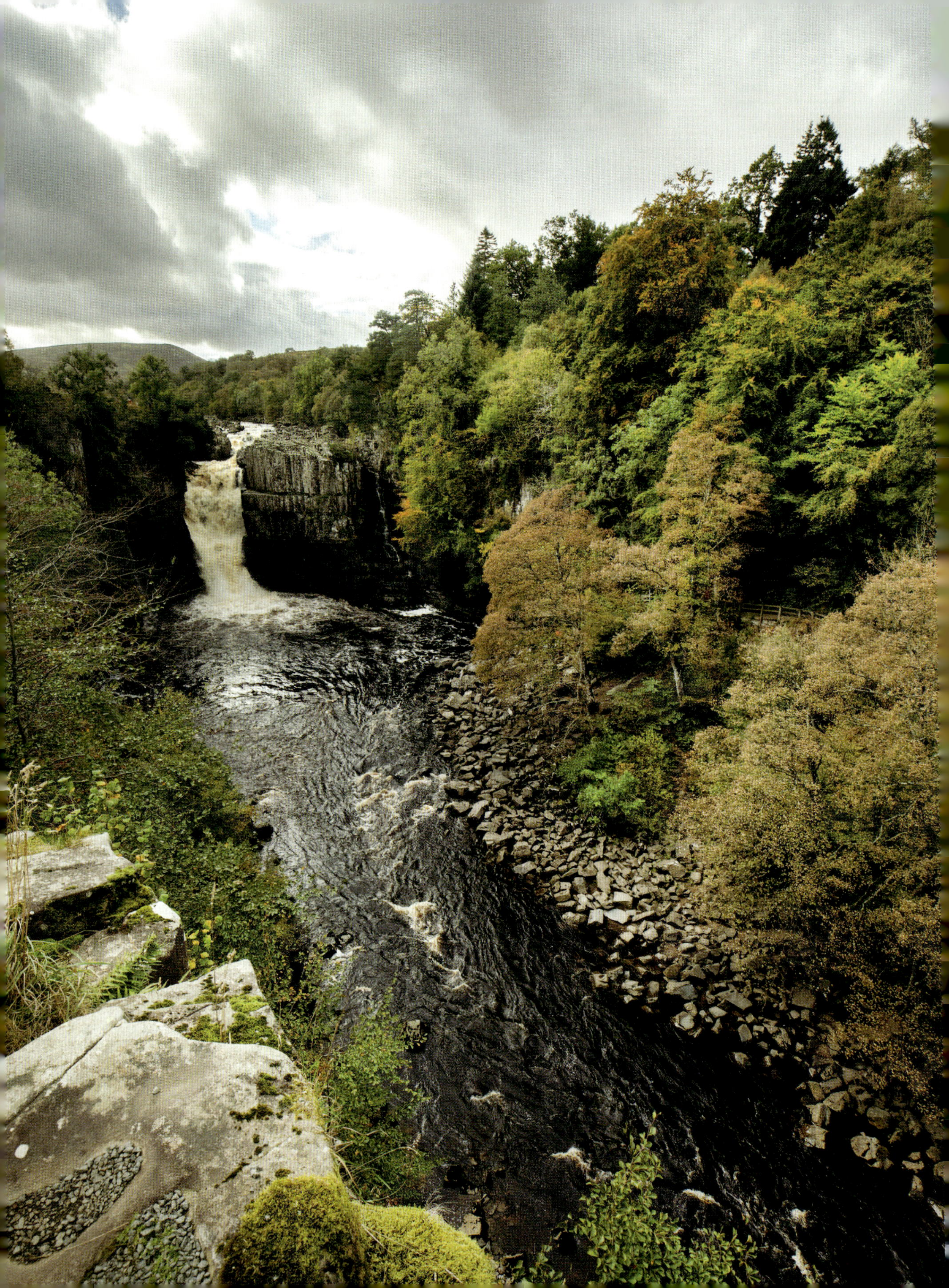

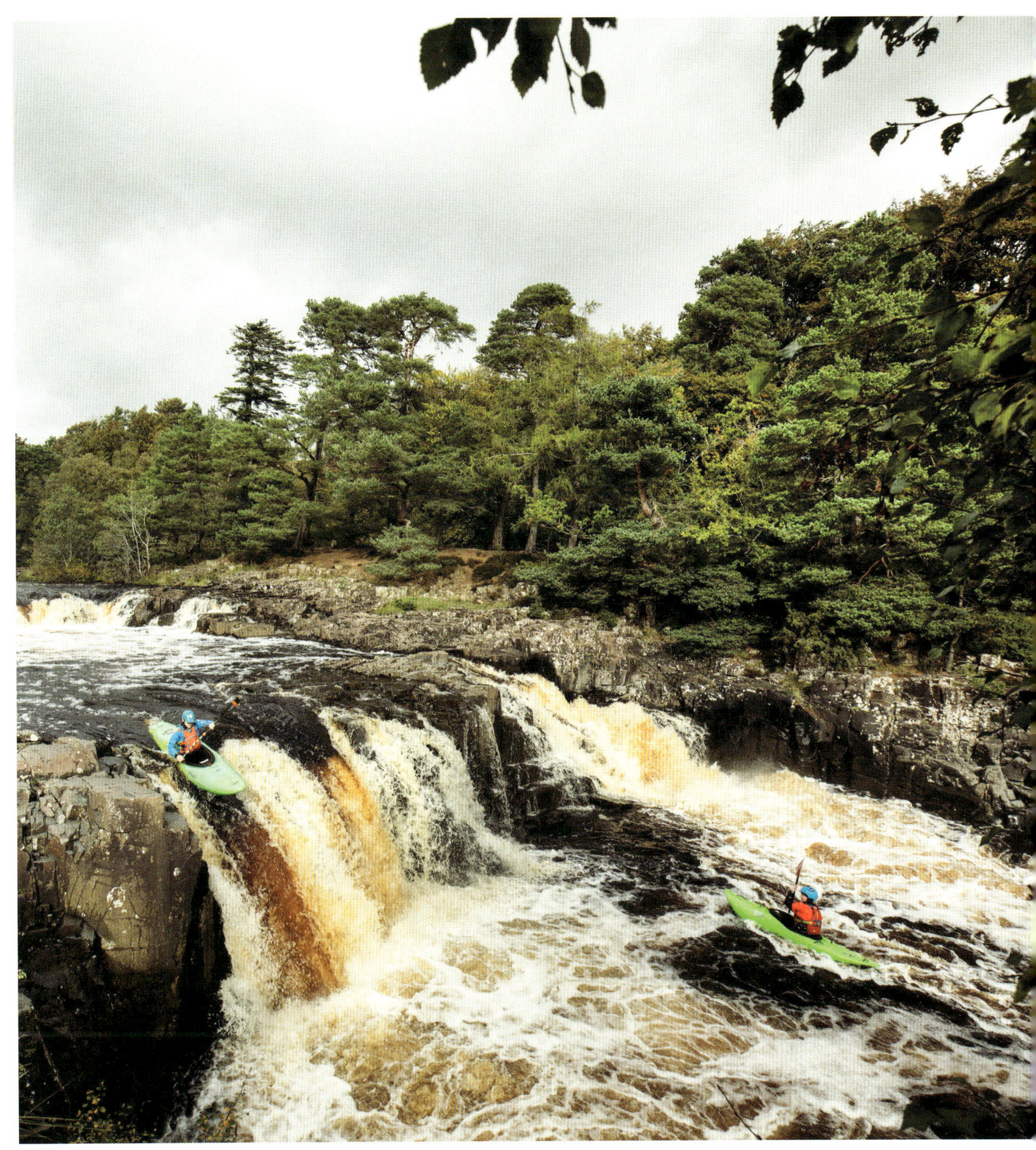

Above: Kayakers on the waterfalls at Low Force, River Tees

Left: High Force, one of the most spectacular waterfalls in England, on the River Tees, as seen from the Pennine Way. The waterfalls are in Forest-in-Teesdale, County Durham

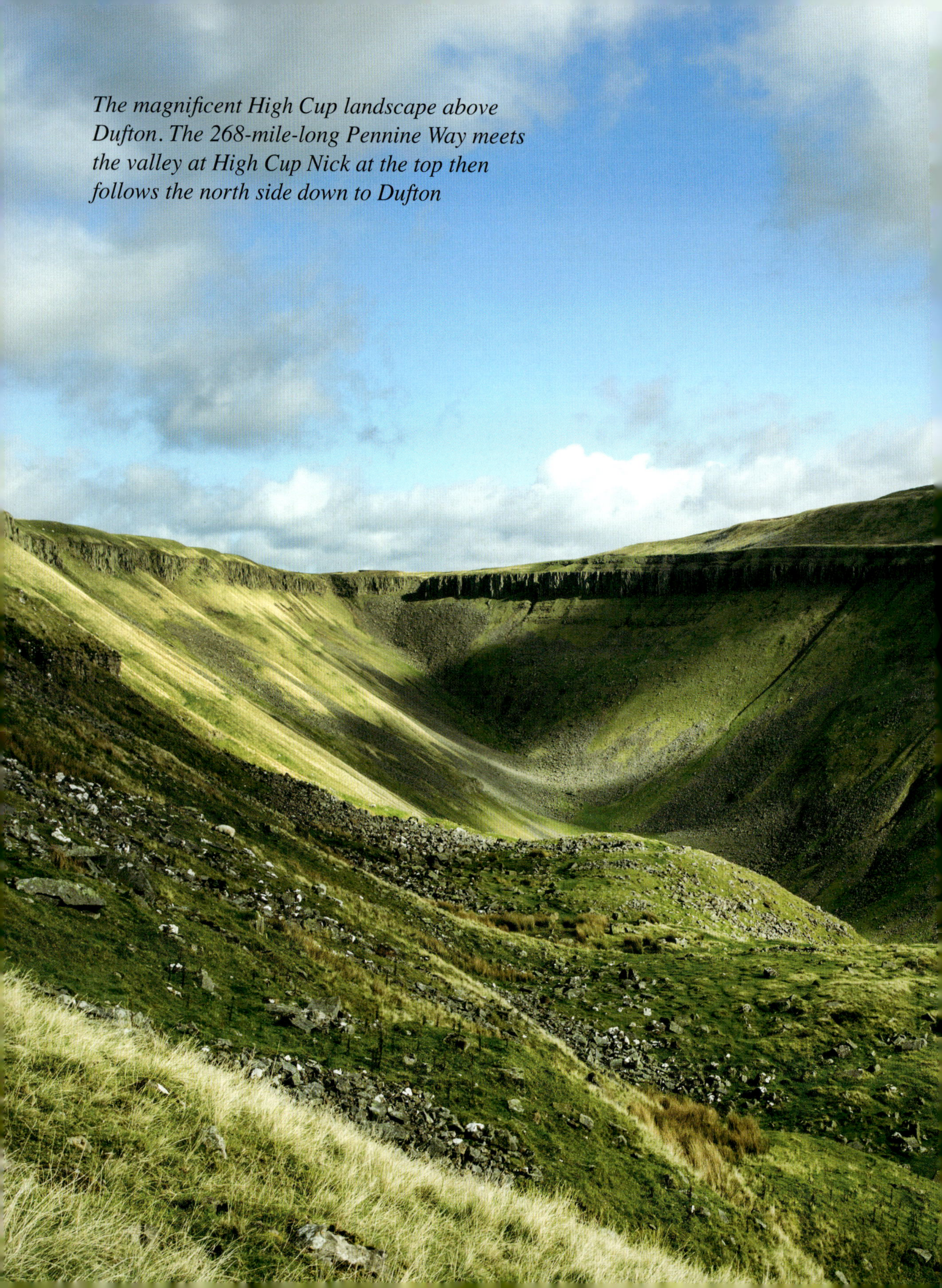

The magnificent High Cup landscape above
Dufton. The 268-mile-long Pennine Way meets
the valley at High Cup Nick at the top then
follows the north side down to Dufton

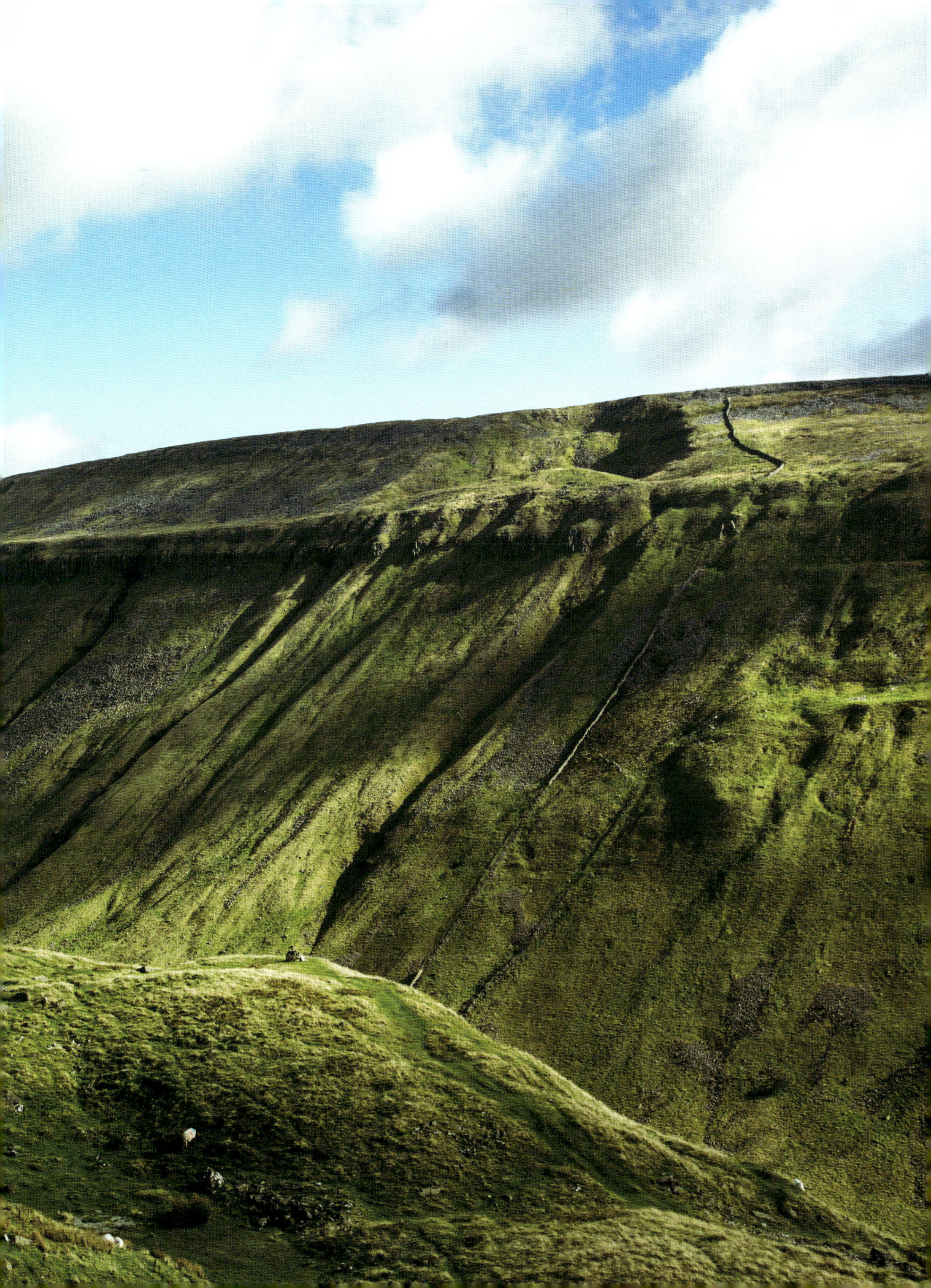

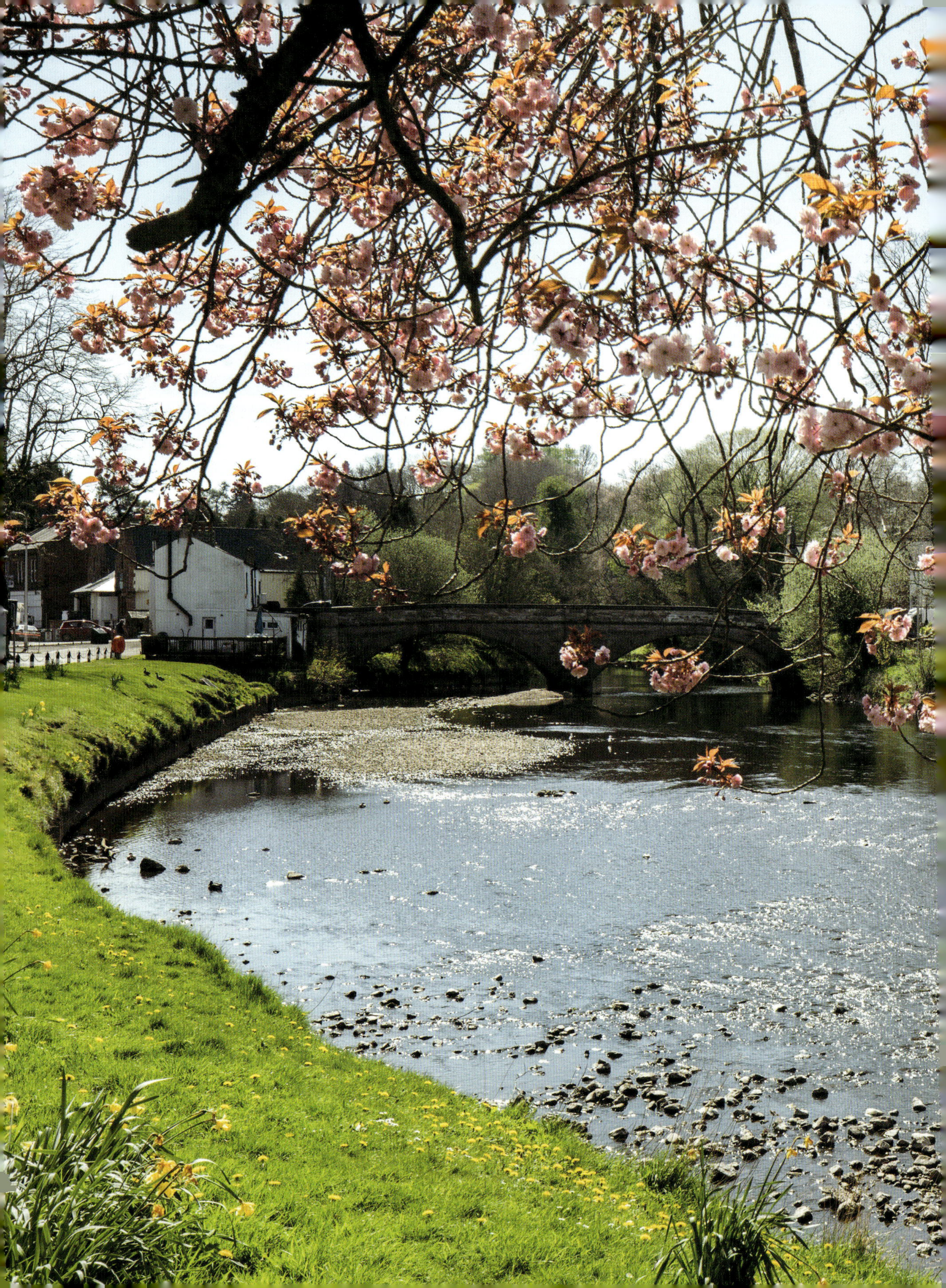

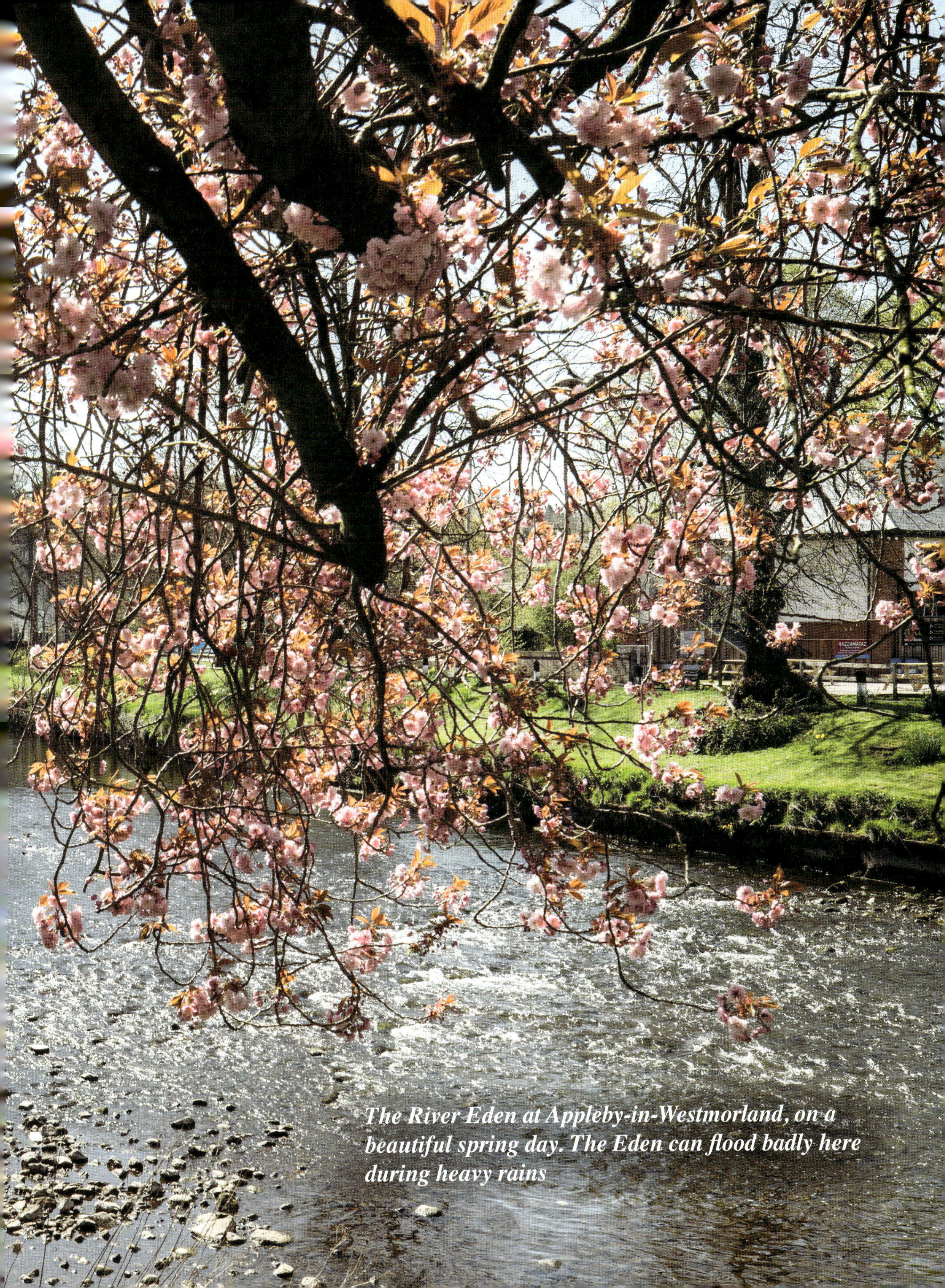

The River Eden at Appleby-in-Westmorland, on a beautiful spring day. The Eden can flood badly here during heavy rains

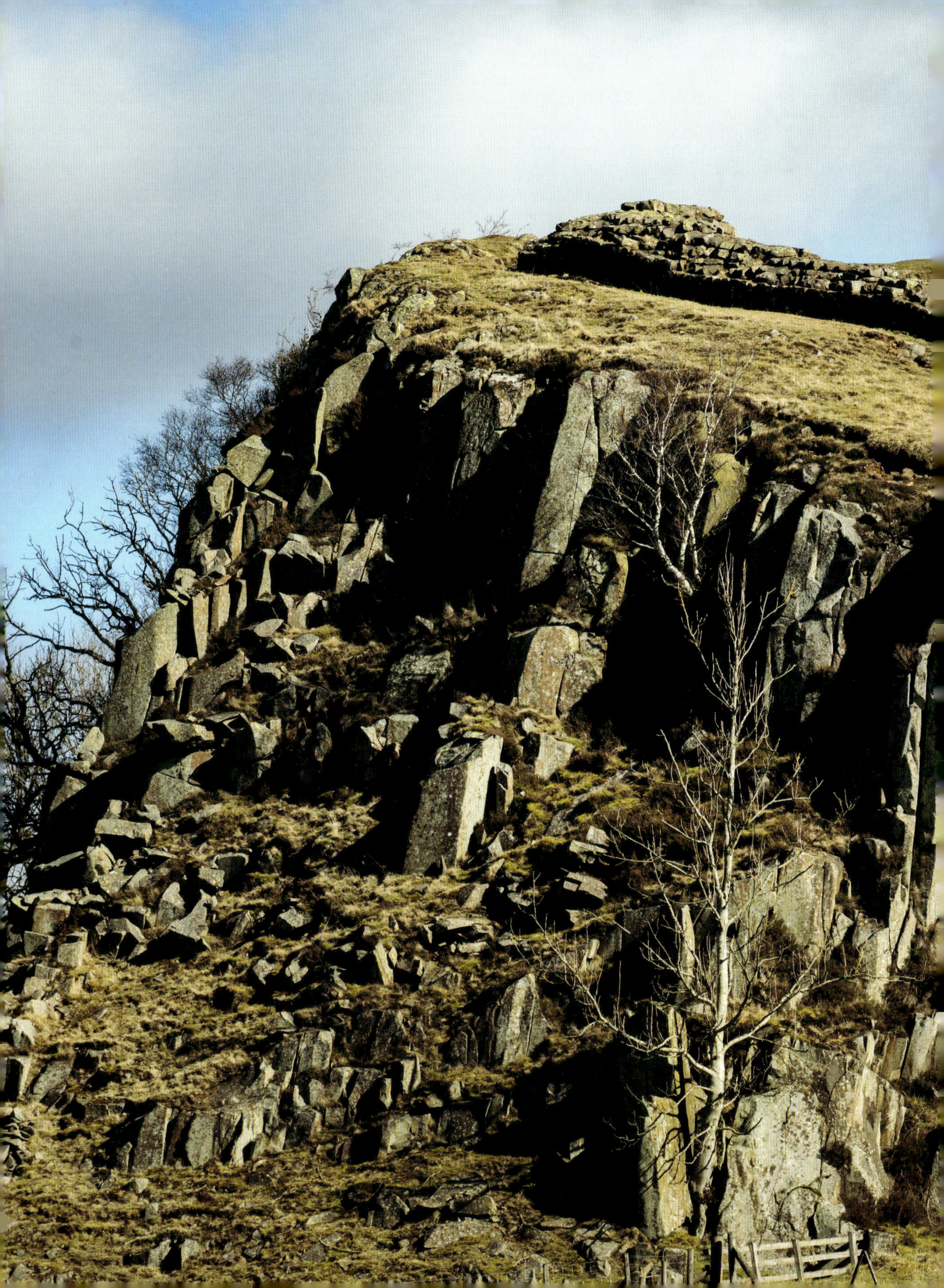

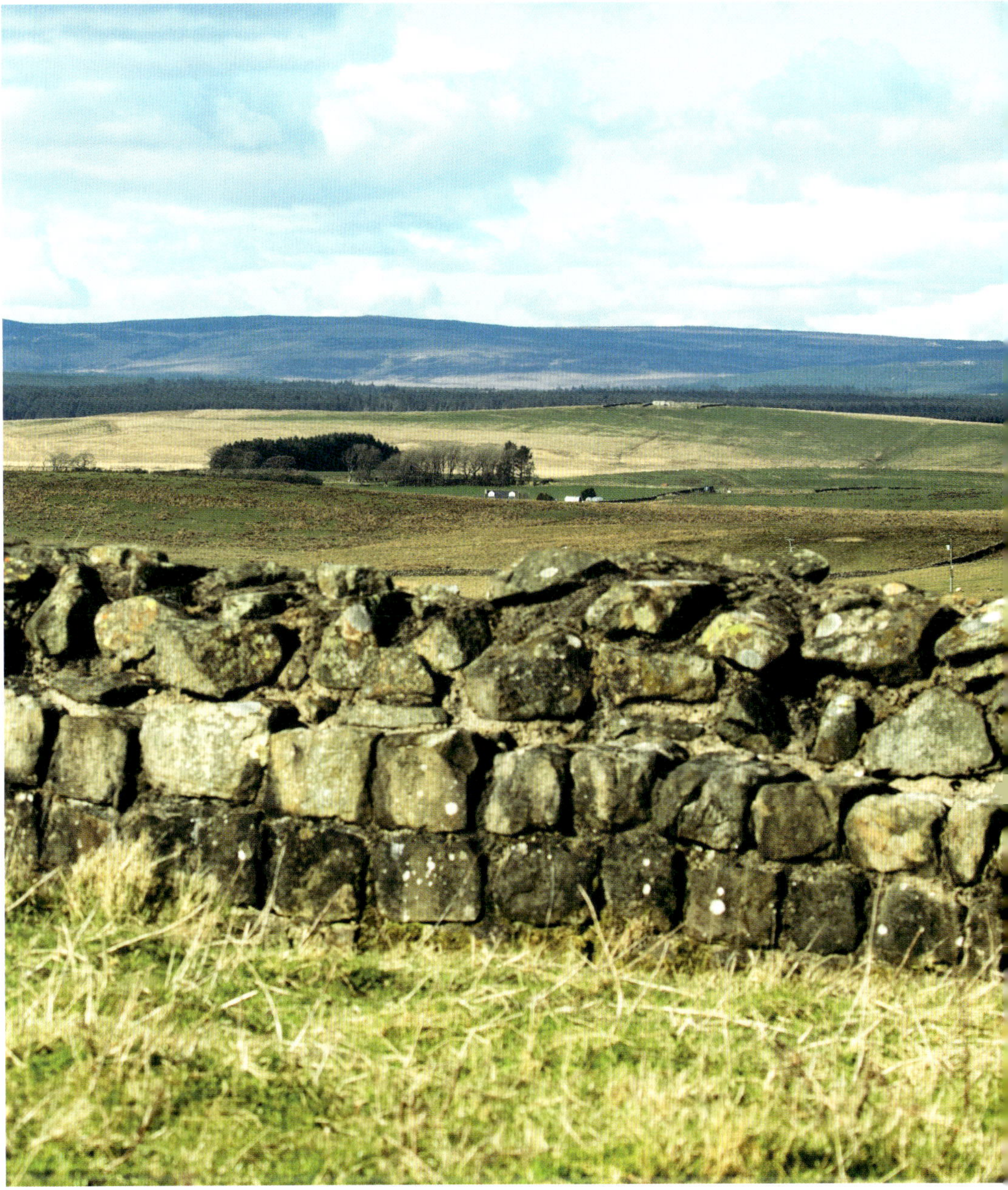

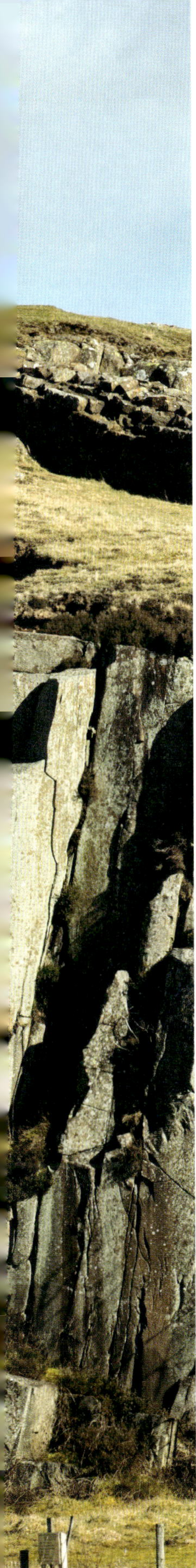

Above: Hadrian's Wall, begun in AD22, looking north towards the land of the tribes it was built to keep out

Left: Hadrian's Wall atop the rocks of the Whin Sill near Walltown Quarry. The wall marked the north-west frontier of the Roman Empire for nearly 300 years

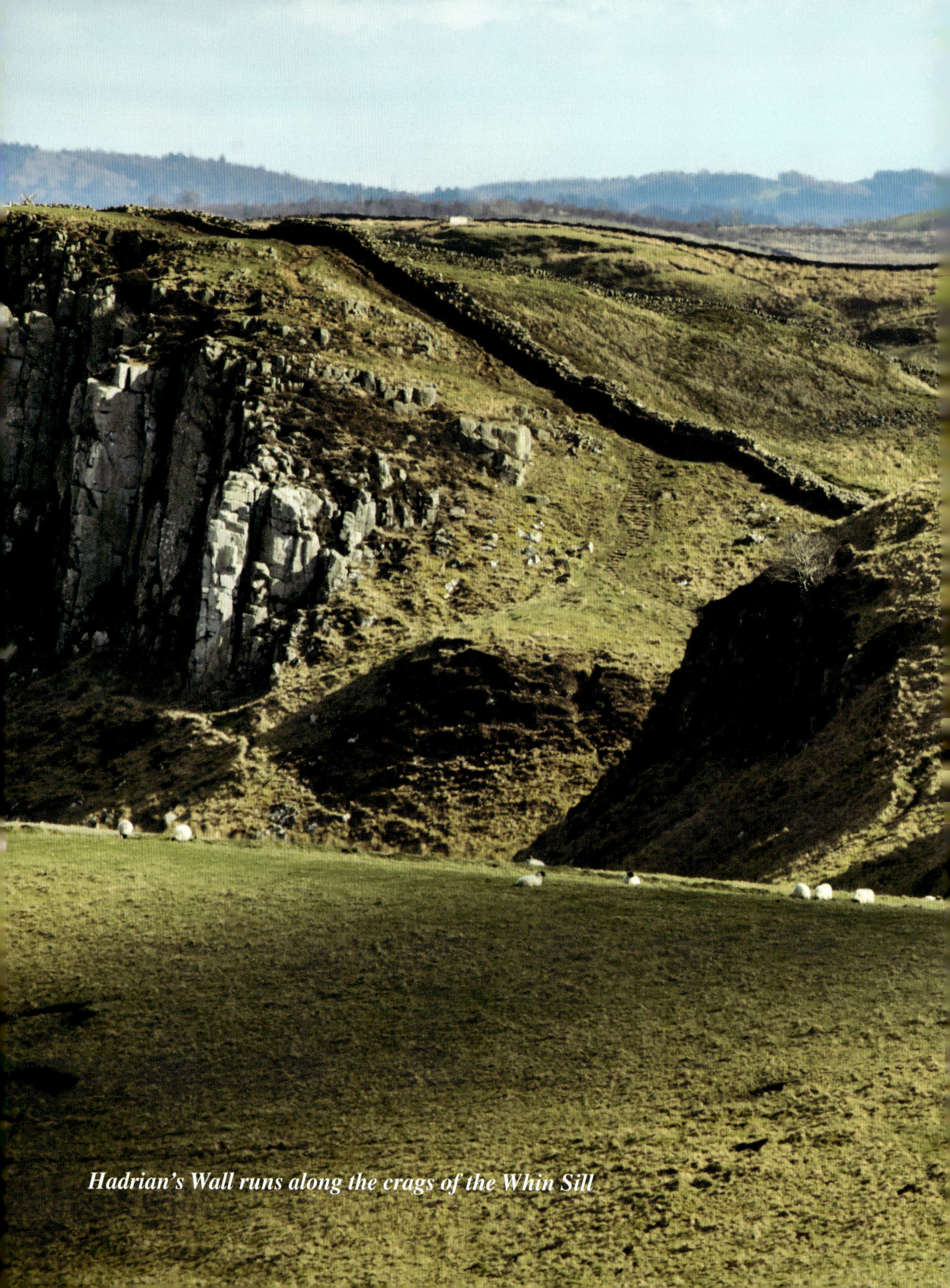

Hadrian's Wall runs along the crags of the Whin Sill

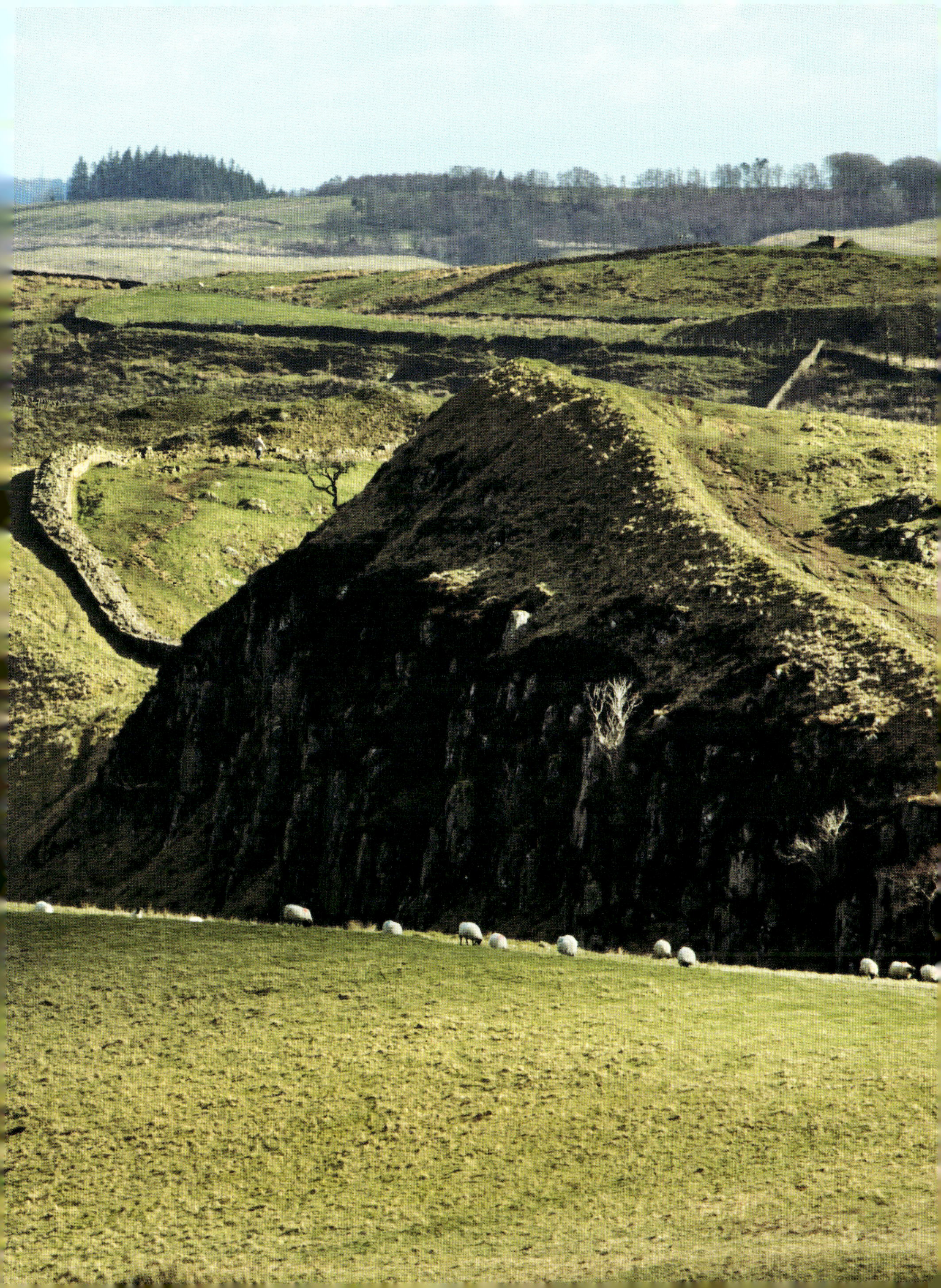

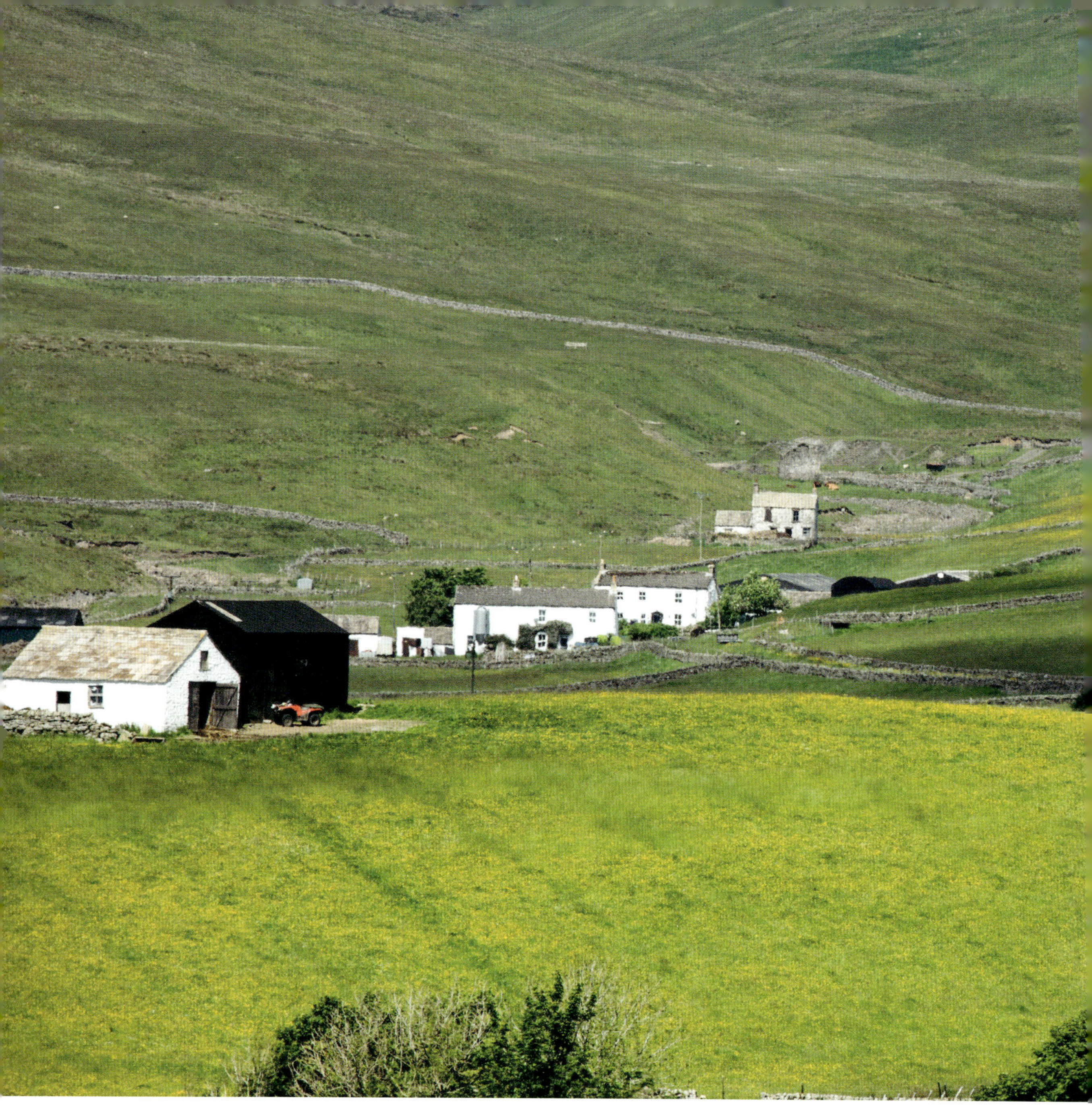

Above: Isolated farms in Upper Teesdale near Harwood

Top right: Old mining trucks, reused as decorative planters outside the Allenheads Inn

Bottom right: The valley of the River South Tyne near Alston

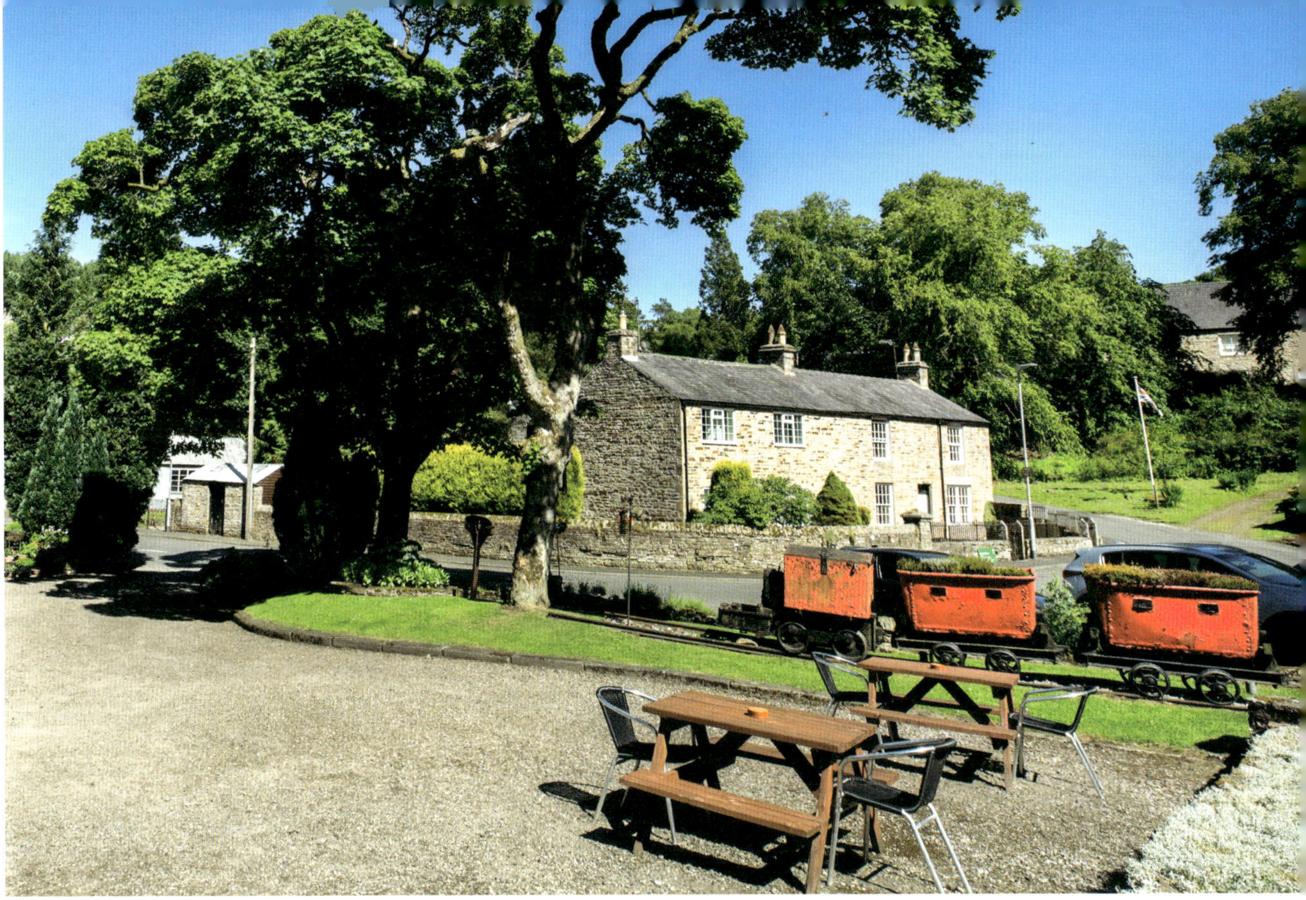

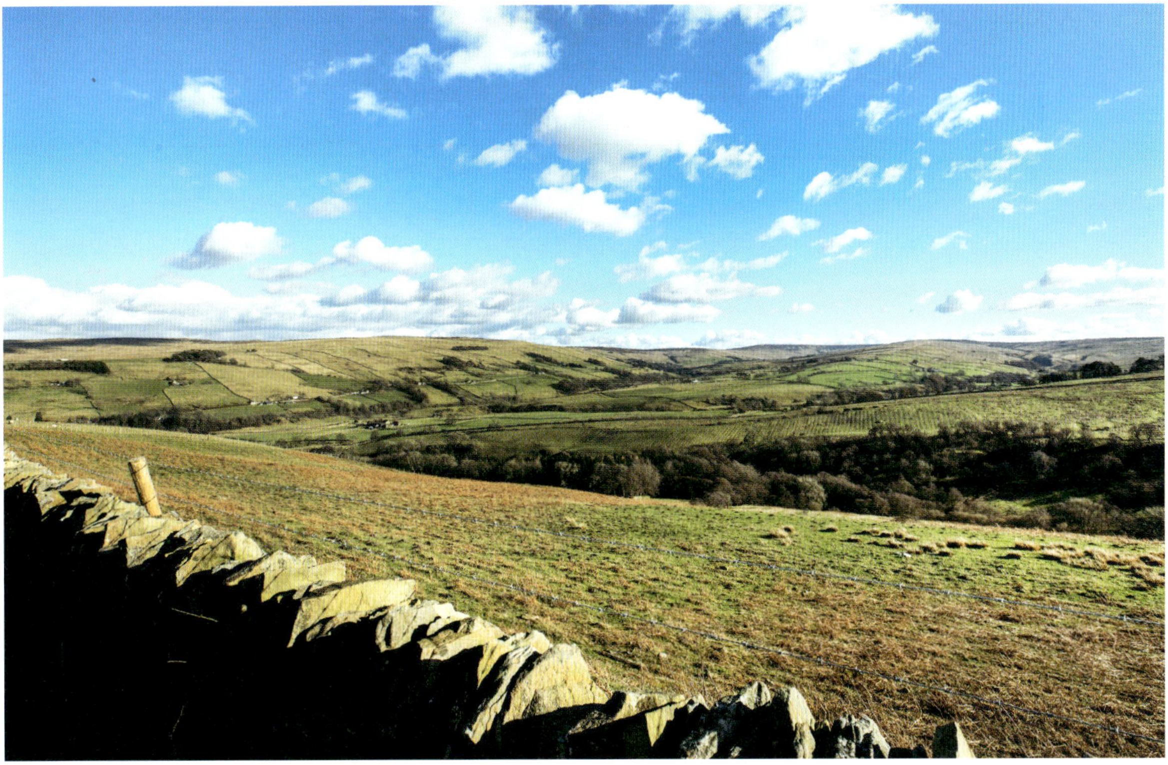

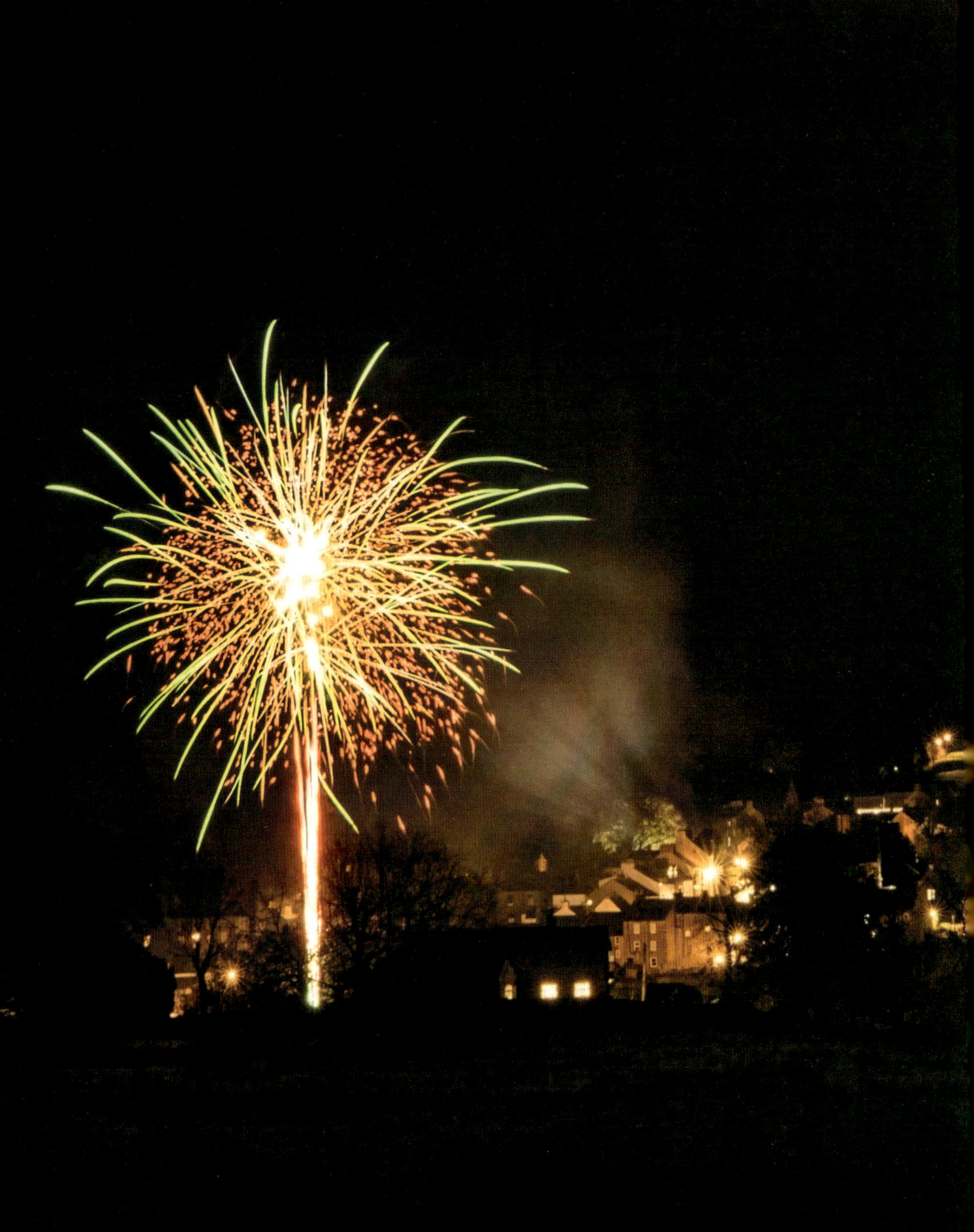

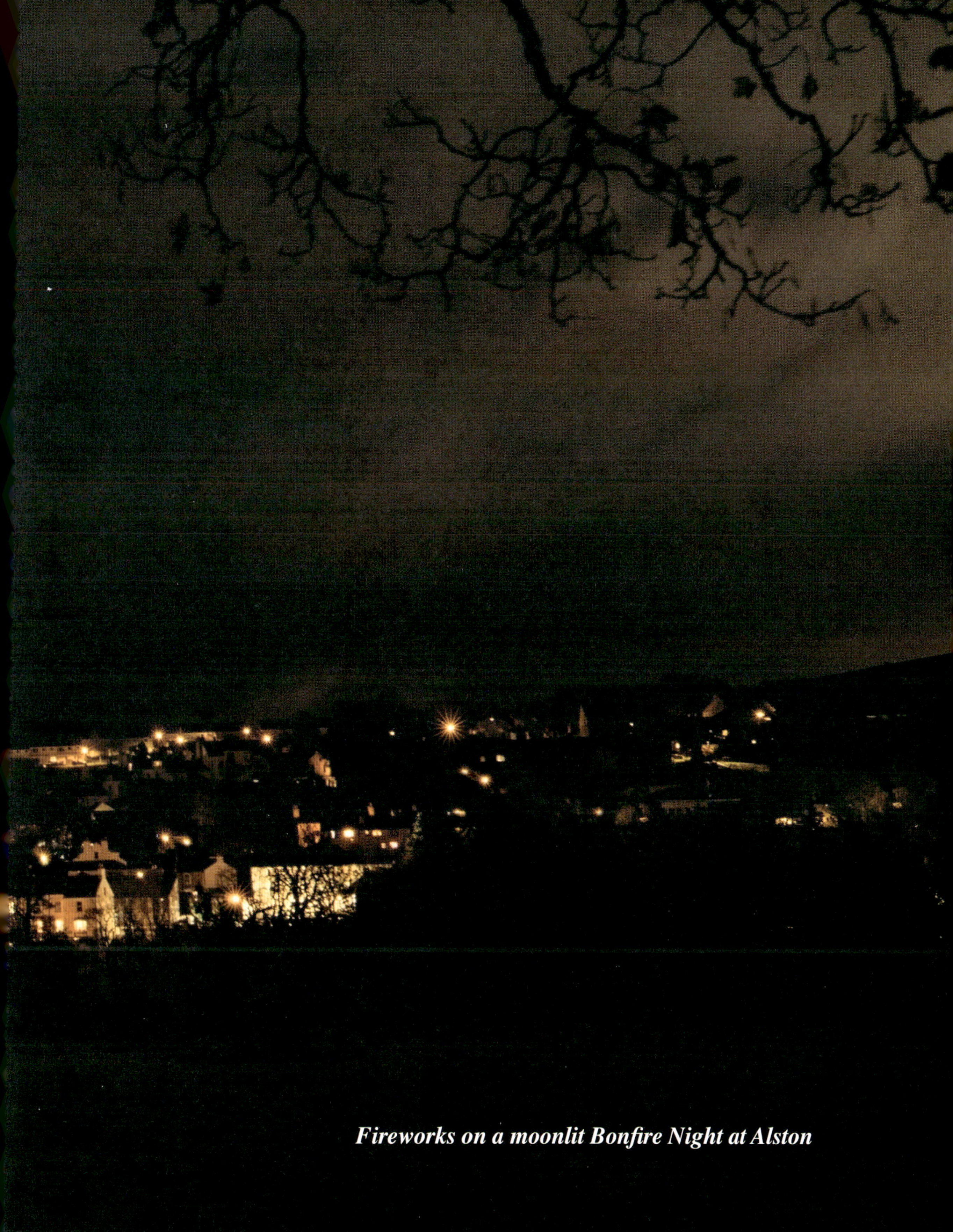

Fireworks on a moonlit Bonfire Night at Alston

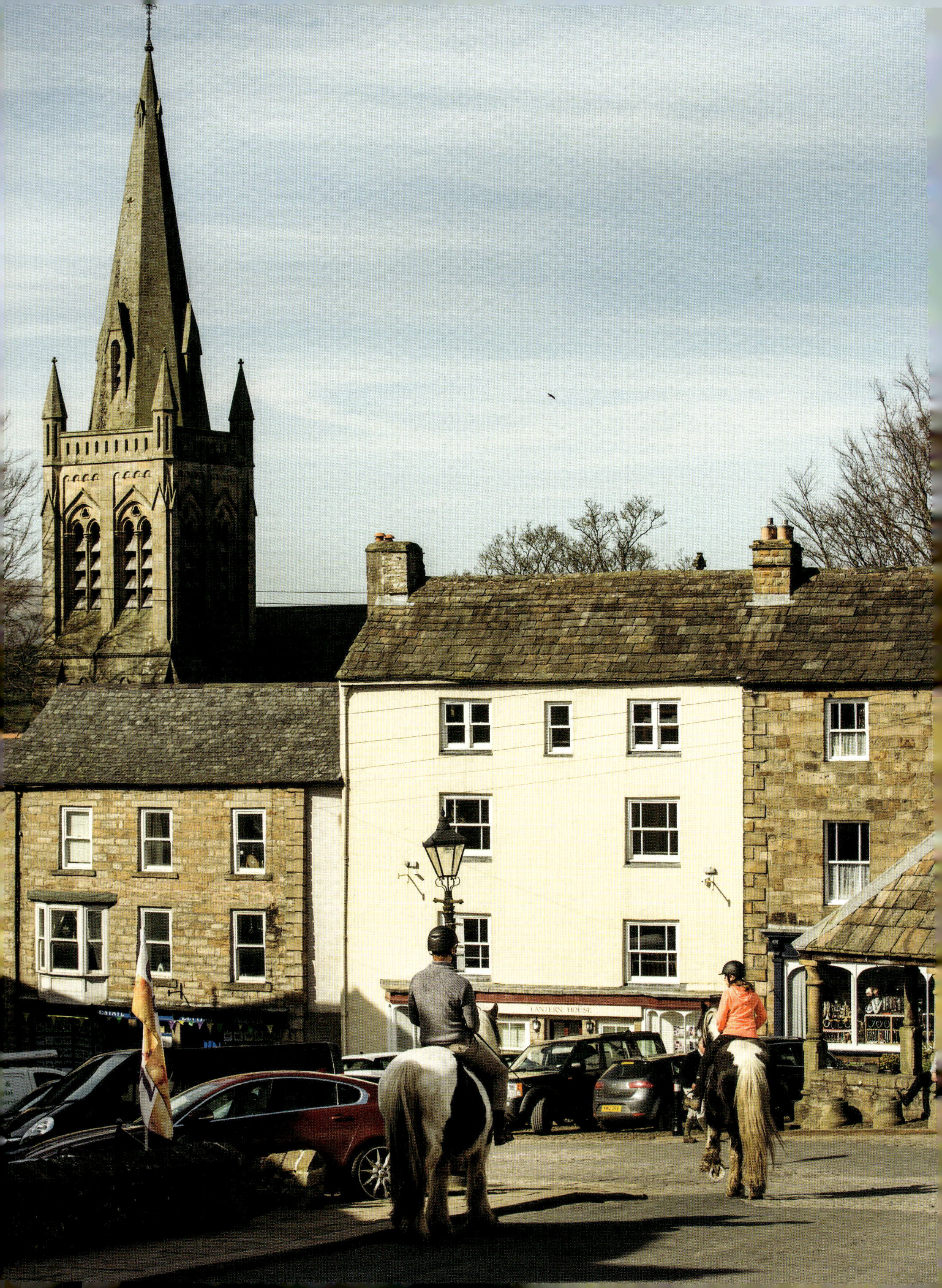

LANTERN HOUSE

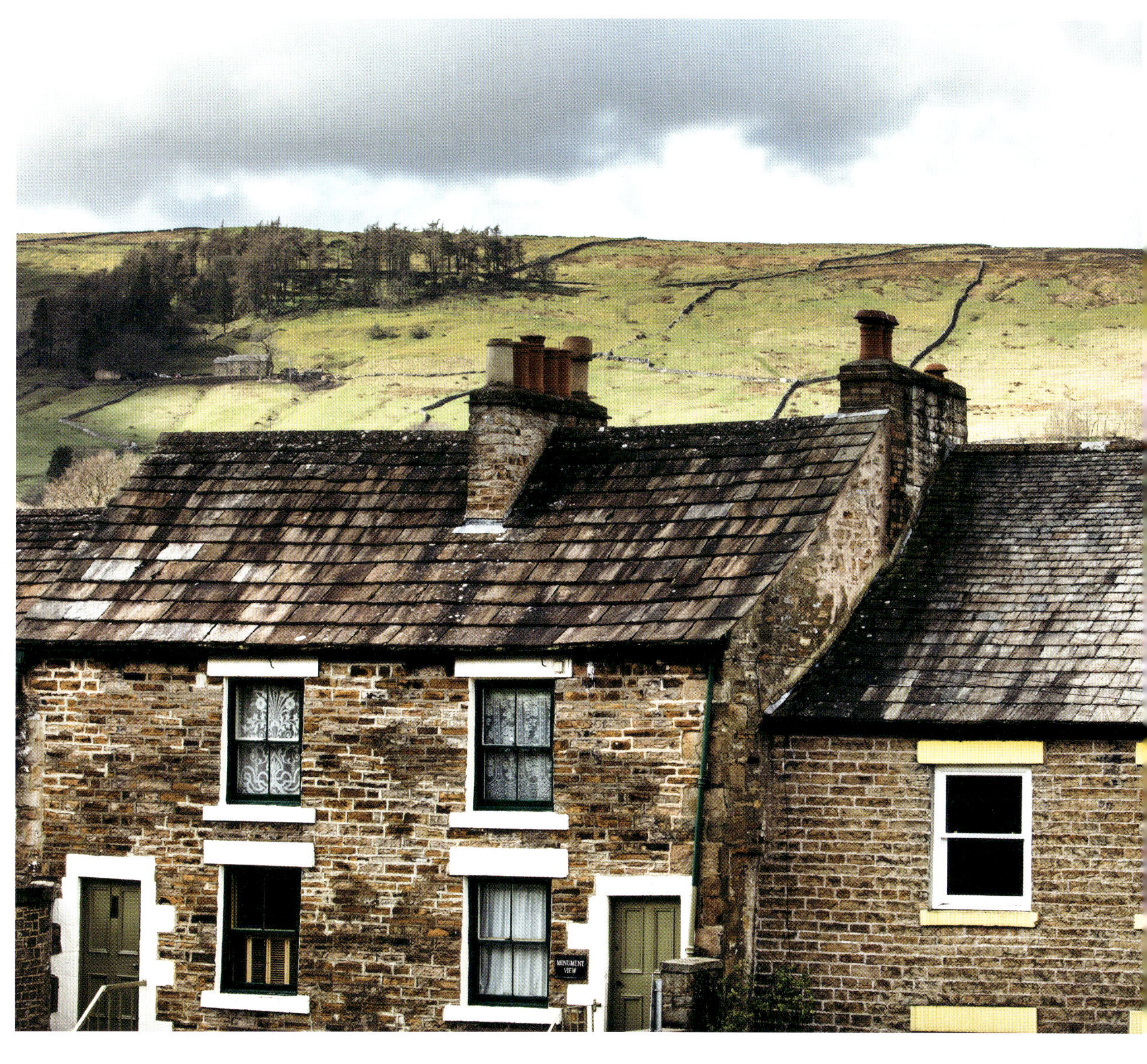

*Above: Cottages in Alston with Park Fell rising in typical North Pennine
fashion behind them*

*Left: Horse riders near the Market Cross on Alston main street with
St Augustine's Church behind*

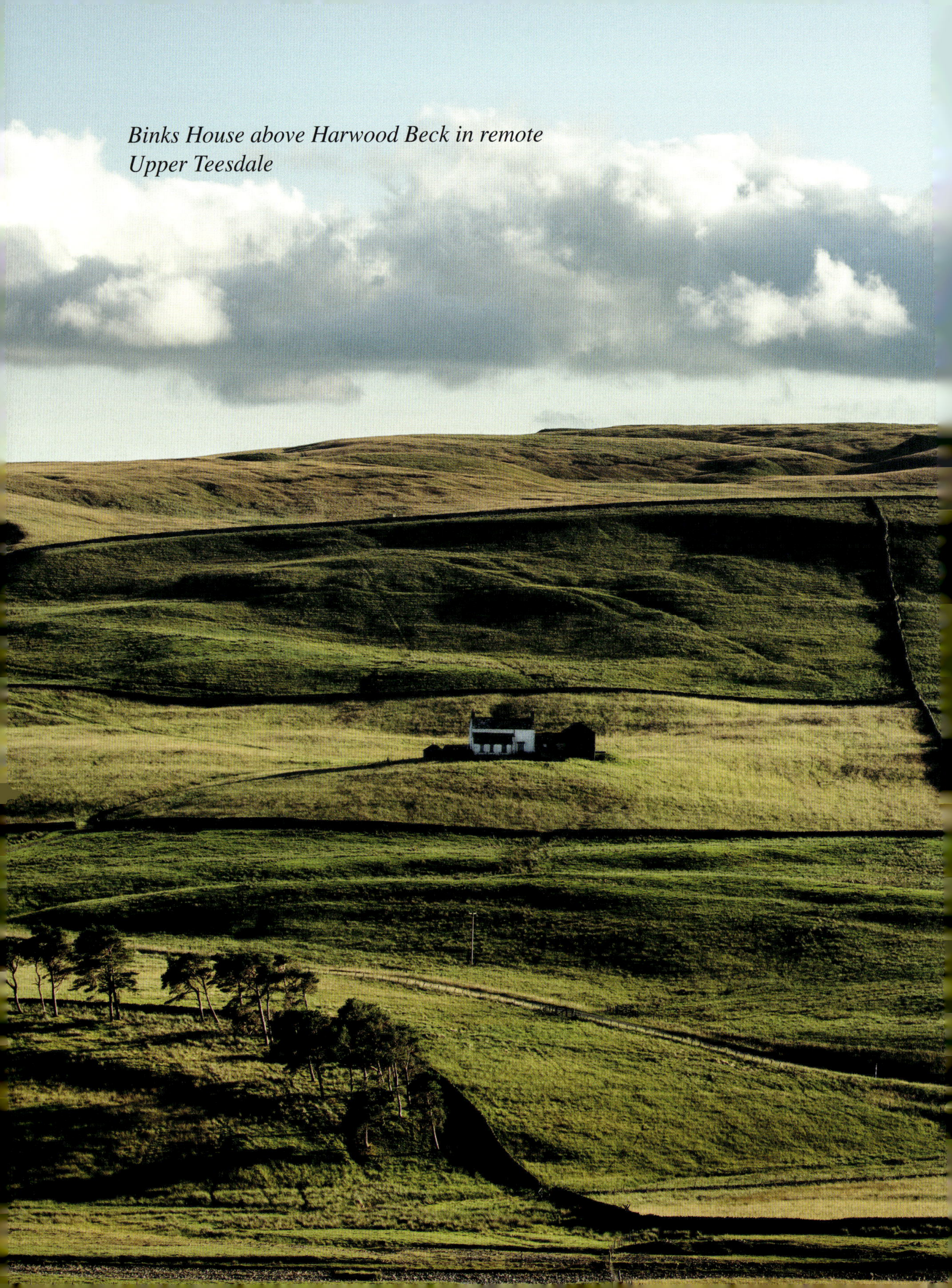

*Binks House above Harwood Beck in remote
Upper Teesdale*

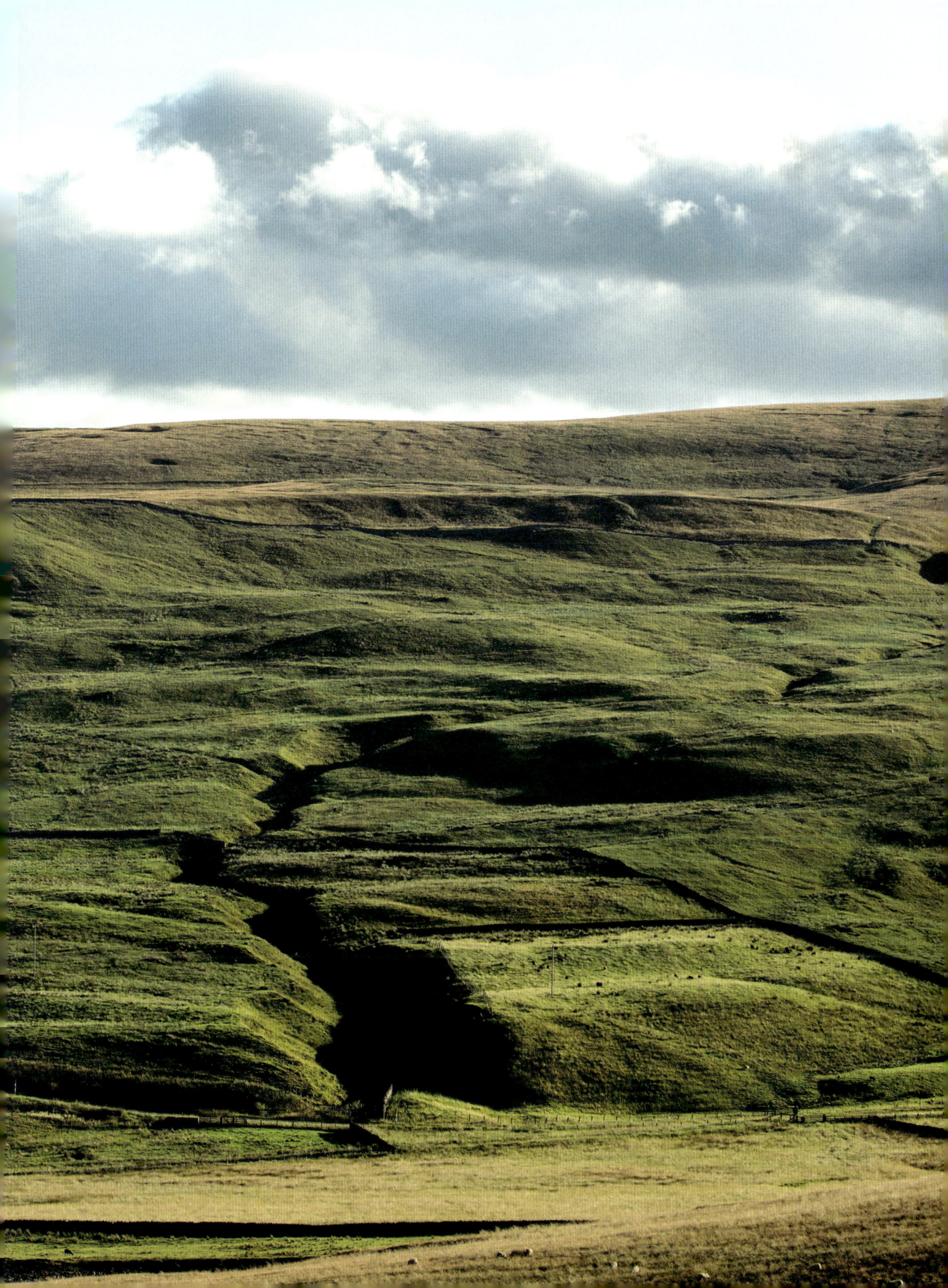

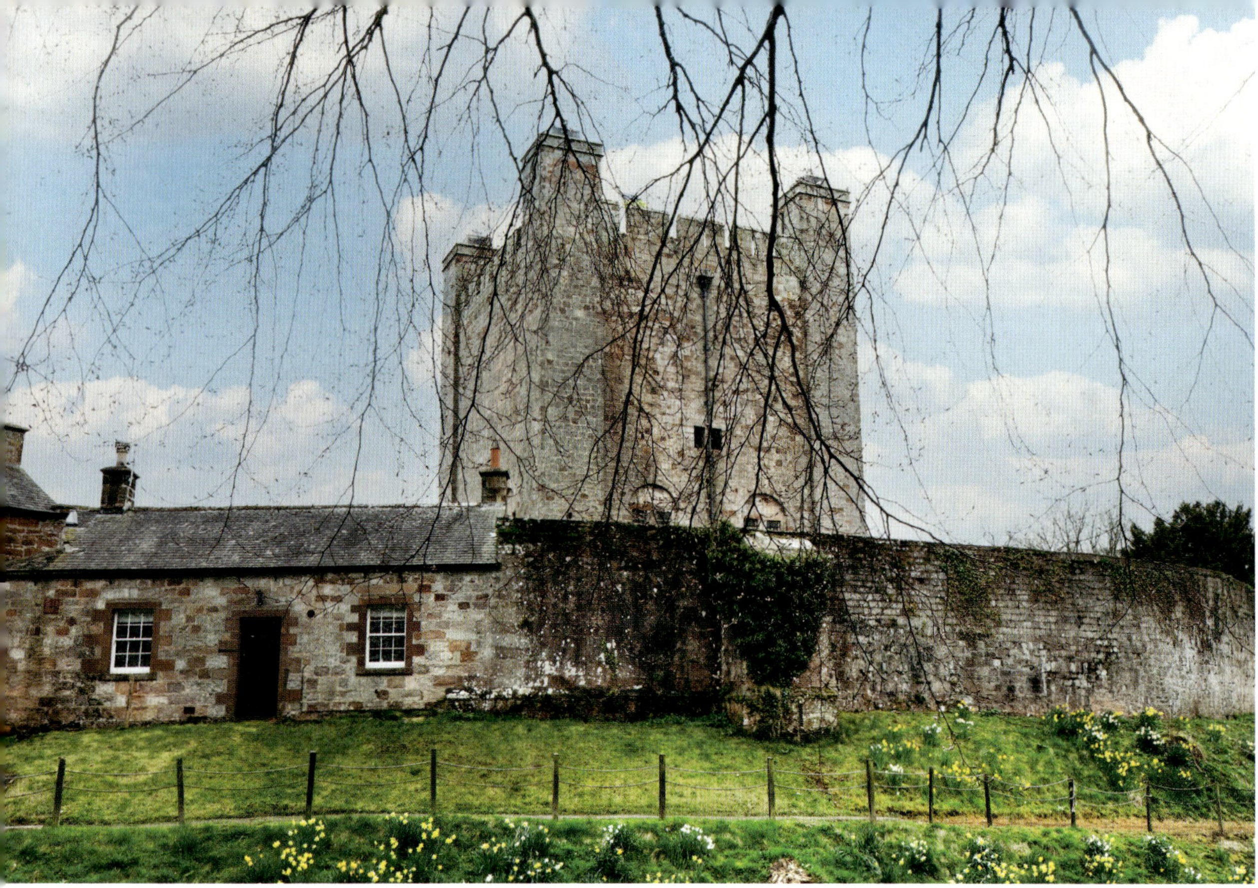

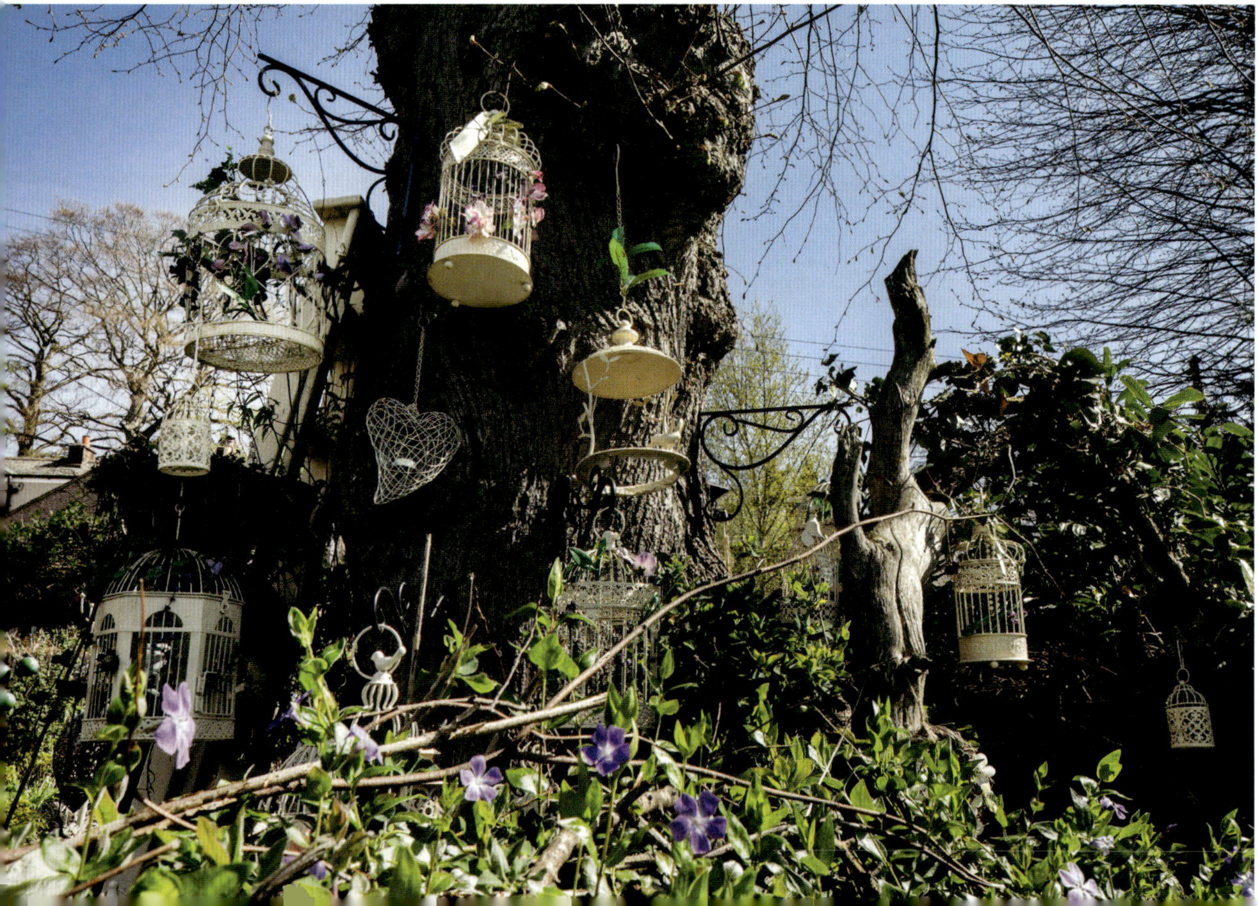

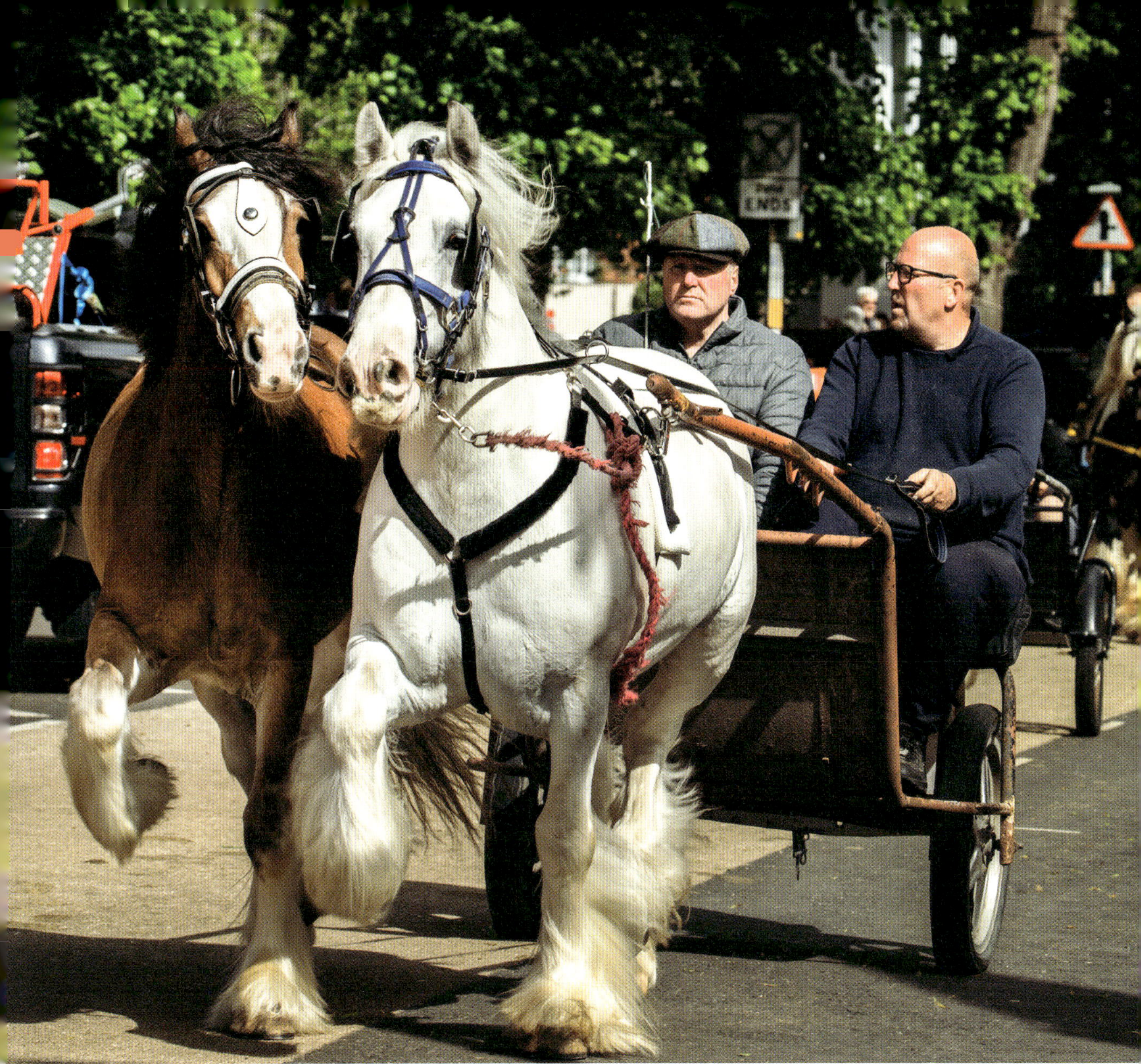

Above: Two magnificent horses pull a trotting cart at Appleby Horse Fair, held over the first week of June every year. It attracts hundreds of Gypsies and travellers from all over the UK and Ireland

Top left: The 12th century Norman castle keep sometimes known as Caesar's Tower, at Appleby-in-Westmorland castle

Bottom left: Pretty bird cages decorate a tree at Appleby-in-Westmorland

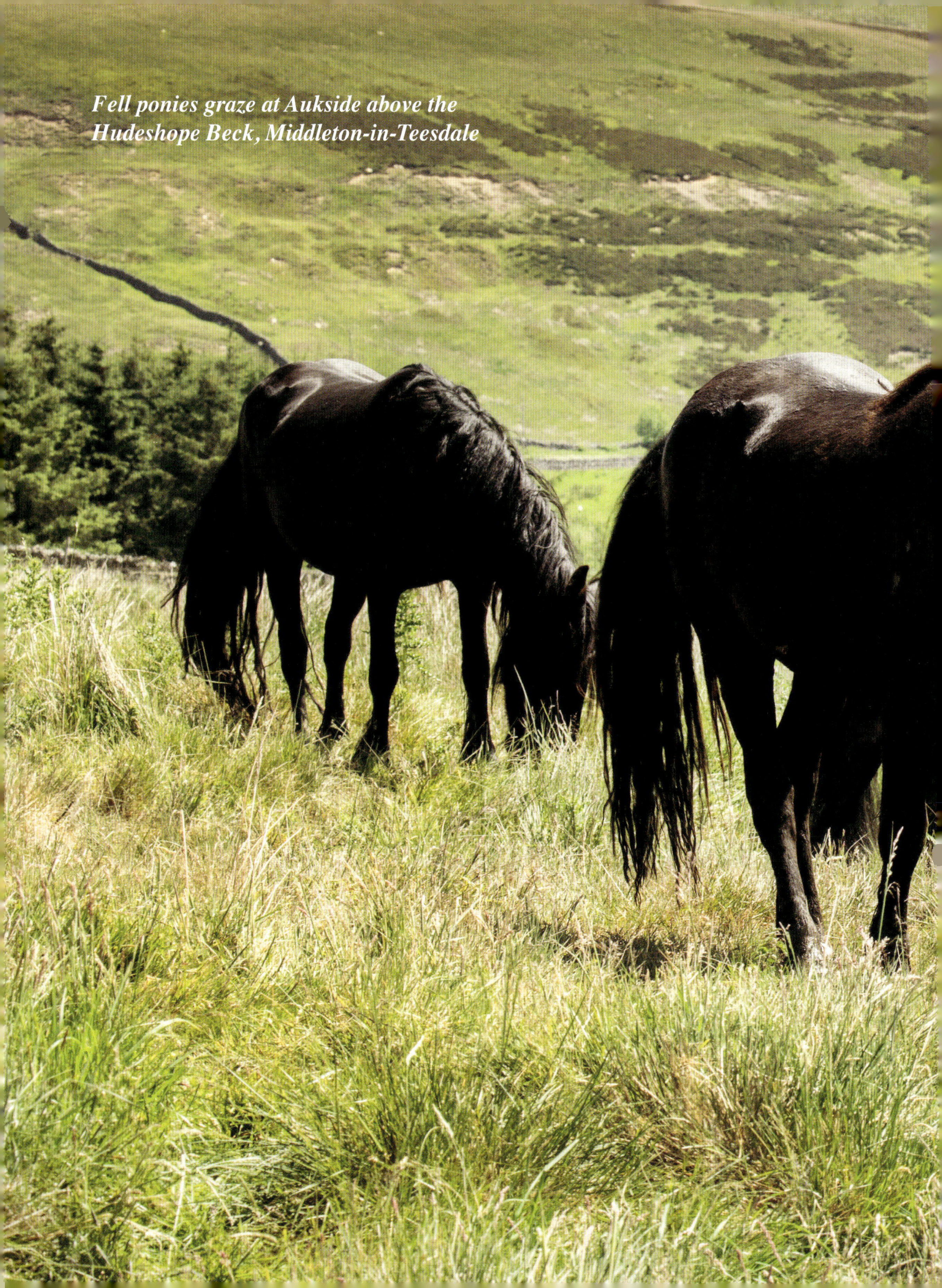

Fell ponies graze at Aukside above the
Hudeshope Beck, Middleton-in-Teesdale

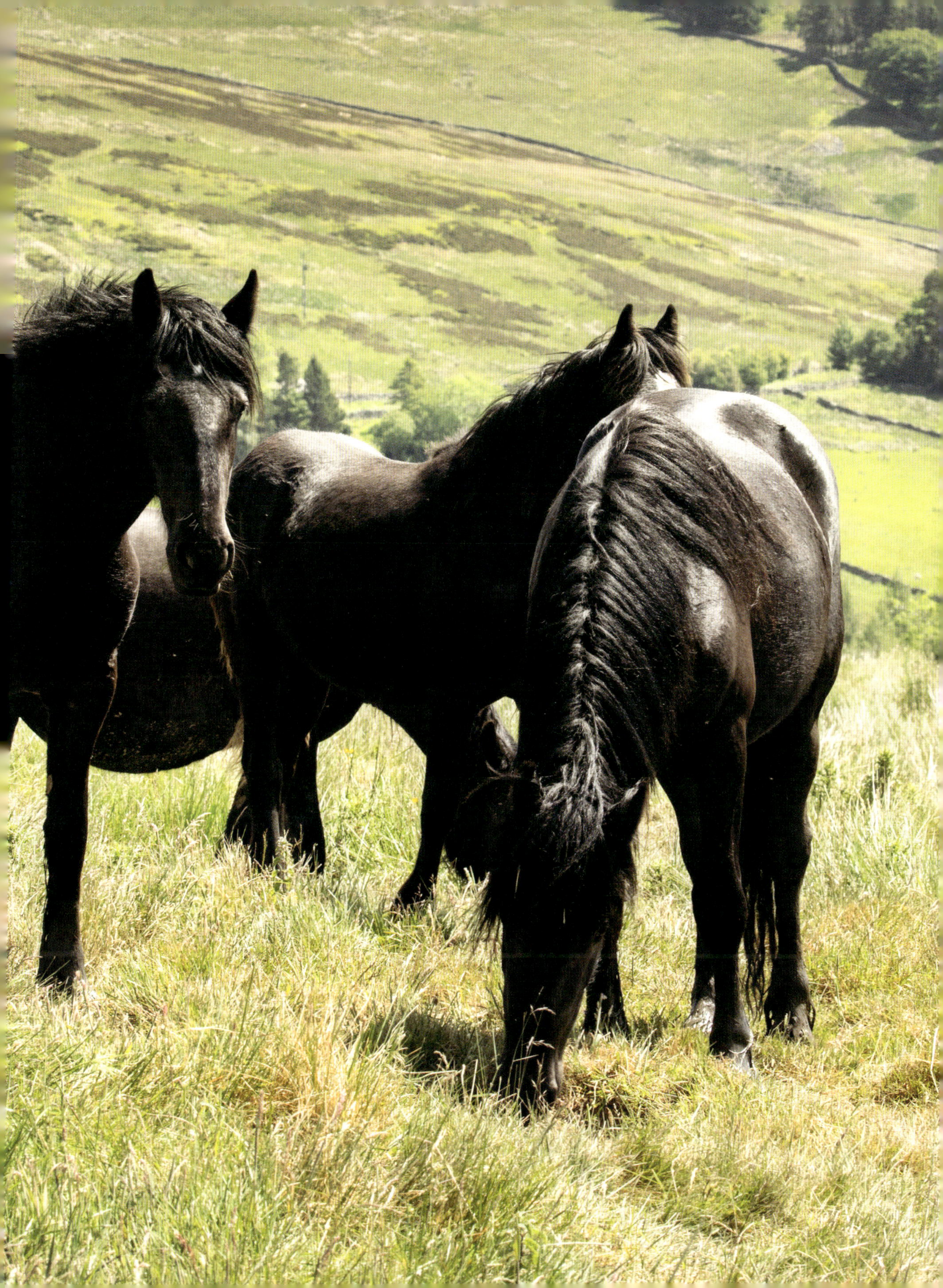

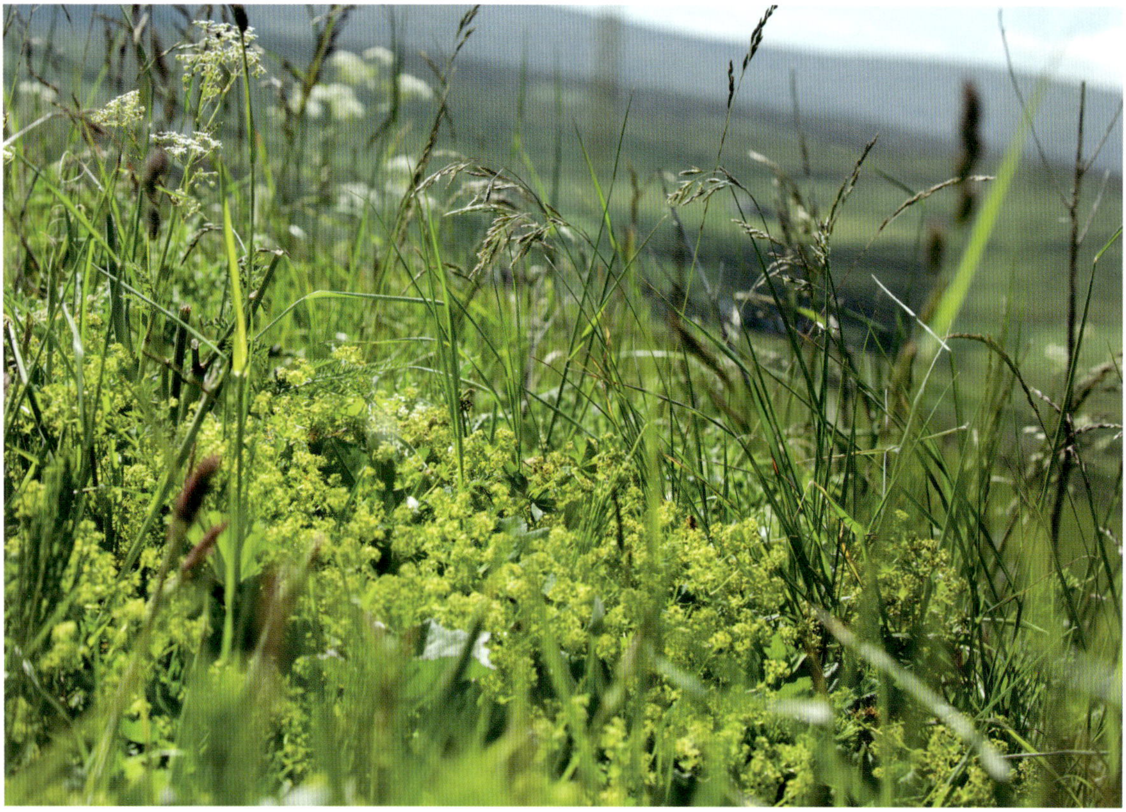

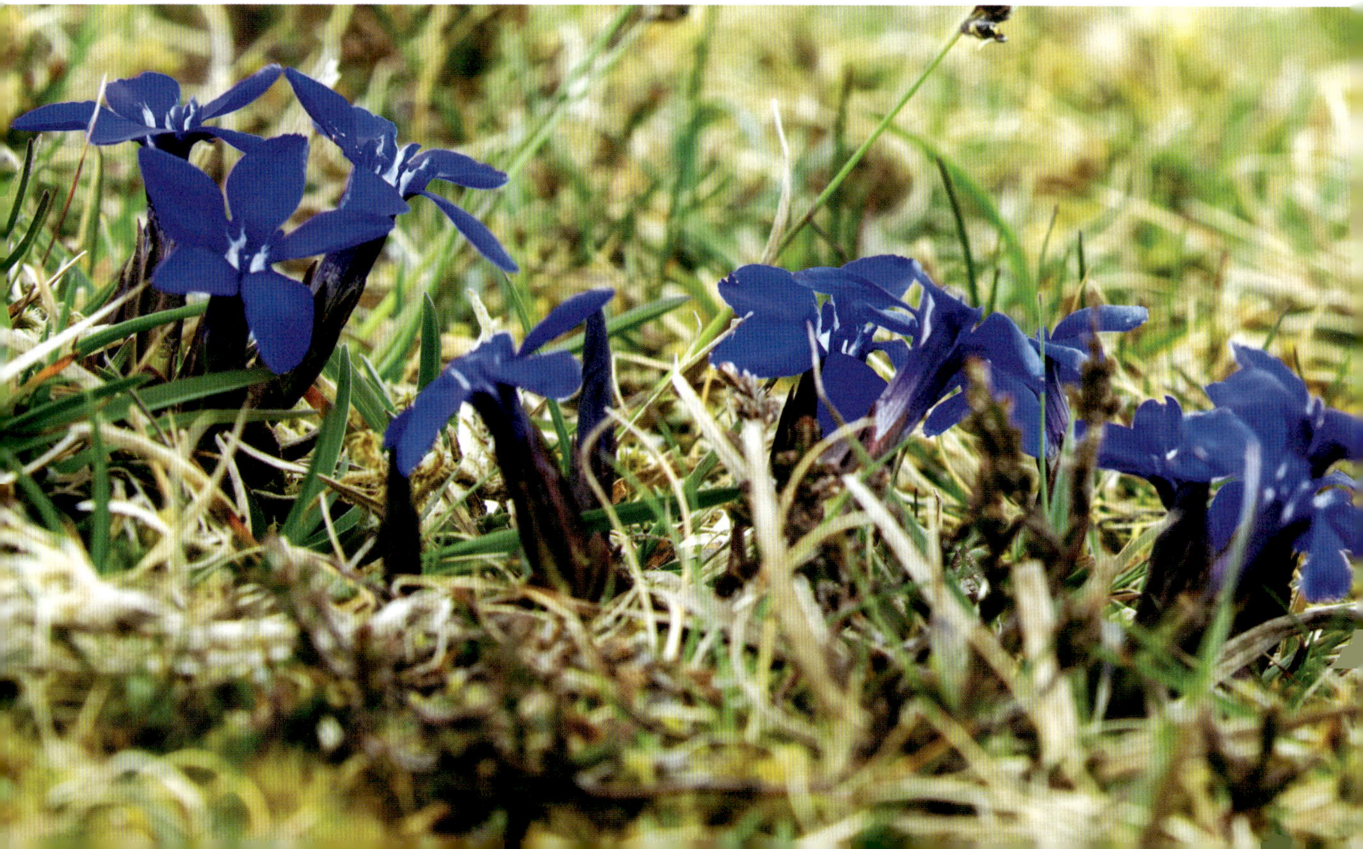

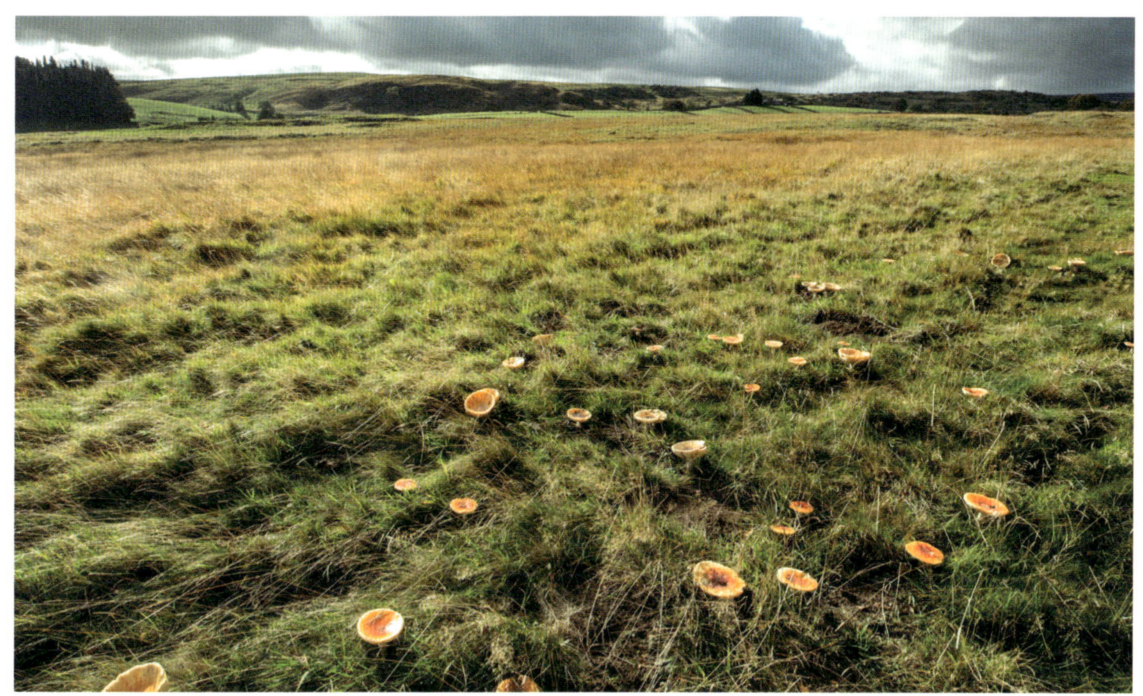

Teesdale is famous for its unique flora and wildflower meadows. Most notable are the incredible spring gentians (below) which flower at Cow Green Reservoir in spring. The fungi are above High Force waterfall

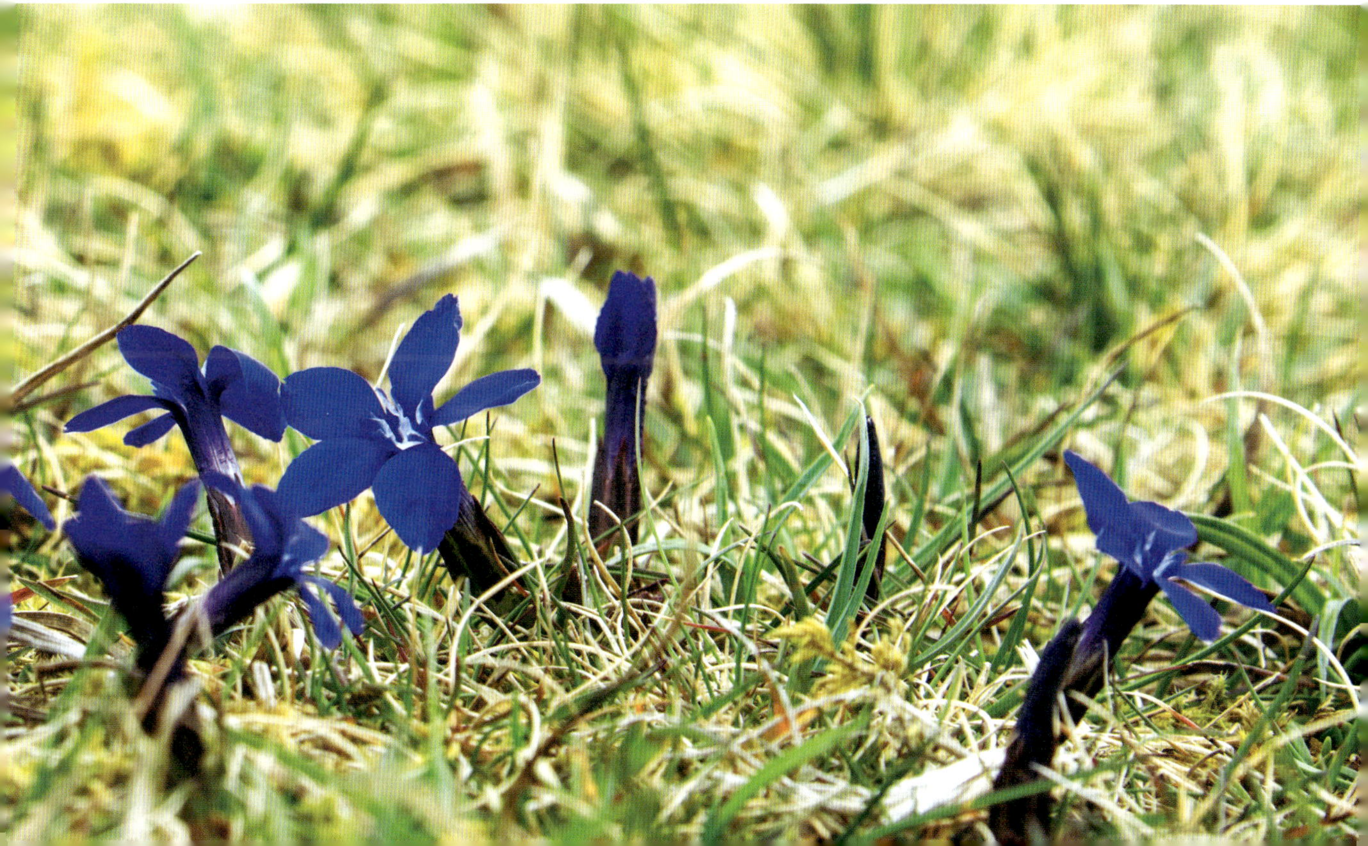

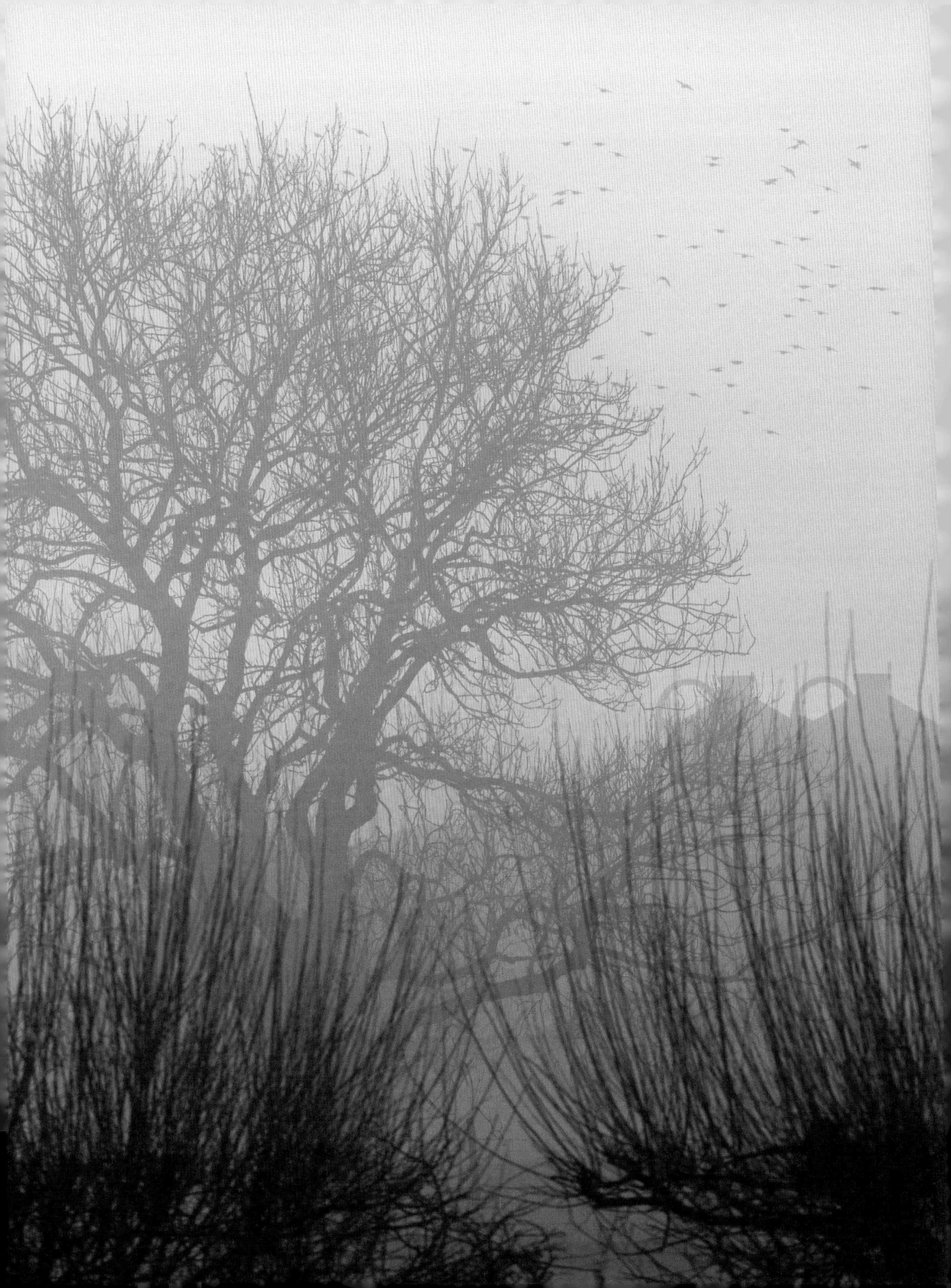

A foggy morning between Bowes and Barnard
Castle. Starlings and redwings fly above the trees

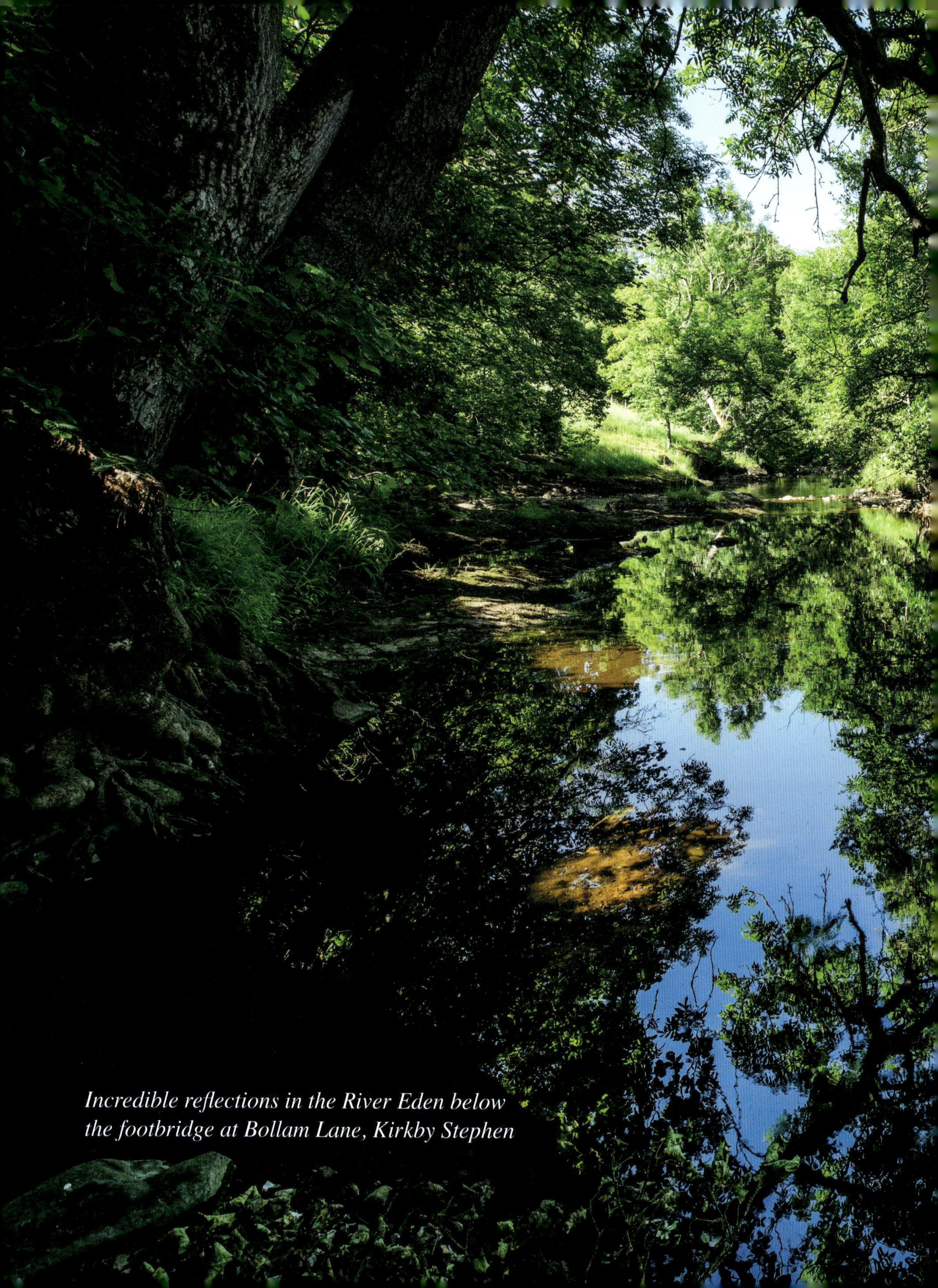

Incredible reflections in the River Eden below the footbridge at Bollam Lane, Kirkby Stephen

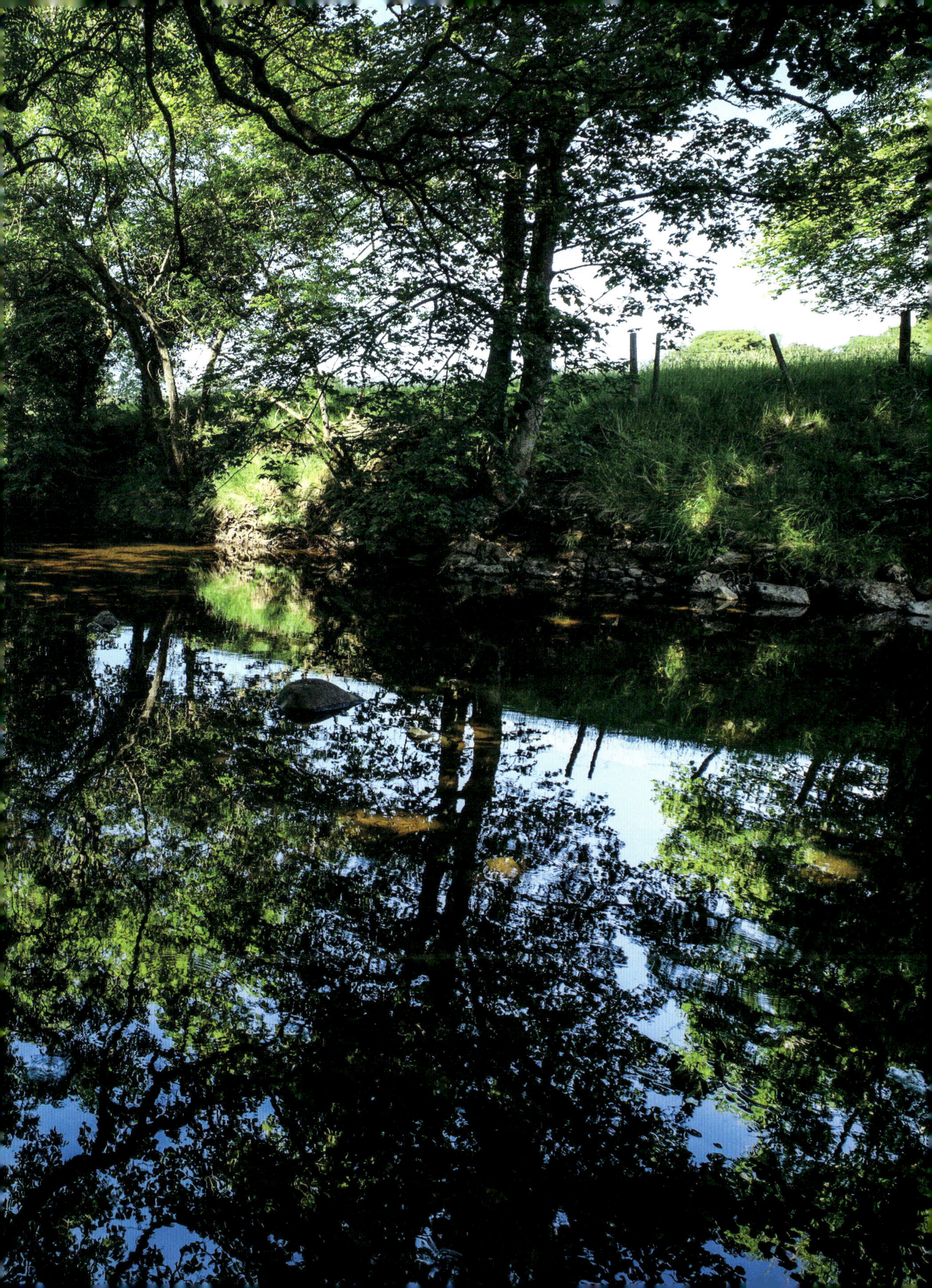

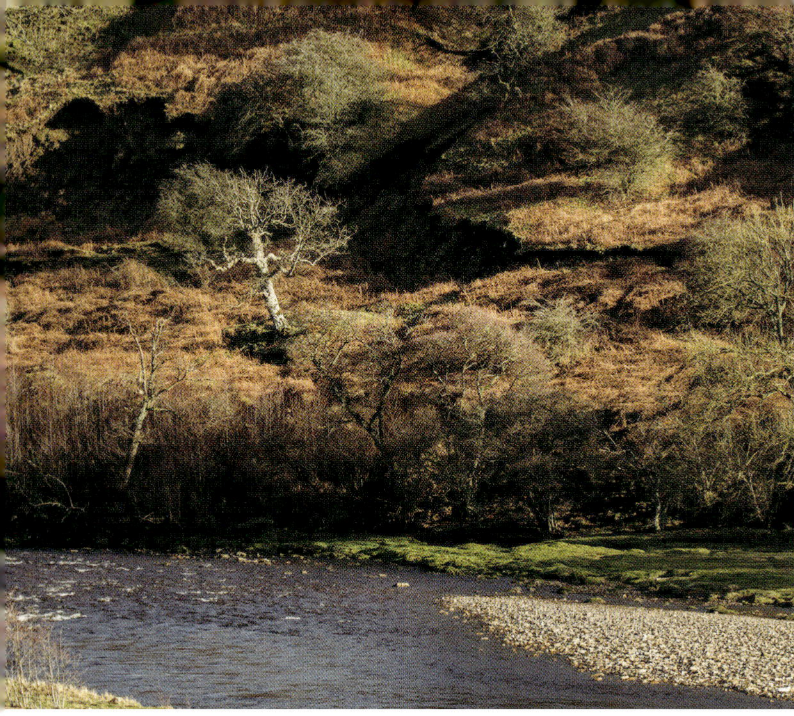

Above: The view of the River South Tyne from the Kirkstyle Inn and Sportsman's Rest at Knarsdale

Right: Knarsdale Hall with Burnstones Arches in front, seen from near Knarsdale Barton

Below: Red grouse mother and four of her chicks amongst the heather near Knarsdale

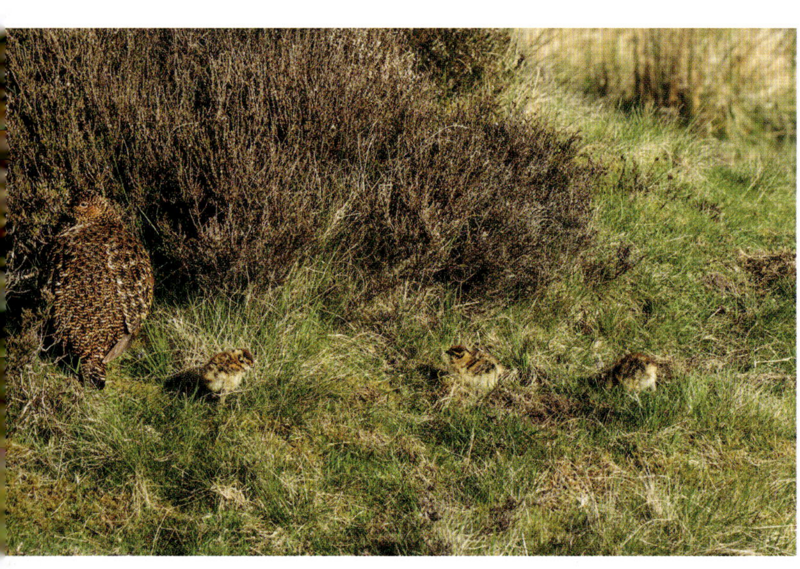

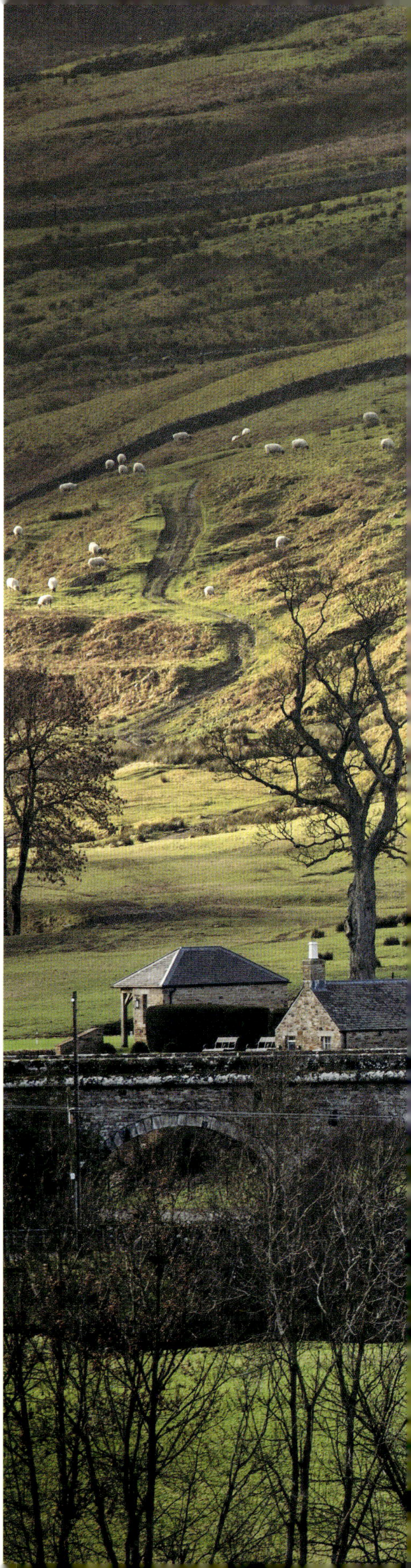

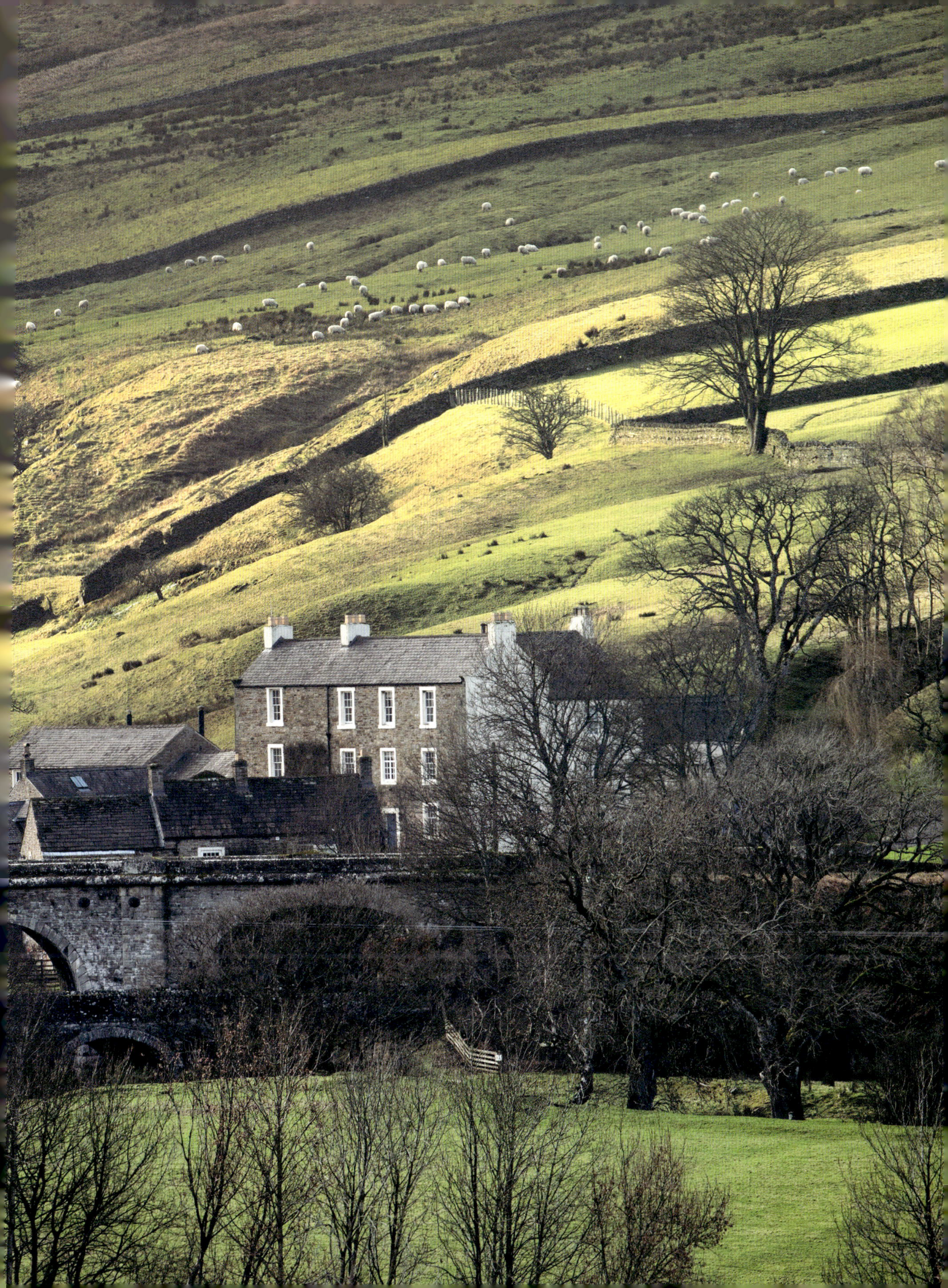

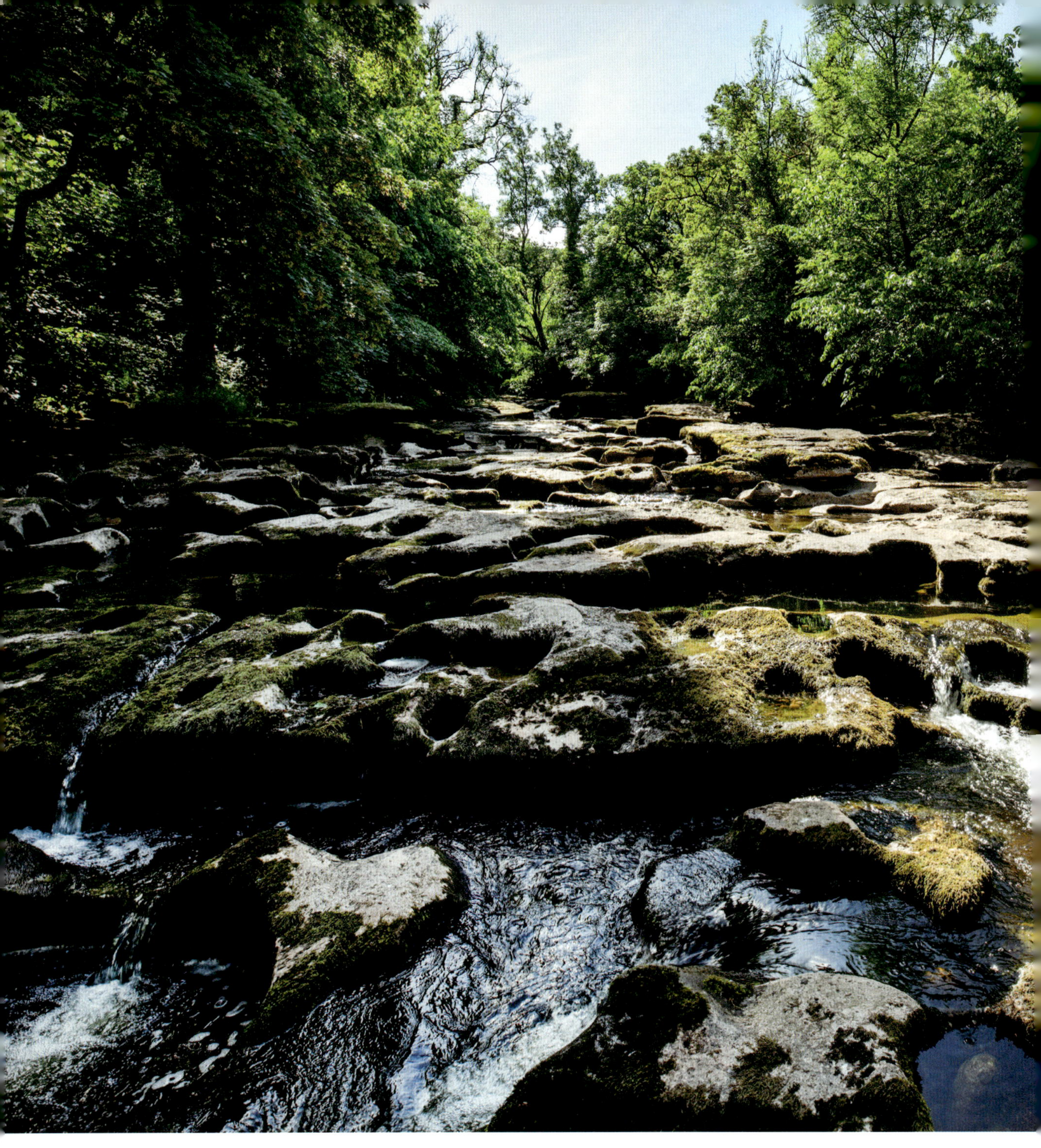

Above: The River Eden at Stenkrith, Kirkby Stephen, where the water has carved potholes in the limestone

Top right: St Stephen's church, Kirkby Stephen, in the Upper Eden Valley

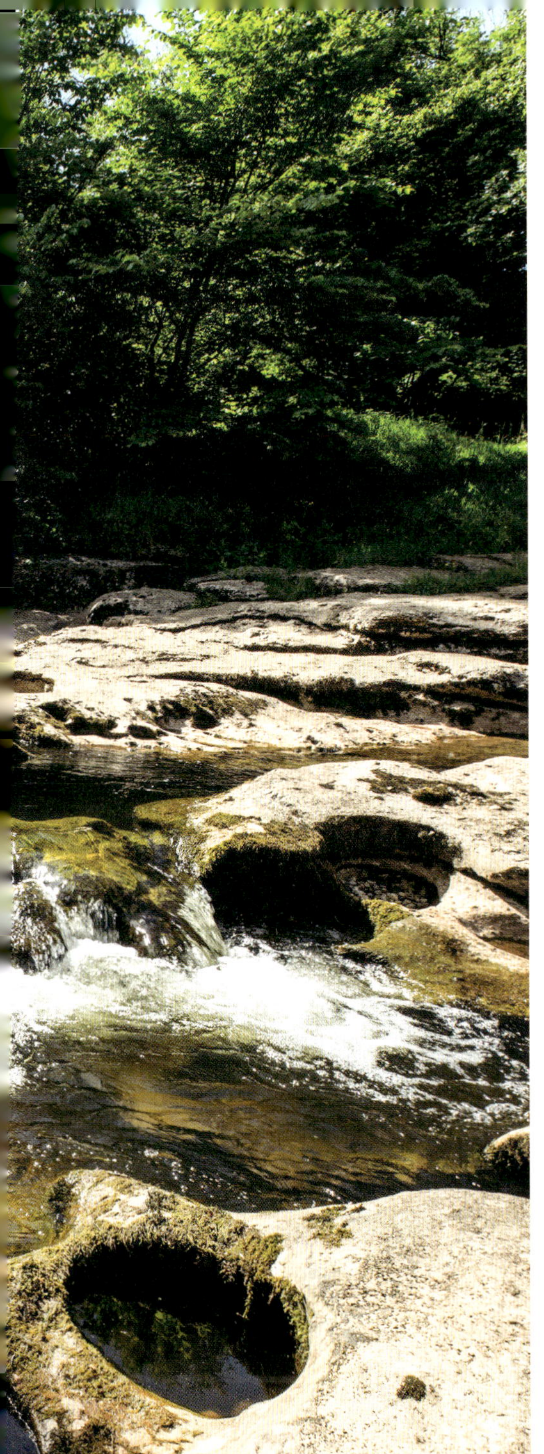

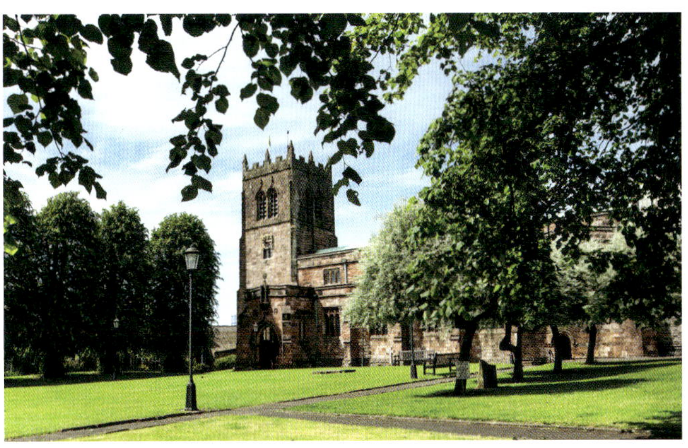

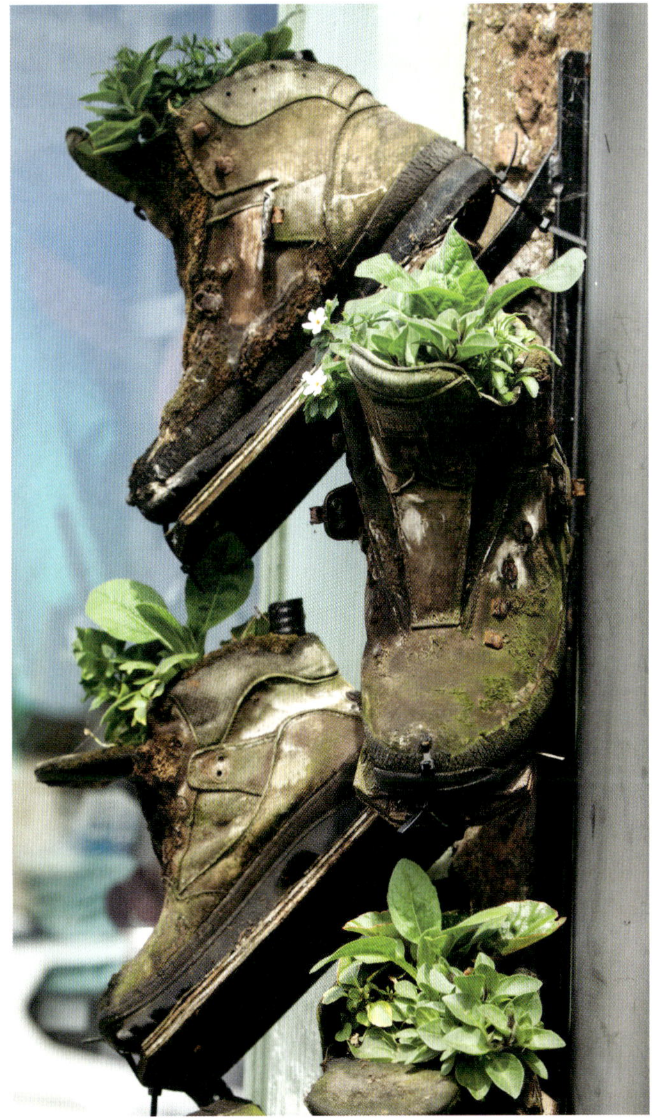

Right: Discarded walkers' boots used as planters at an outdoors shop in Kirkby Stephen. The town is the centre of regional walking tours

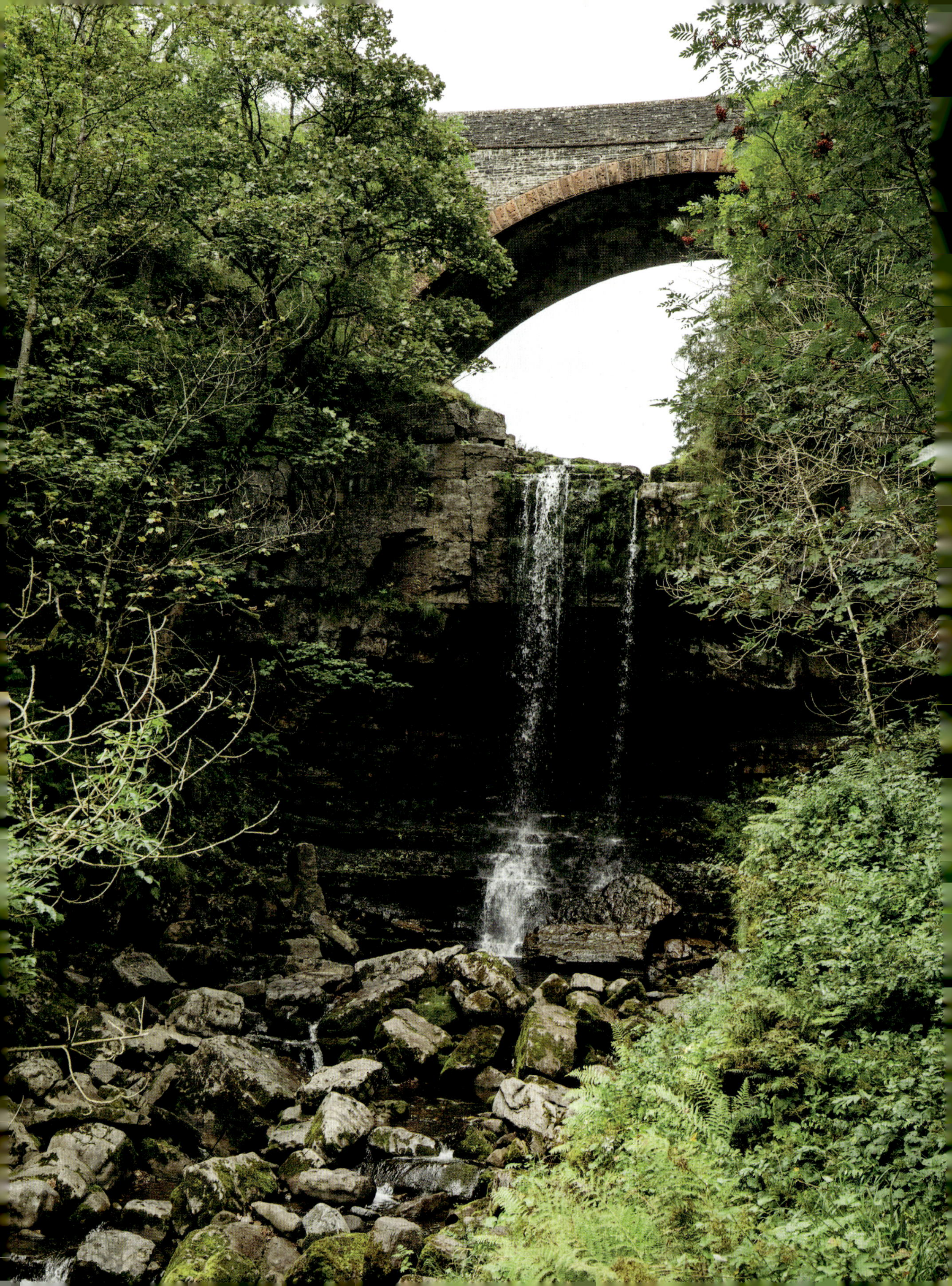

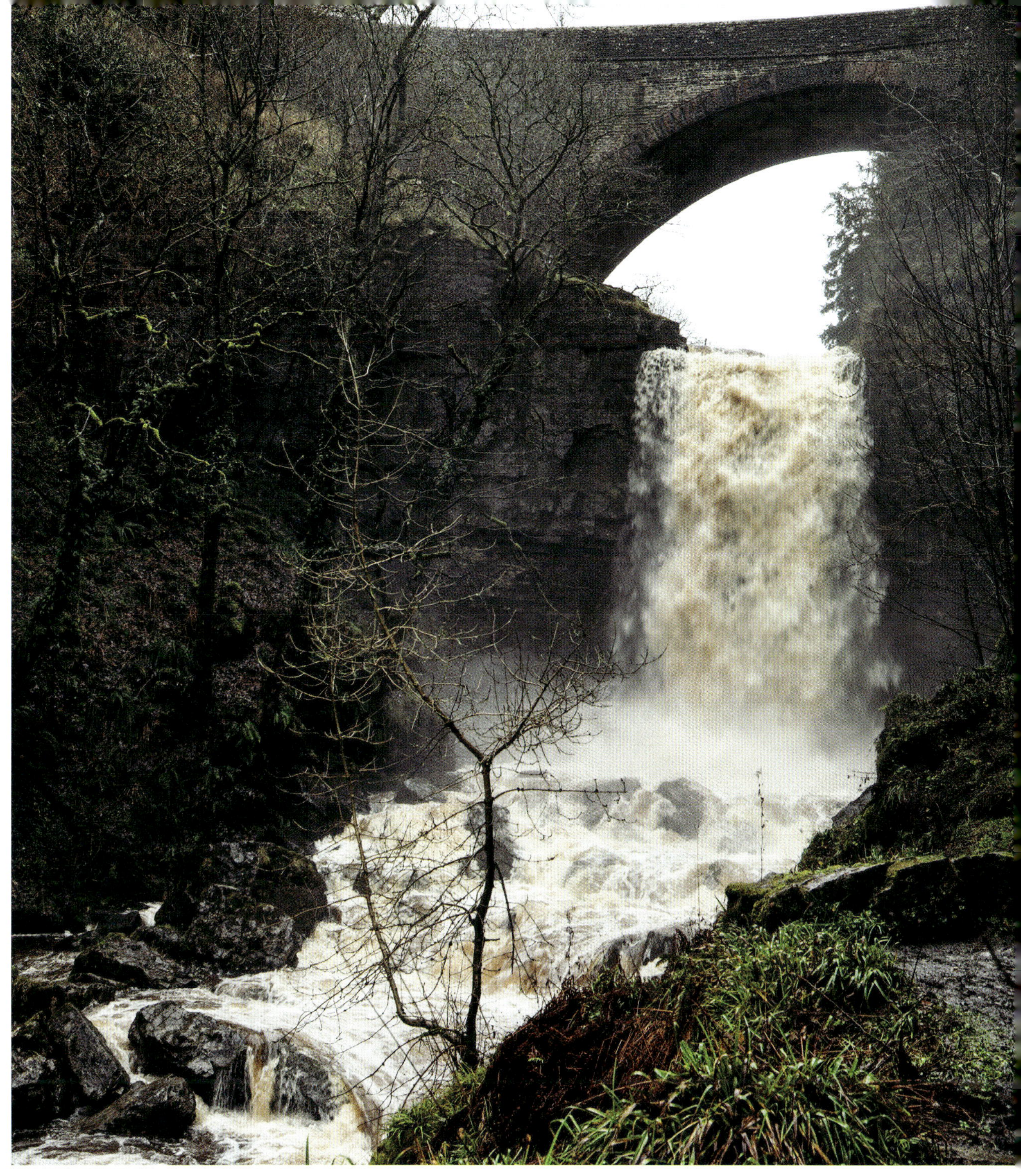

What a difference the rain makes. Ashgill Force on Ash Gill near Garrigill, Cumbria, in the summer (left) and in winter spate (right). Ash Gill joins the River South Tyne shortly after the waterfall. It is possible, when the waterfall is NOT in spate, to walk behind the veil of water and in summer to dip into the little pools lower down

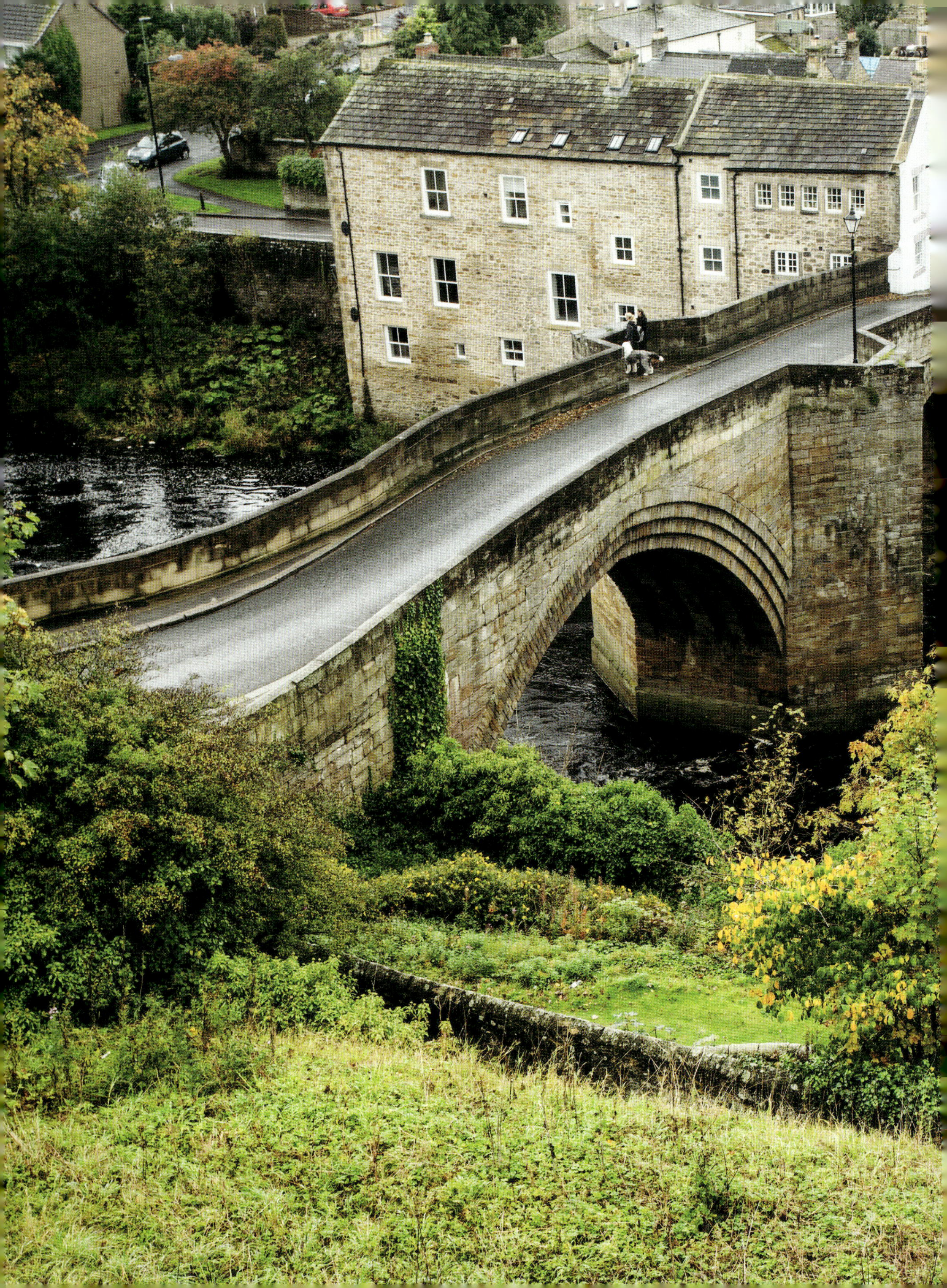

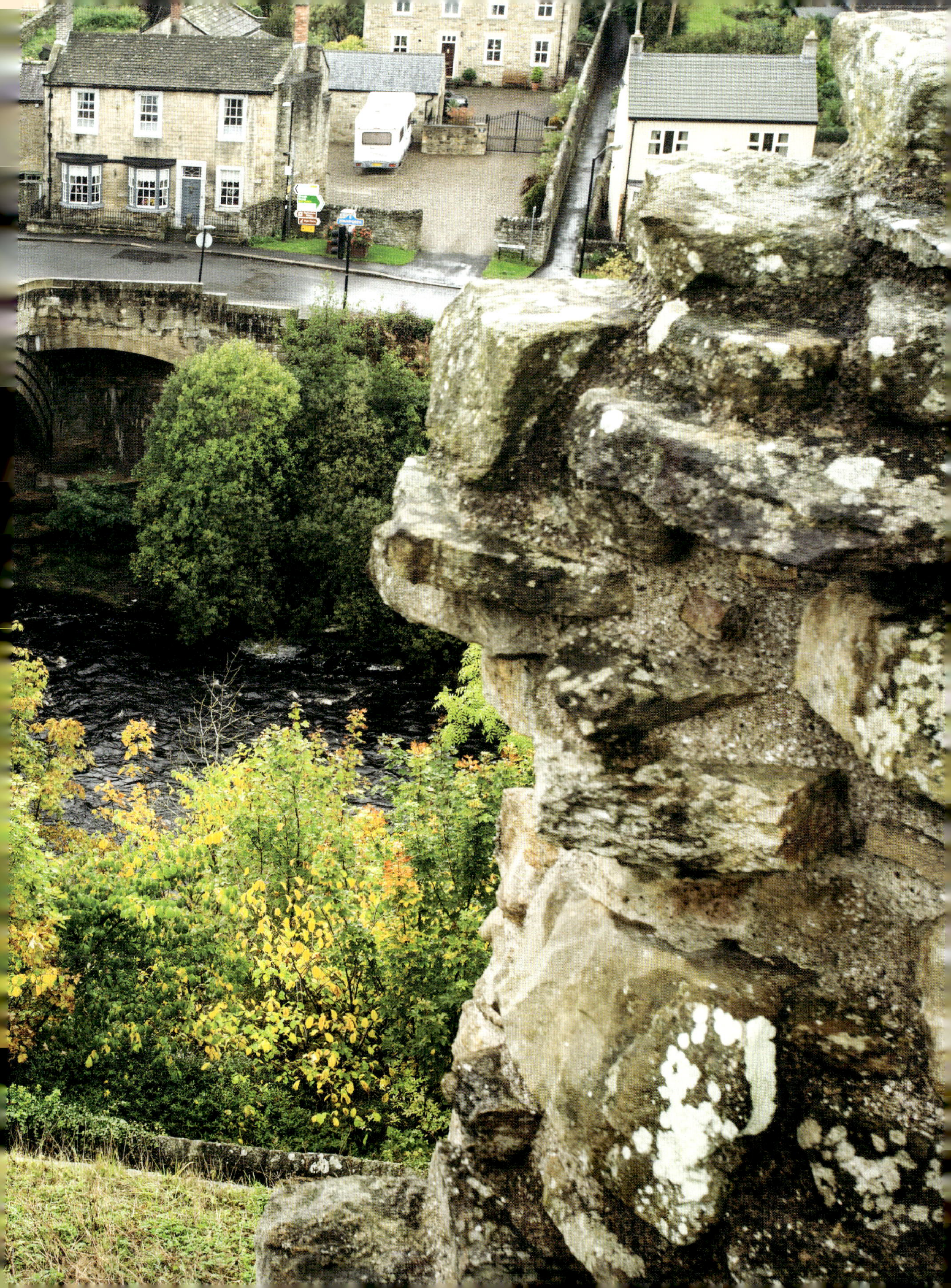

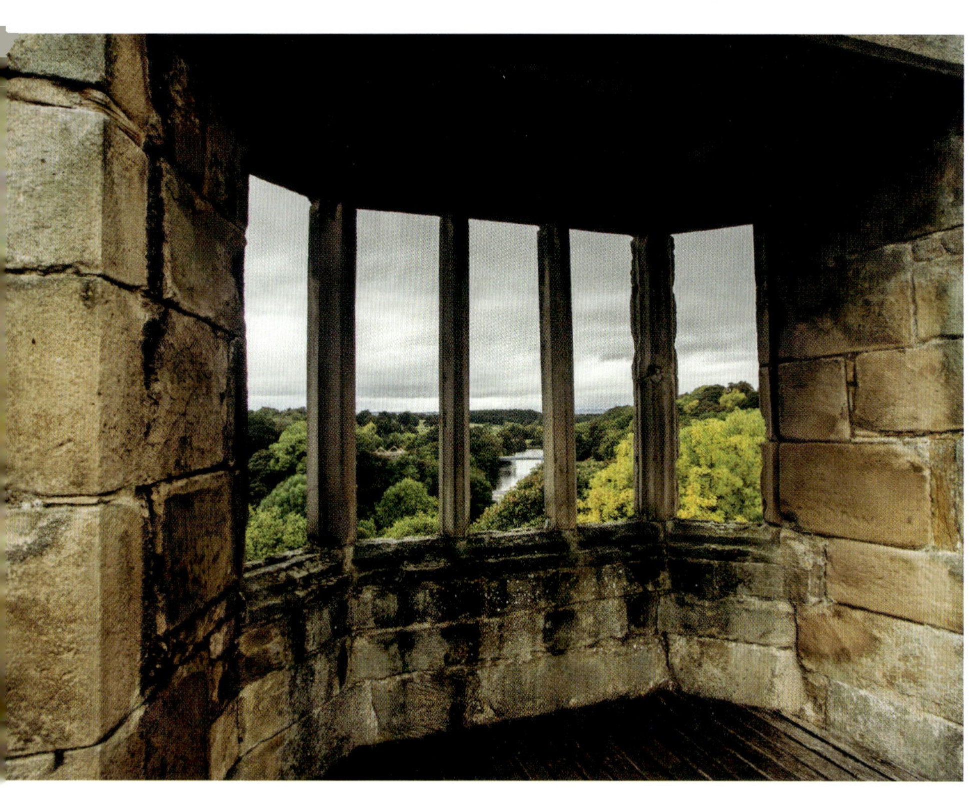

Above: The oriel window of the castle ramparts at Barnard Castle, looking upriver to the River Tees. The window was added by Richard III

Previous Page: The Grade I listed 14th century County Bridge over the River Tees as seen from the castle ramparts

Right: The Bowes Museum and art gallery at Barnard Castle. Built in 1892 in the style of a French chateau, it has paintings by El Greco, Canaletto and Goya

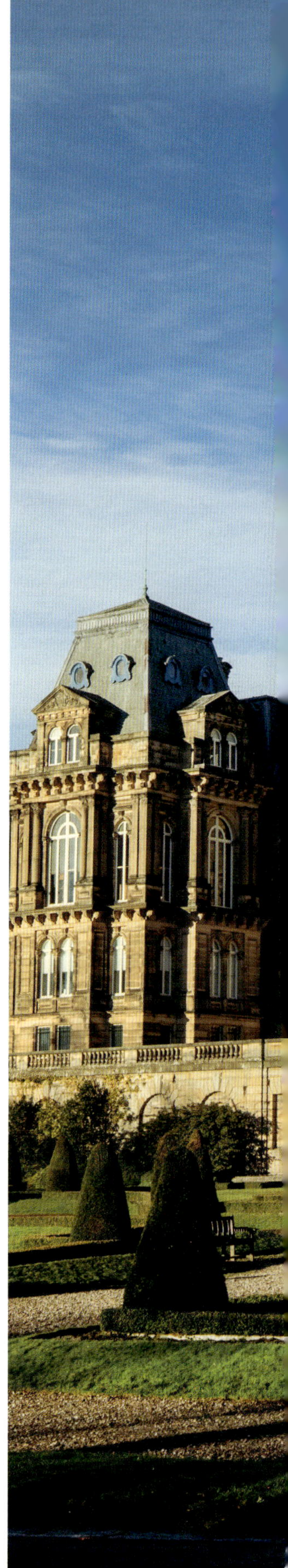

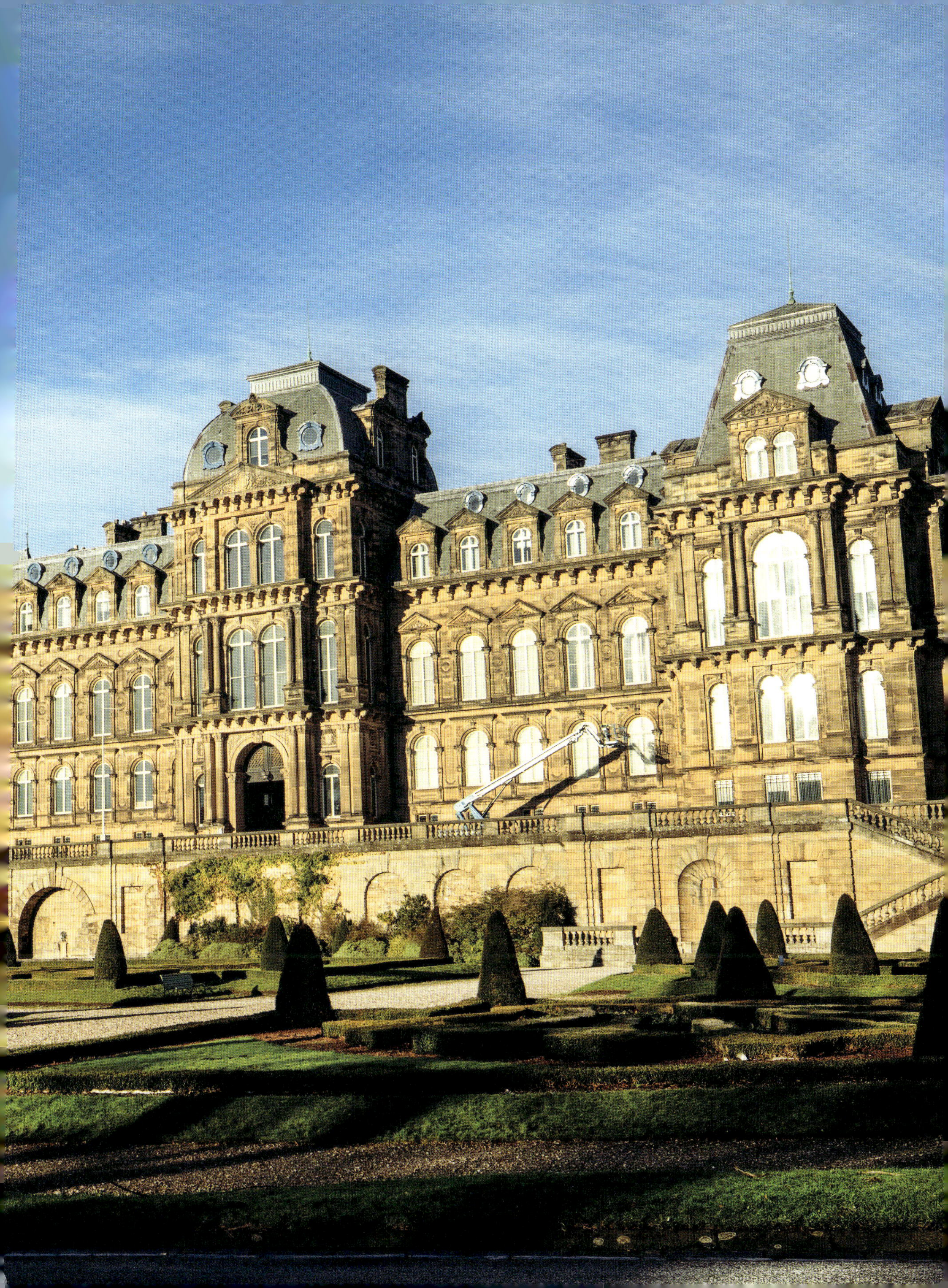

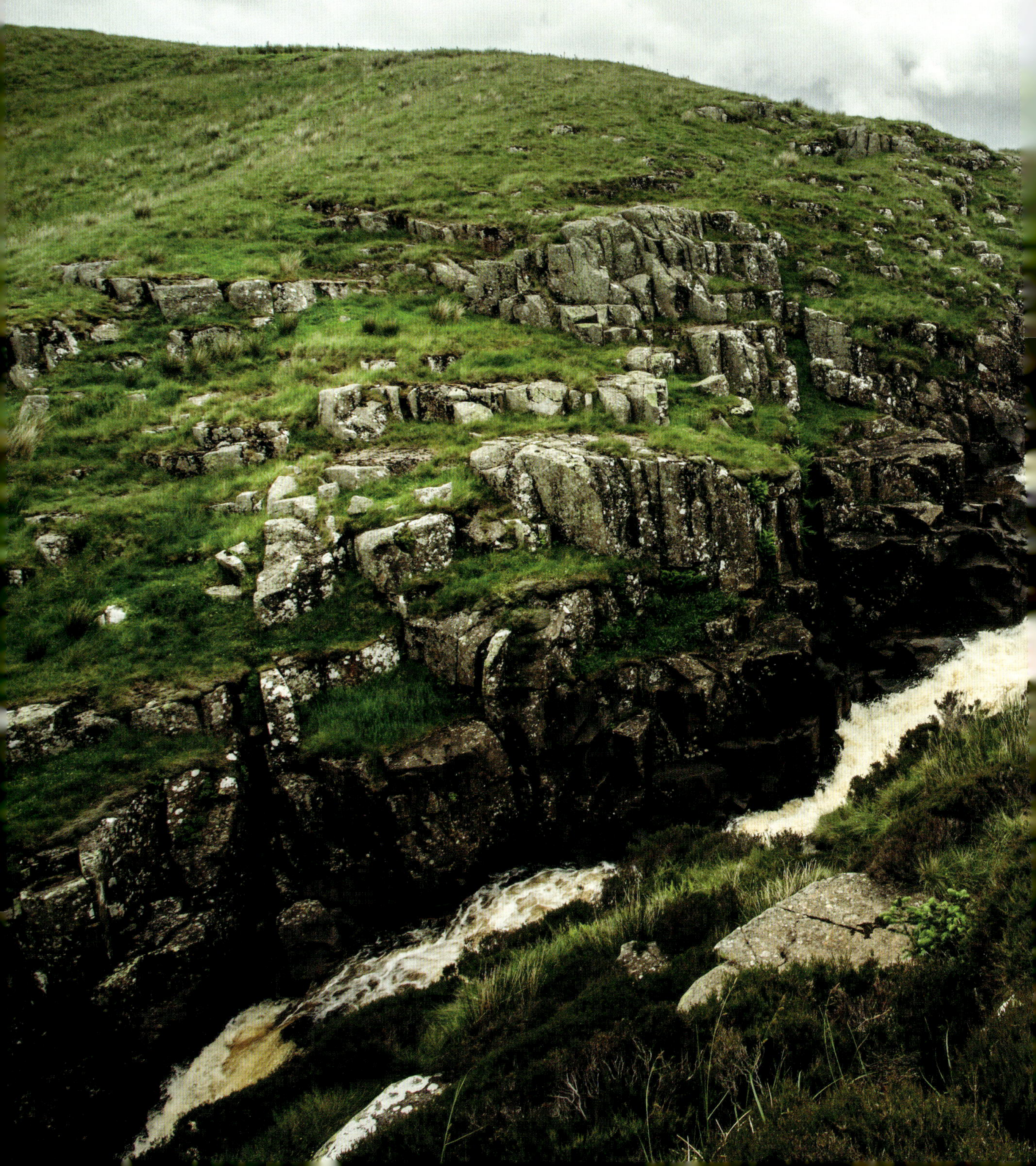

The Pennine Way on the right of Cauldron Snout Waterfall on the River Tees. In the background can be seen the dam of Cow Green Reservoir. Cauldron Snout is the longest waterfall in England, stretching 200 yards

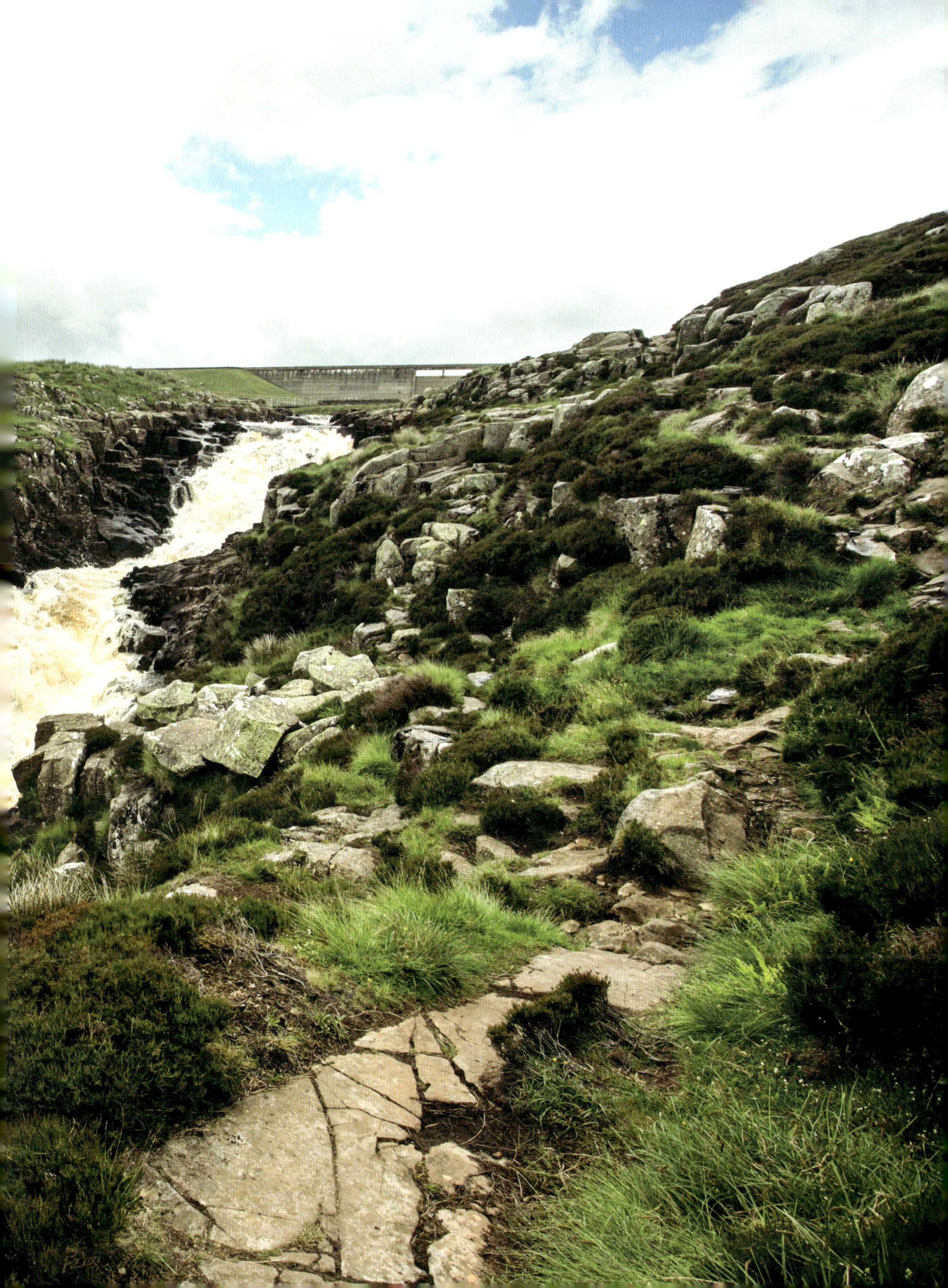

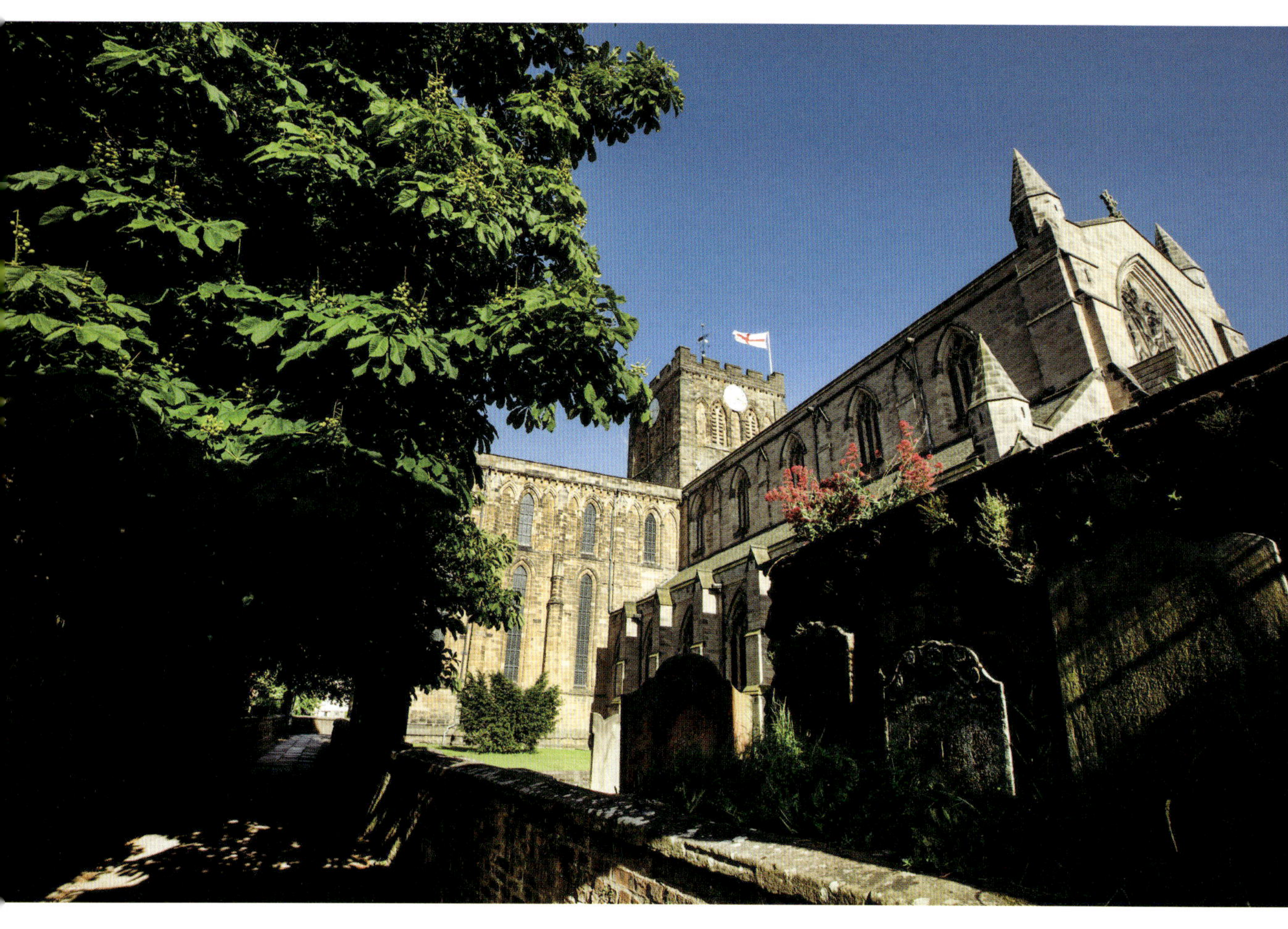

Above: The 12th century Hexham Abbey. There has been a church here for over 1300 years and a Saxon crypt still remains

Right: Market Street, Hexham, a town on the banks of the River Tyne with Viking roots, an Abbey and the oldest gaol in England built around 1332

Overleaf: National Hunt racing: approaching the finishing post at Hexham Racecourse, which is 760 feet above Hexham at High Yarridge

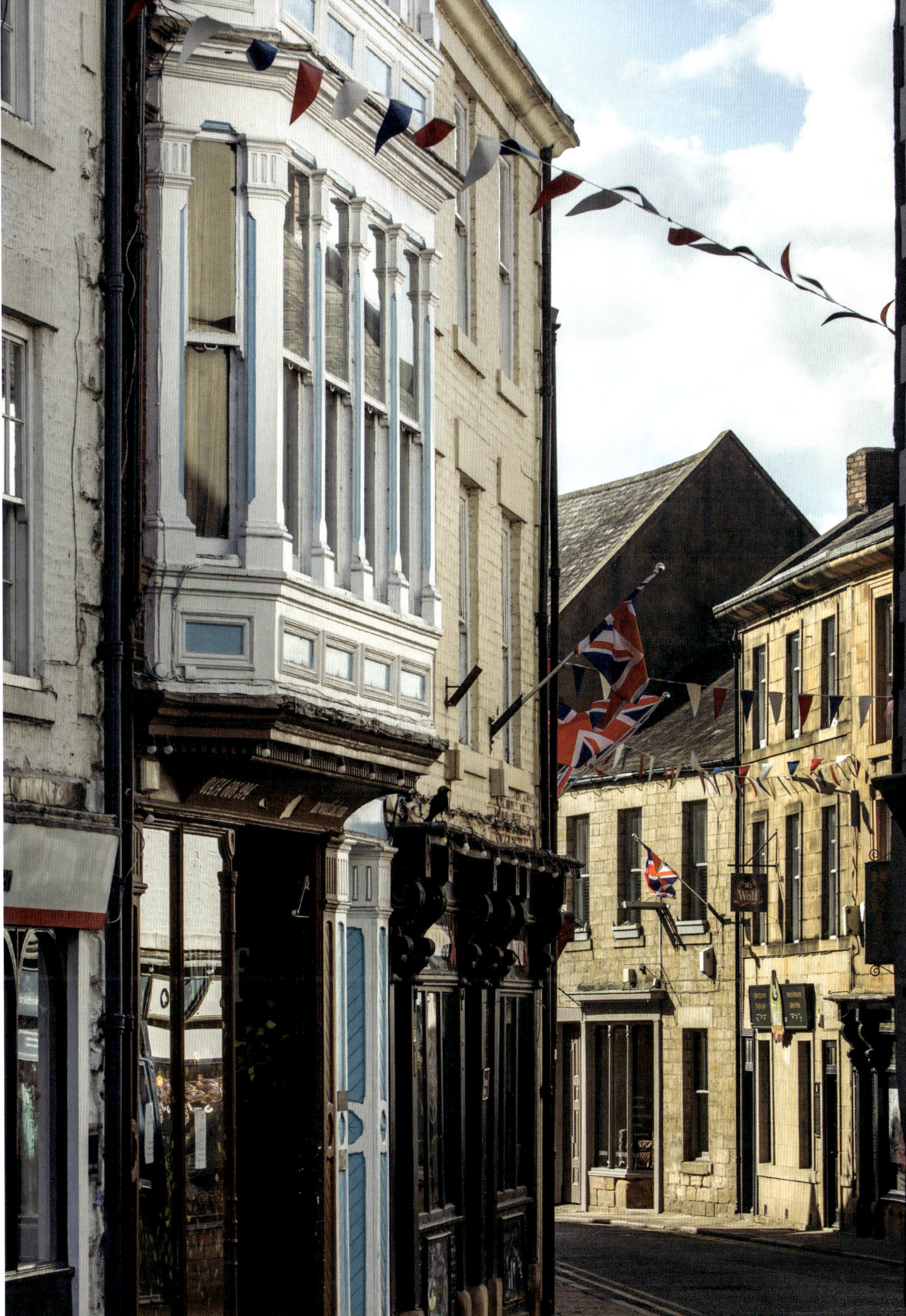

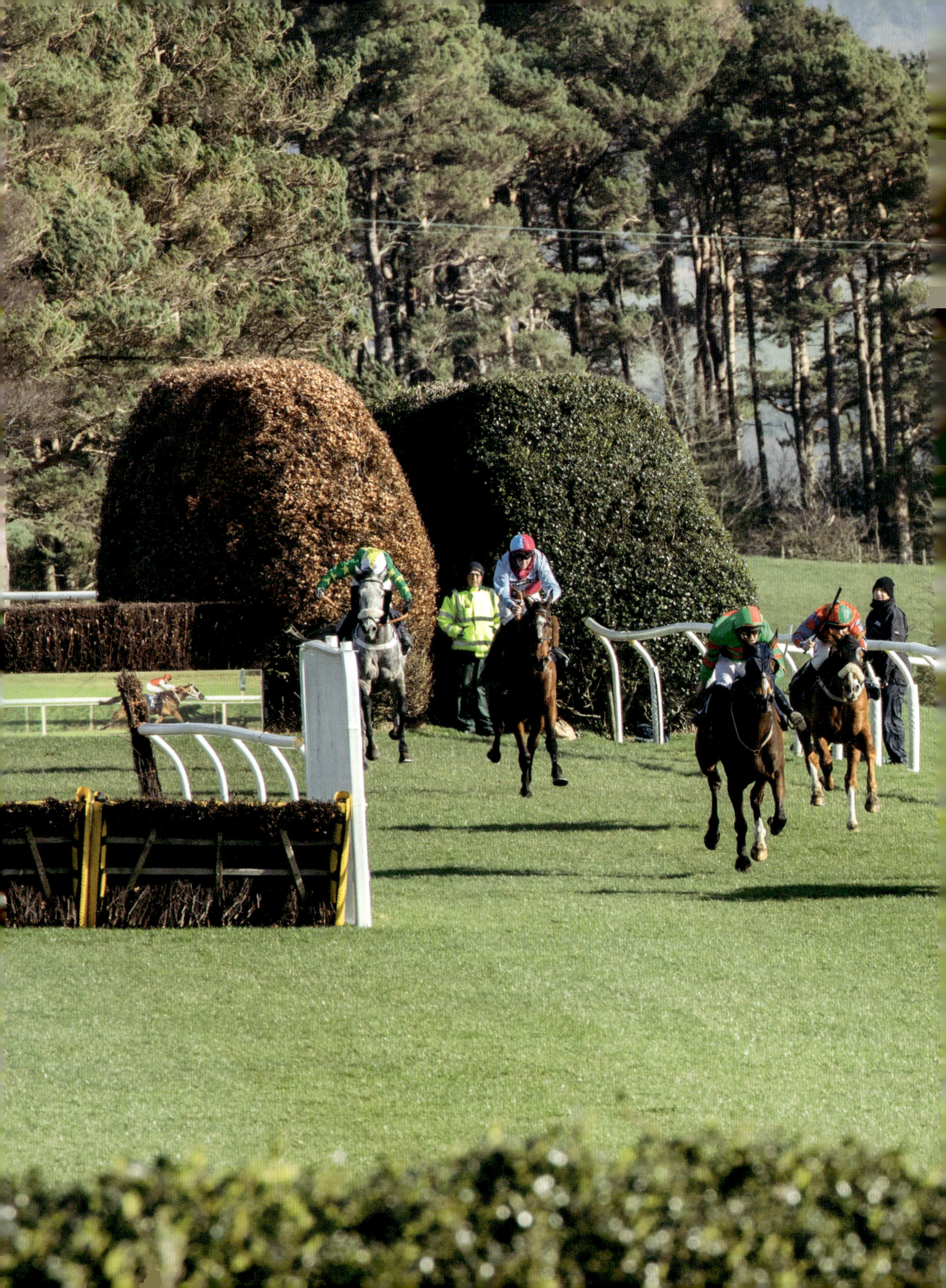

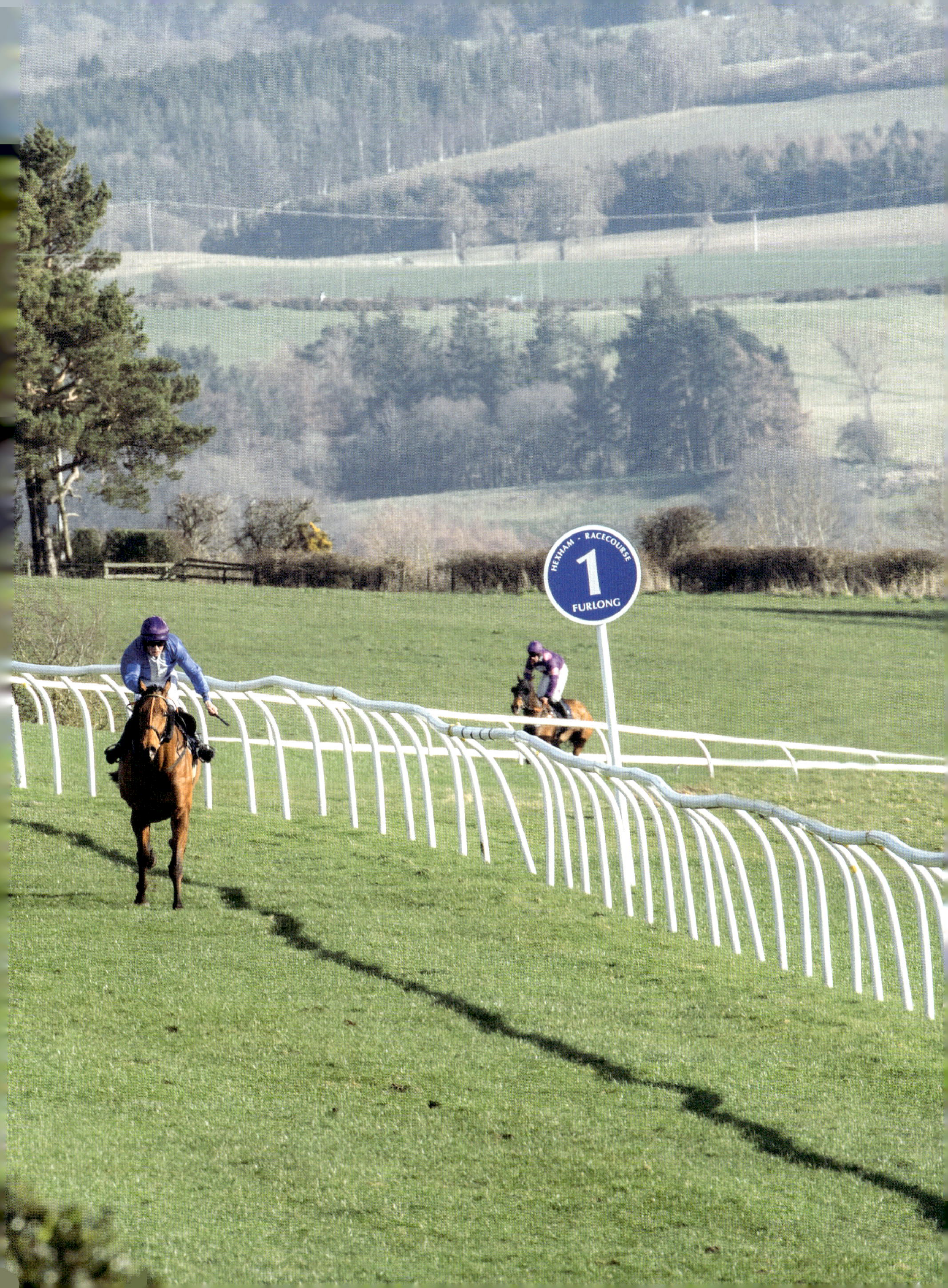

HEXHAM - RACECOURSE
1
FURLONG

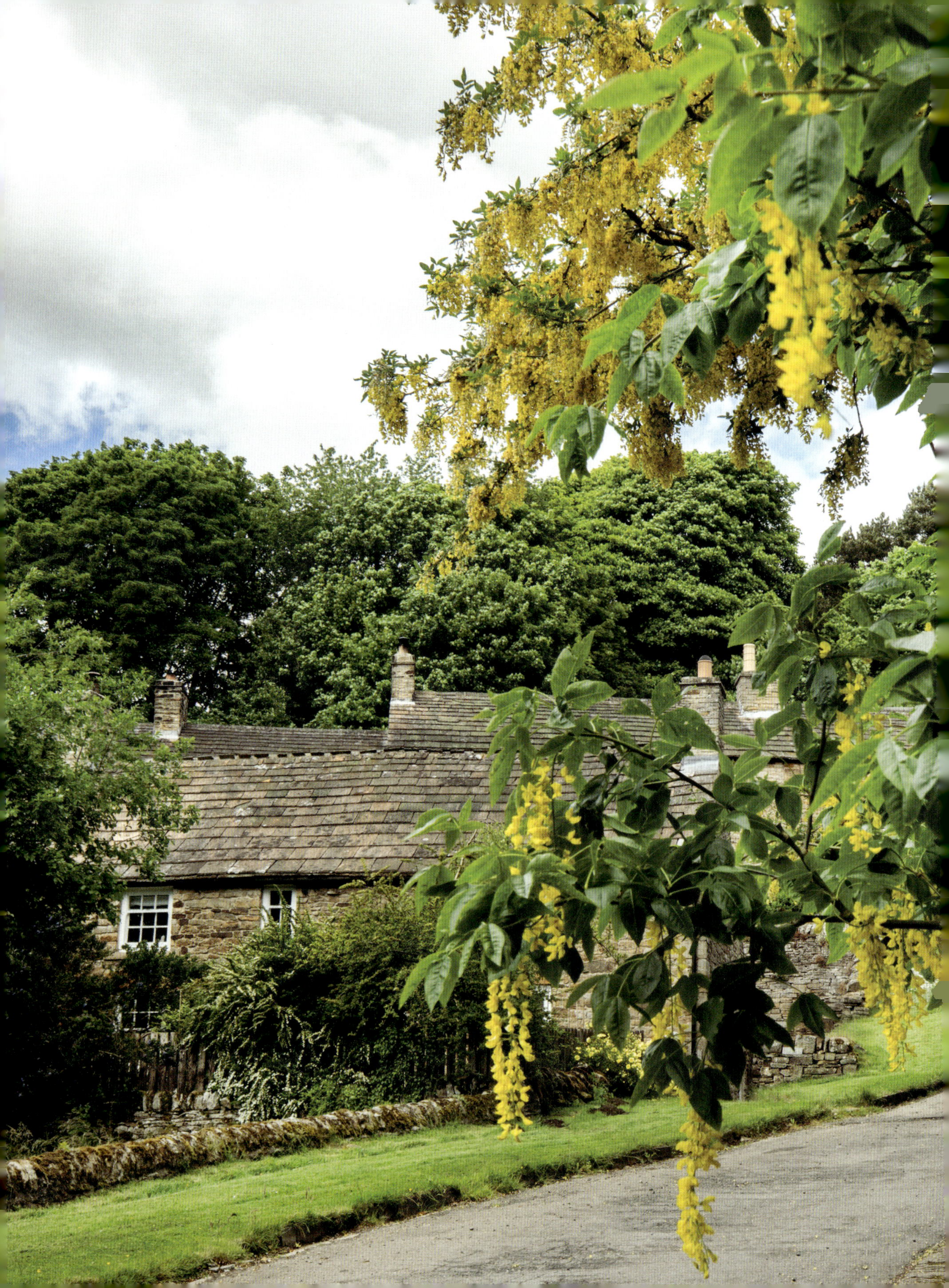

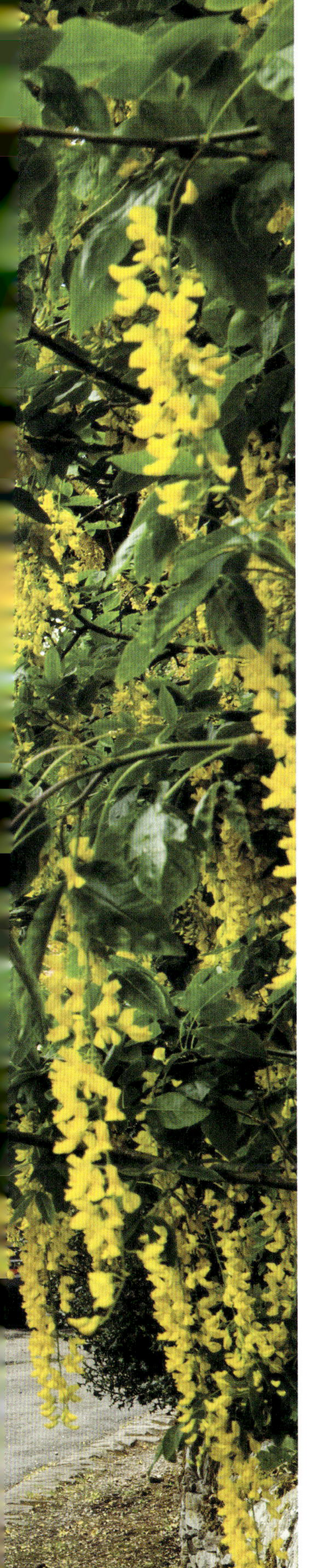

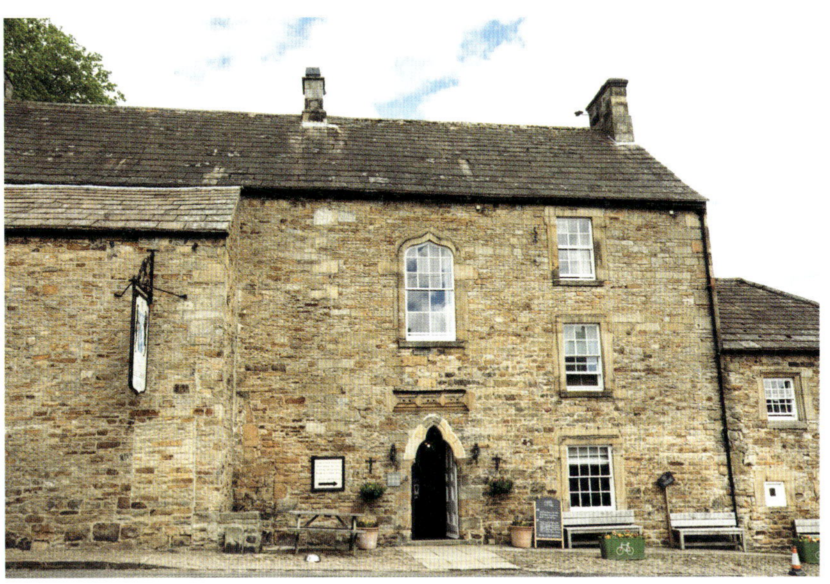

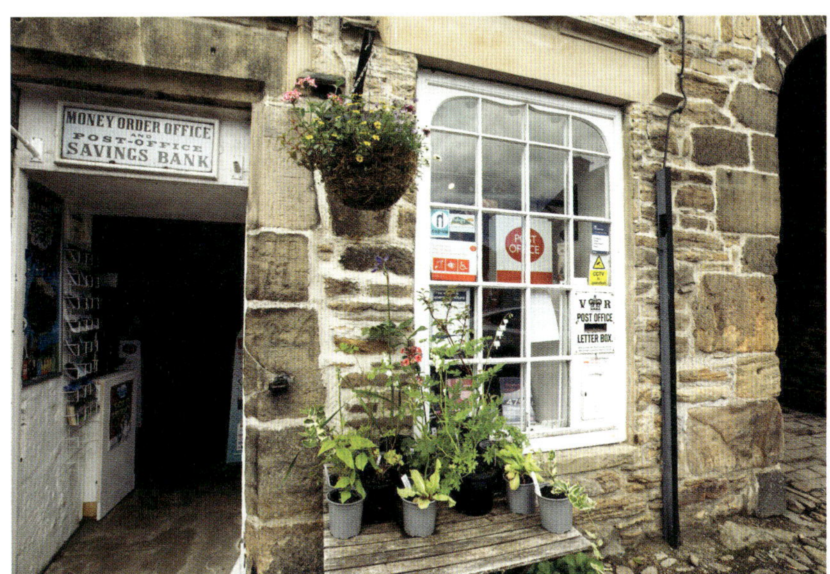

Above: The Lord Crewe Arms which started out as a guest house for Blanchland Abbey in 1165. Below is Blanchland's traditional Post Office

Left: Blanchland is a picture-perfect little village, with its medieval roots, later becoming the centre of the lead mining community in early Victorian times

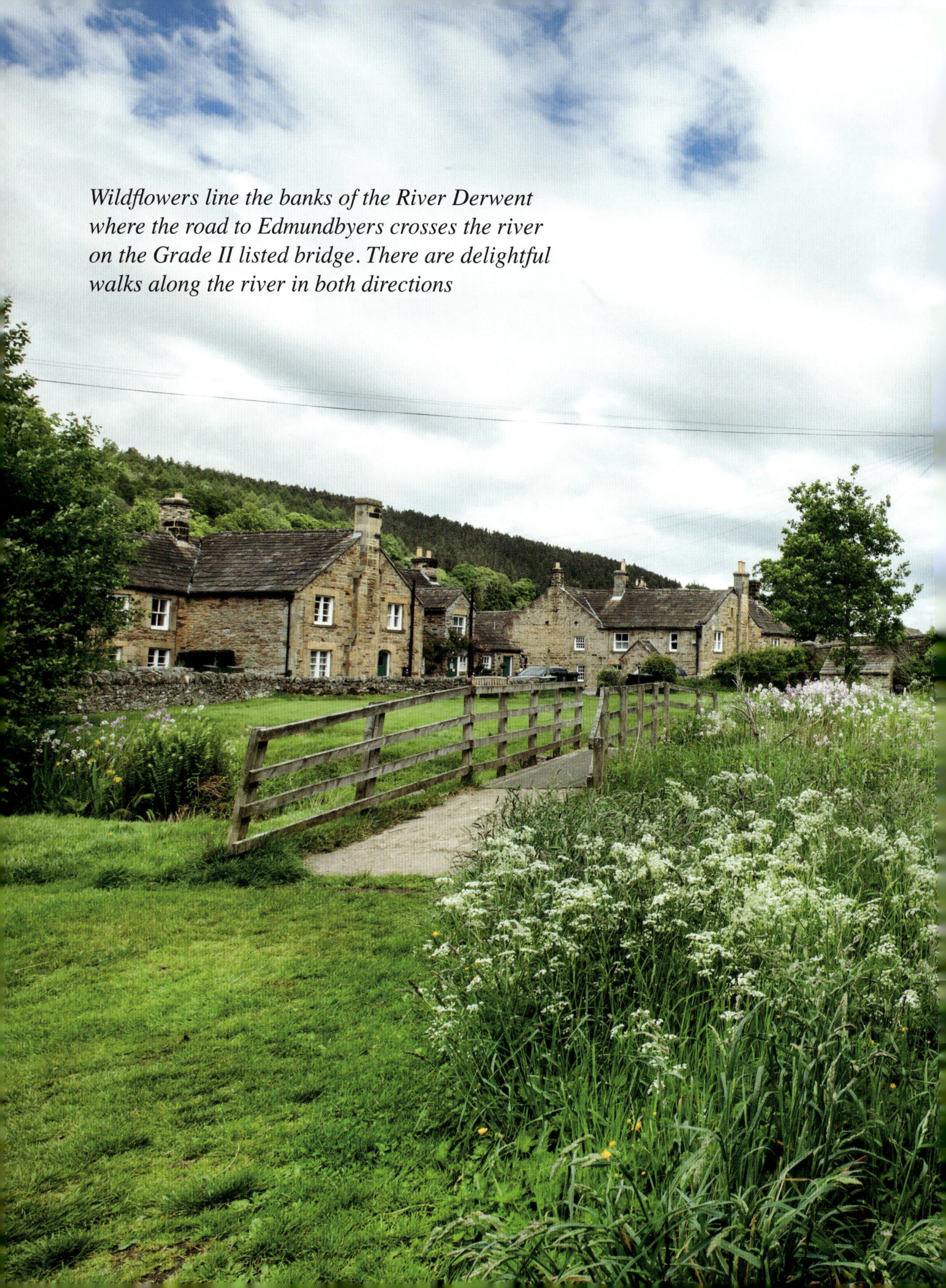
Wildflowers line the banks of the River Derwent
where the road to Edmundbyers crosses the river
on the Grade II listed bridge. There are delightful
walks along the river in both directions

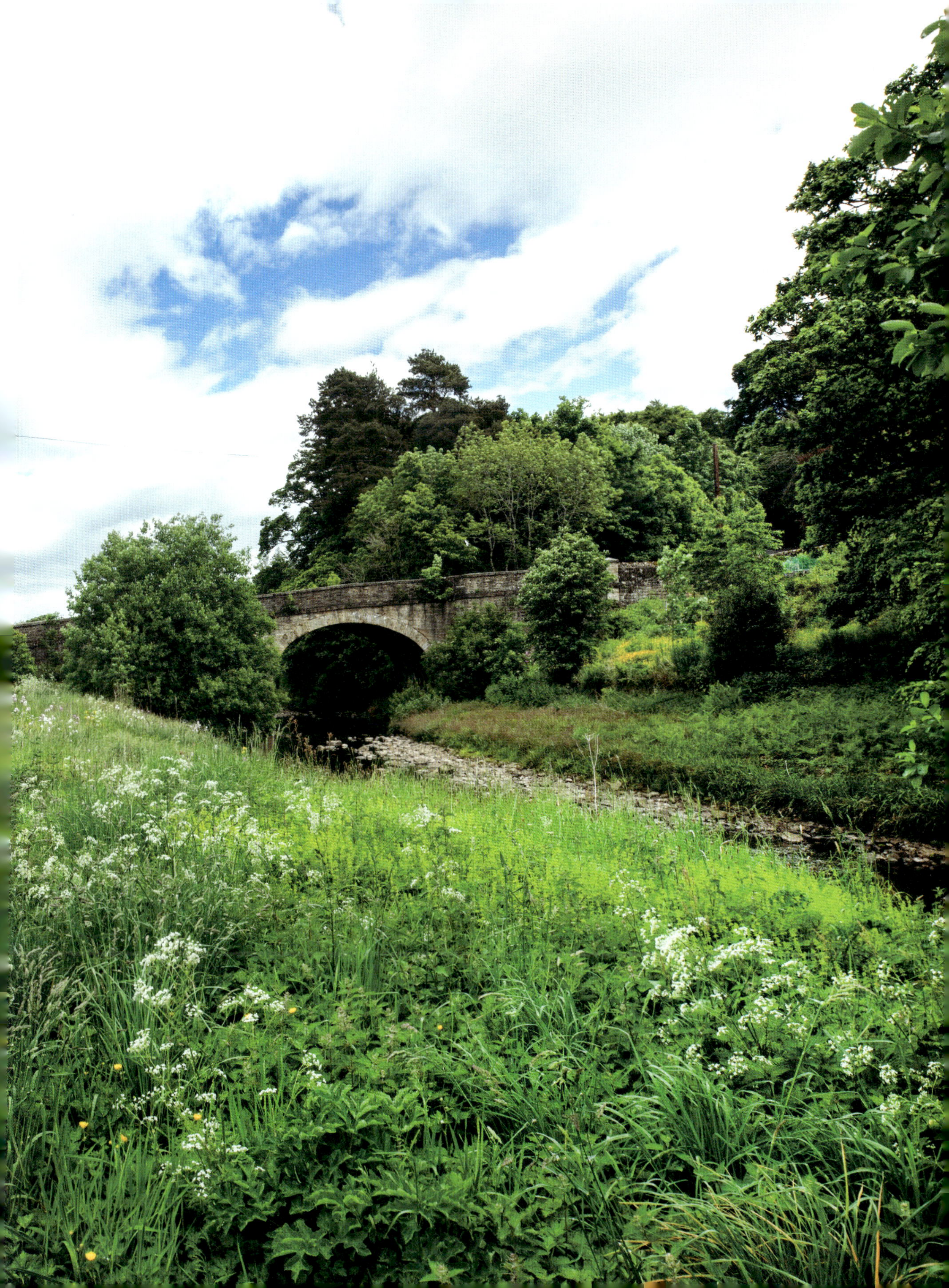

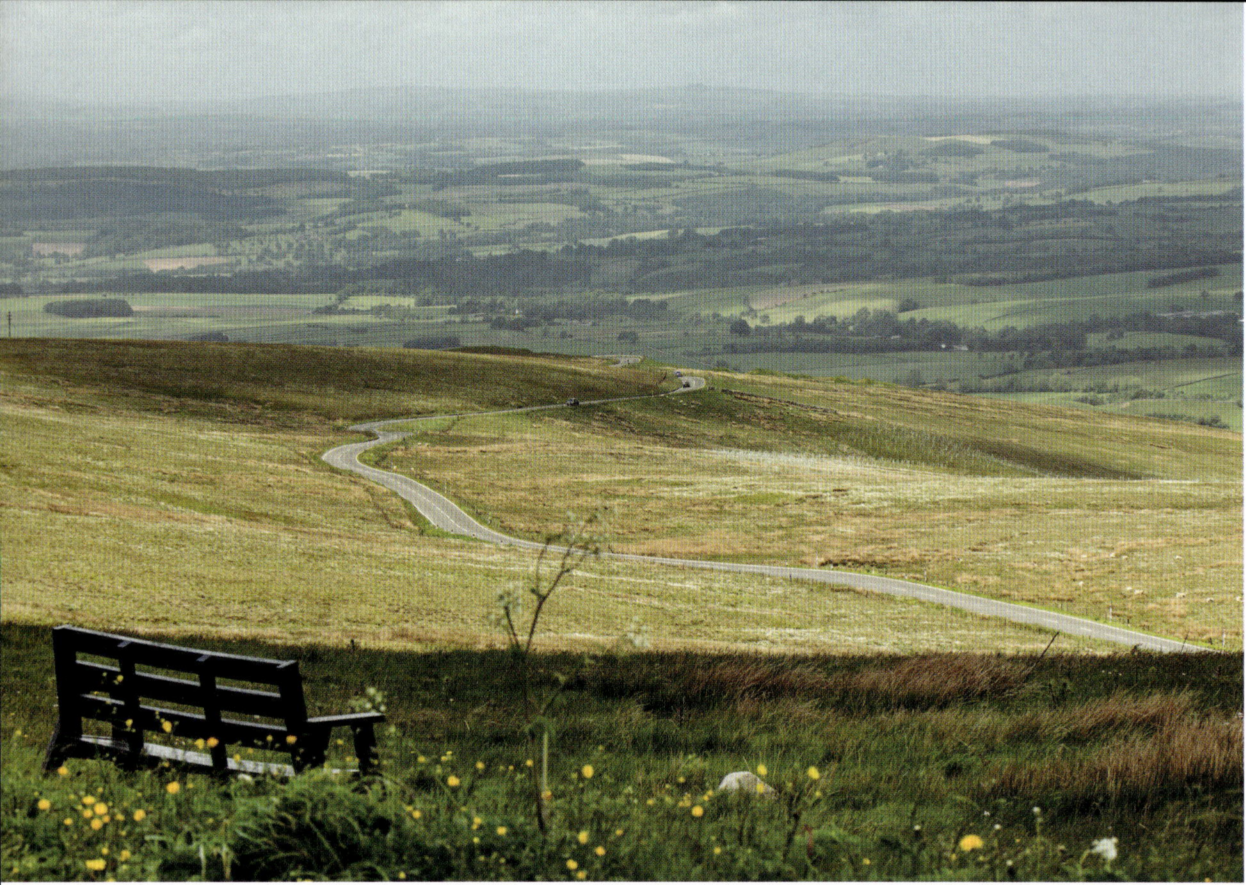

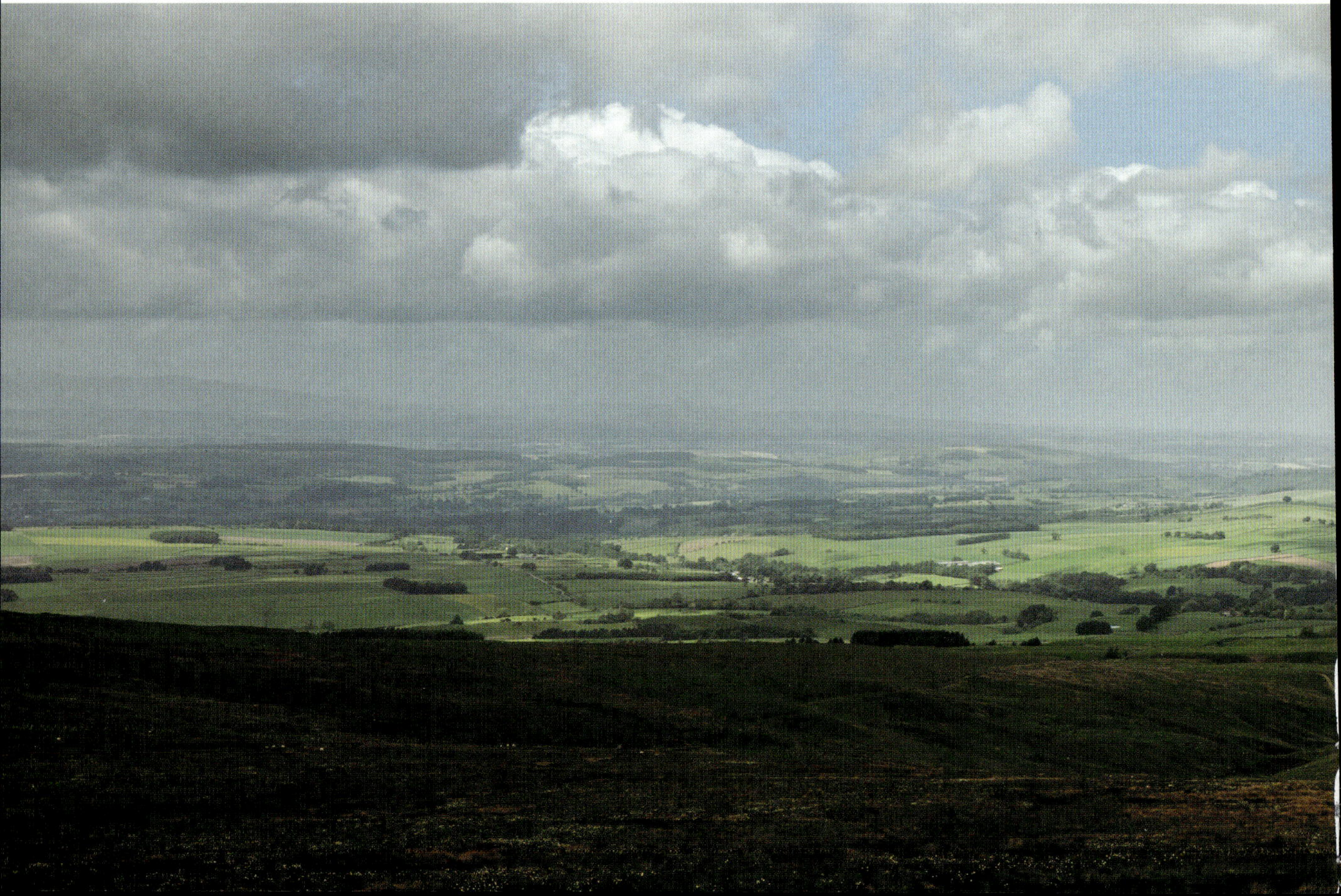

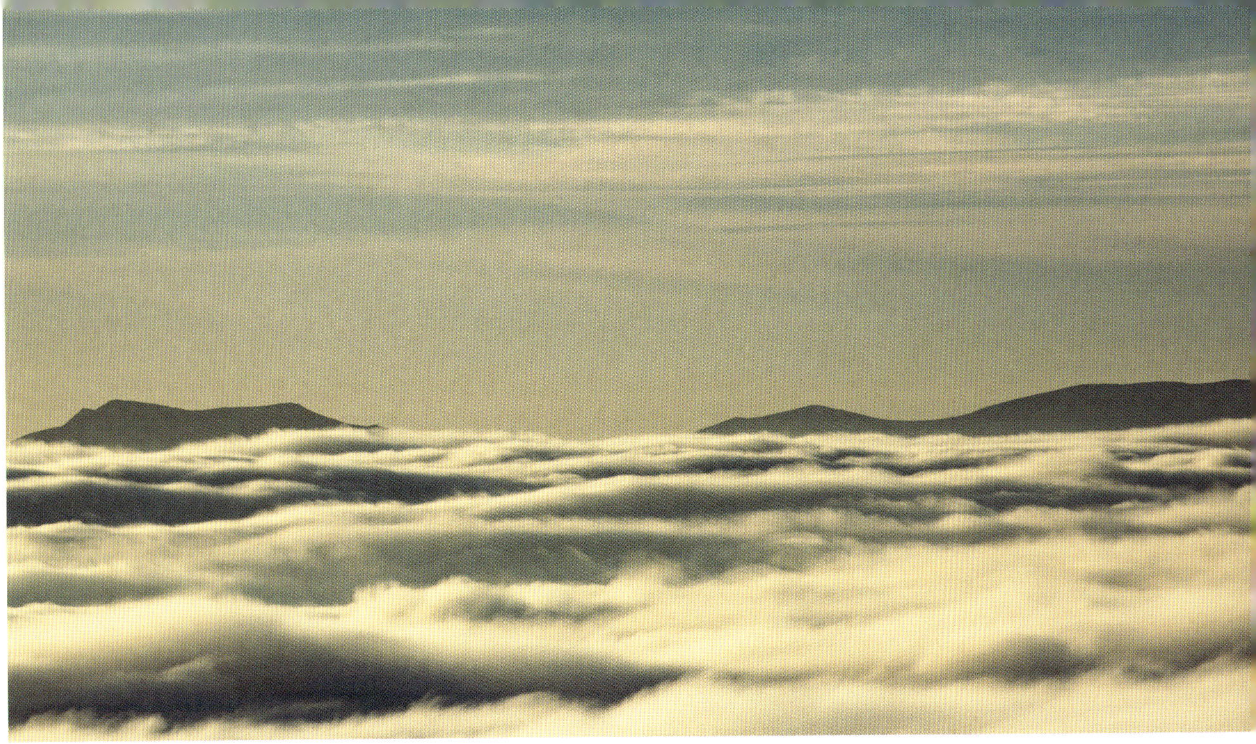

Hartside Pass, between Melmerby and Alston, rises to 1904 feet. The views from the summit stretch as far as the Solway Firth and (above) Blencathra and the Lake District mountains

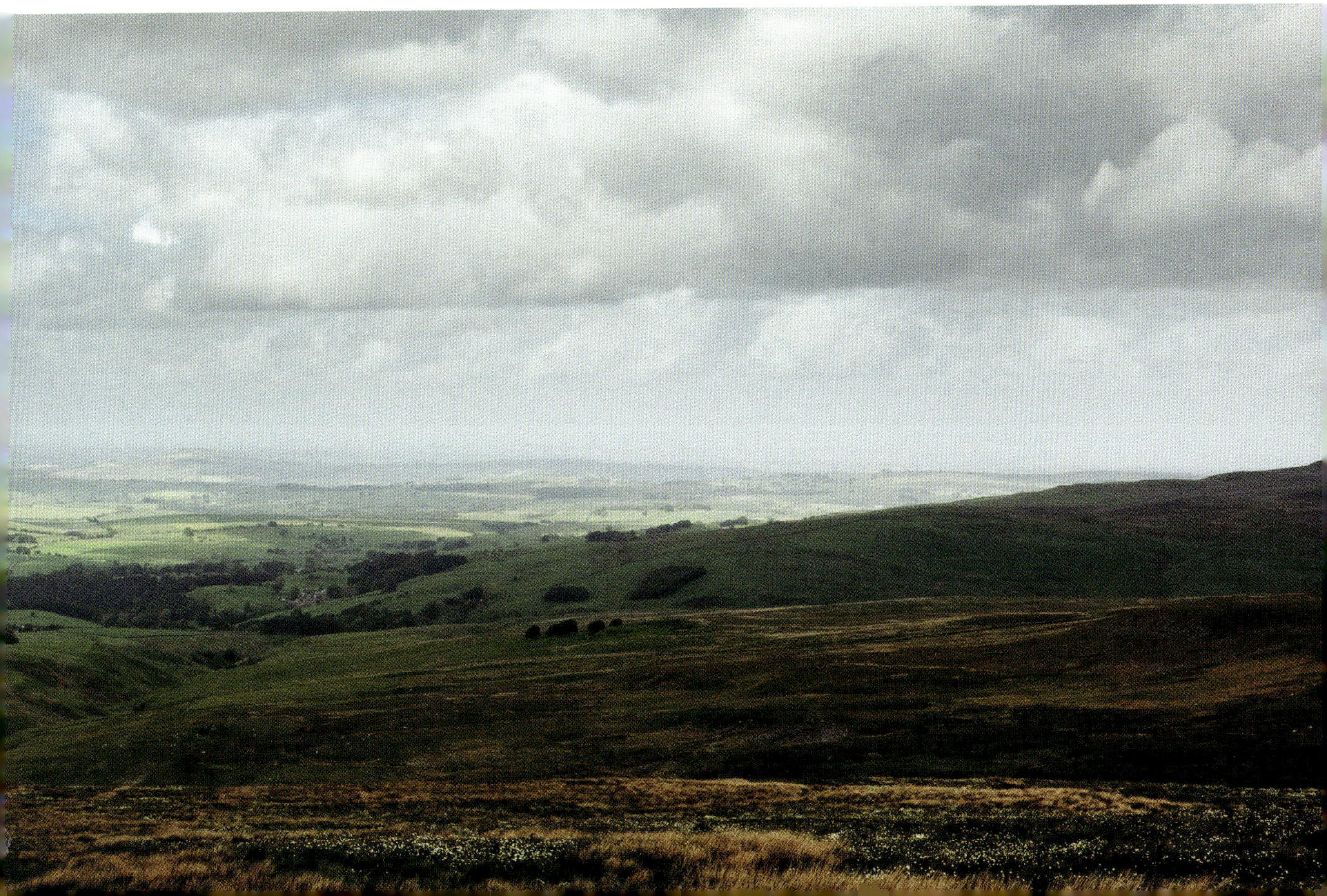

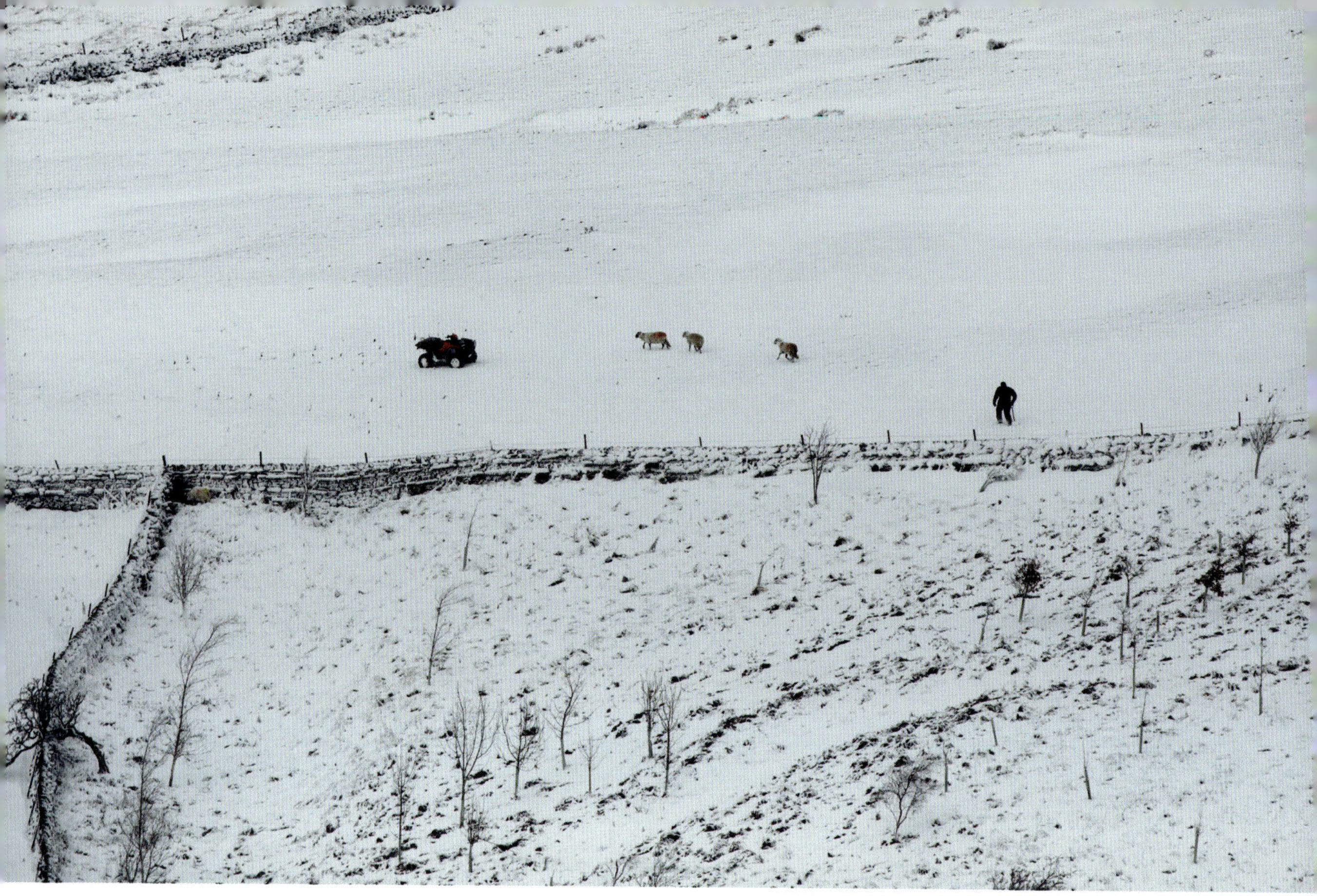

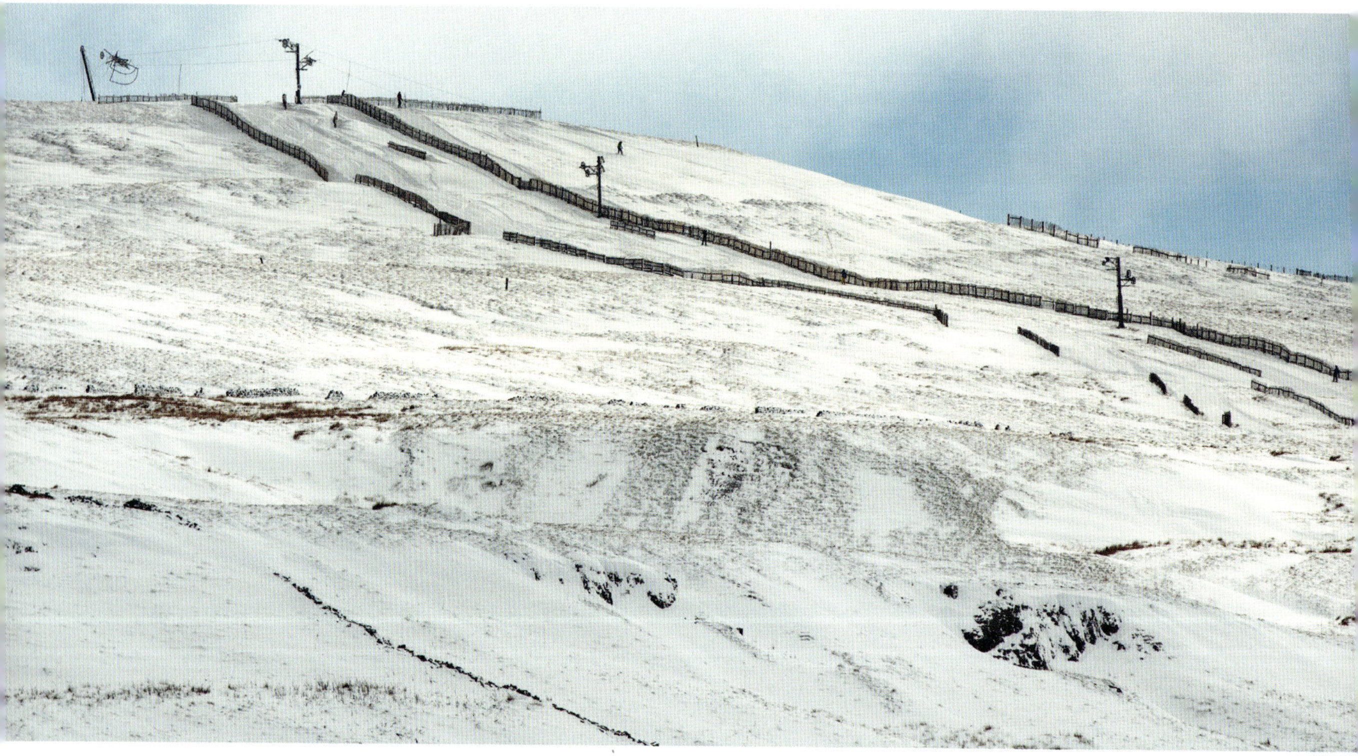

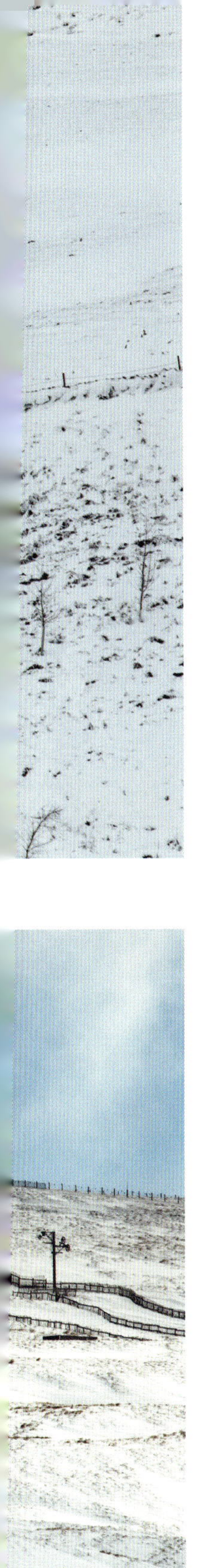

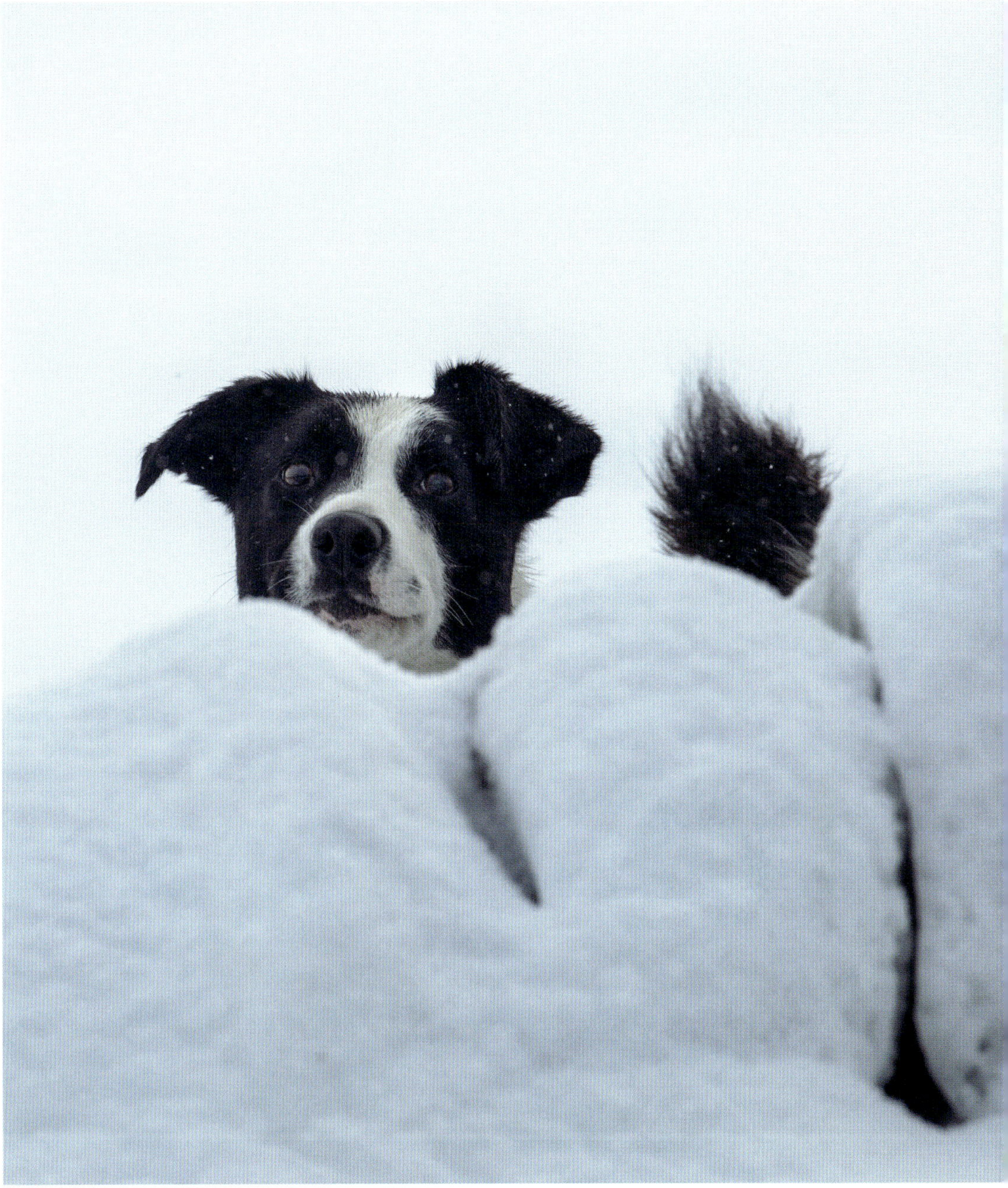

Winters in the North Pennines can be very harsh and there are frequent
heavy snowfalls, so much so that there is a ski run and ski tows at Yad
Moss (left) in the upper Tyne Valley and at several other locations in the
area. No matter the weather, farmers have to feed and check on their
sheep (top left) and faithful sheepdogs are always ready to work. Moss
(above) lives at High Crossgill Farm outside Garrigill

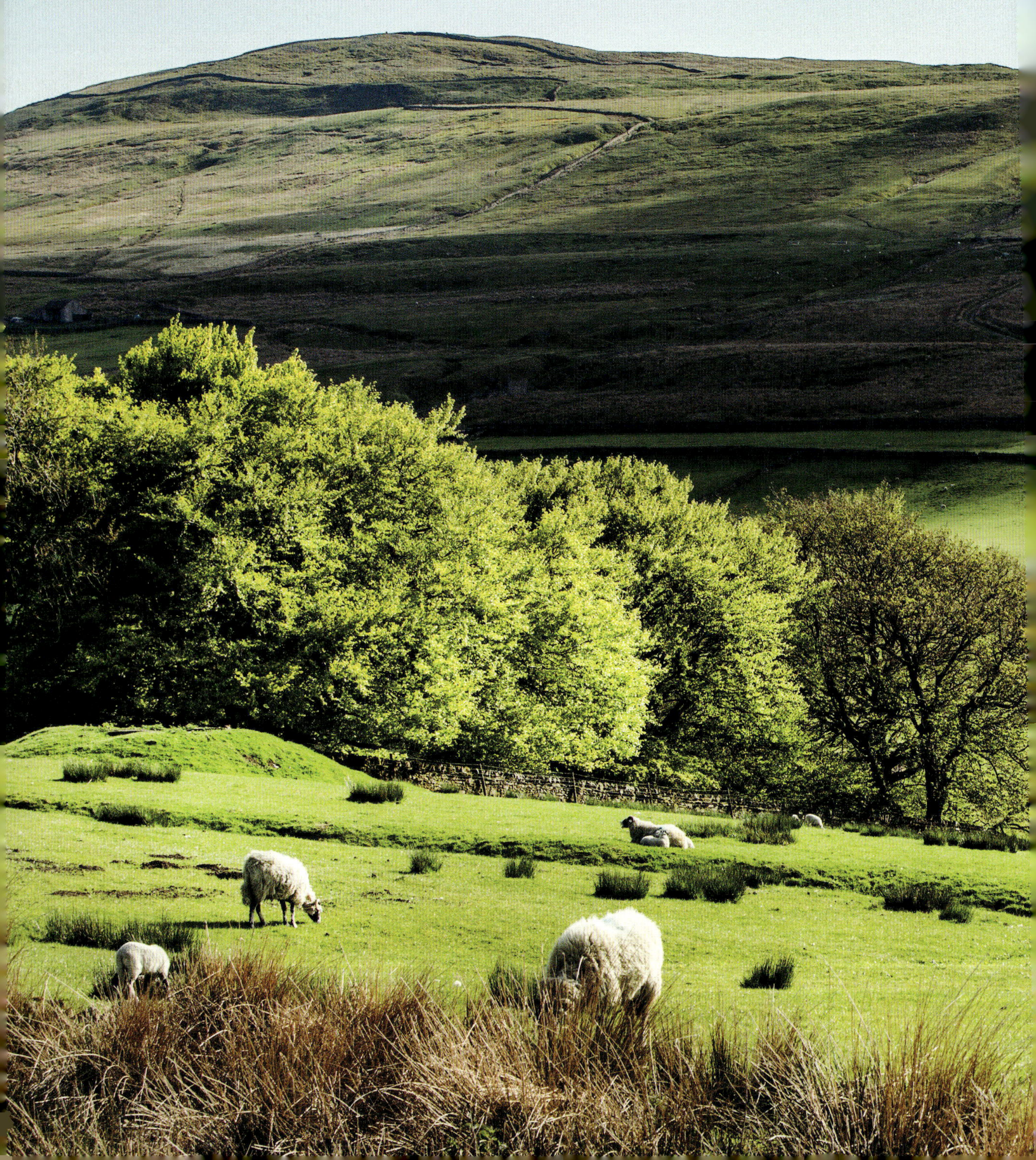

Middle Lee, the photographer/author's home. The property lies south of Garrigill close to the source of the River South Tyne and on the lower slopes of Cross Fell to the west

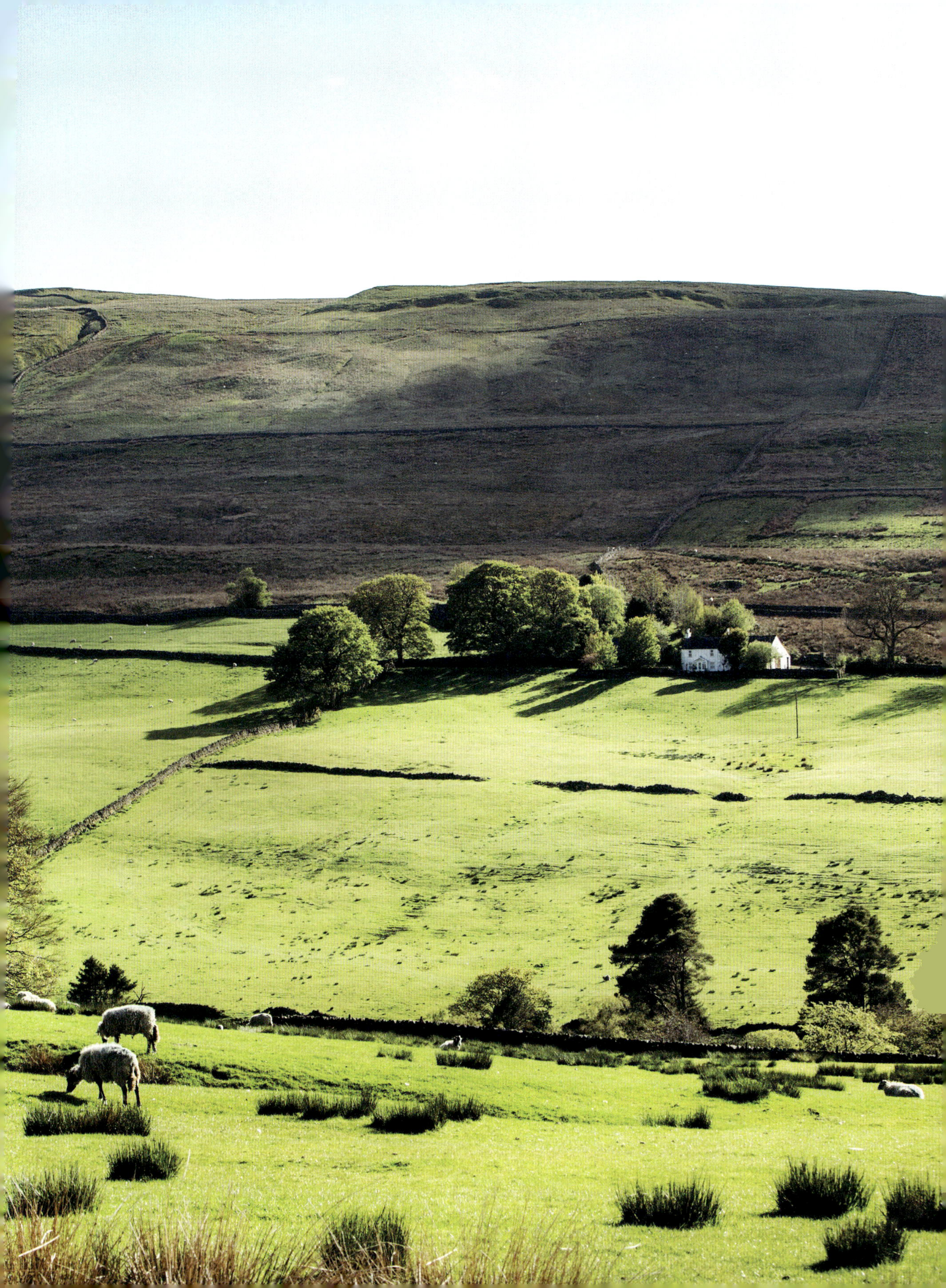

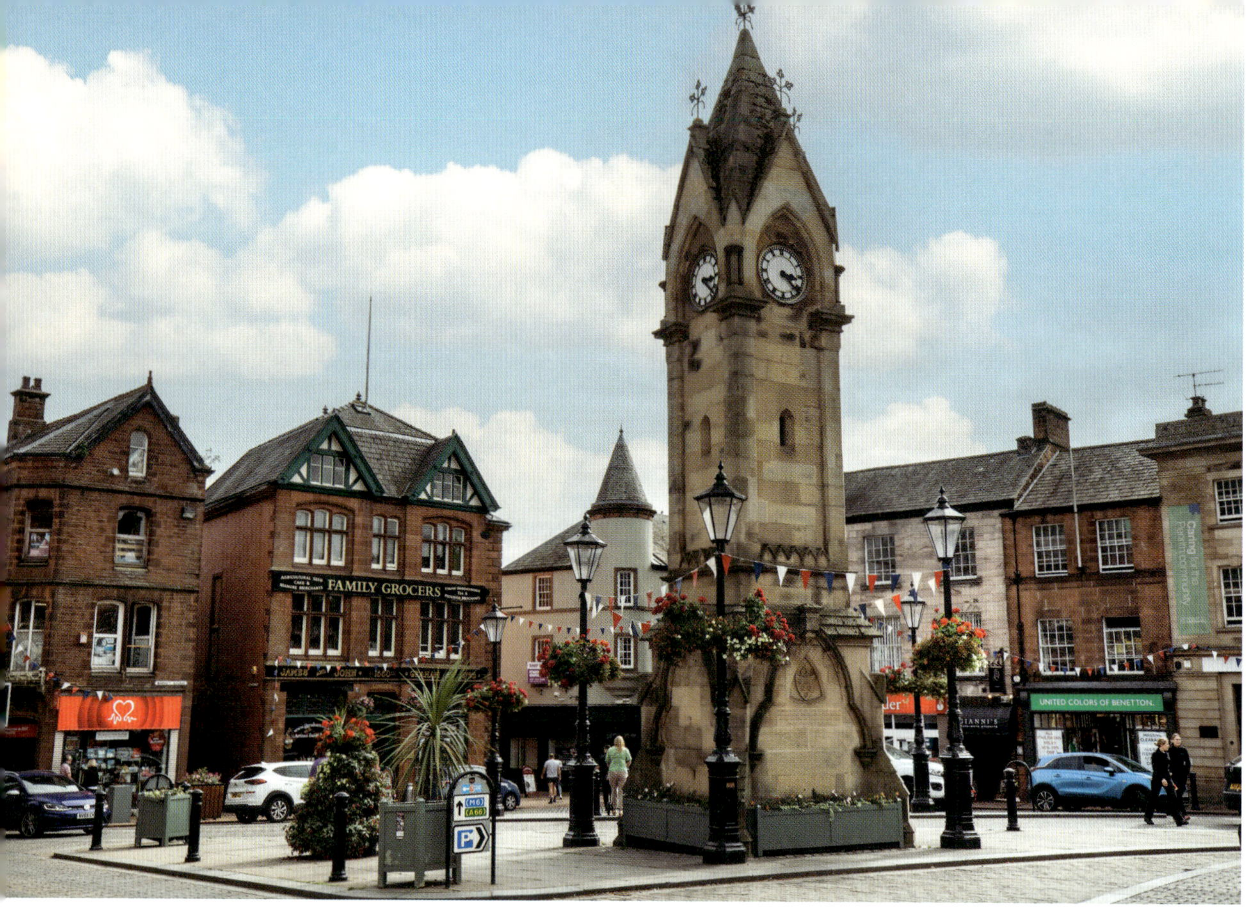

Penrith, in the Eden Valley. The clock tower in Market Square is also known as the Musgrave Monument. The 14th century castle was built on the site of an earlier Roman fort and is overlooked by Penrith Beacon, built in 1719

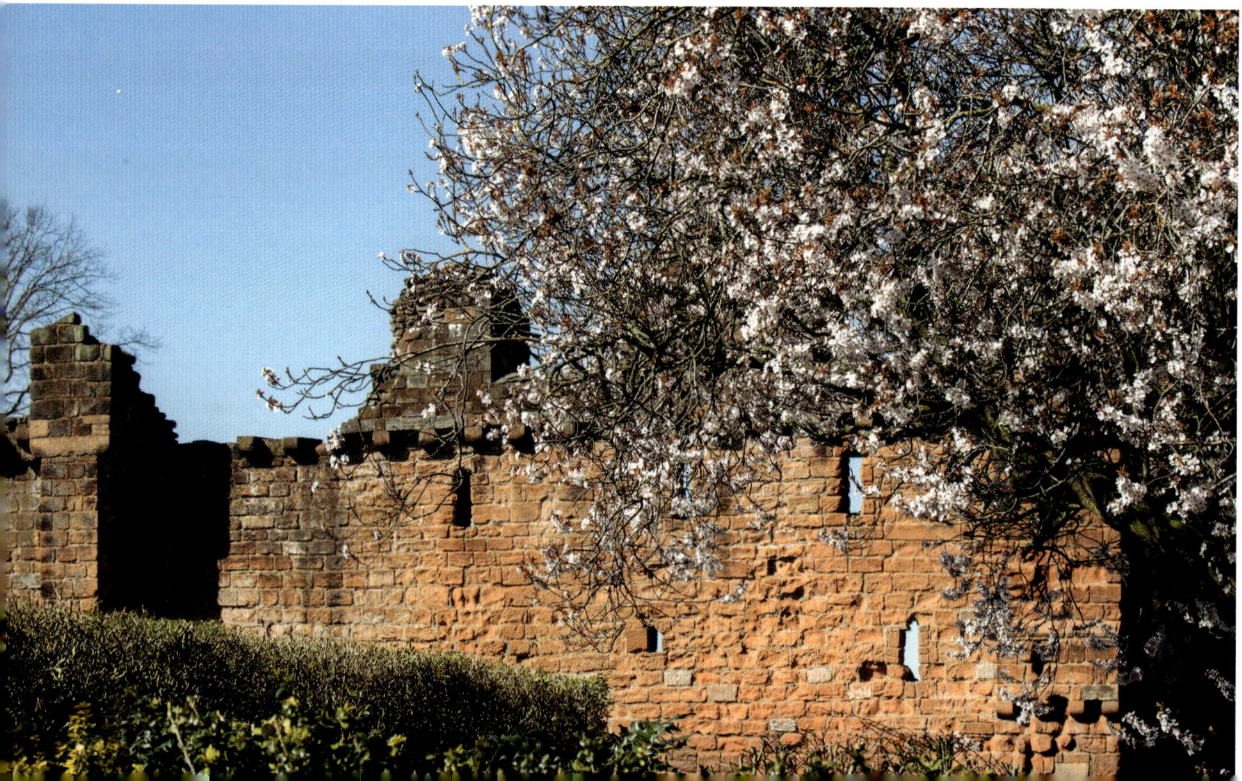

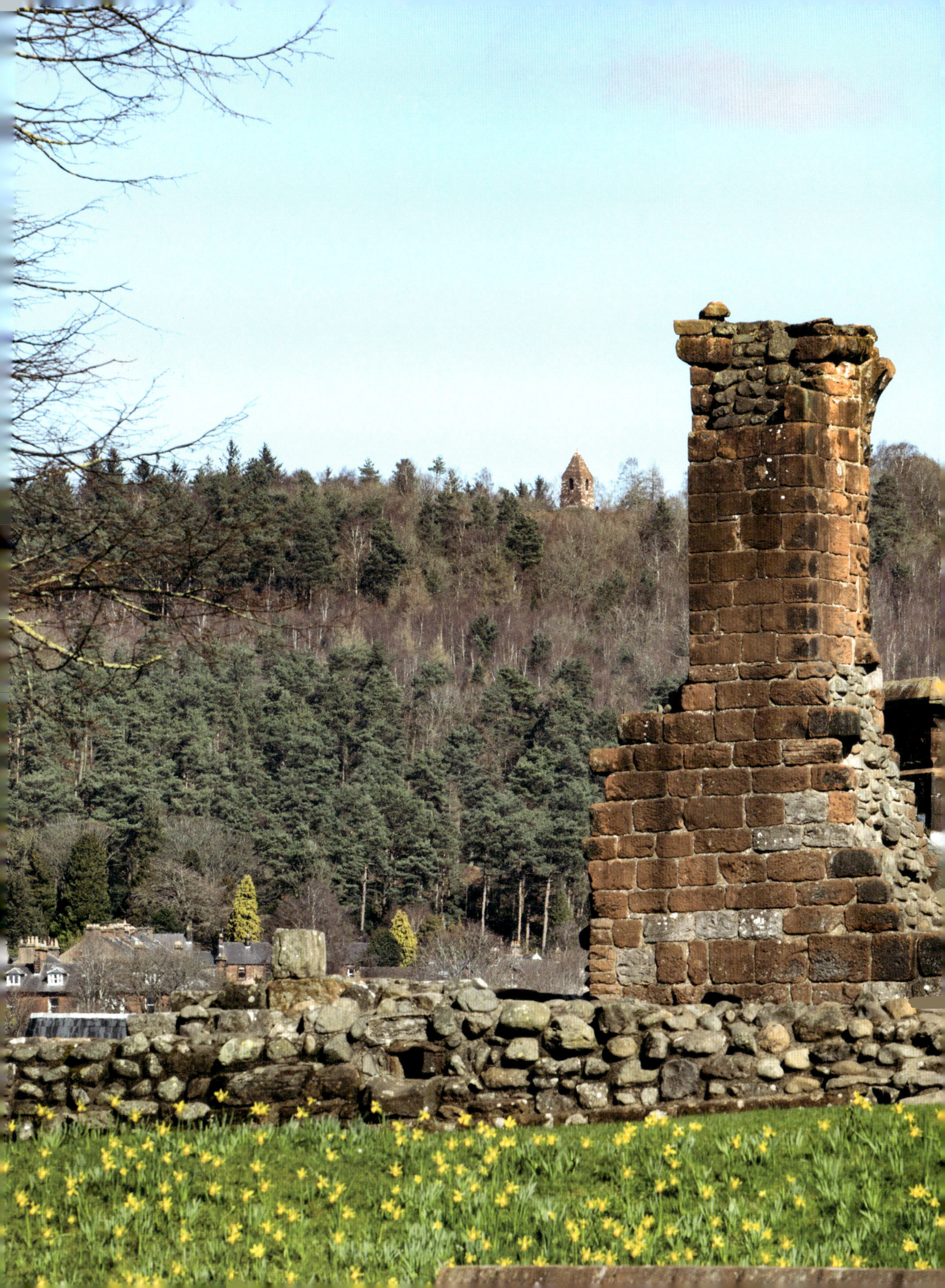

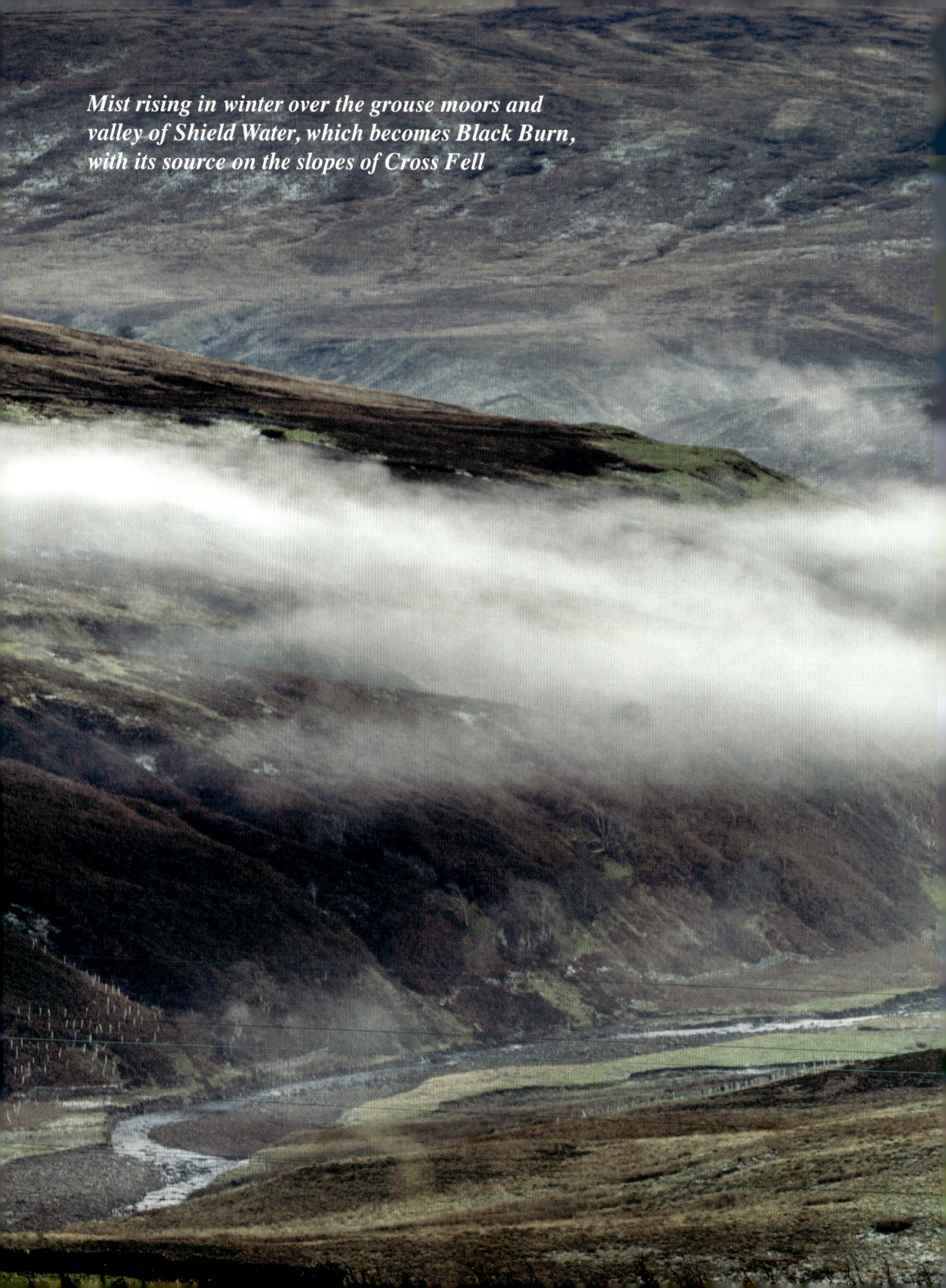

Mist rising in winter over the grouse moors and
valley of Shield Water, which becomes Black Burn,
with its source on the slopes of Cross Fell

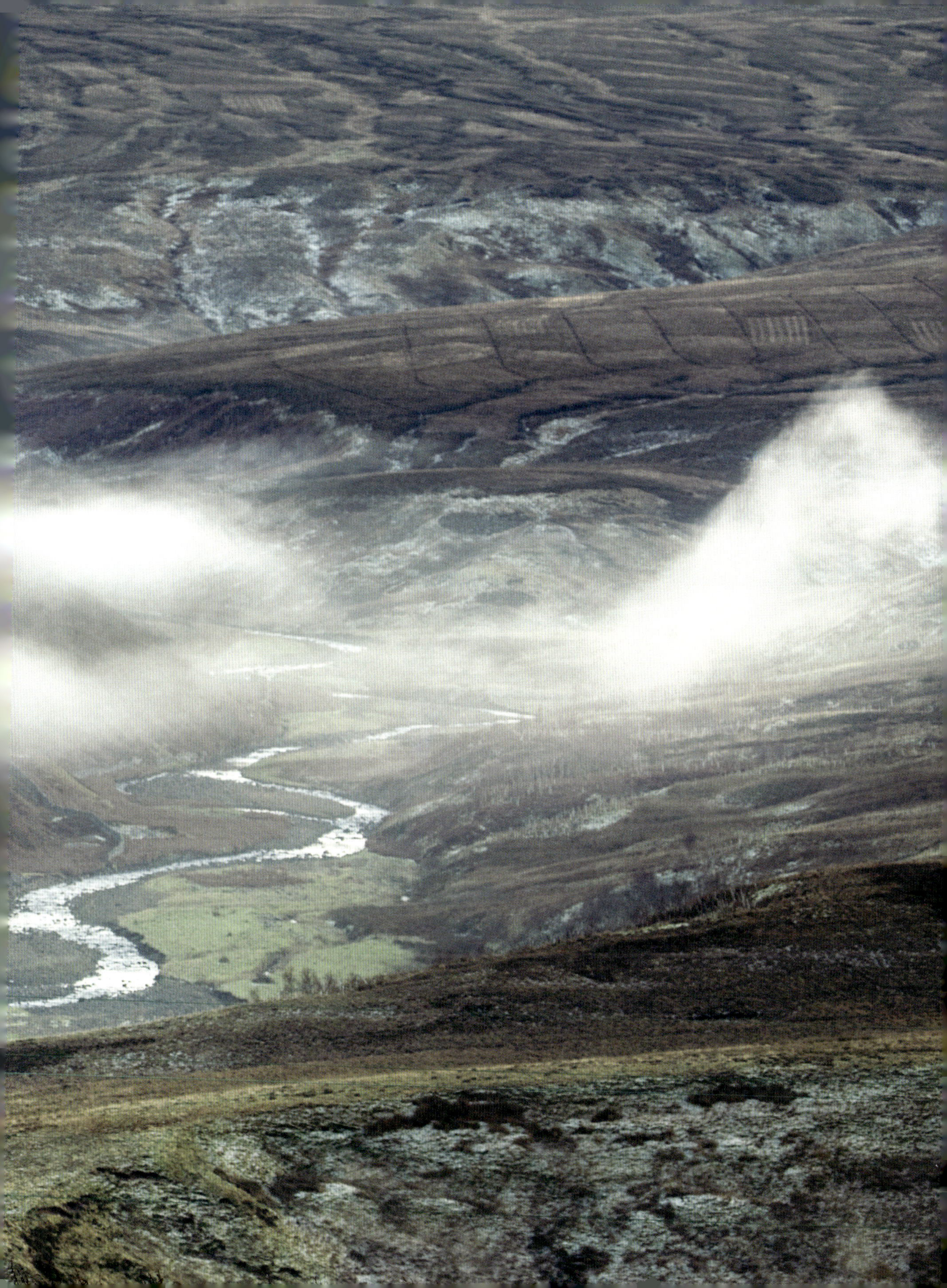

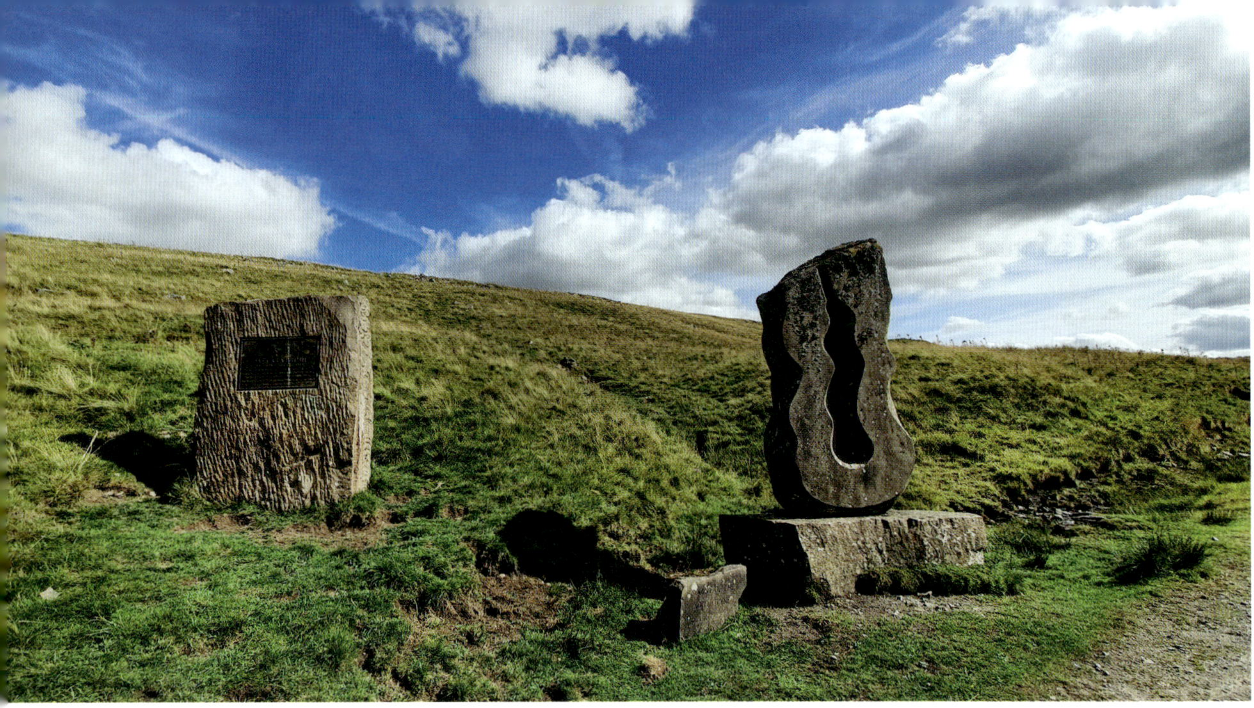

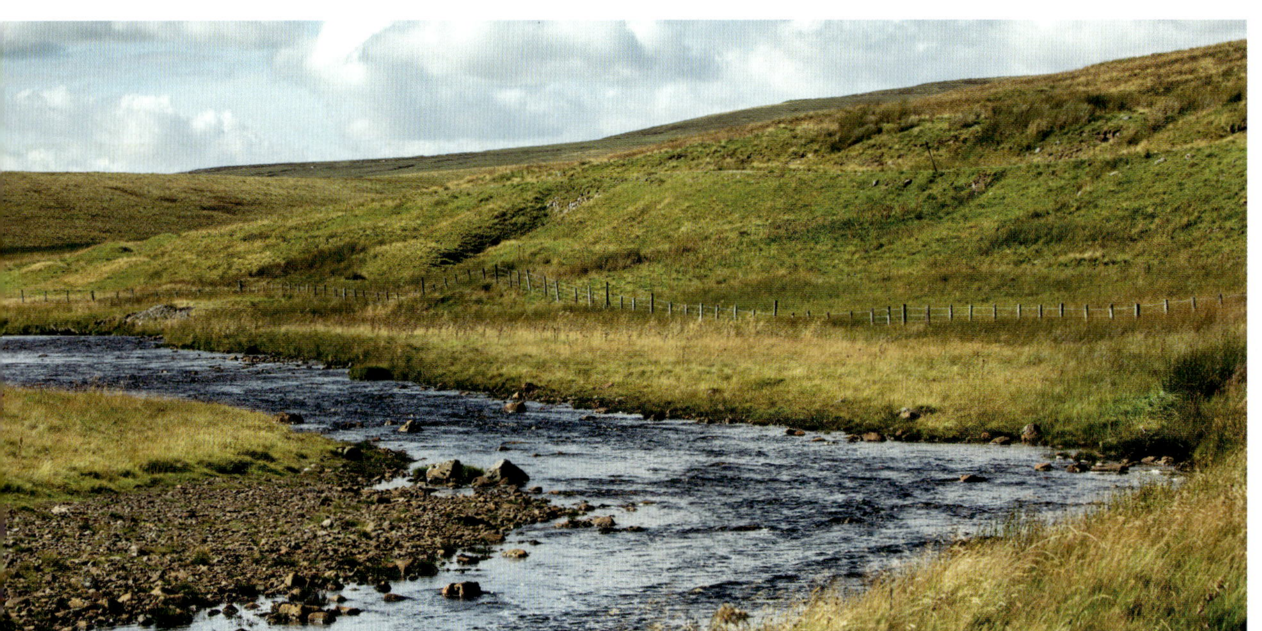

Top: Sculpture by Gilbert Ward marking the source of the River South Tyne 4 miles south of Garrigill

Middle: The River Tees at Troutbeck Foot around 2 miles from its source on Cross Fell

Right: The infant River South Tyne at Tynehead. The sources of the Tees and the South Tyne are close together on the slopes of Cross Fell

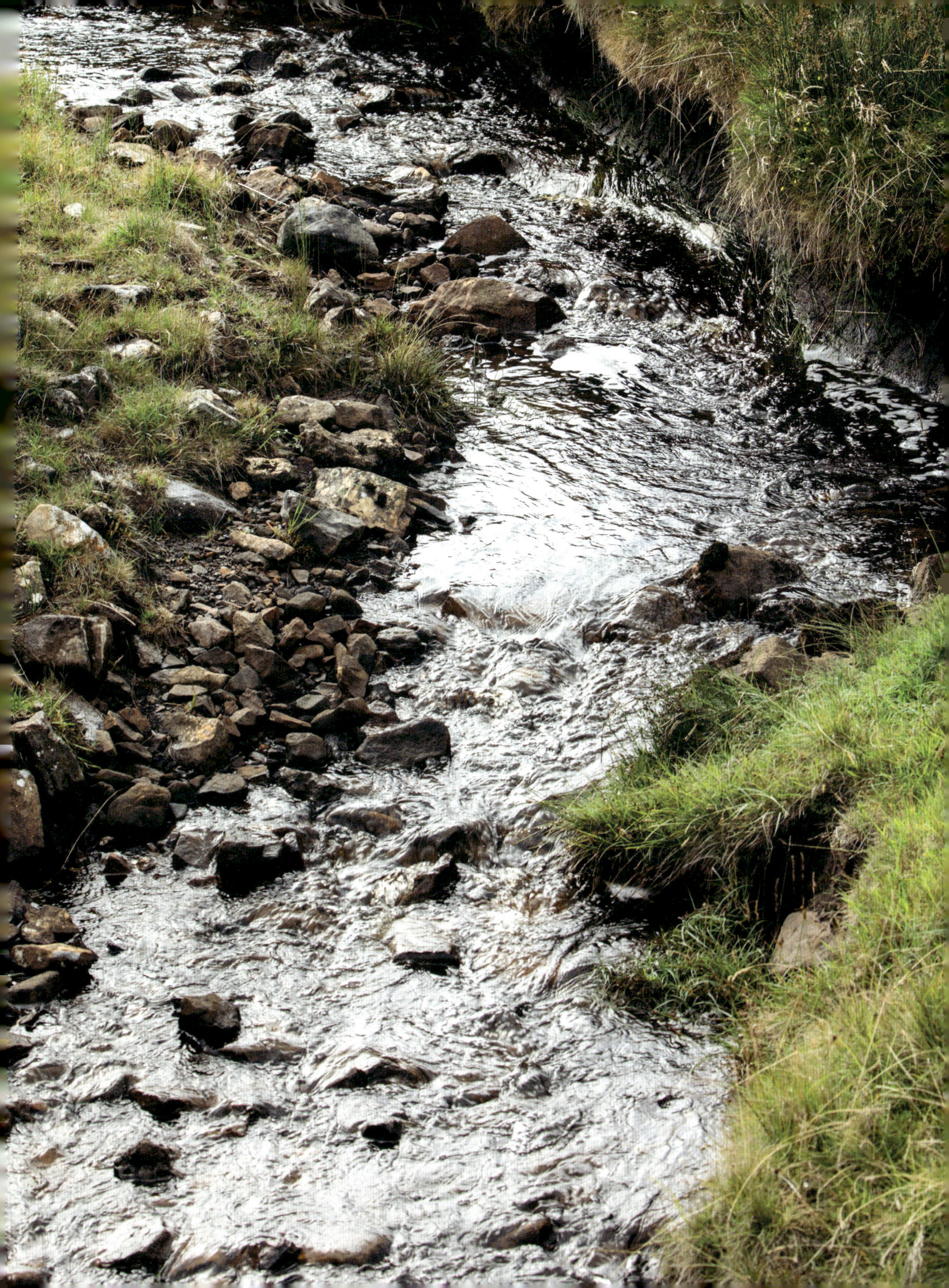

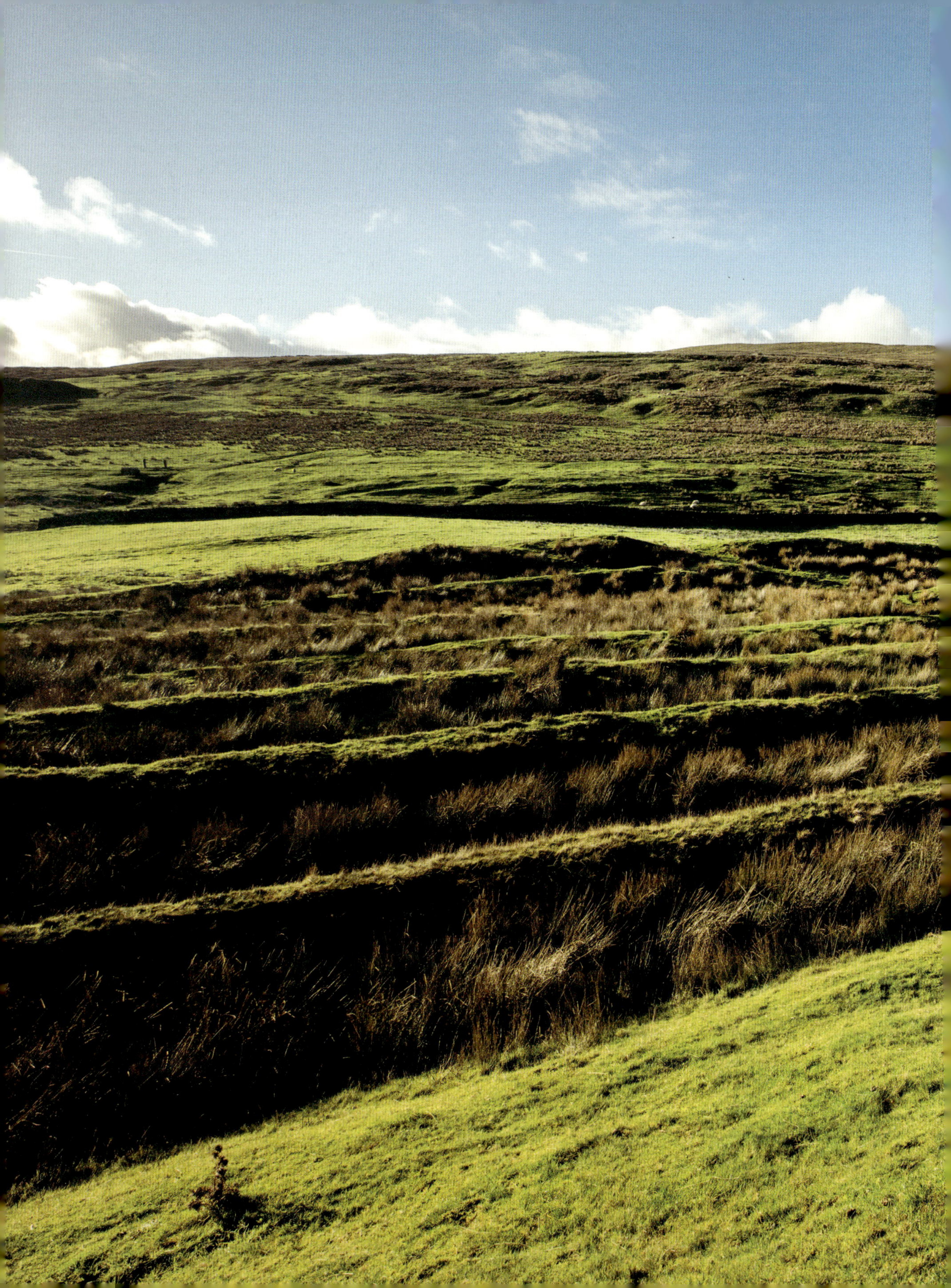

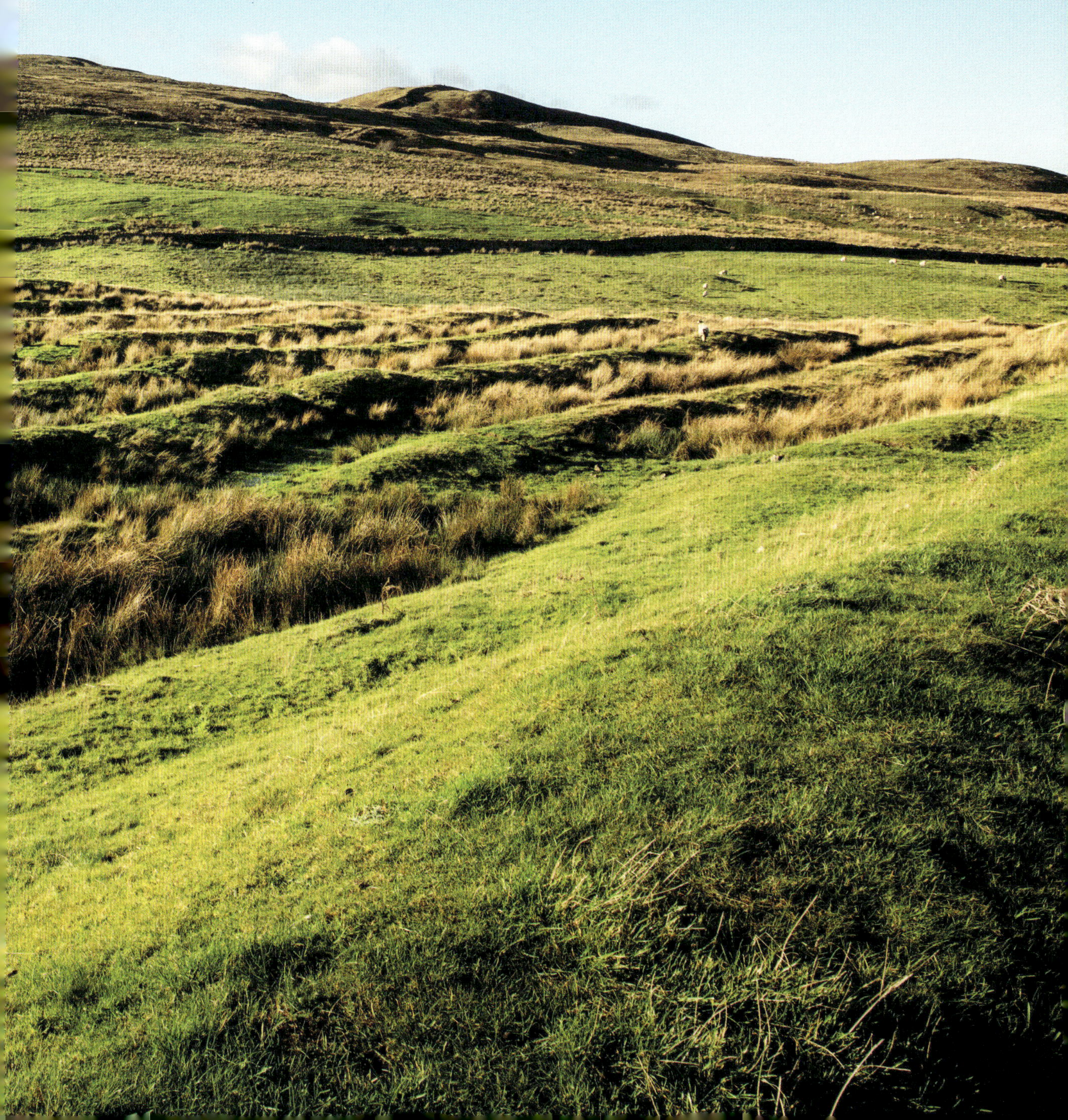

Epiacum Roman Fort (previously called Whitley Castle) north west of
Alston at Castle Nook Farm. It has the most complex defensive earthworks
of any known fort in the Roman Empire and sits on the Maiden Way, a
Roman road linking the Eden Valley to Hadrian's Wall. The Pennine Way
runs past the fort

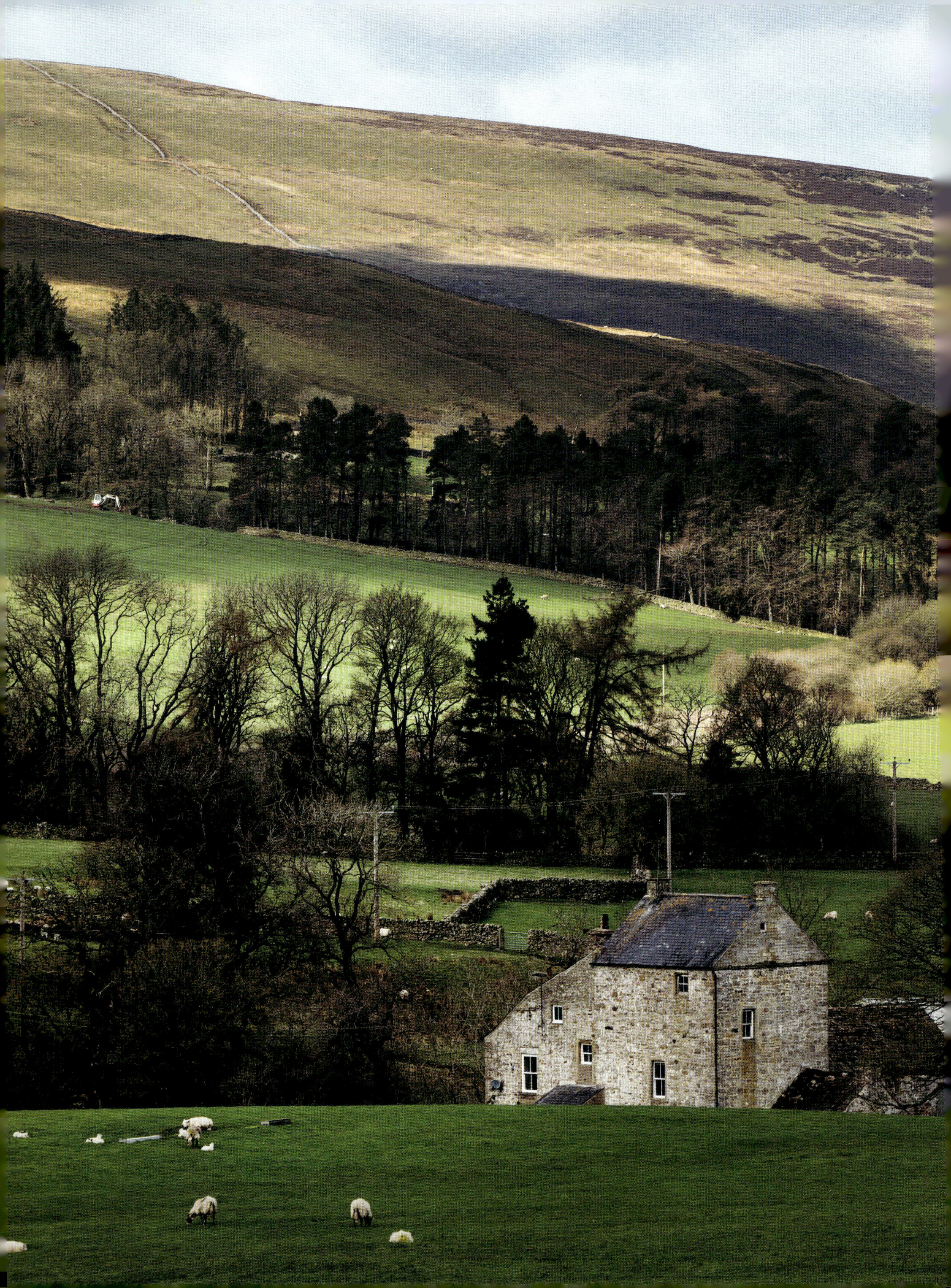

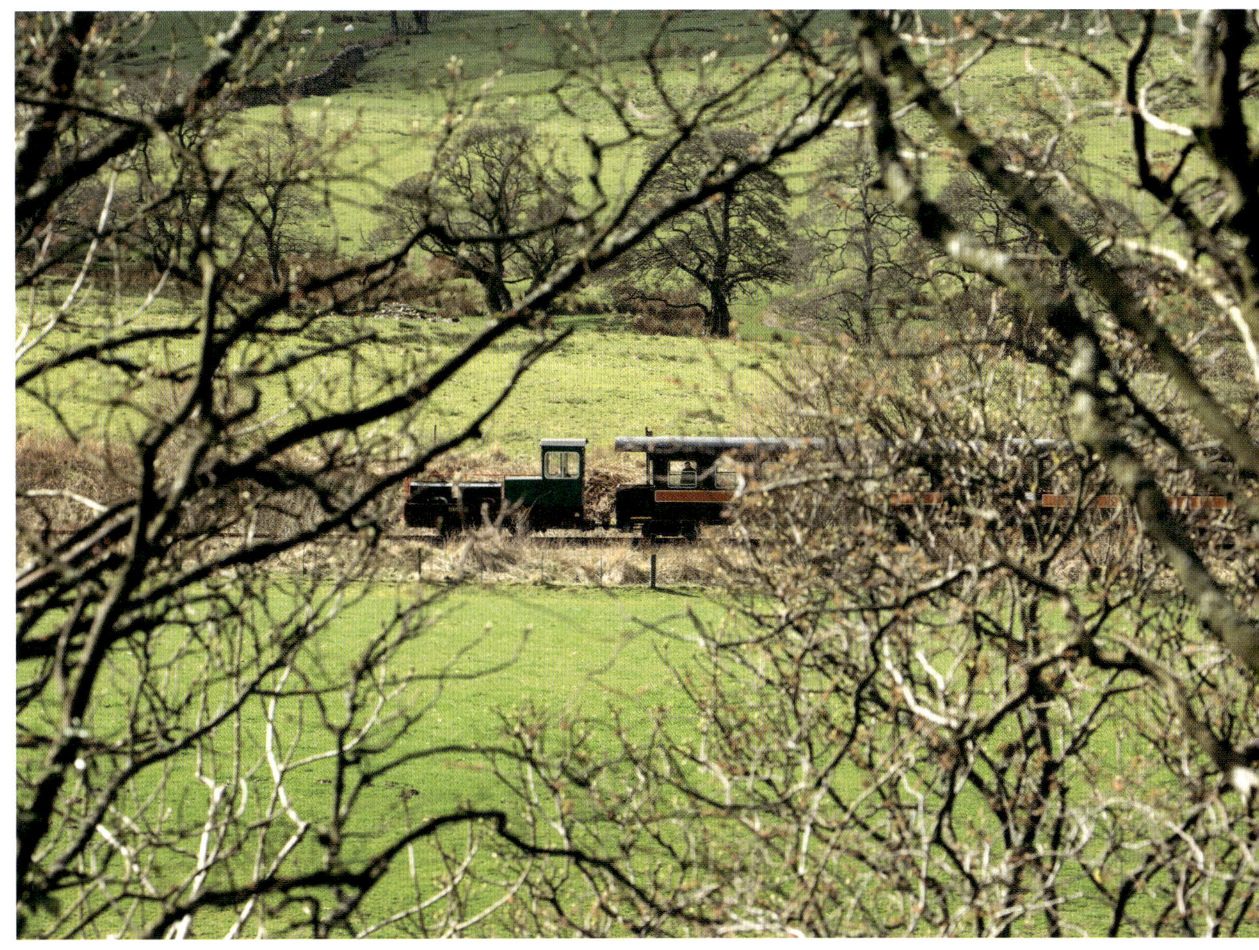

Above: A glimpse of the popular South Tynedale Railway, a heritage line running between Alston and Slaggyford

Left: Randalholme, incorporating a 14th century peel tower (a fortified tower house or keep) with Great Heaplaw and Thornhope Fell behind, near Kirkhaugh in the valley of the River South Tyne

Overleaf: Signpost for Isaac's Tea Trail walk near Kirkhaugh. The walk is a 36 mile circular loop between Allendale and Alston, visiting Ninebanks, Nenthead and Carrshield on the way. The walk shadows the route taken by Isaac Holden, former lead miner turned itinerant tea seller, fundraiser and preacher in the mid 1800s. Isaac raised money for a well to provide clean drinking water for his community and became famous across the north of England

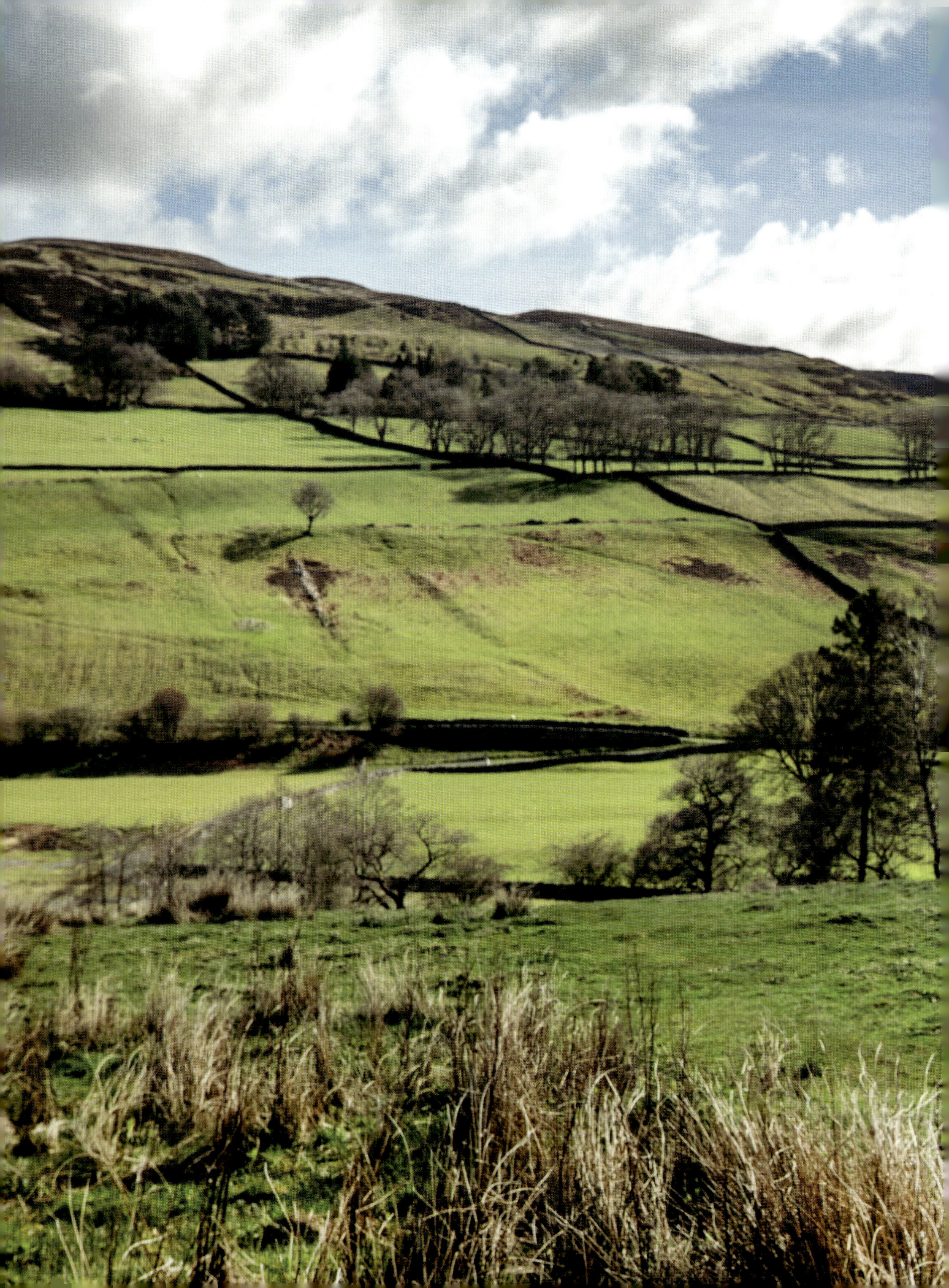

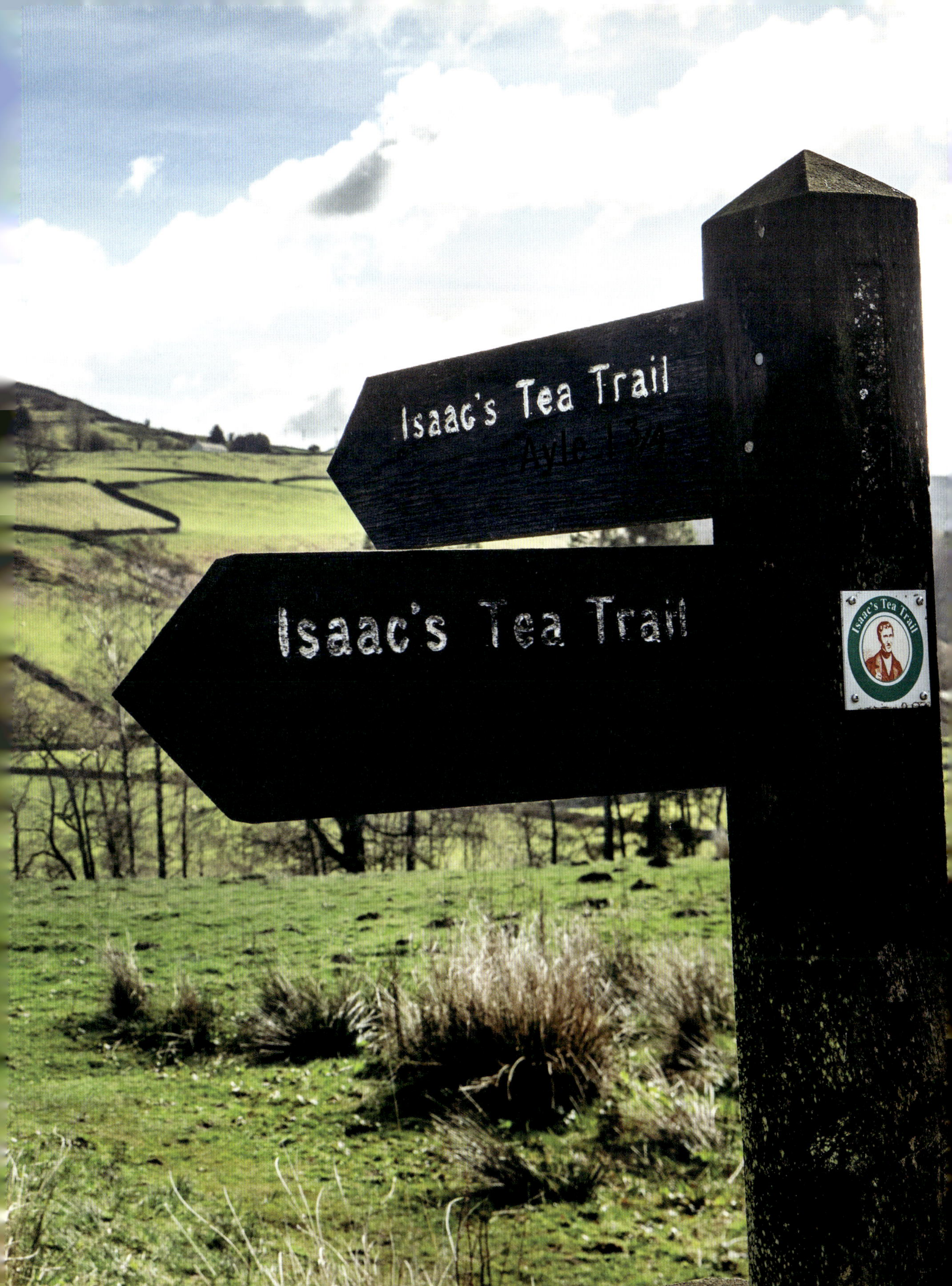

Isaac's Tea Trail
Ayle 1¾
Isaac's Tea Trail
Isaac's Tea Trail

*Smoke rises from a cottage chimney as evening mists cloak
the fells on a freezing winter day in the South Tyne valley*

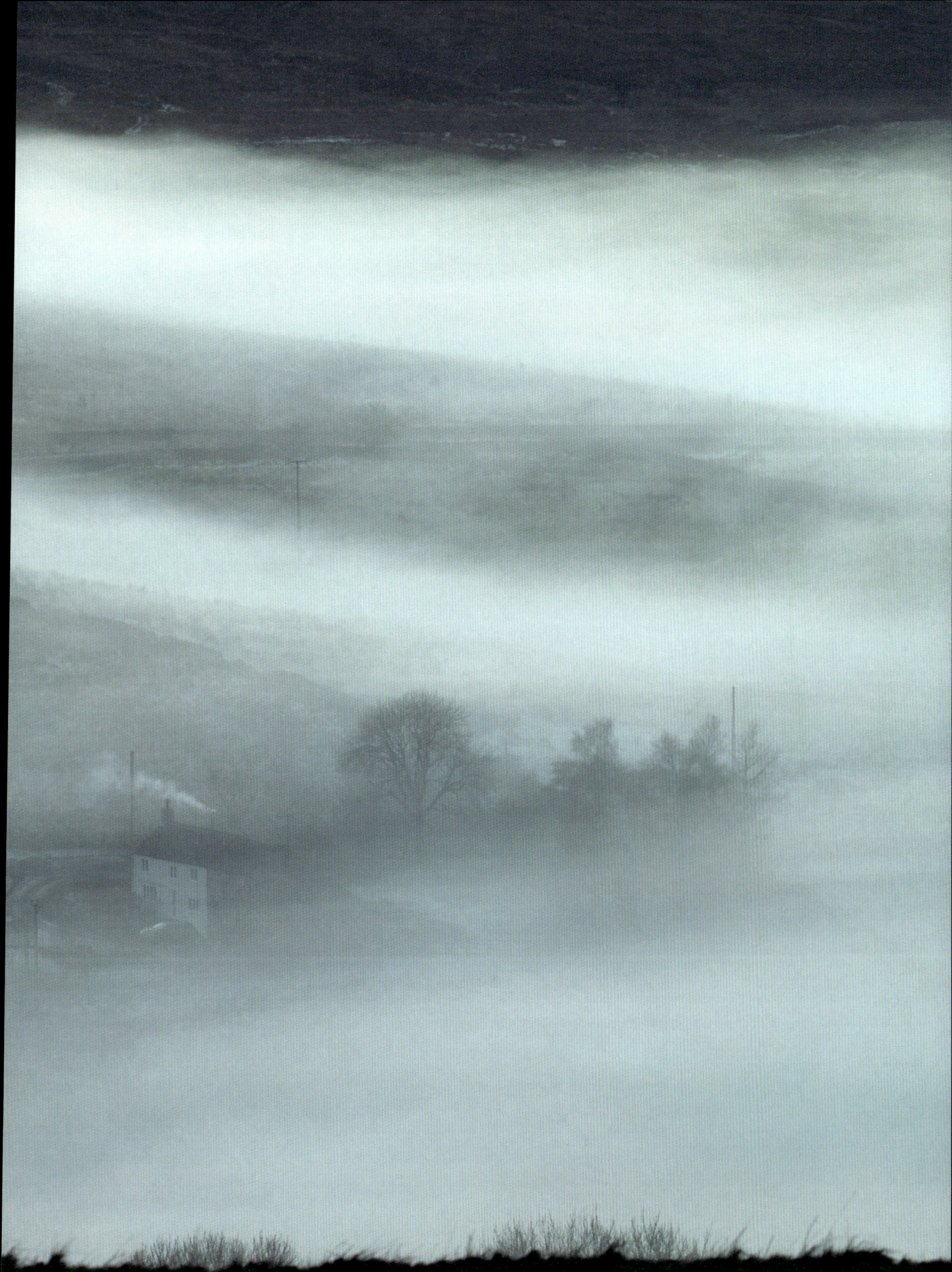

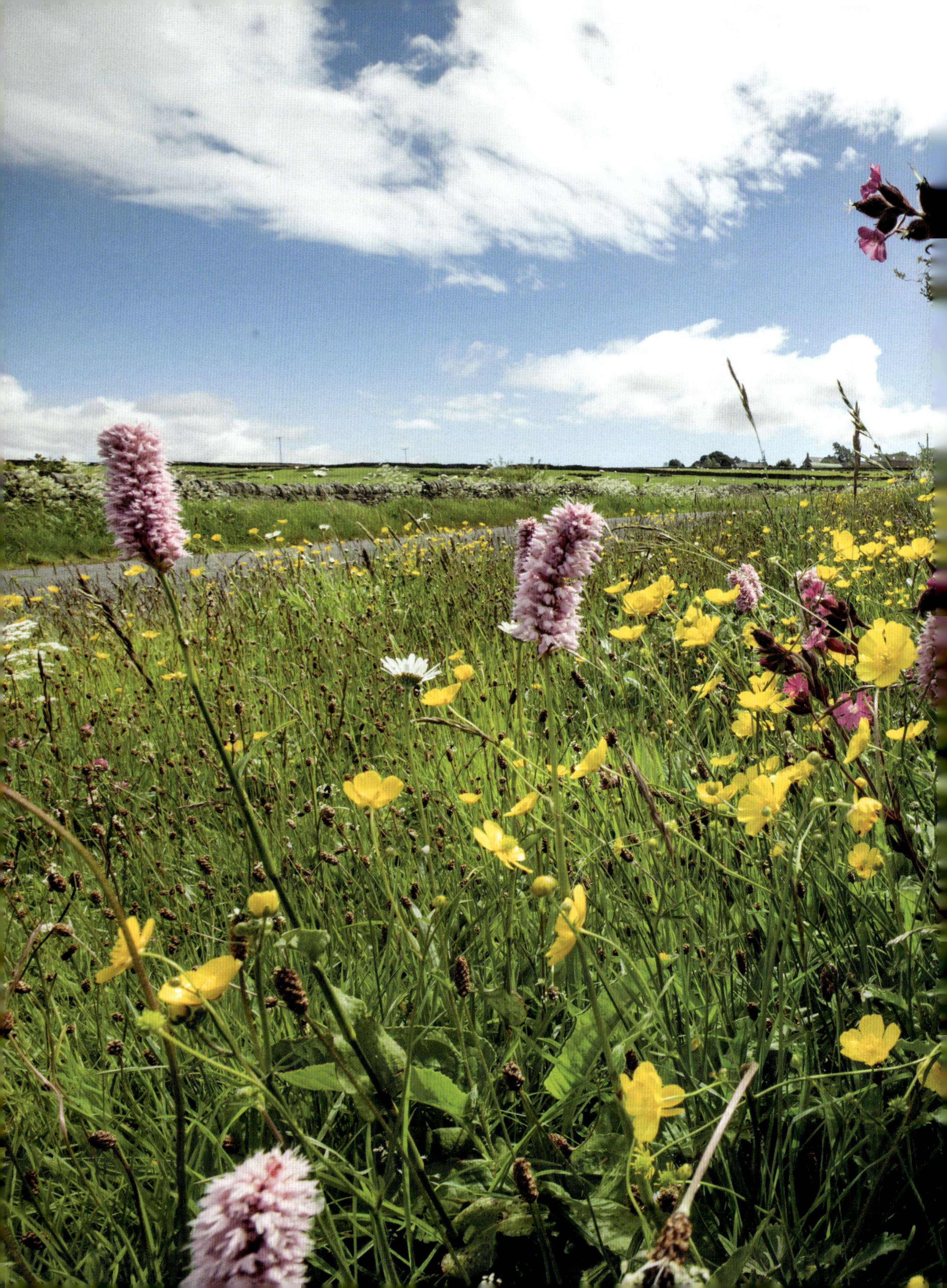

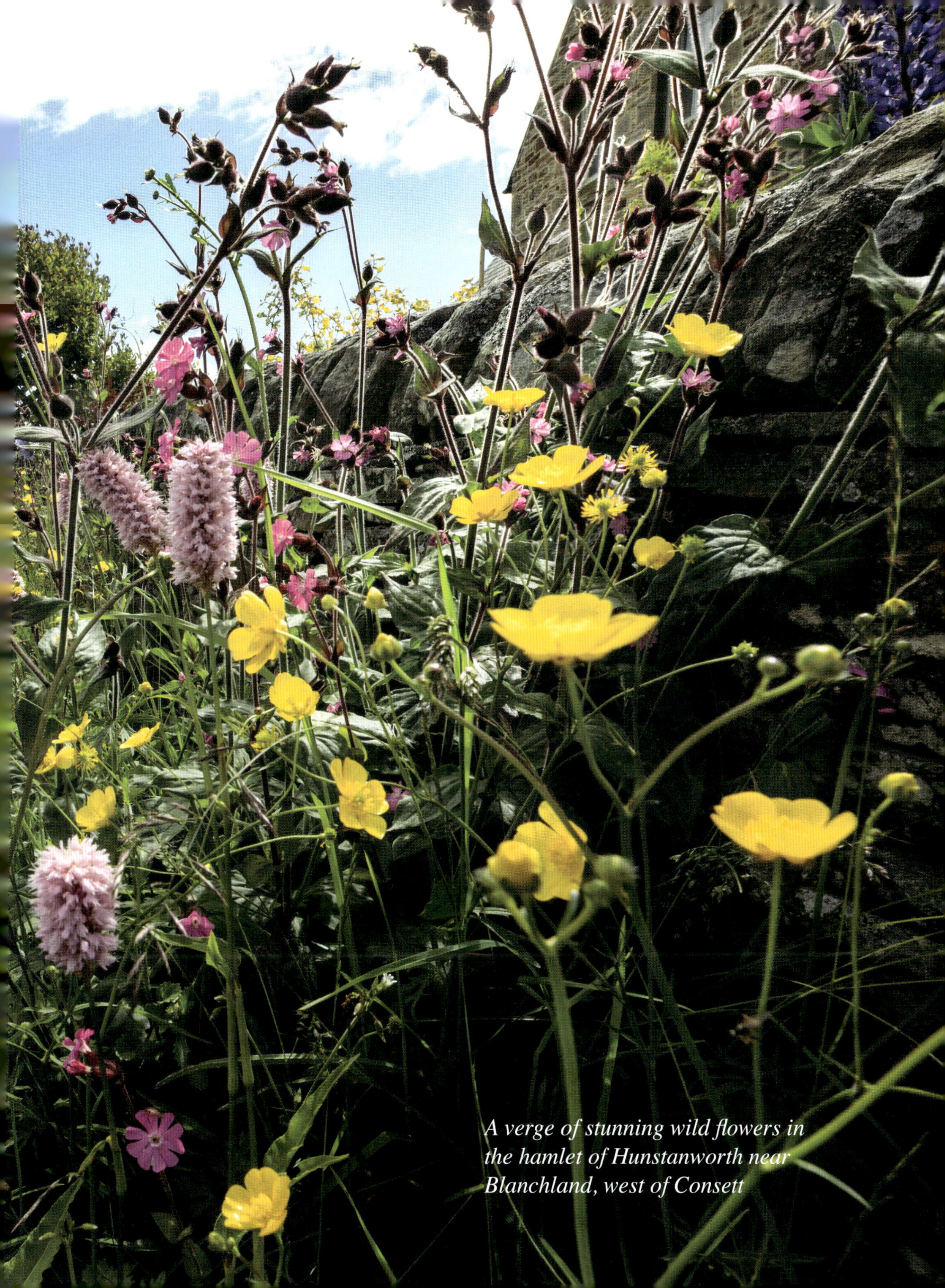

A verge of stunning wild flowers in the hamlet of Hunstanworth near Blanchland, west of Consett

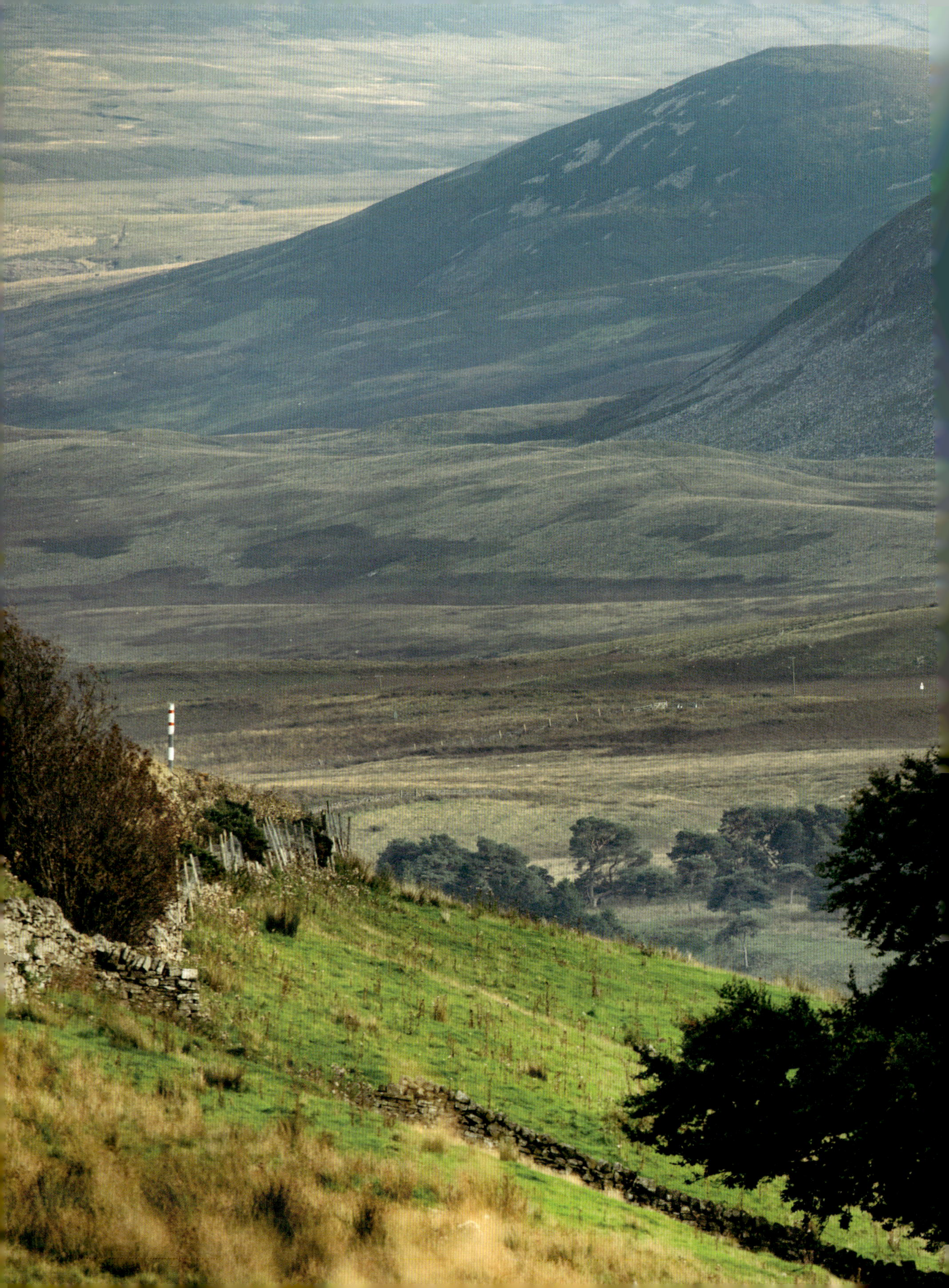

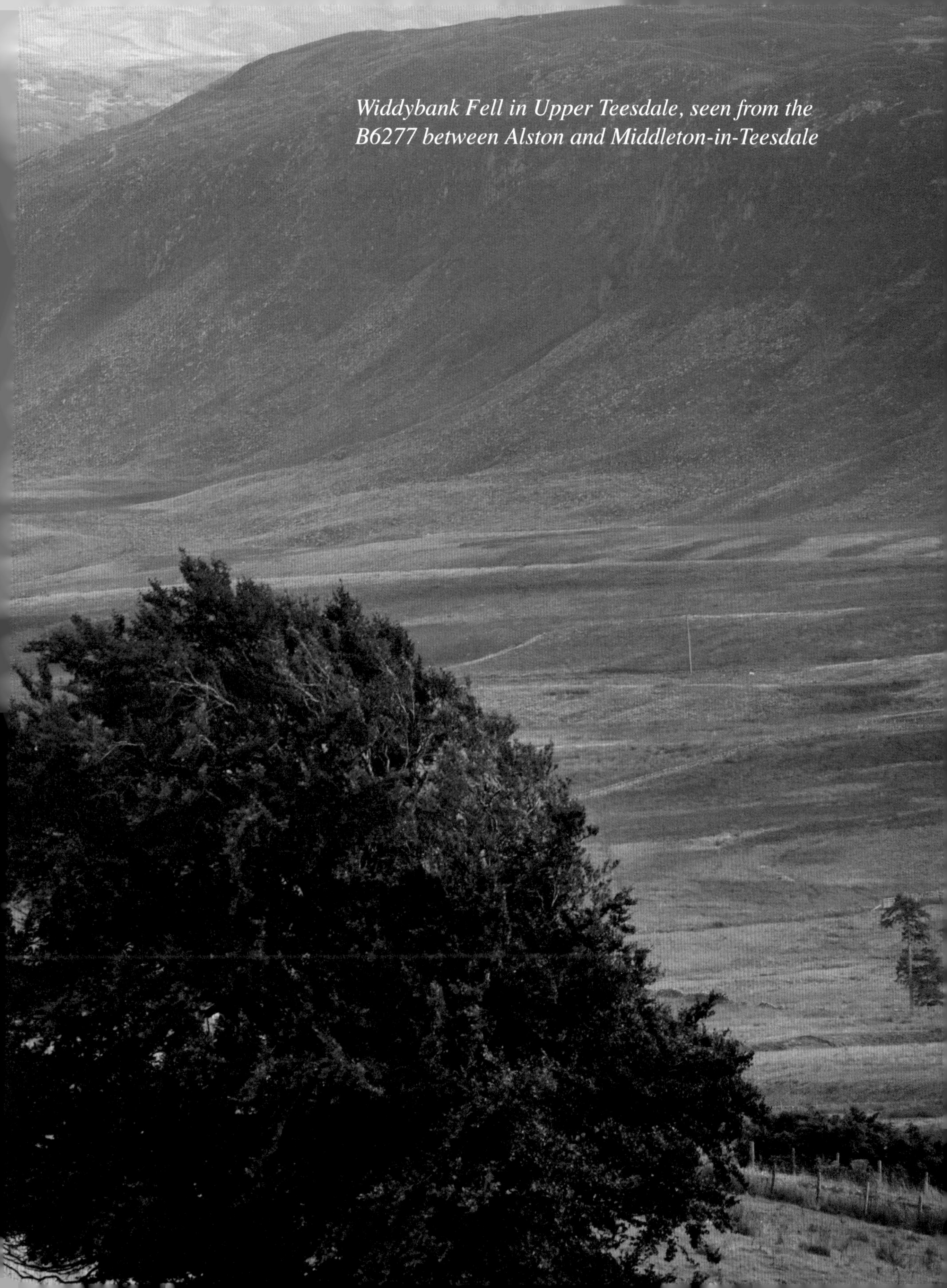

Widdybank Fell in Upper Teesdale, seen from the
B6277 between Alston and Middleton-in-Teesdale

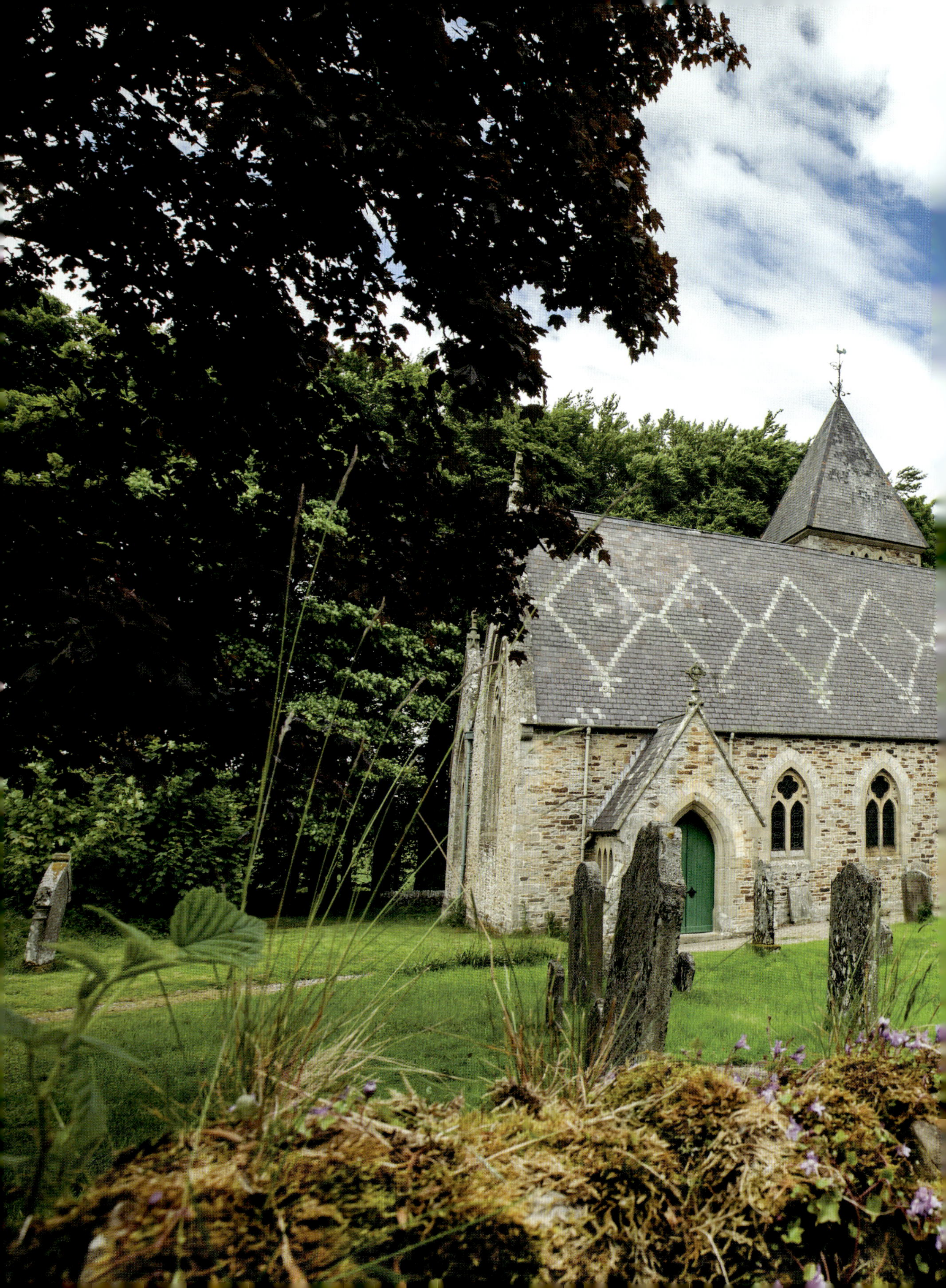

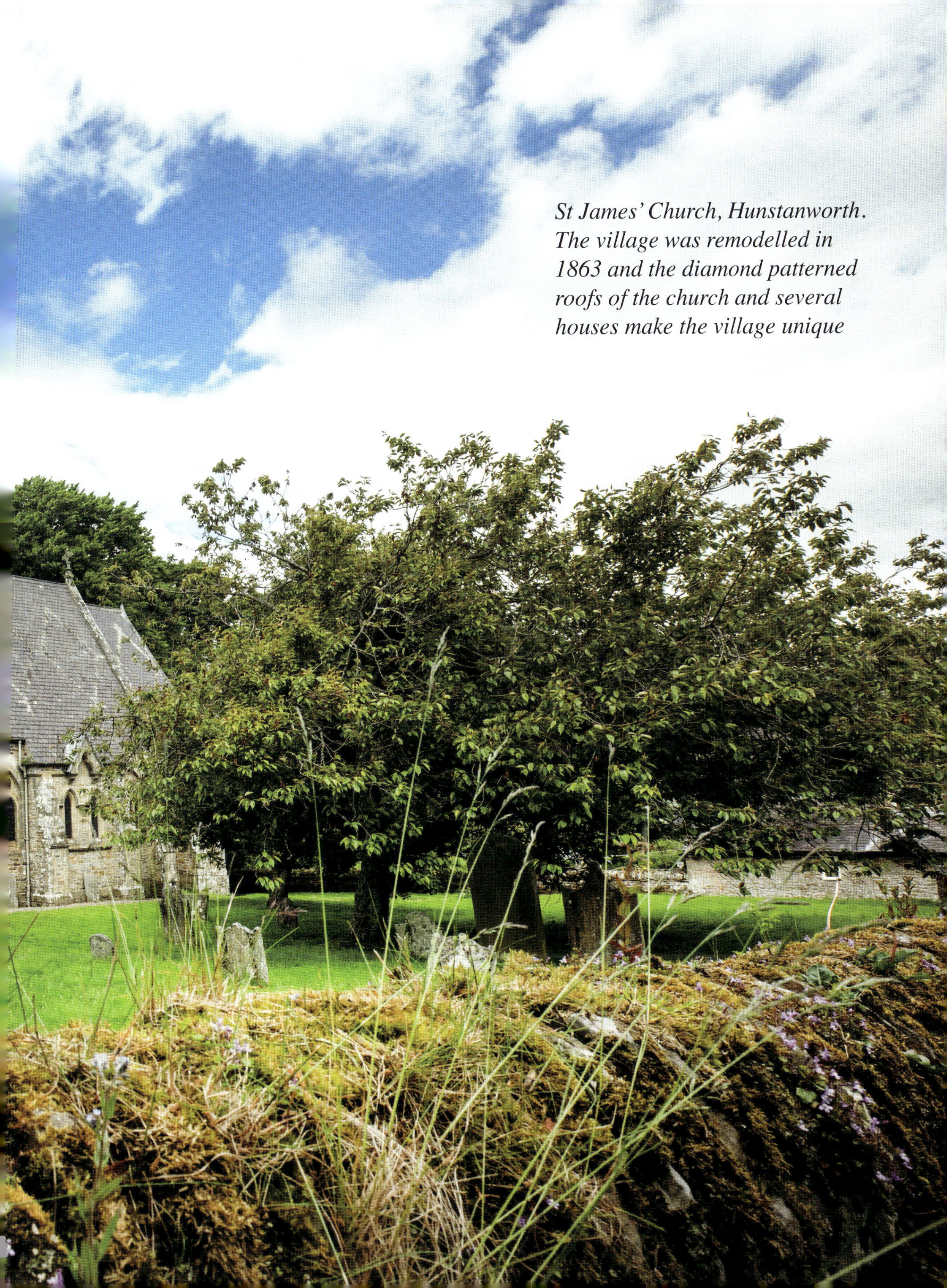

*St James' Church, Hunstanworth.
The village was remodelled in
1863 and the diamond patterned
roofs of the church and several
houses make the village unique*

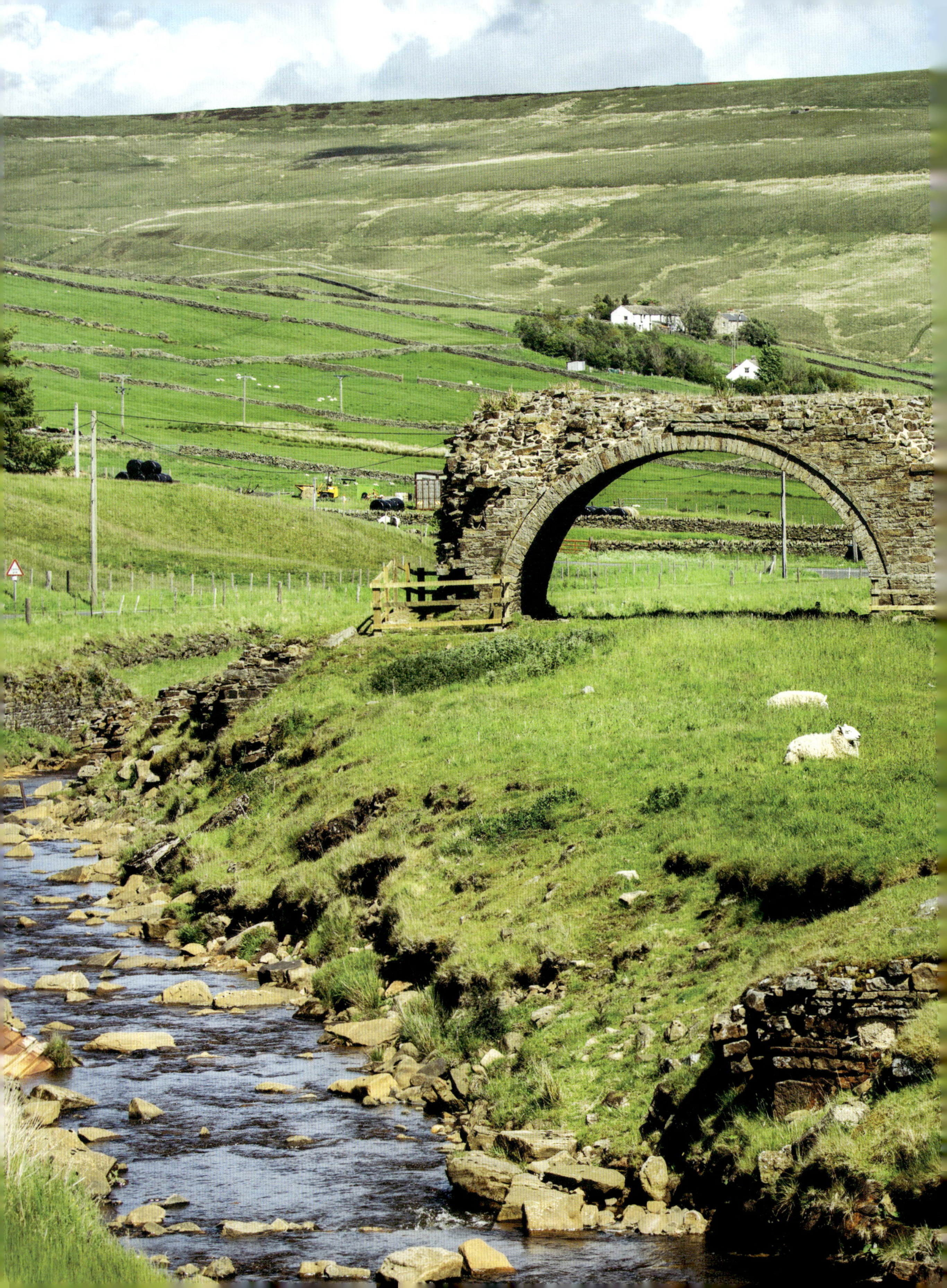

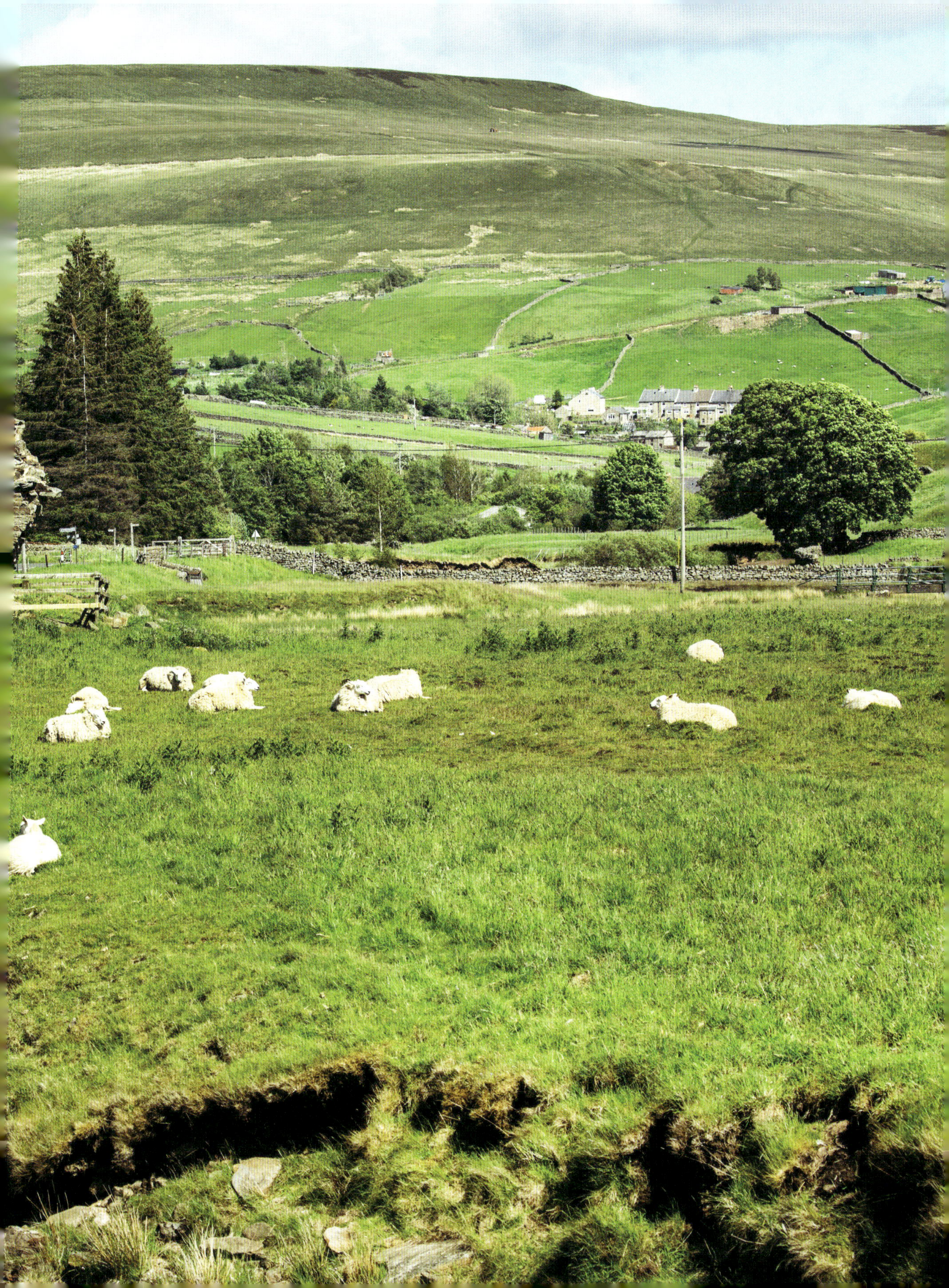

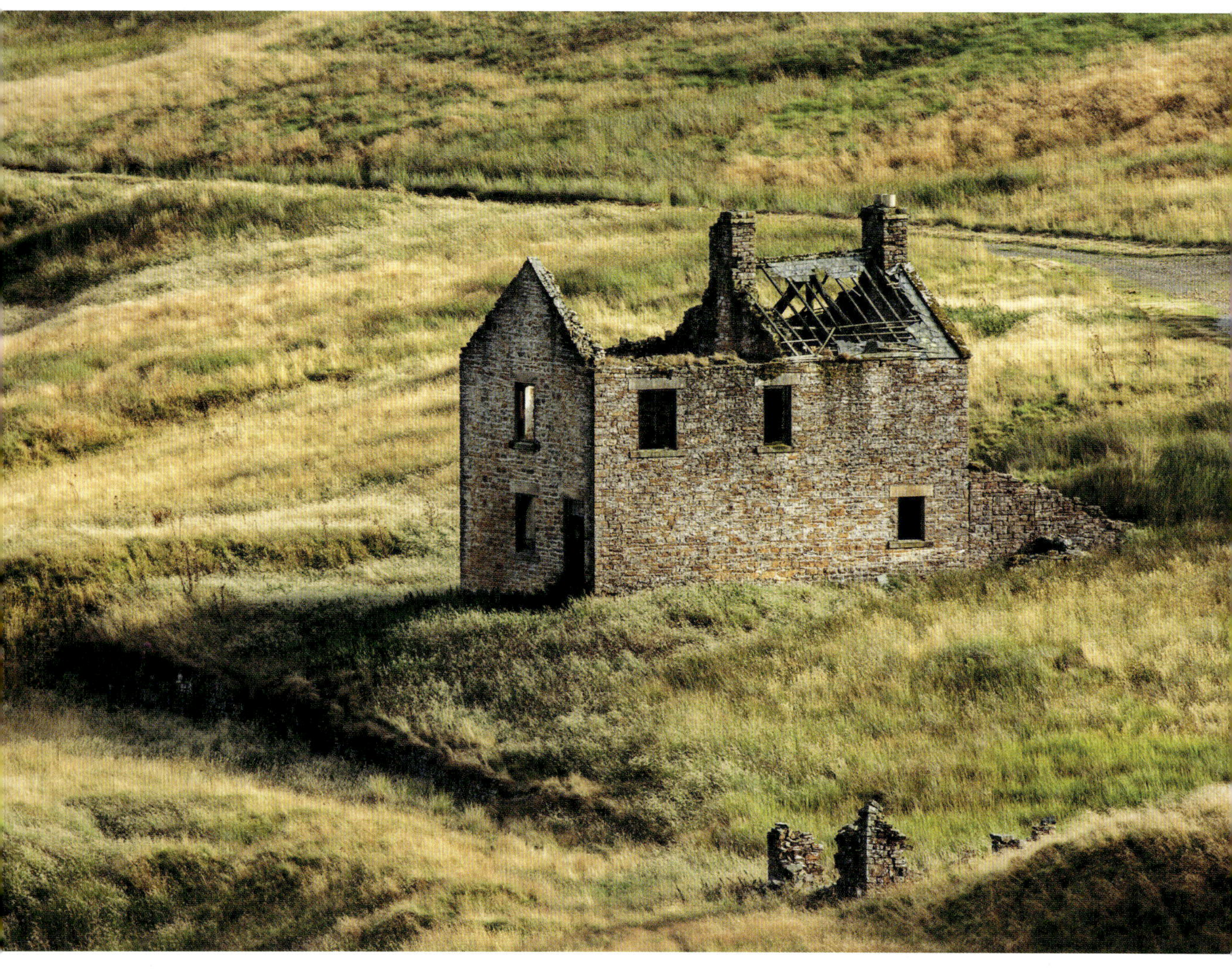

Above and right: Groverake Mine above Rookhope has the last remaining headframe (right) in County Durham. The mine opened in the 17th century for ironstone followed by lead, and in the 1930s for fluorspar. It finally closed in 1999

Previous page: The Rookhope or Lintzgarth Arch near Stanhope is all that is left of a mill to smelt lead ore from the mines in the valley of the Rookhope Burn, lying between Weardale and Blanchland. The name 'Lintz' derives from German miners and refers to linden (lime) trees

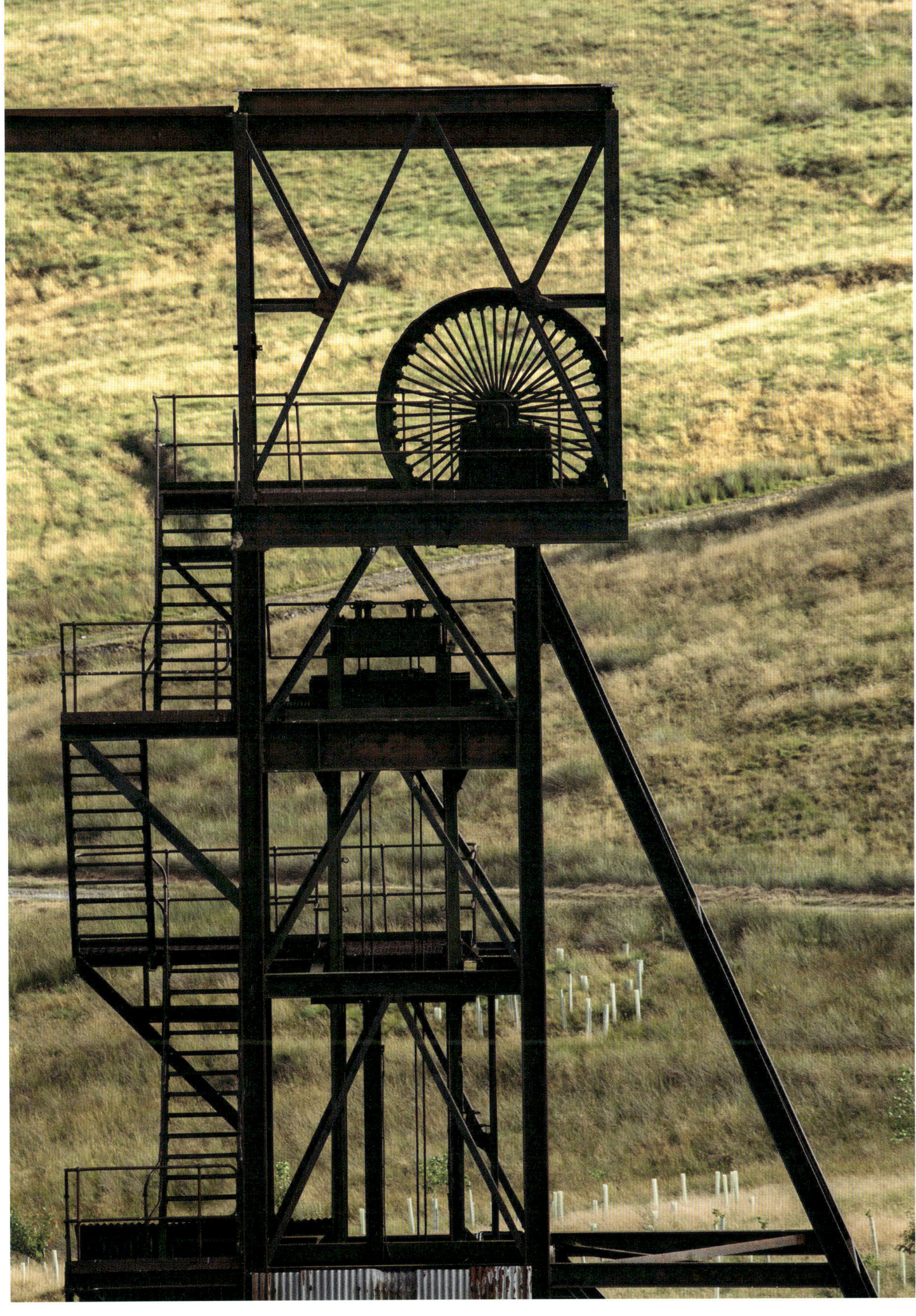

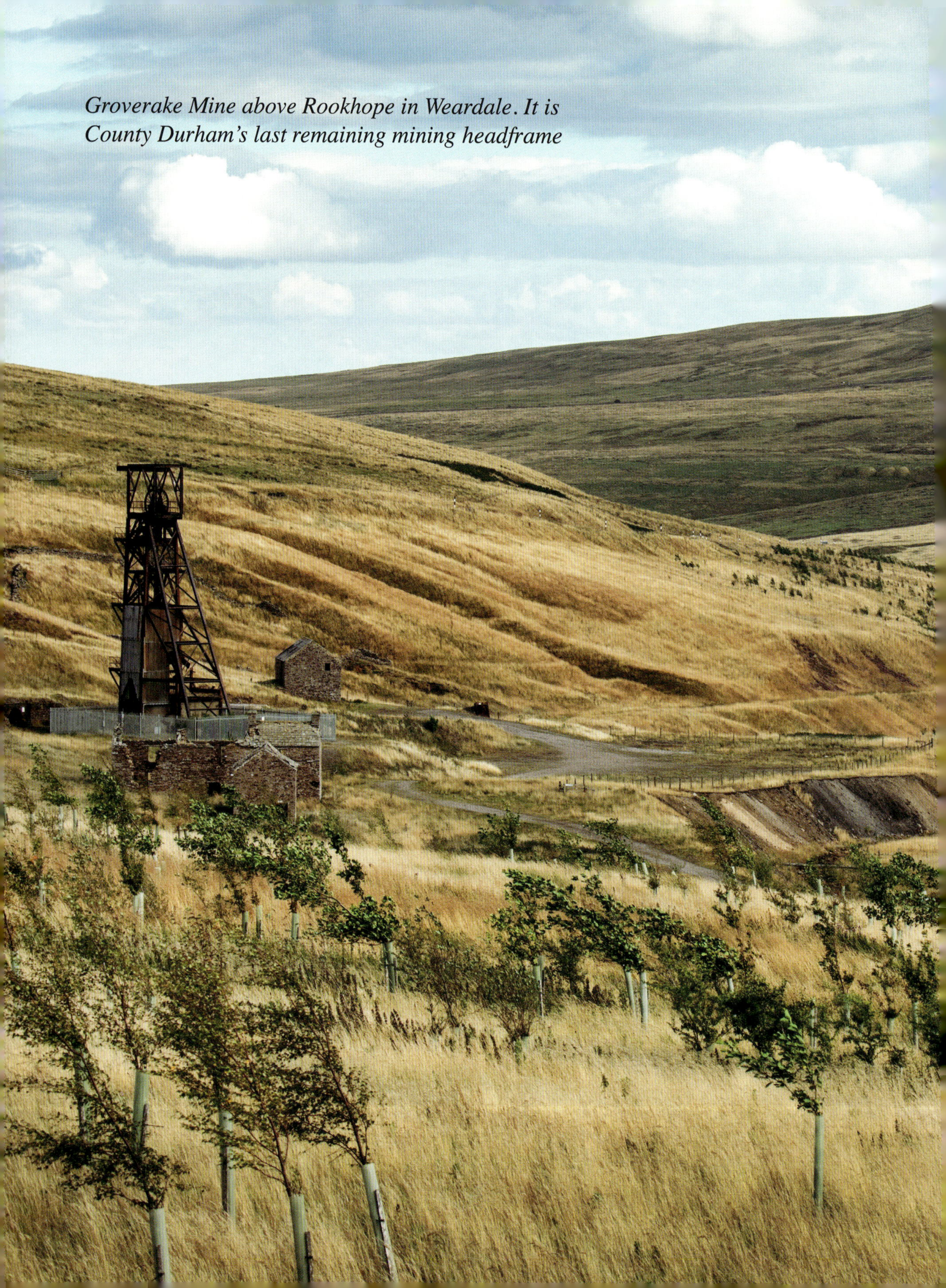

Groverake Mine above Rookhope in Weardale. It is
County Durham's last remaining mining headframe

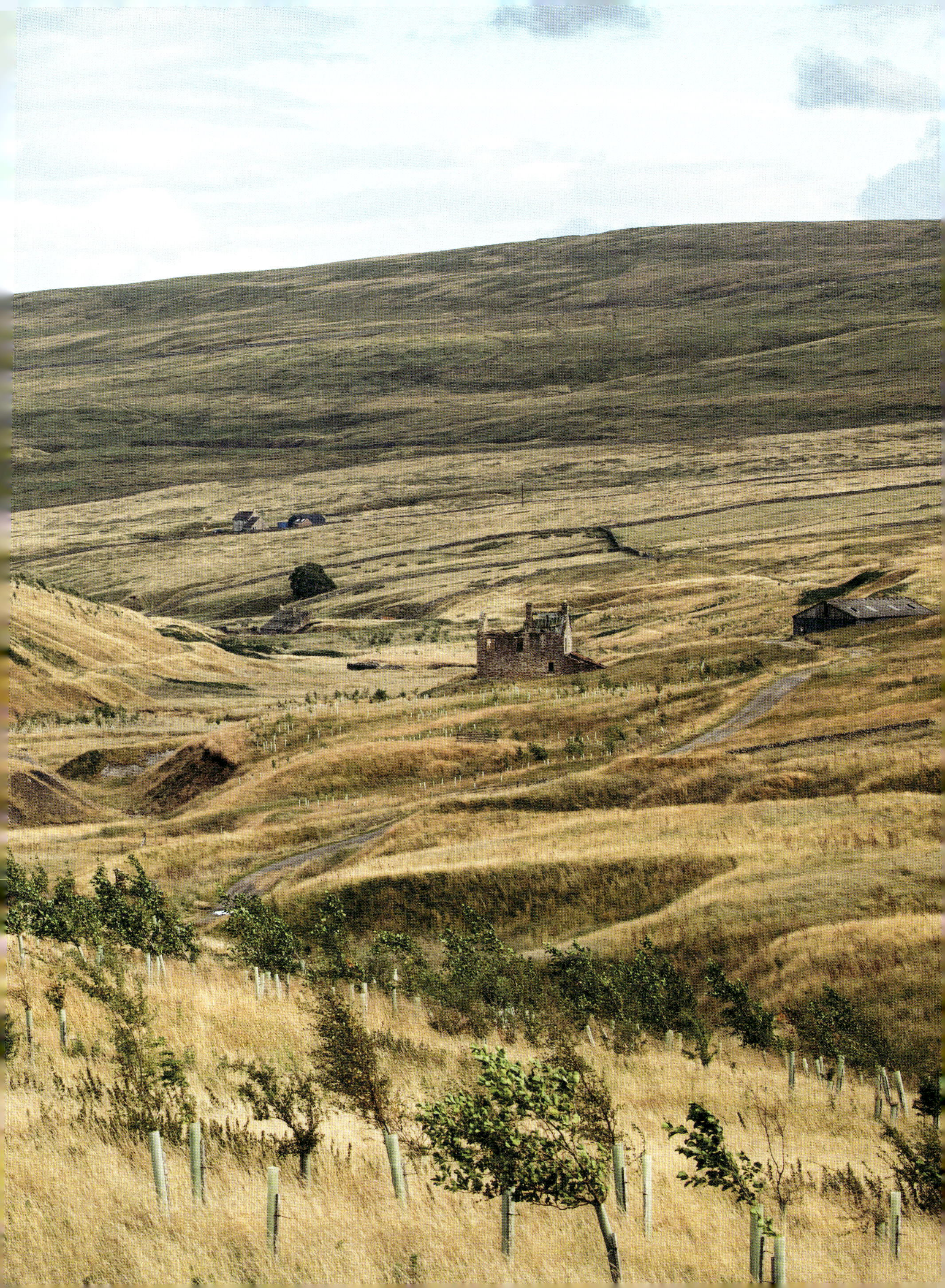

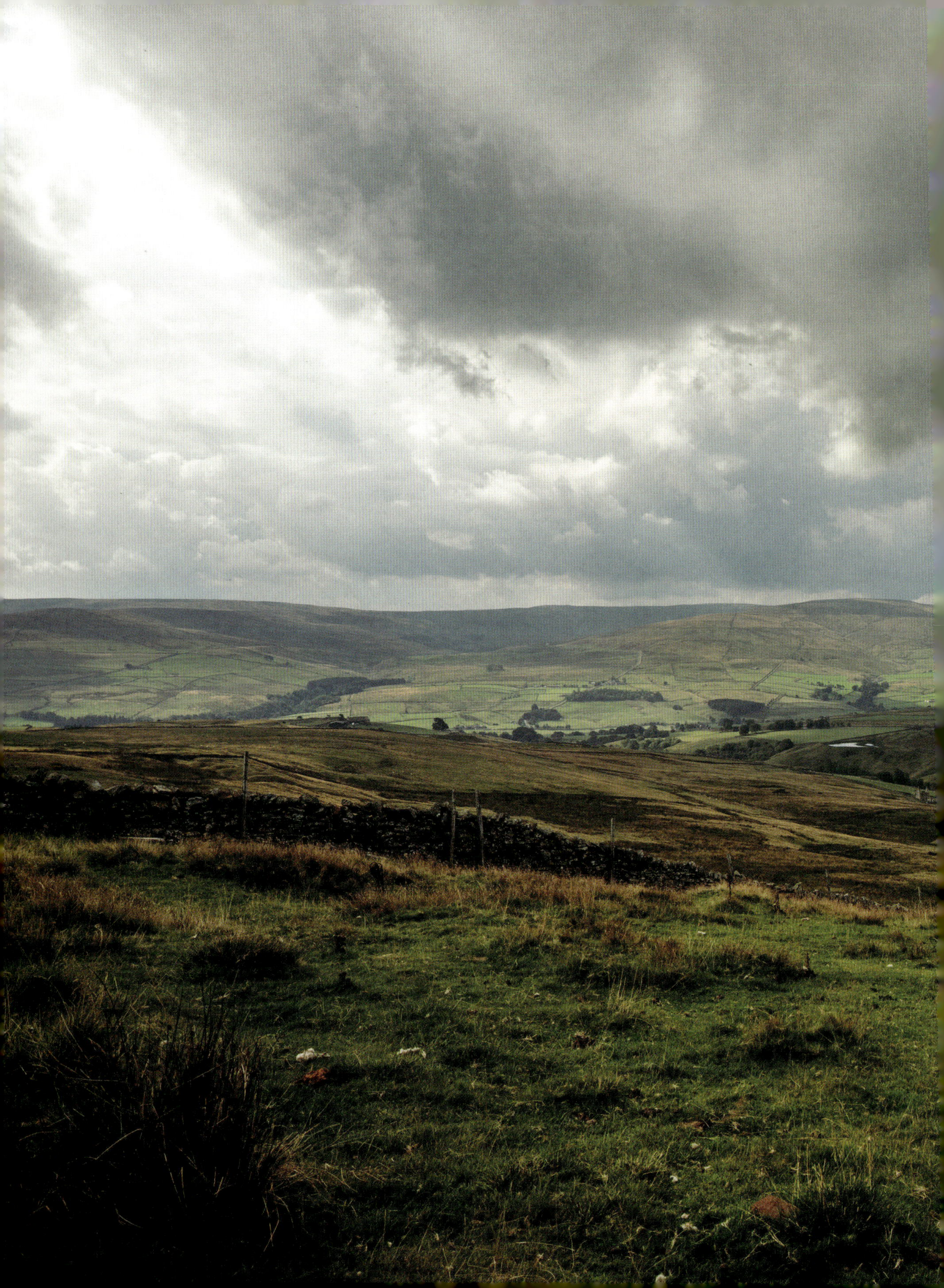

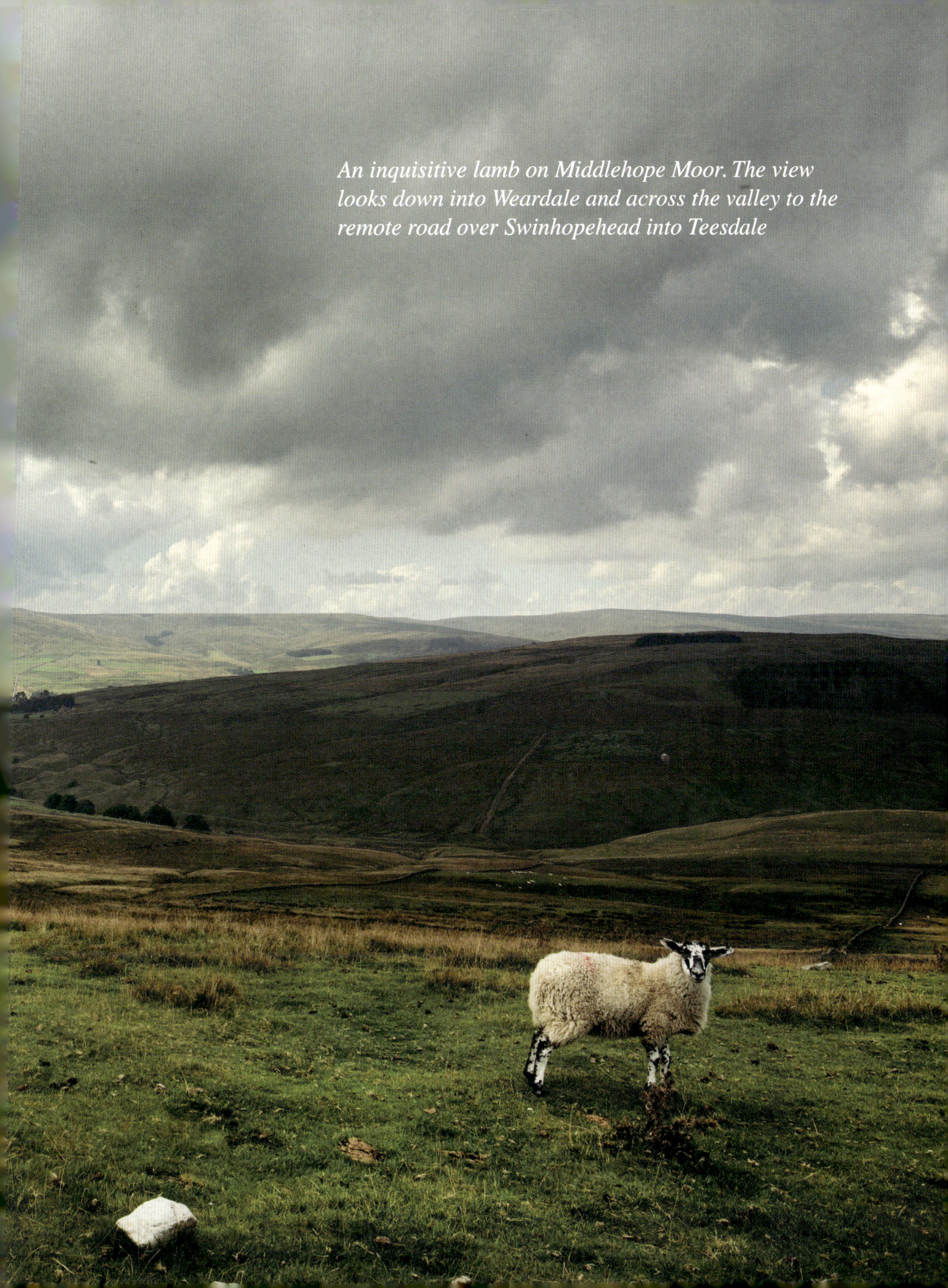

An inquisitive lamb on Middlehope Moor. The view looks down into Weardale and across the valley to the remote road over Swinhopehead into Teesdale

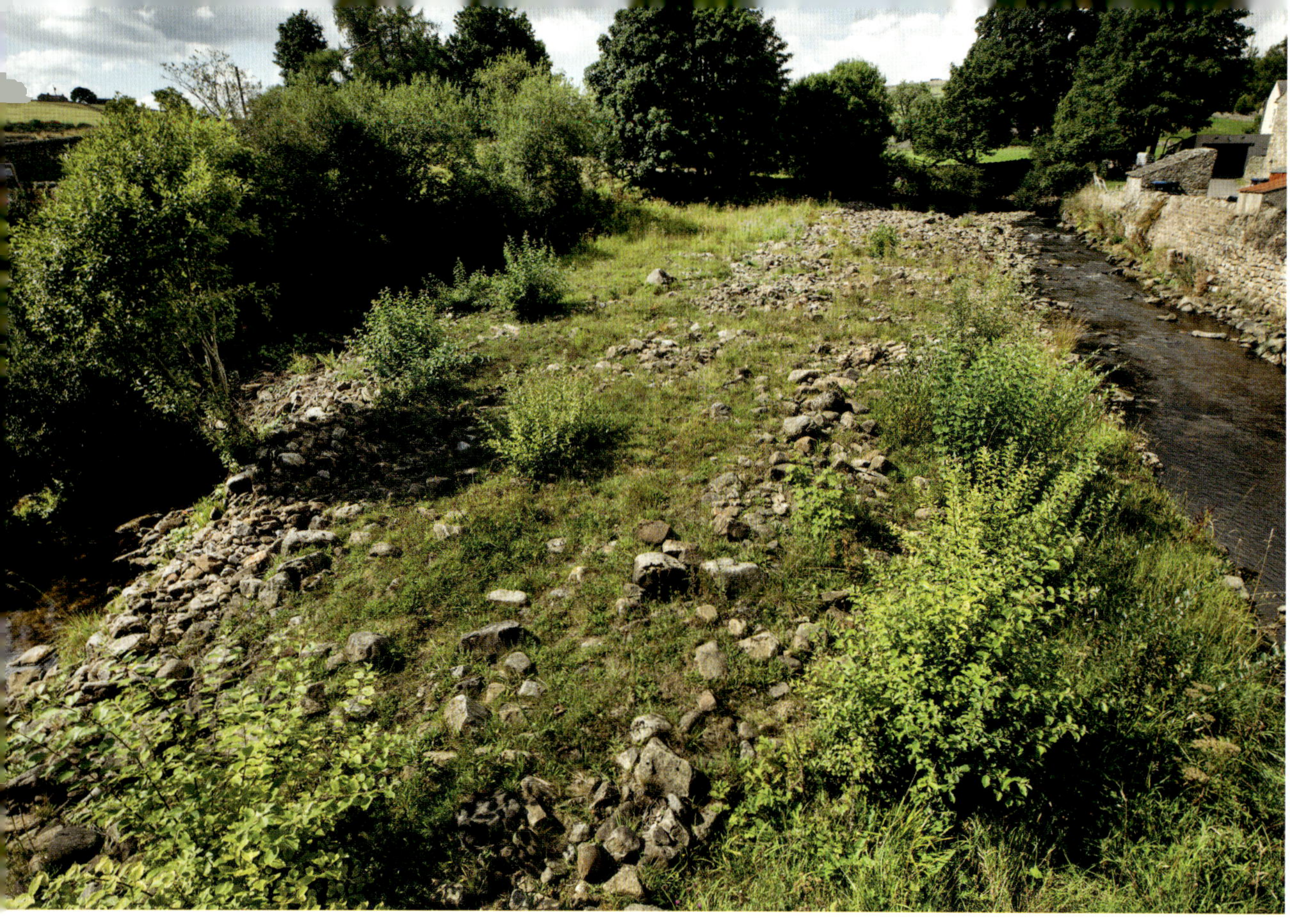

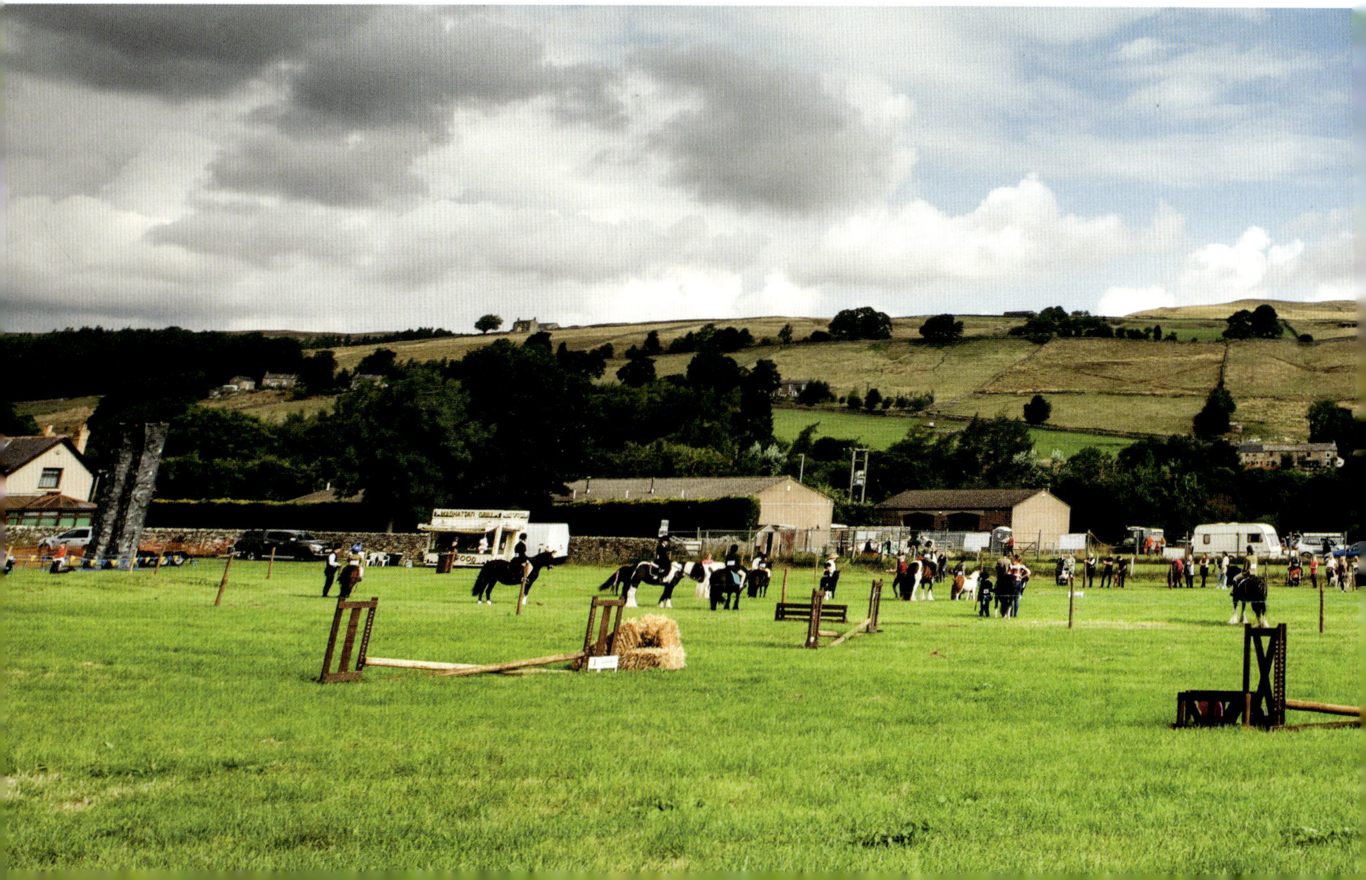

Left: the source of the River
Wear at Wearhead where the
Killhope and Burnhope Burns
combine to form the River Wear

Right and bottom: Weardale
Show, held at St John's Chapel
at the end of August, is a
key highlight of the year and
attracts everyone from the
youngest competitors upwards!
The country show has been
running for about 150 years

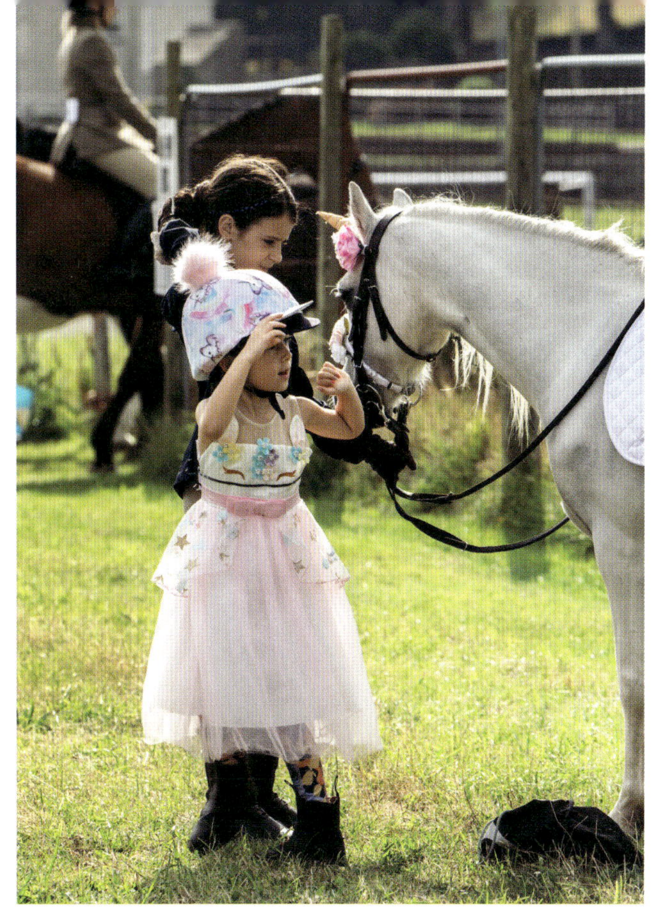

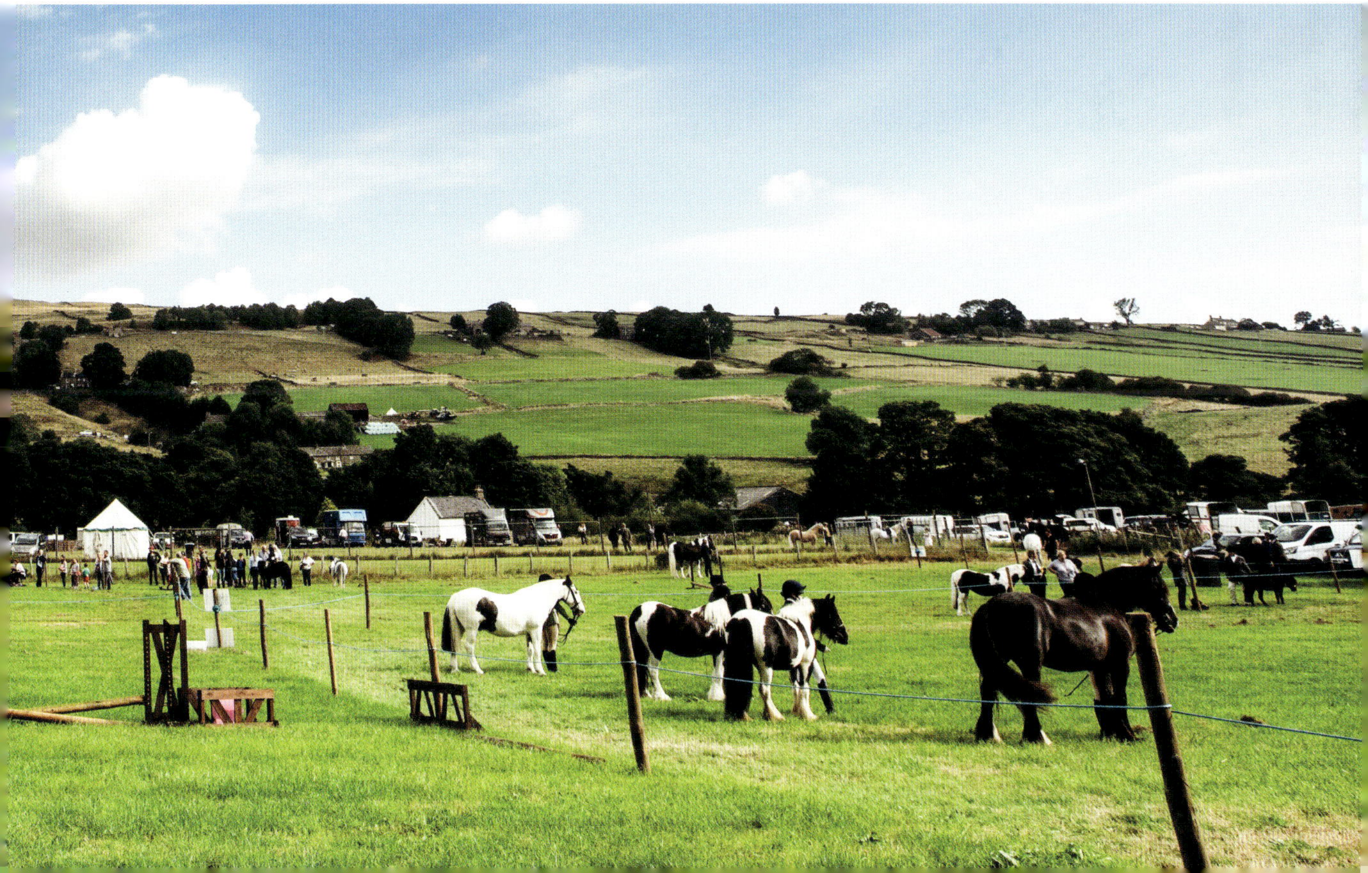

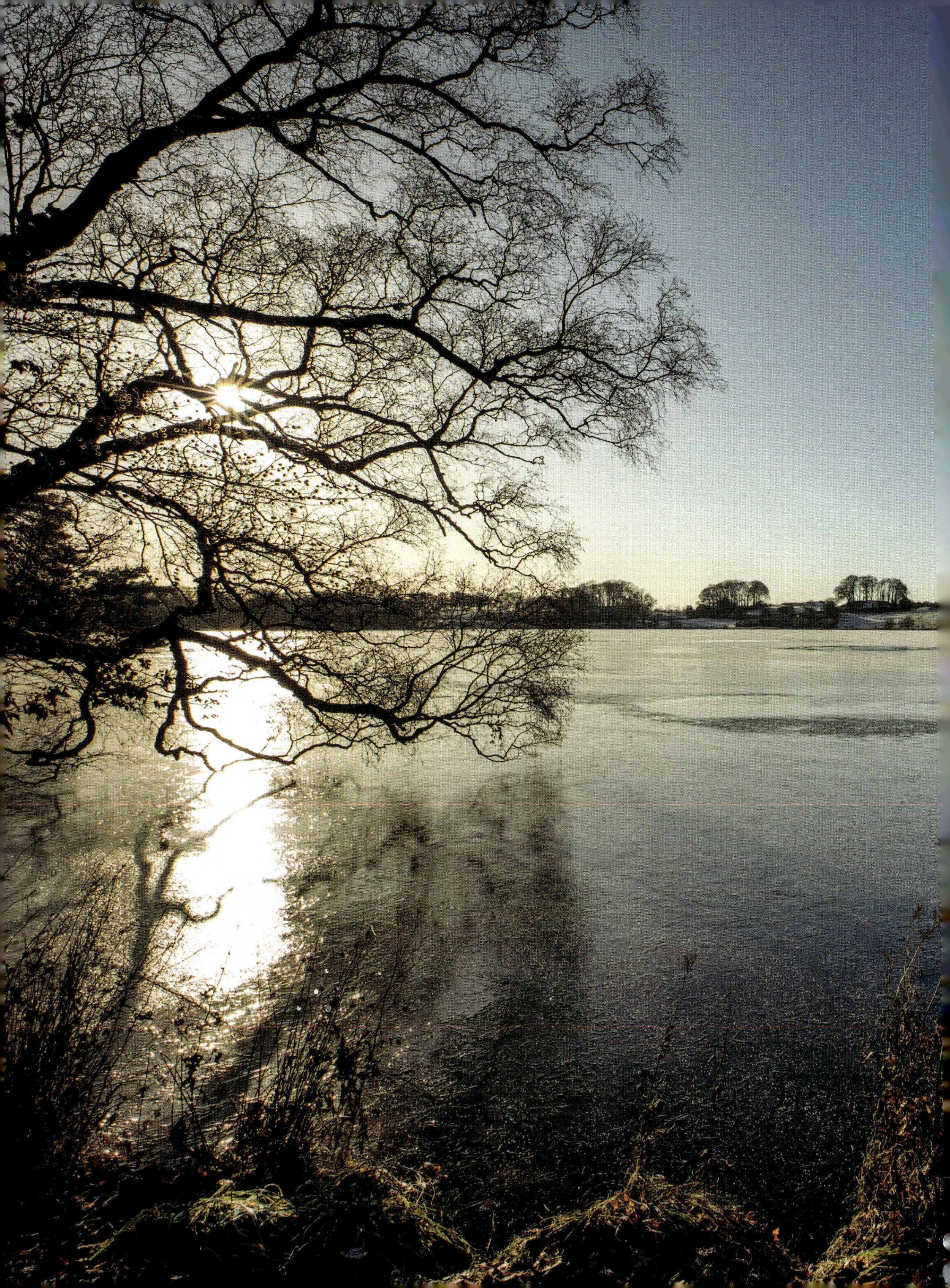

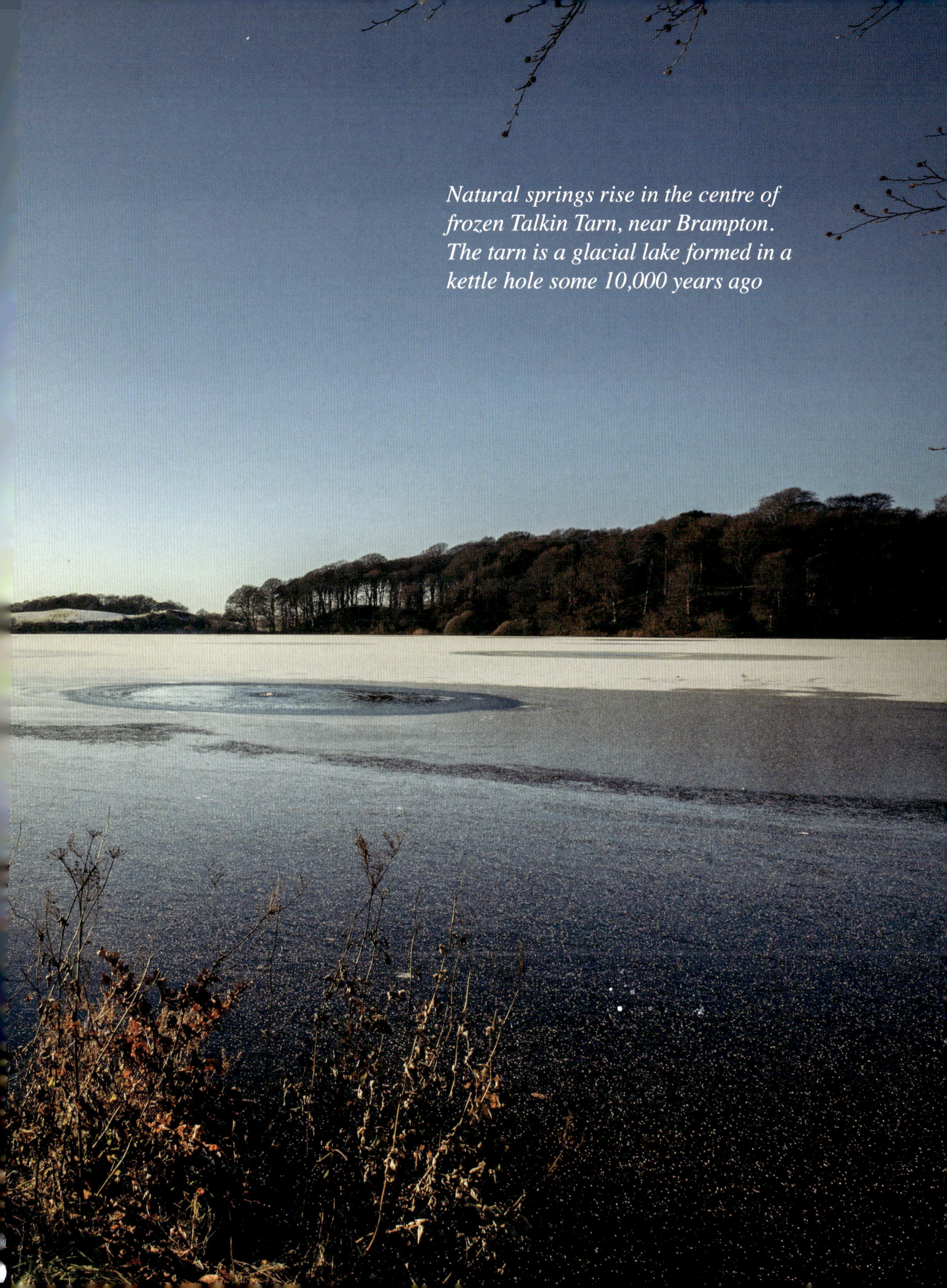

Natural springs rise in the centre of
frozen Talkin Tarn, near Brampton.
The tarn is a glacial lake formed in a
kettle hole some 10,000 years ago

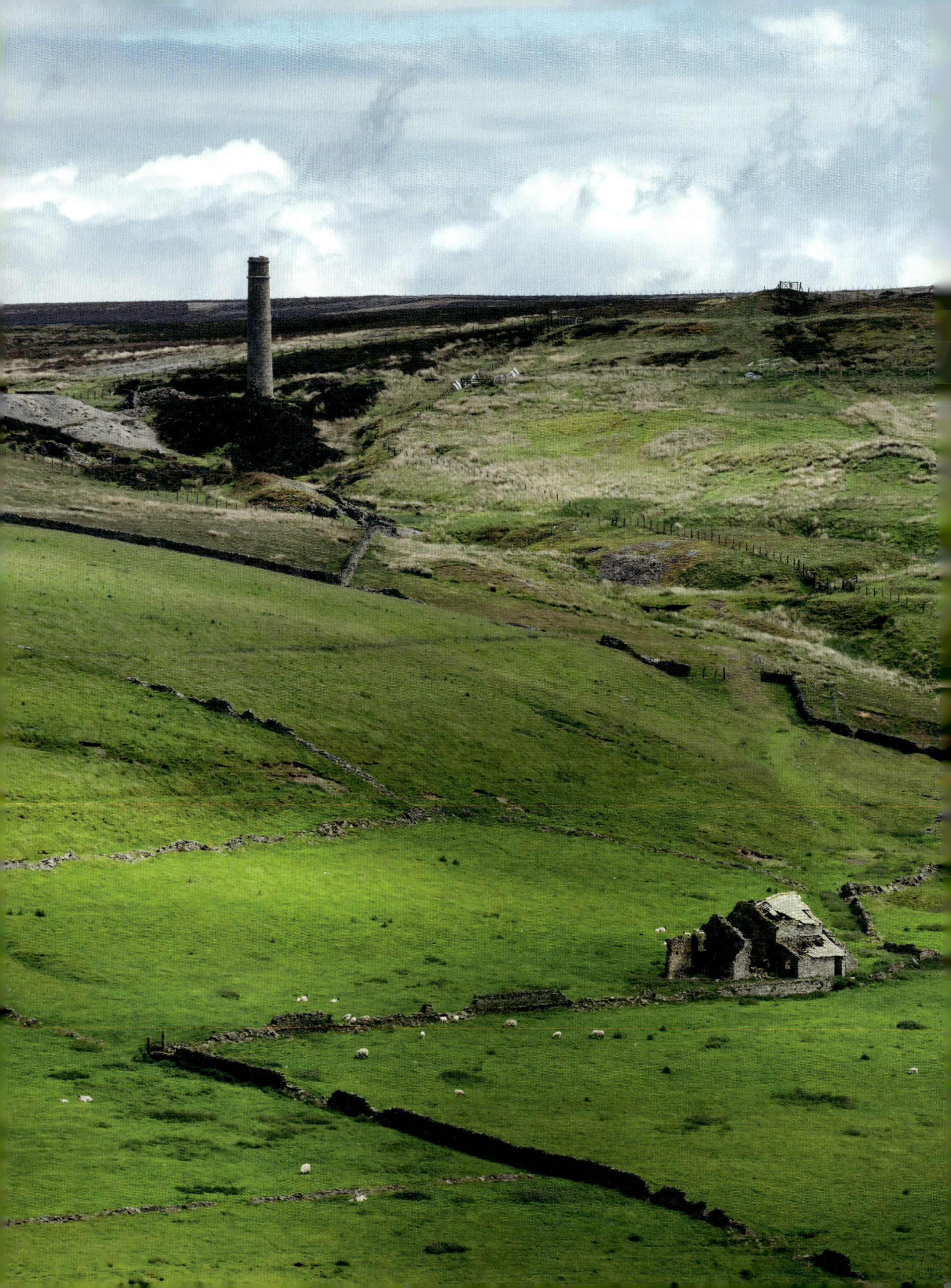

The chimney of the engine house at Sikehead
Lead Mine, Ramshaw near Hunstanworth

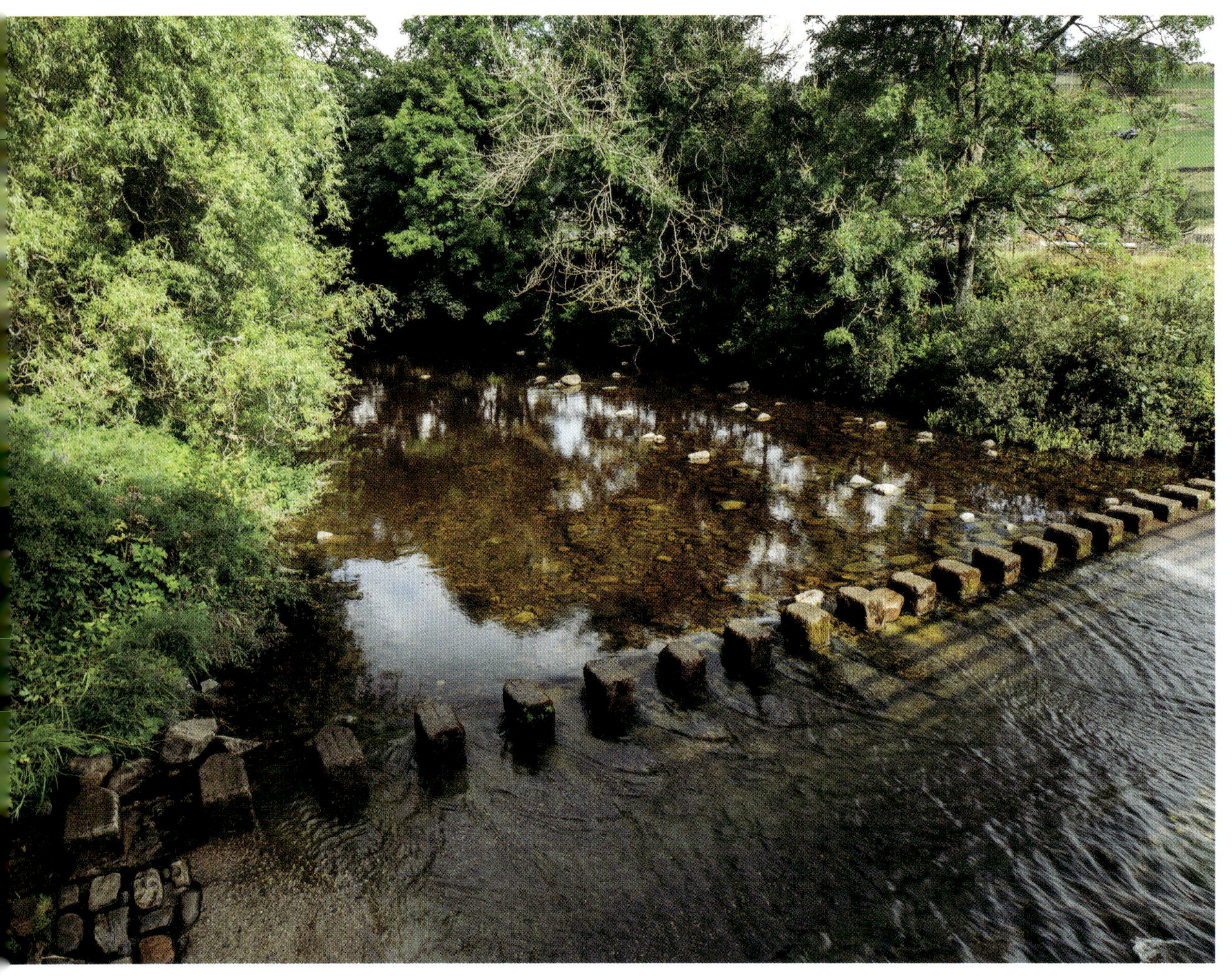

Above: Stepping stones and a ford on the River Wear at Huntshield Ford, St John's Chapel. It is thought there was a ford and stone crossing here even in medieval times. Today there is also a footbridge

Right: Ford across the River East Allen at Low Huntwell near Spartylea in East Allendale. There are several small roads in the area with pretty little fords, sometimes perhaps a bit risky when the streams are in spate!

Overleaf: A frozen footpath leading to Brackenthwaite from near Garth Head in Geltsdale, Castle Carrock

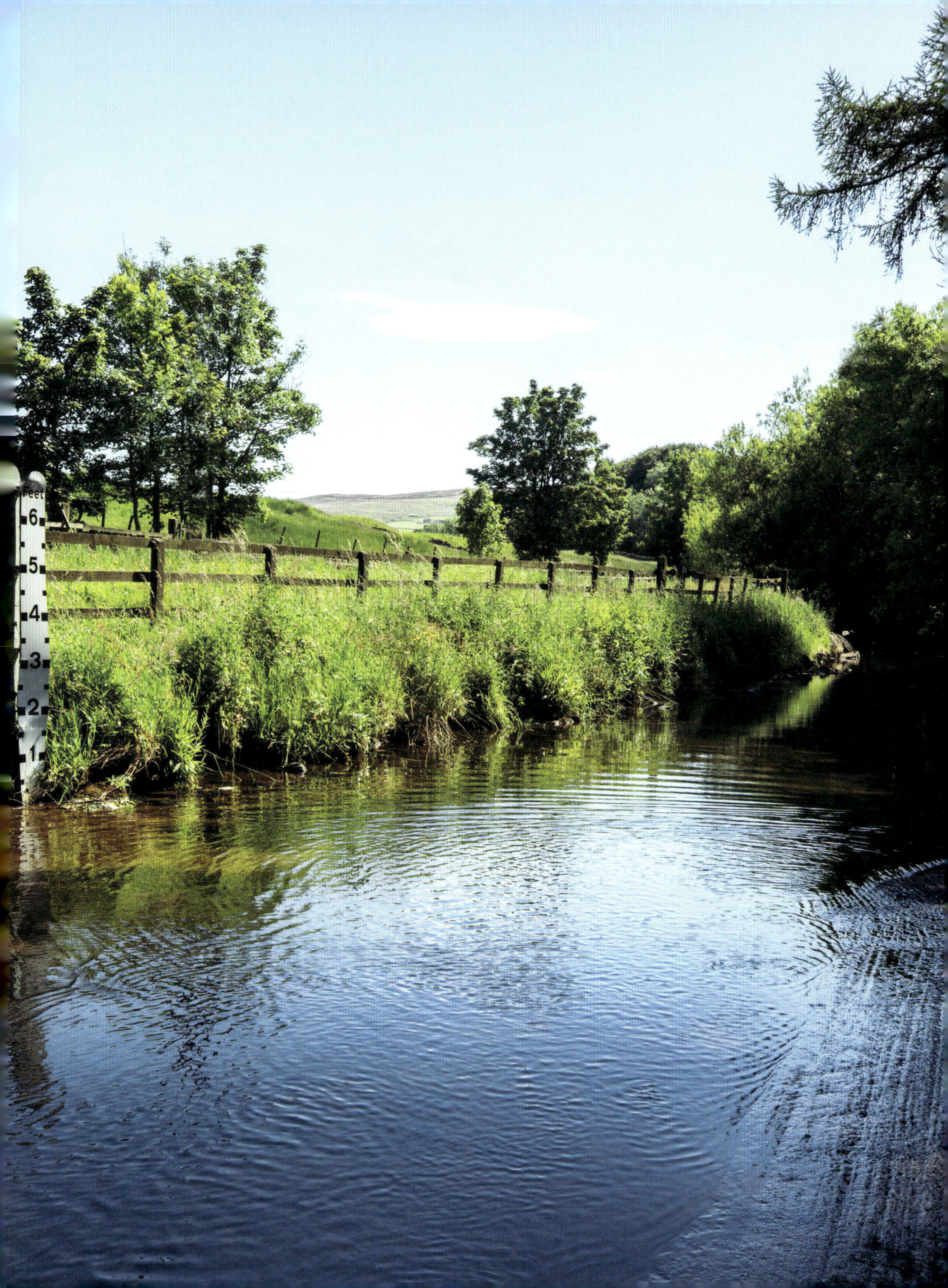

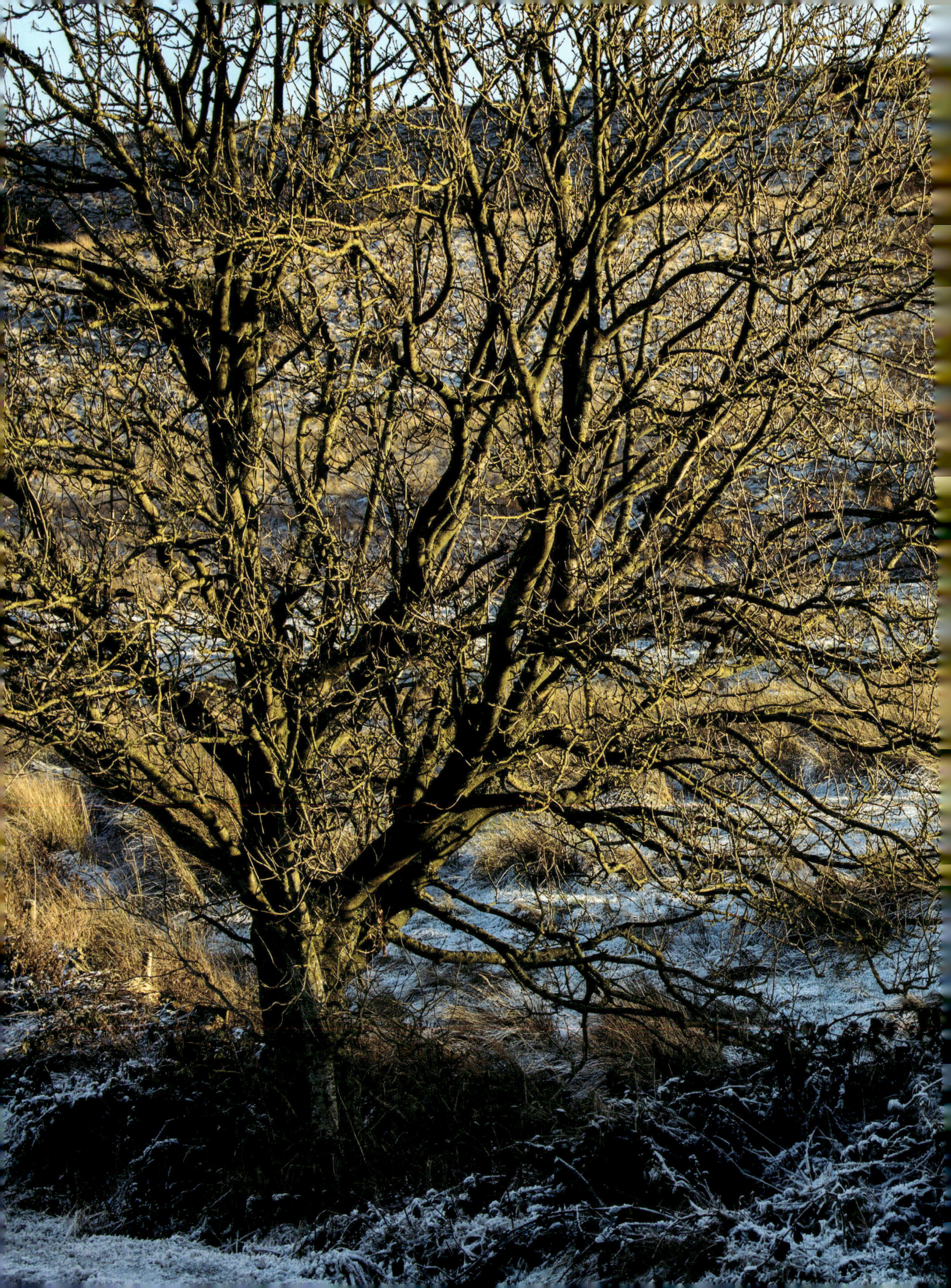

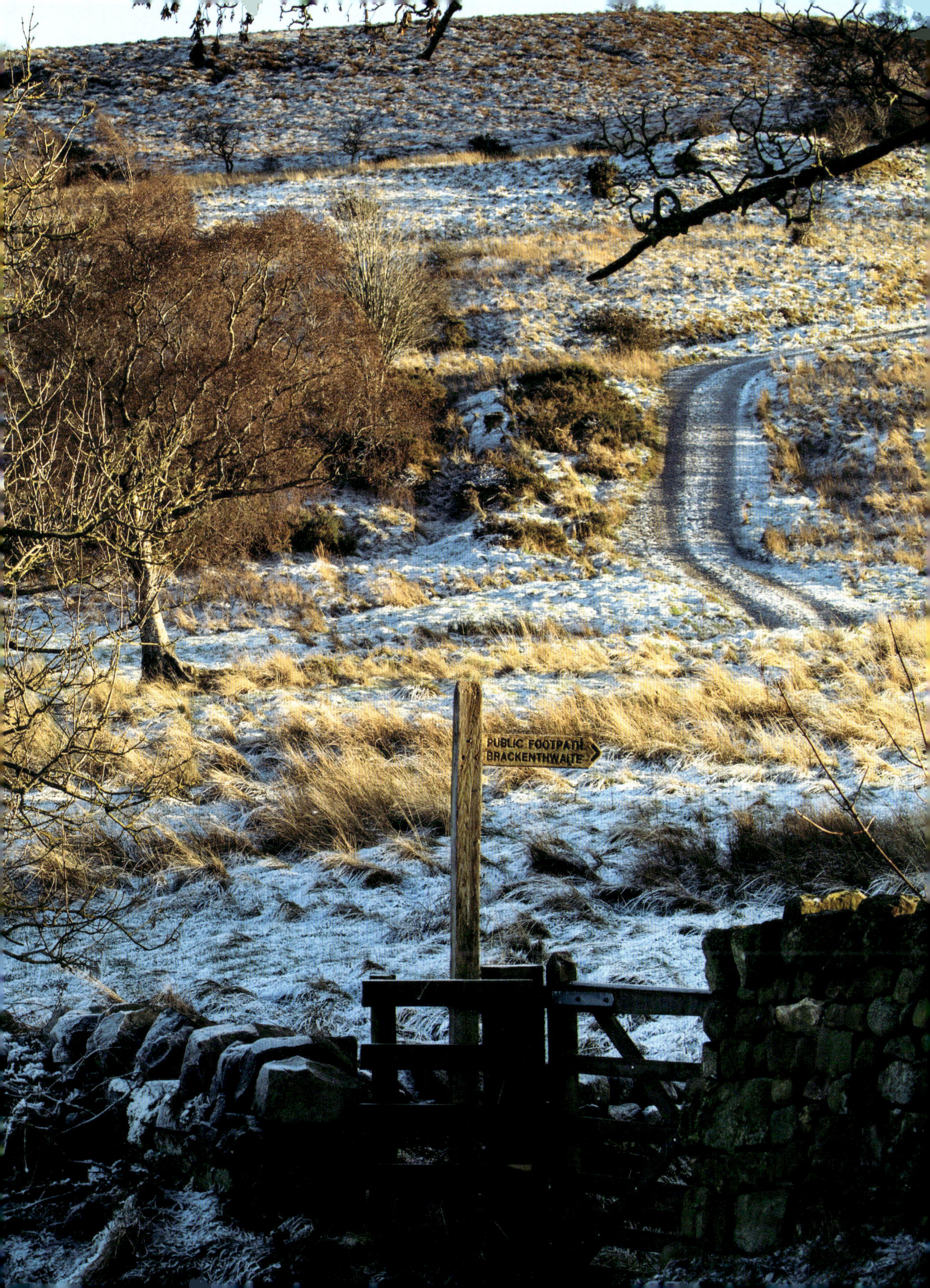

PUBLIC FOOTPATH
BRACKENTHWAITE

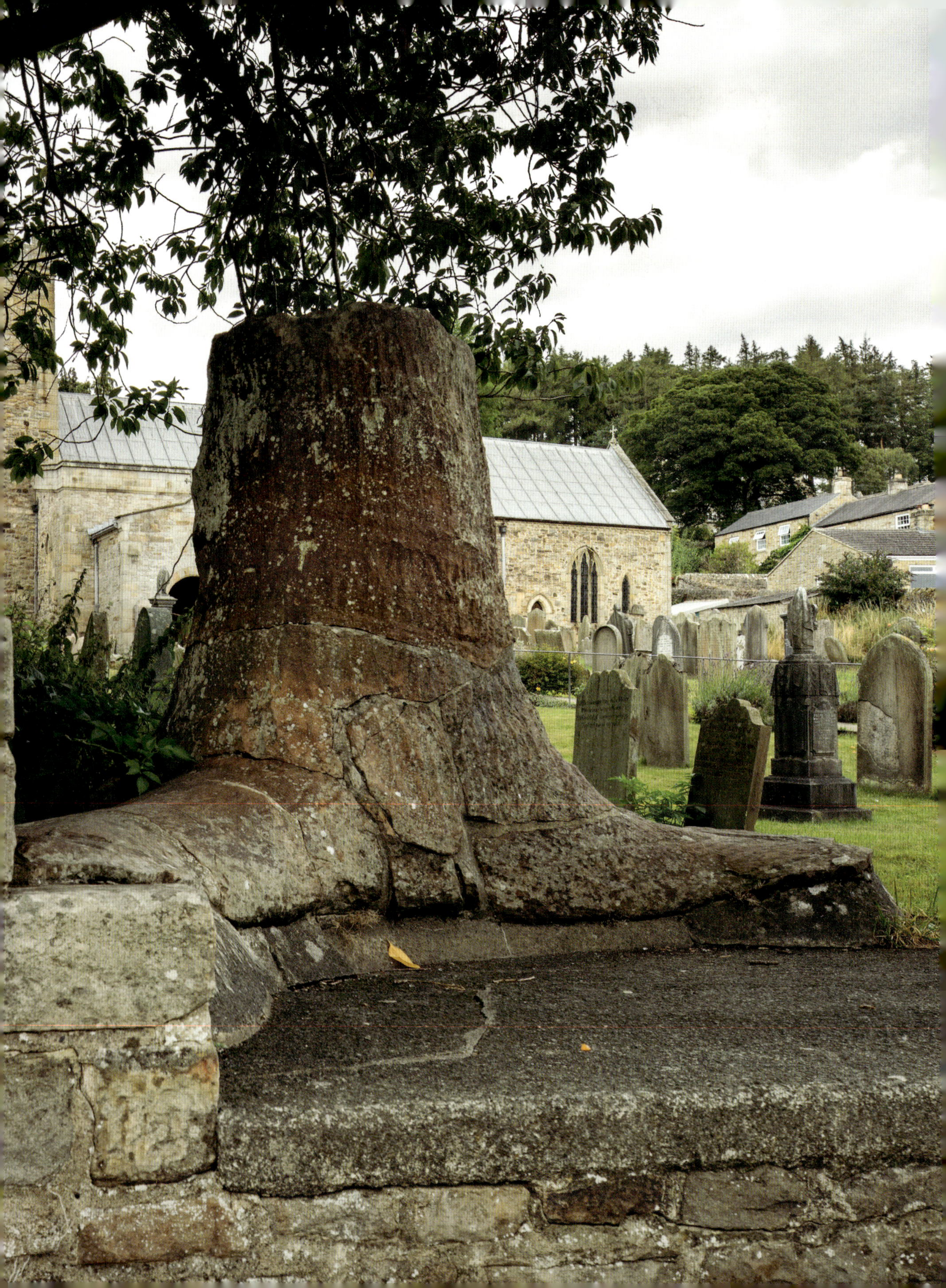

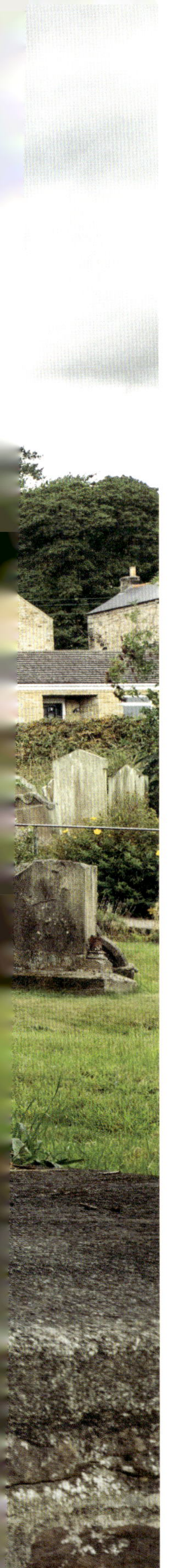

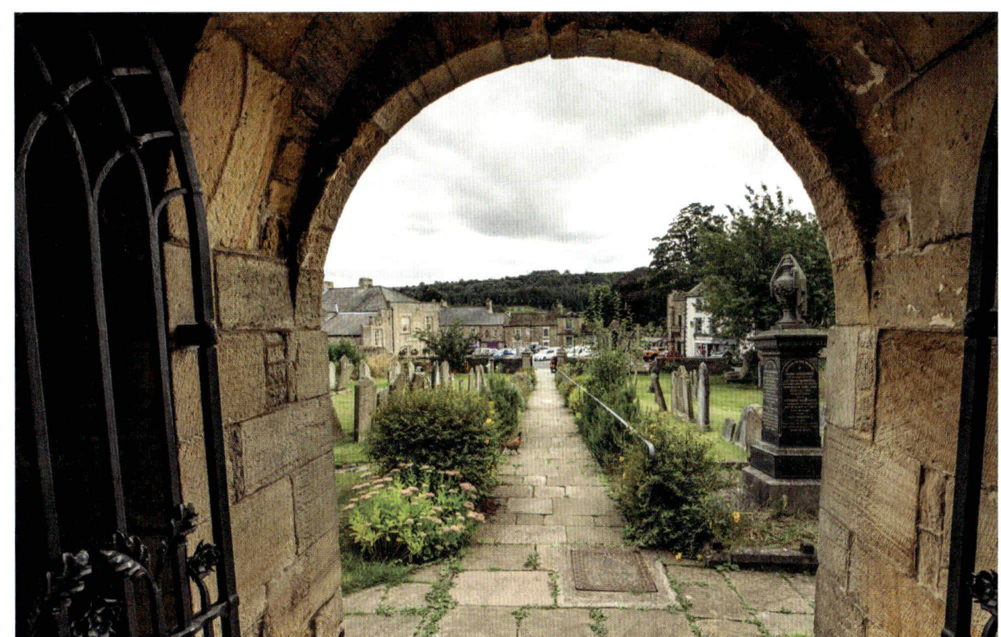

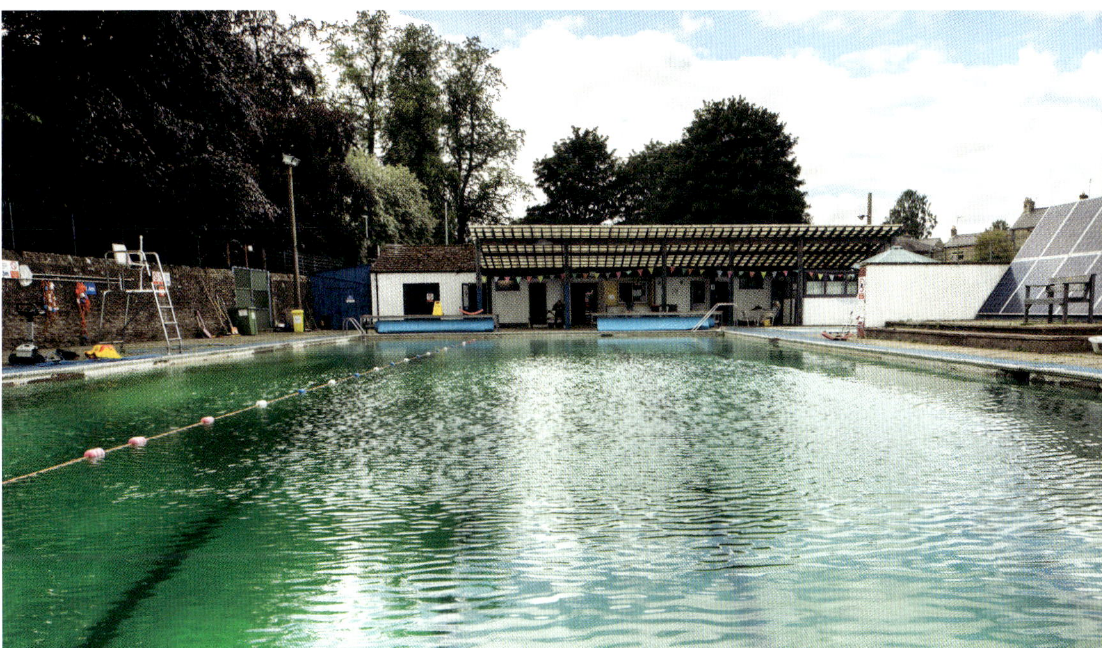

Stanhope. This quaint market town is at the heart of the Durham Dales in Weardale. The 13th century St Thomas the Apostle Church is built on Saxon foundations and has a fossilised tree (left) in the churchyard. The tree was discovered in a sandstone quarry at Edmundbyers in 1915. Stanhope swimming pool is one of only a few open air pools in the North East

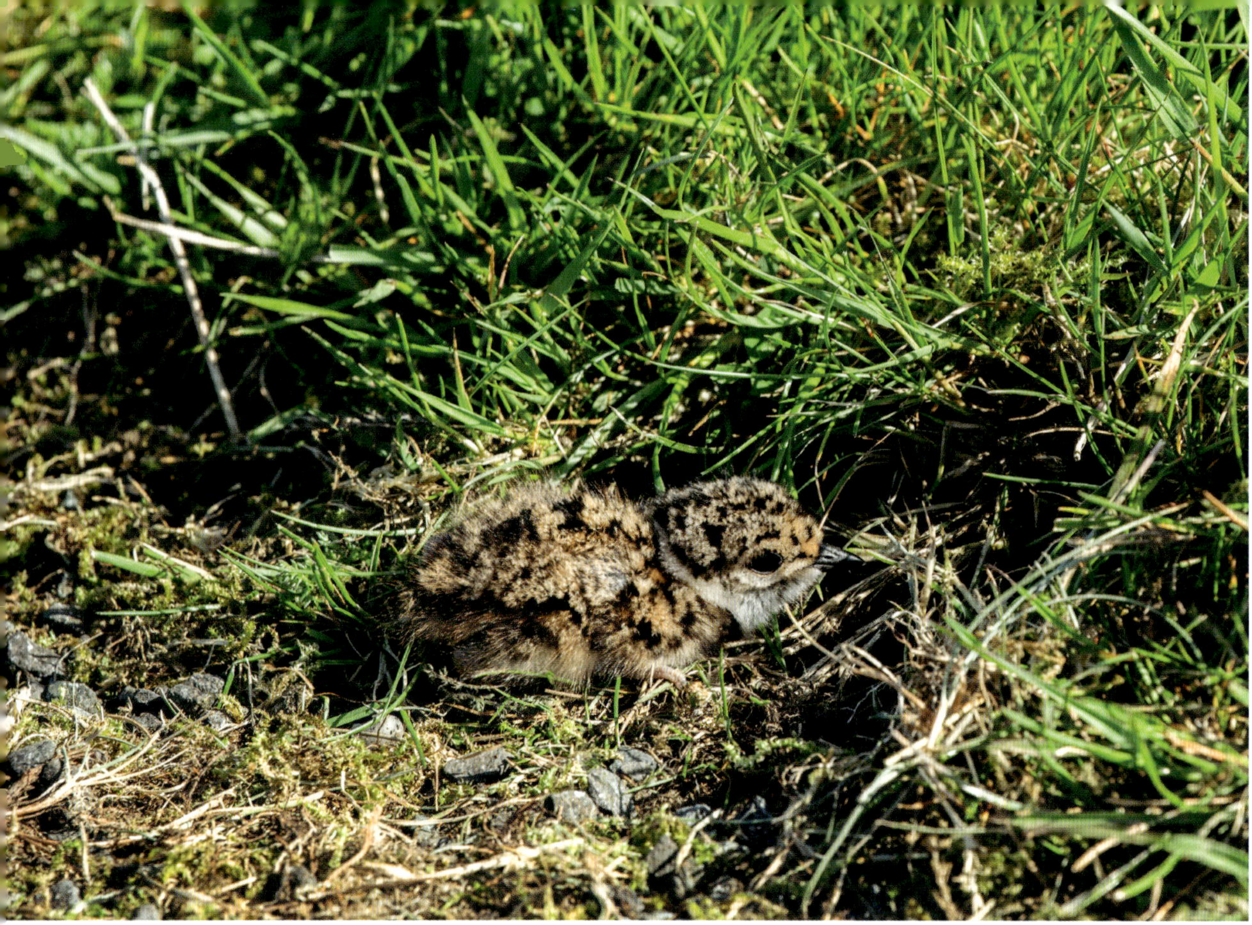

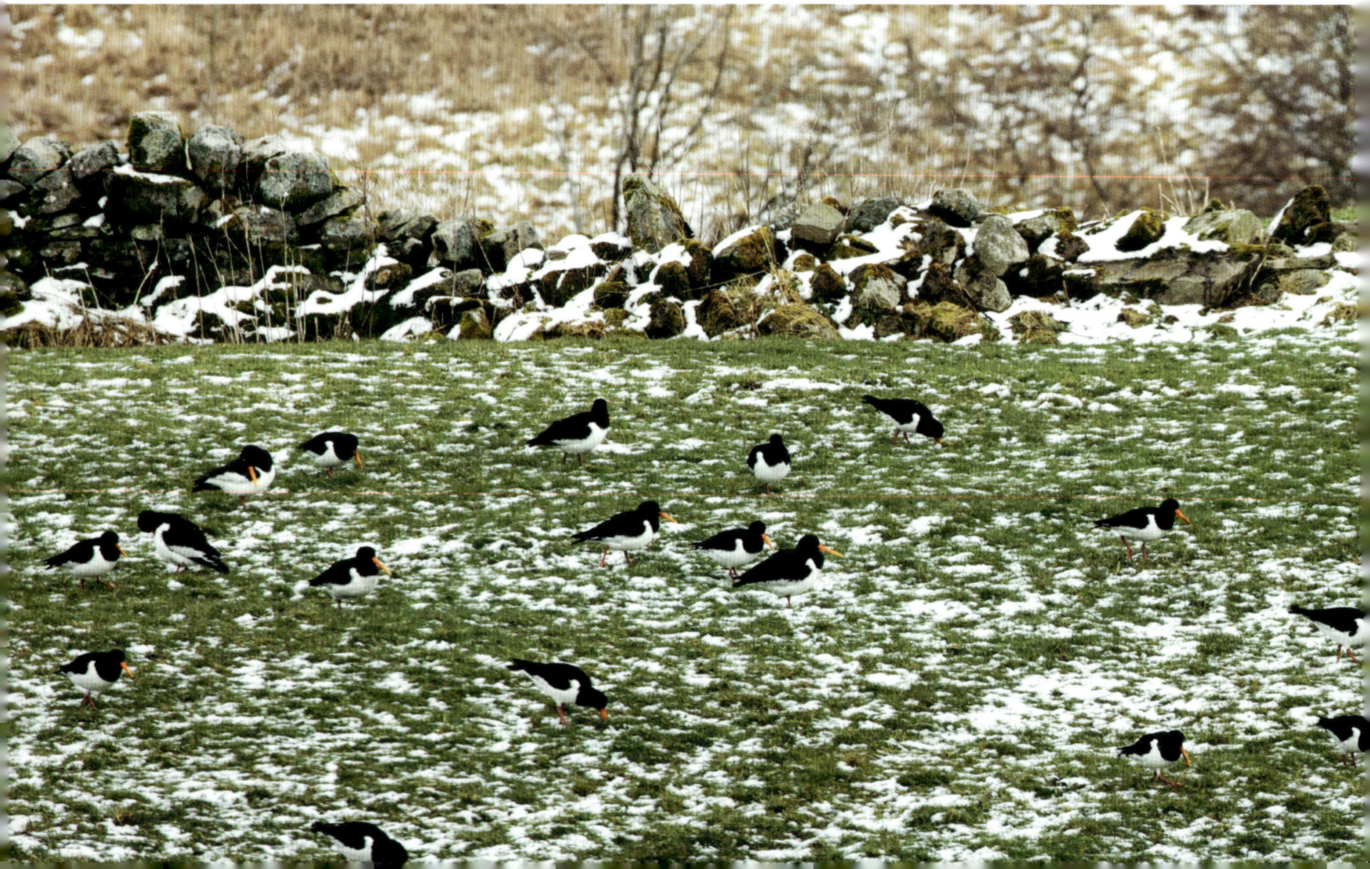

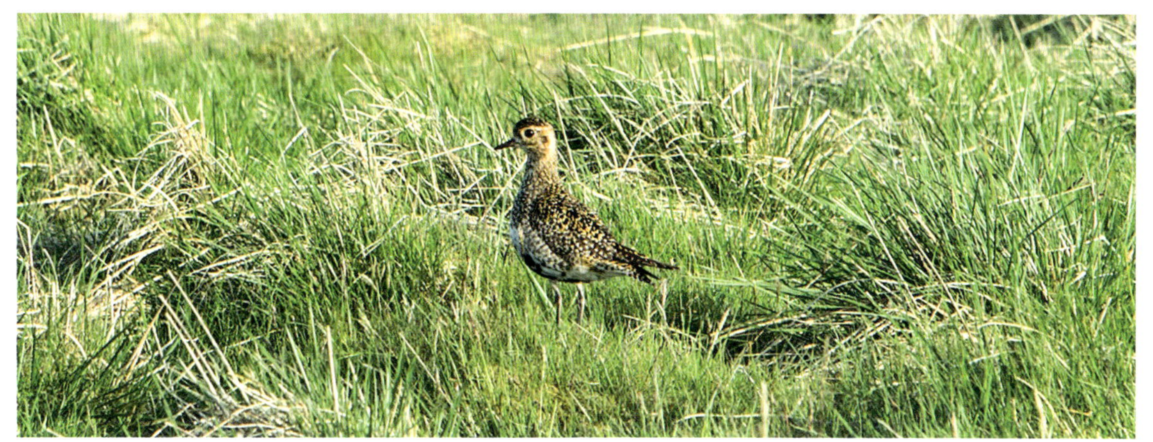

The North Pennines are a vital landscape for wading and ground-nesting birds

Above: Golden Plover, often difficult to see, but a sign that spring is on its way

Left: Lapwing chick with excellent camouflage

Below: Oystercatchers gather on a snowy field at Middle Lee, the photographer/ author's home. When inland they probe grassy areas for worms and invertebrates

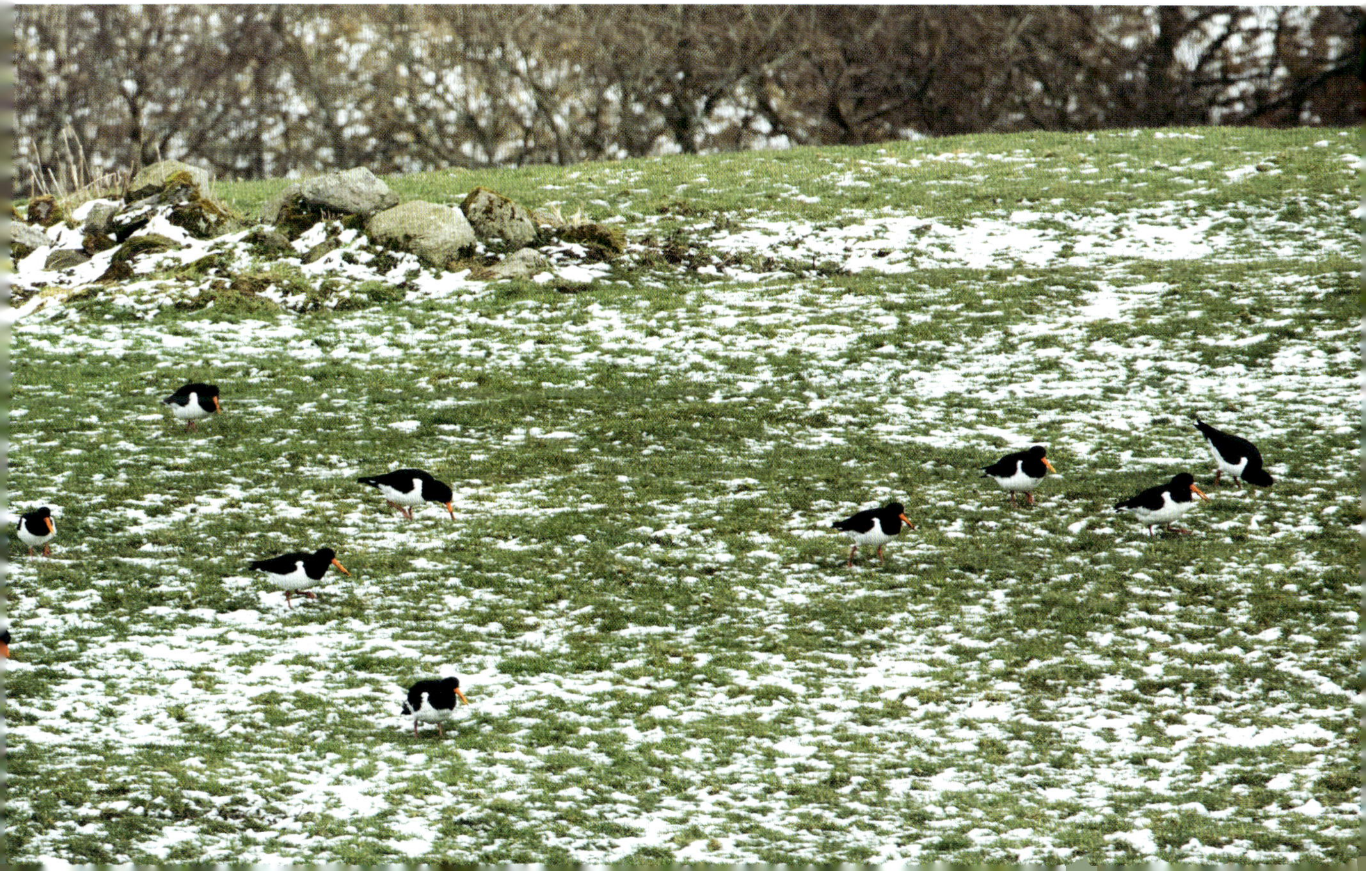

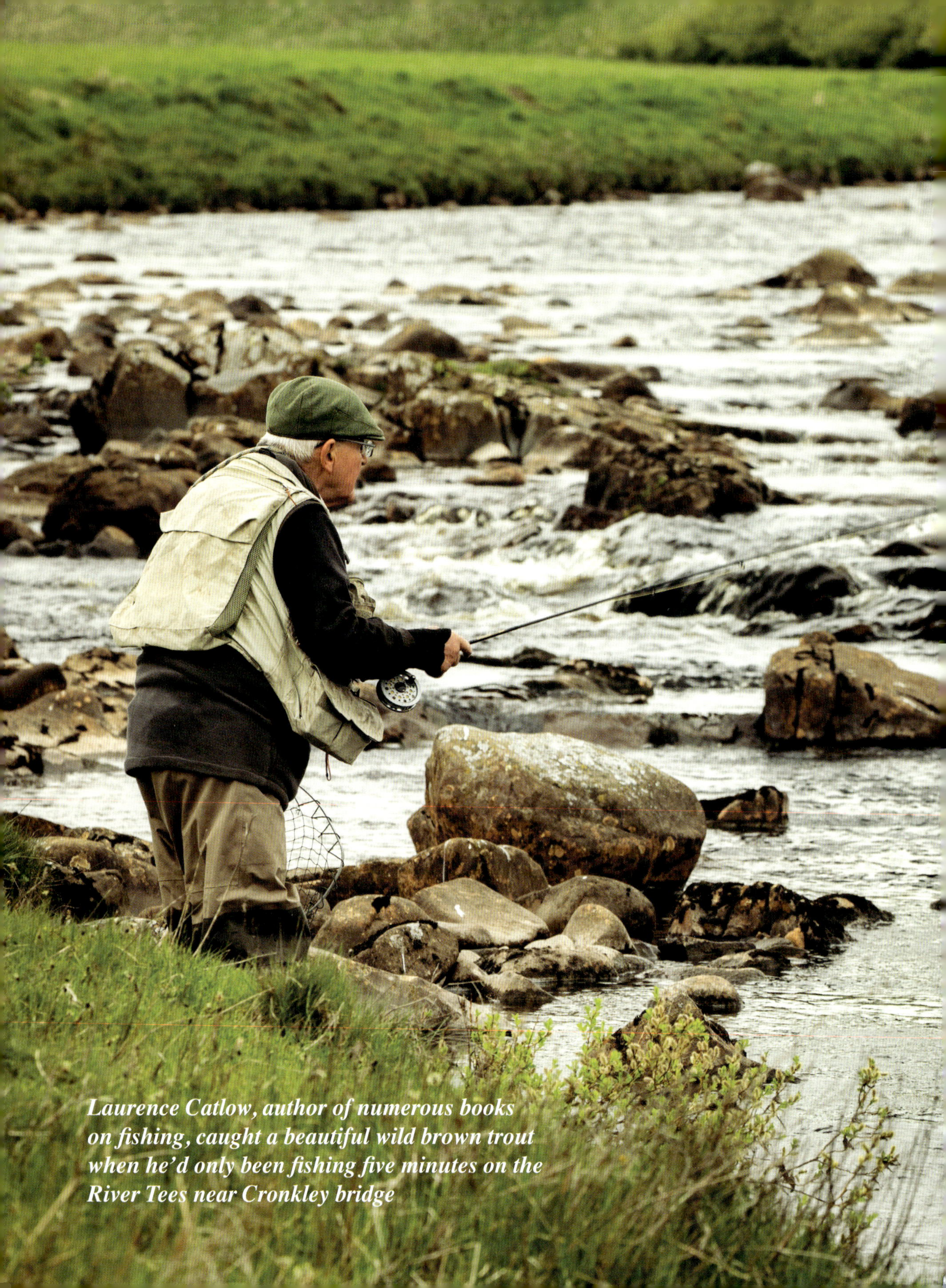

Laurence Catlow, author of numerous books on fishing, caught a beautiful wild brown trout when he'd only been fishing five minutes on the River Tees near Cronkley bridge

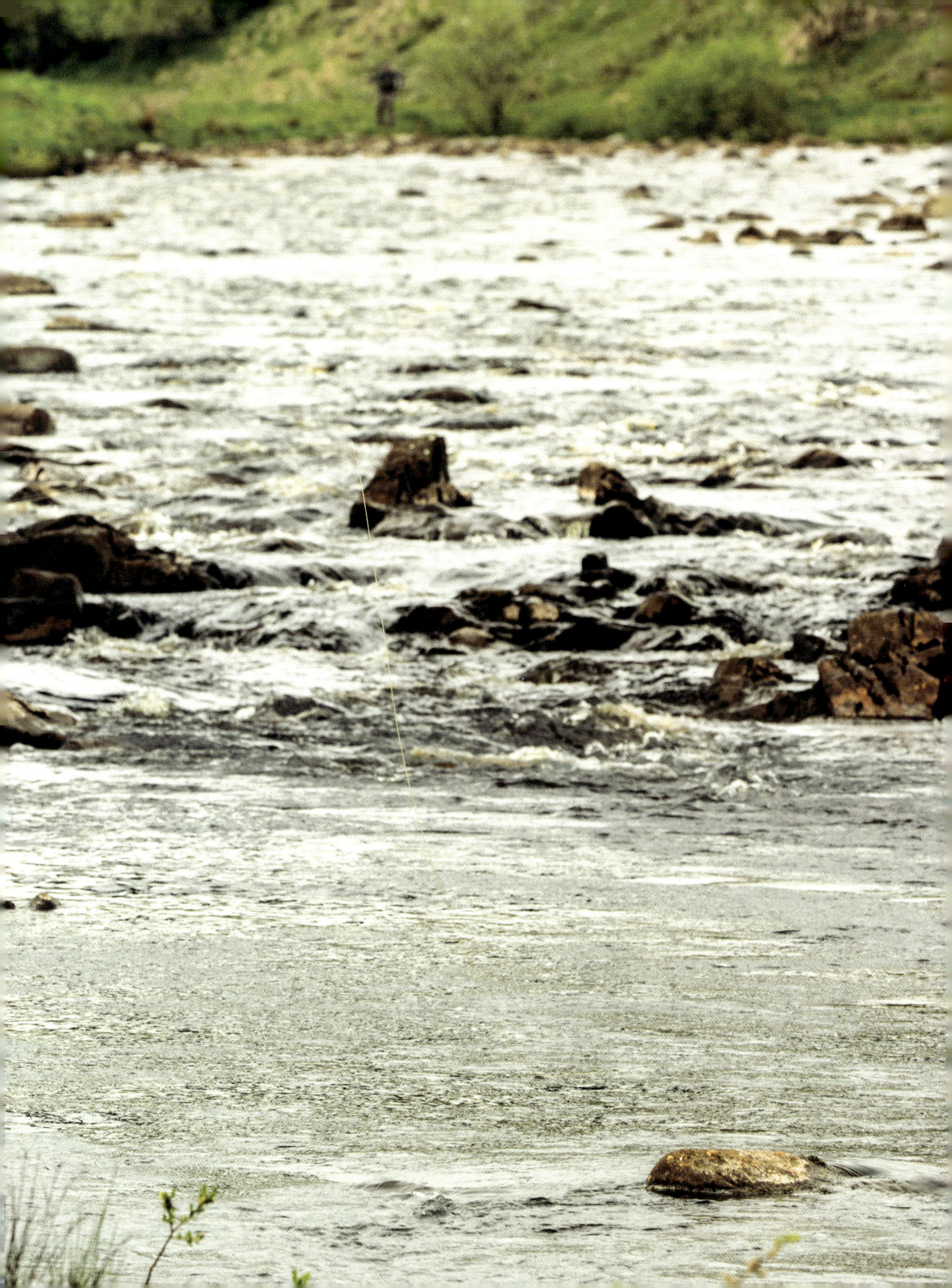

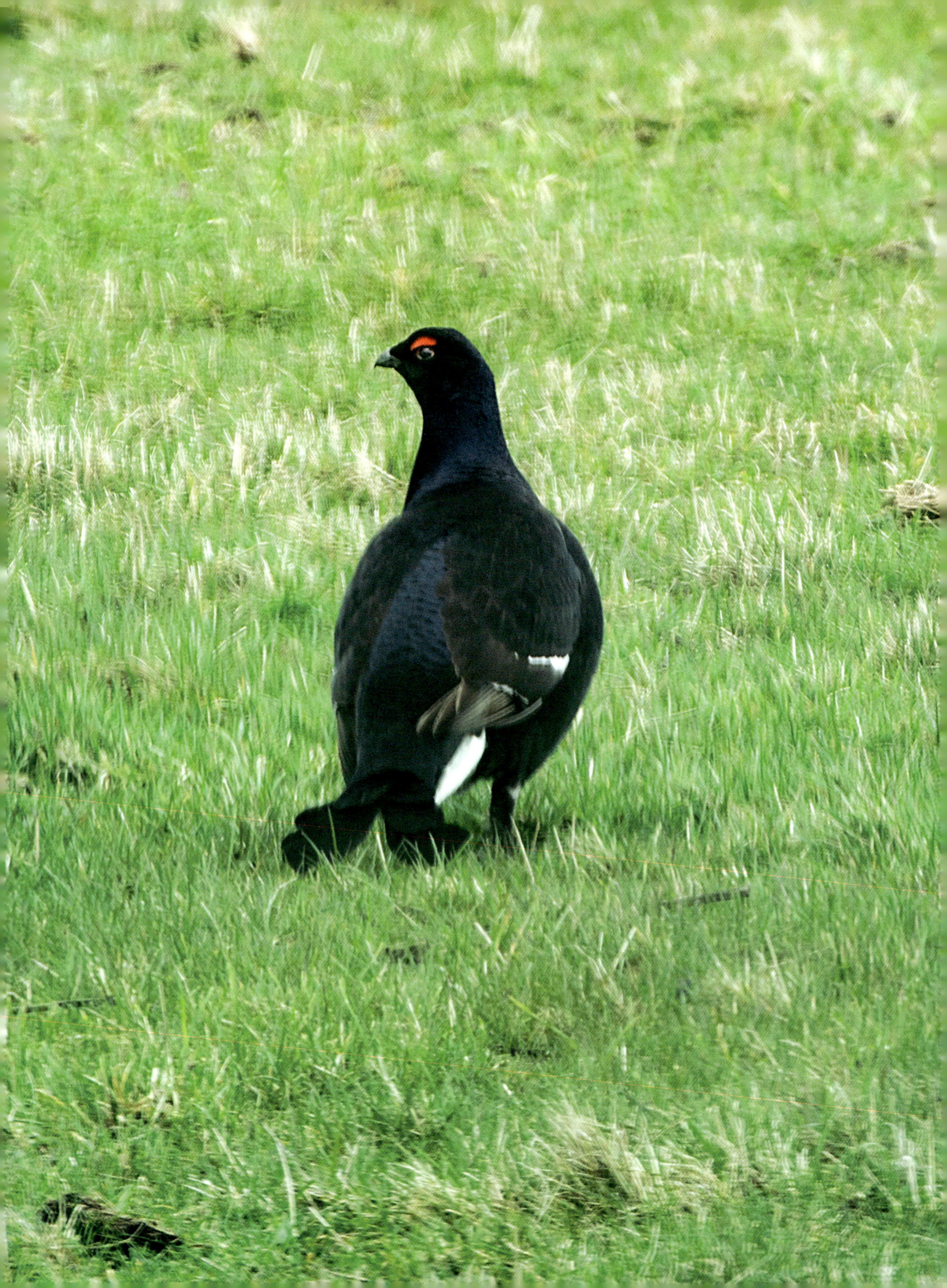

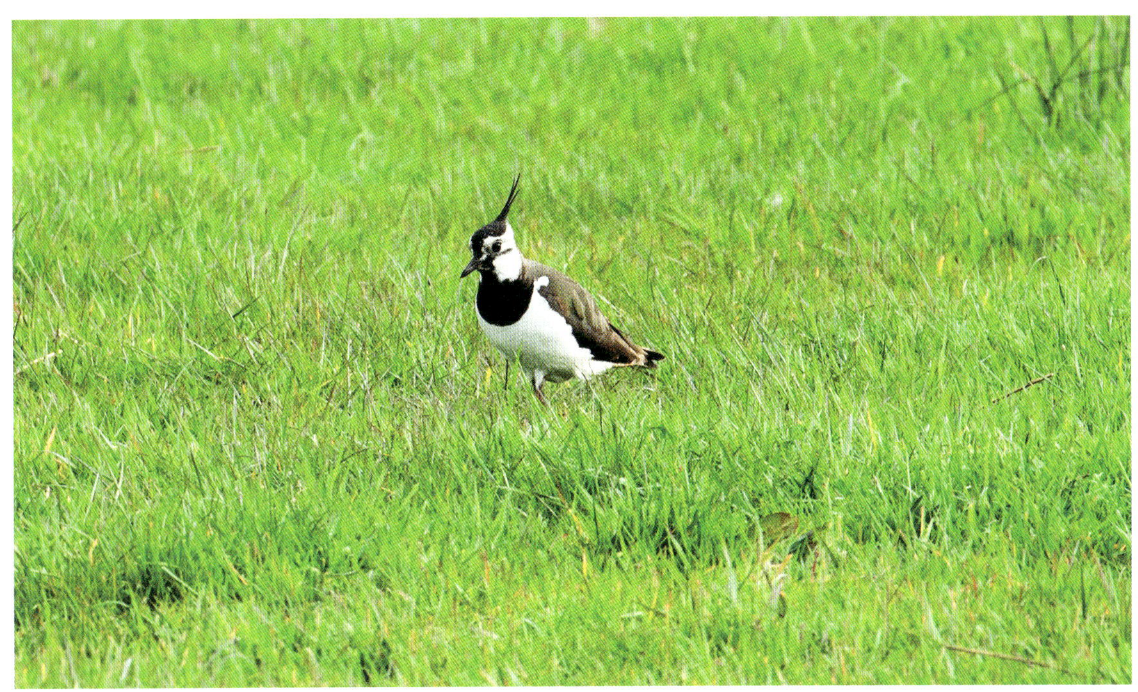

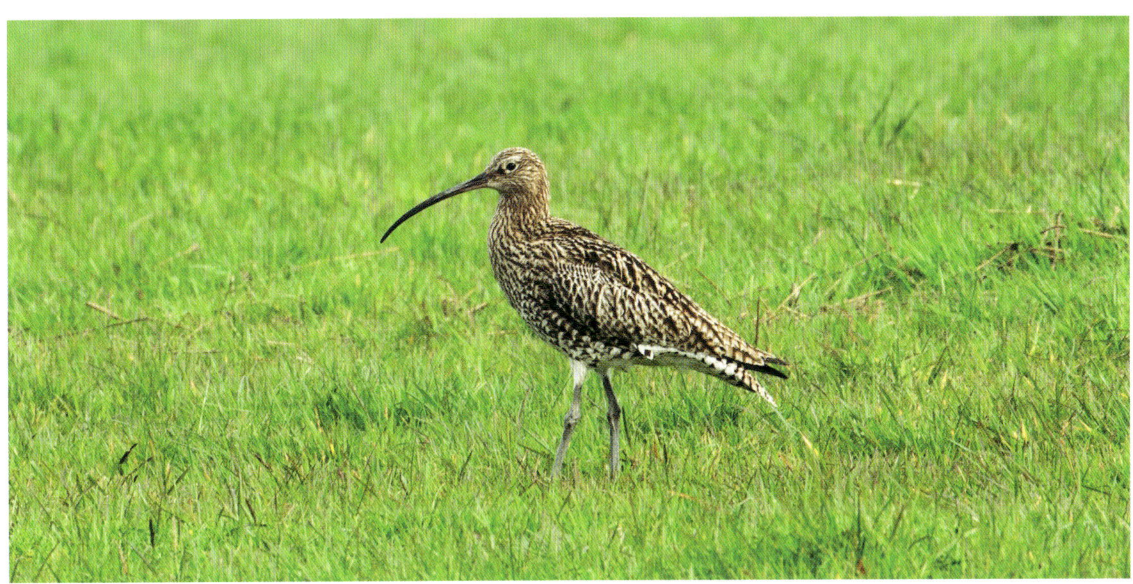

Top: Lapwings are fairly easy to spot and photograph in the area

Middle: Curlews particularly like the rough grasslands, moorlands and bogs of the North Pennines

Left: Black Grouse. 80% of England's Black Grouse population is found in the North Pennines

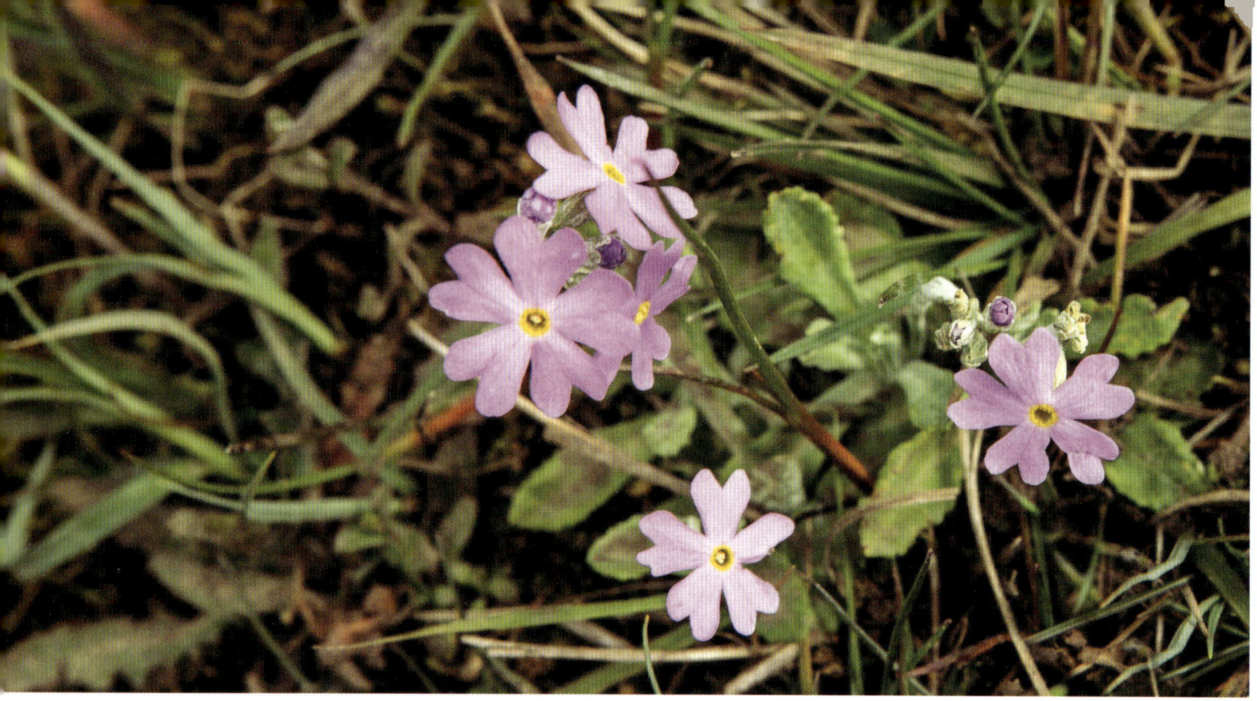

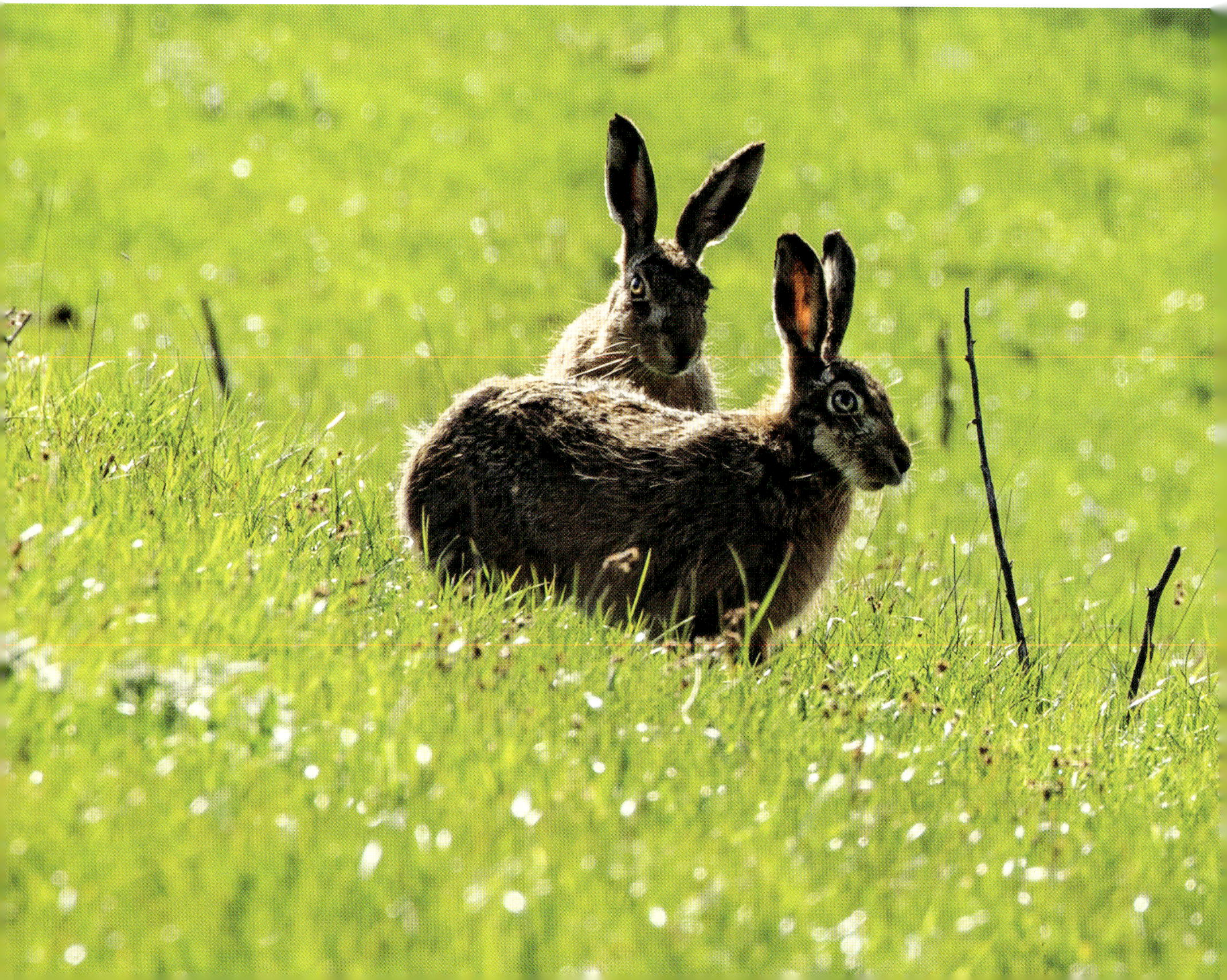

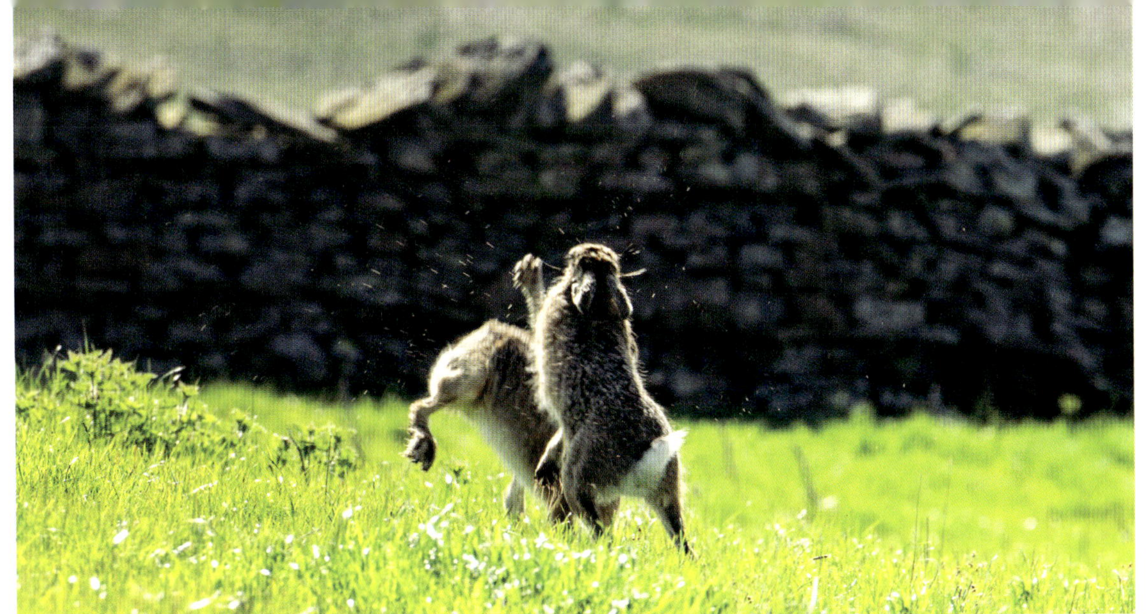

Birds Eye primroses and boxing hares; there were about 20 visible in this upland field in spring

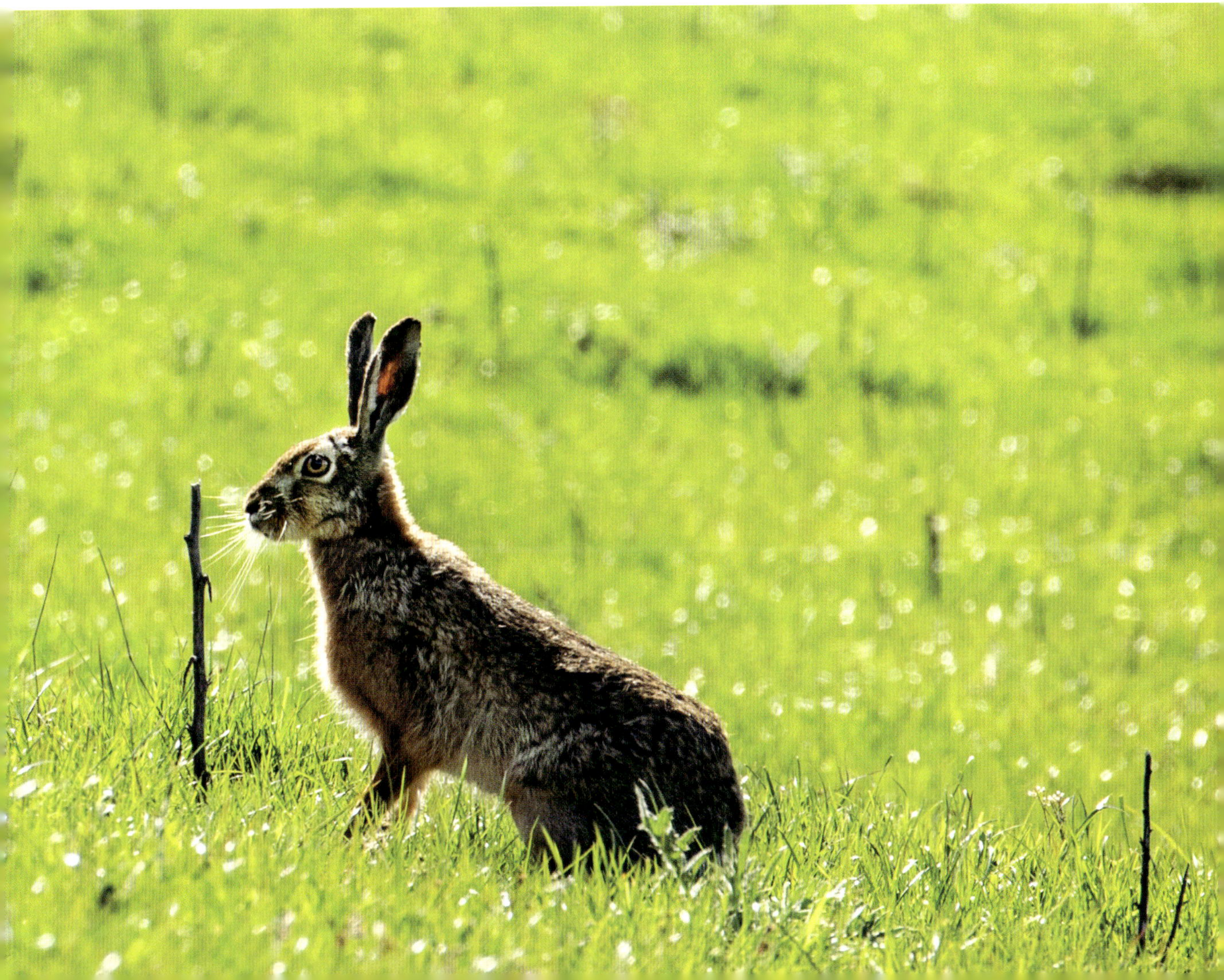

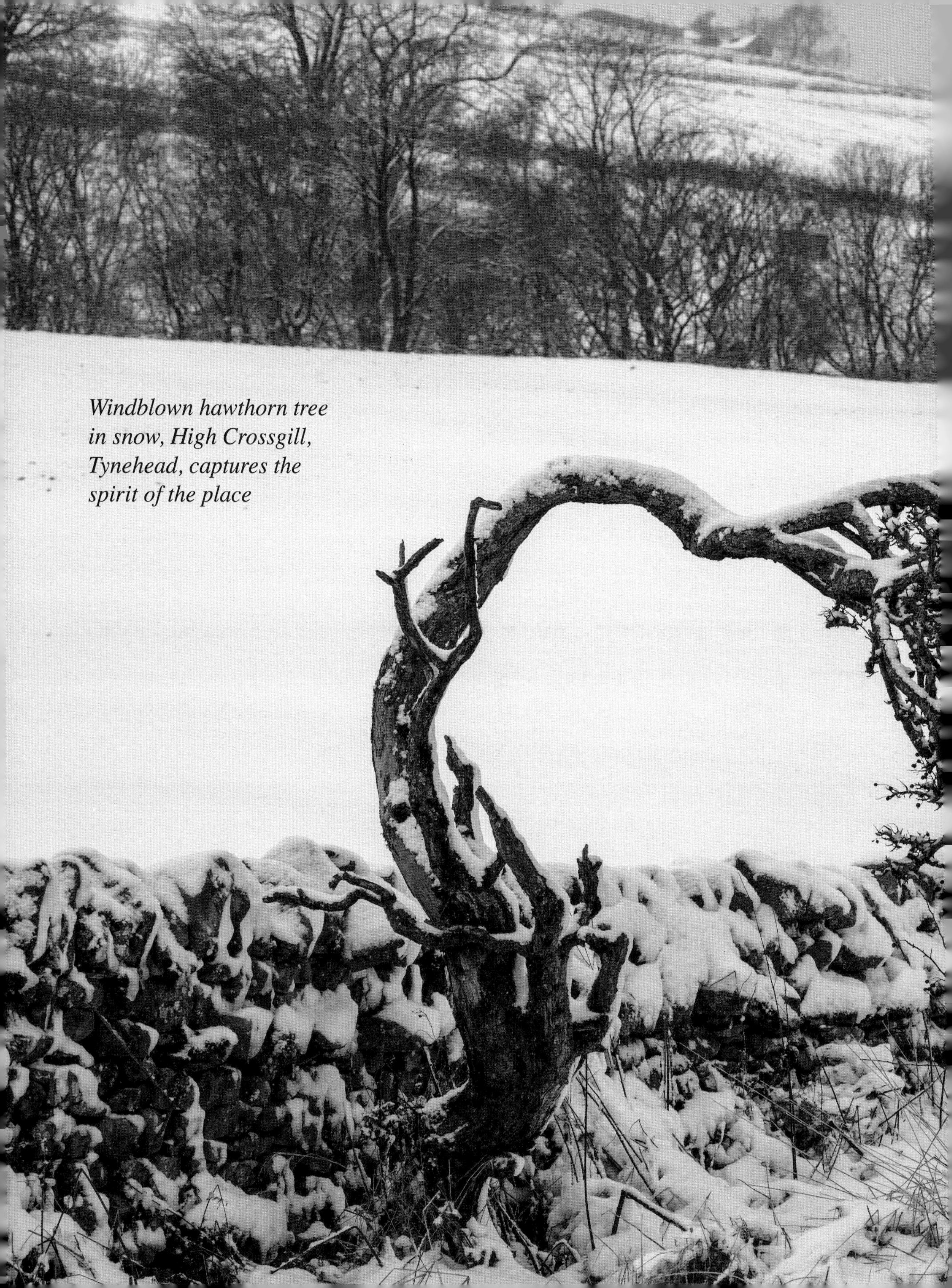

Windblown hawthorn tree in snow, High Crossgill, Tynehead, captures the spirit of the place

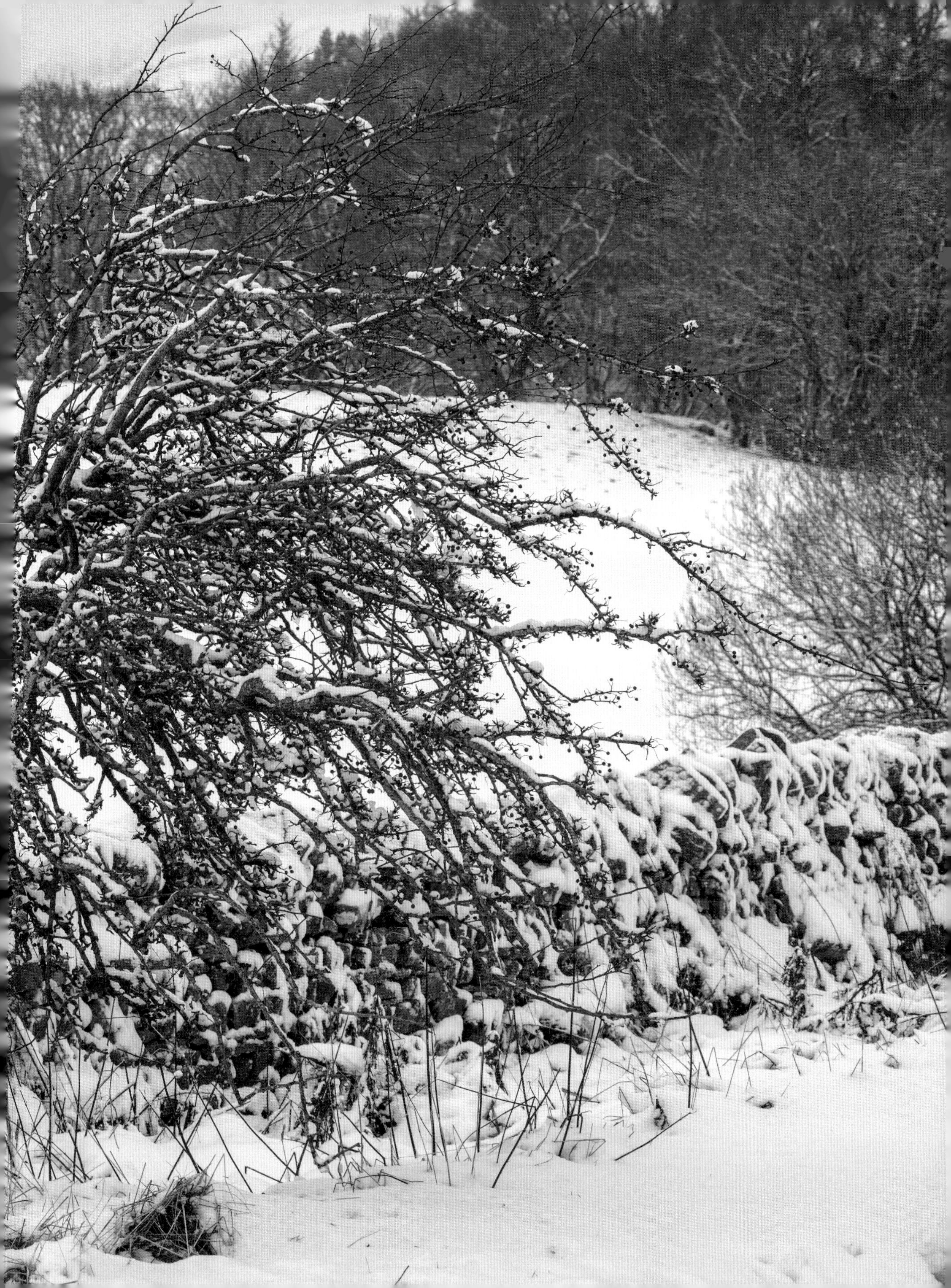

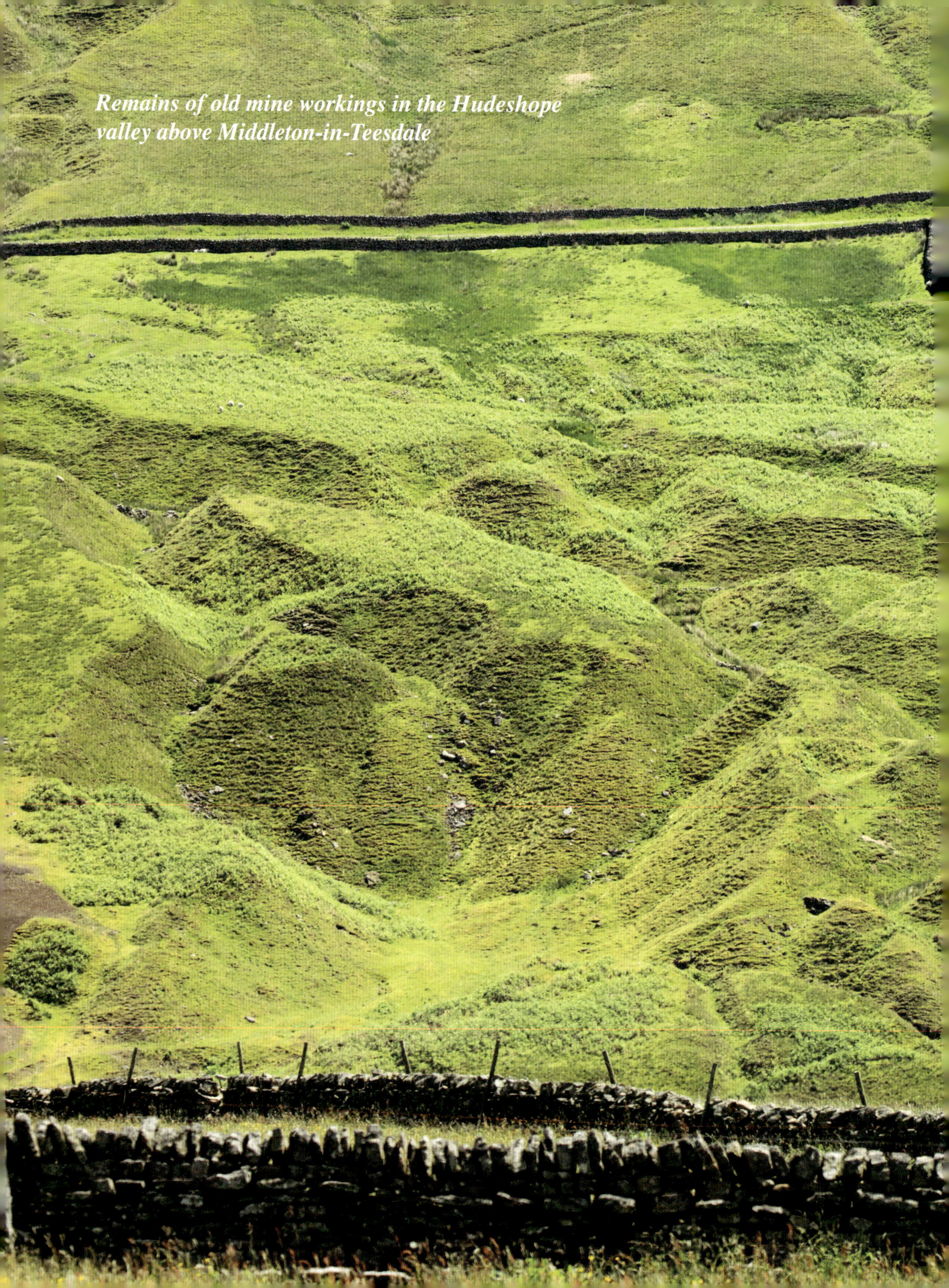

Remains of old mine workings in the Hudeshope
valley above Middleton-in-Teesdale

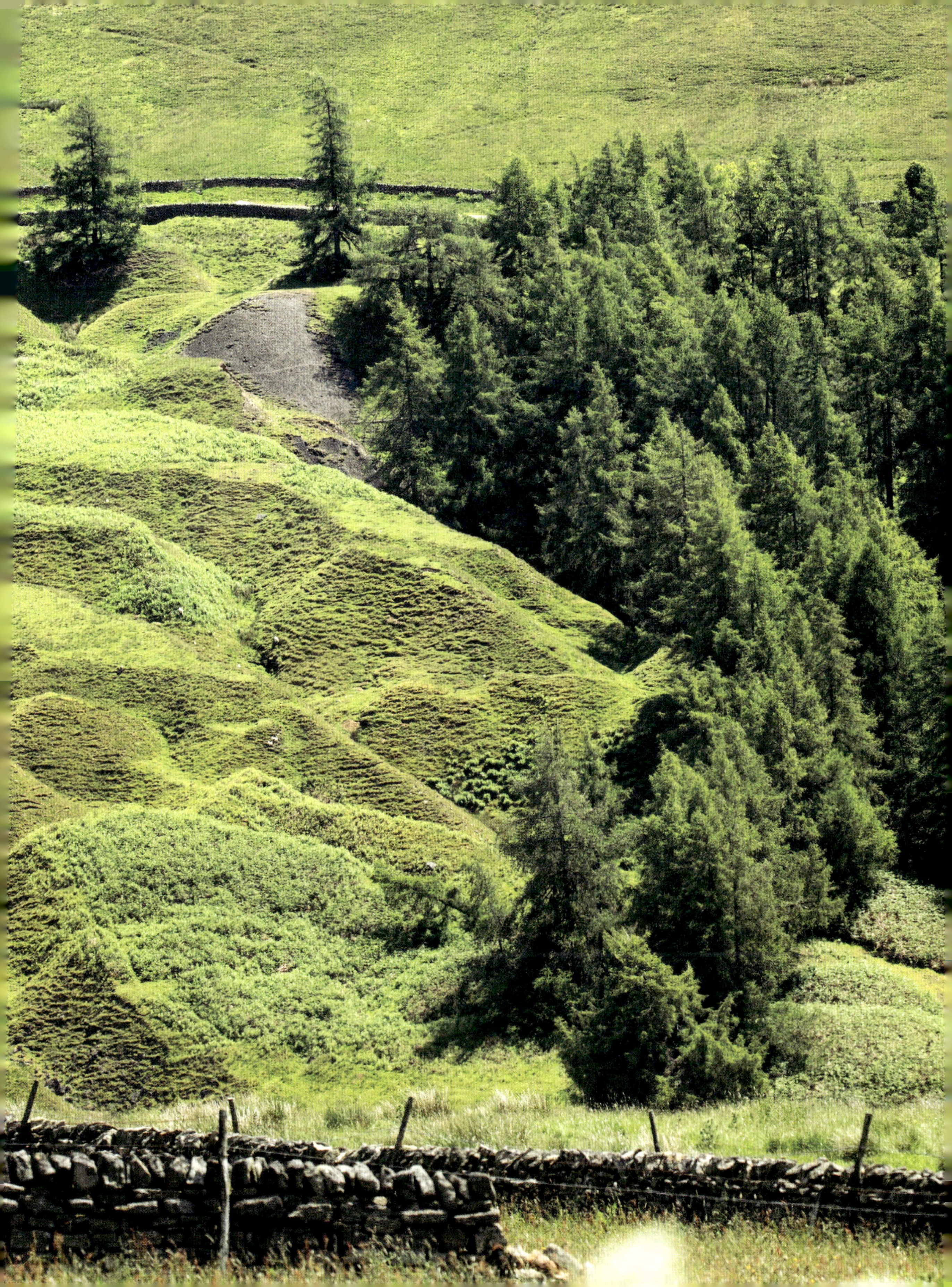

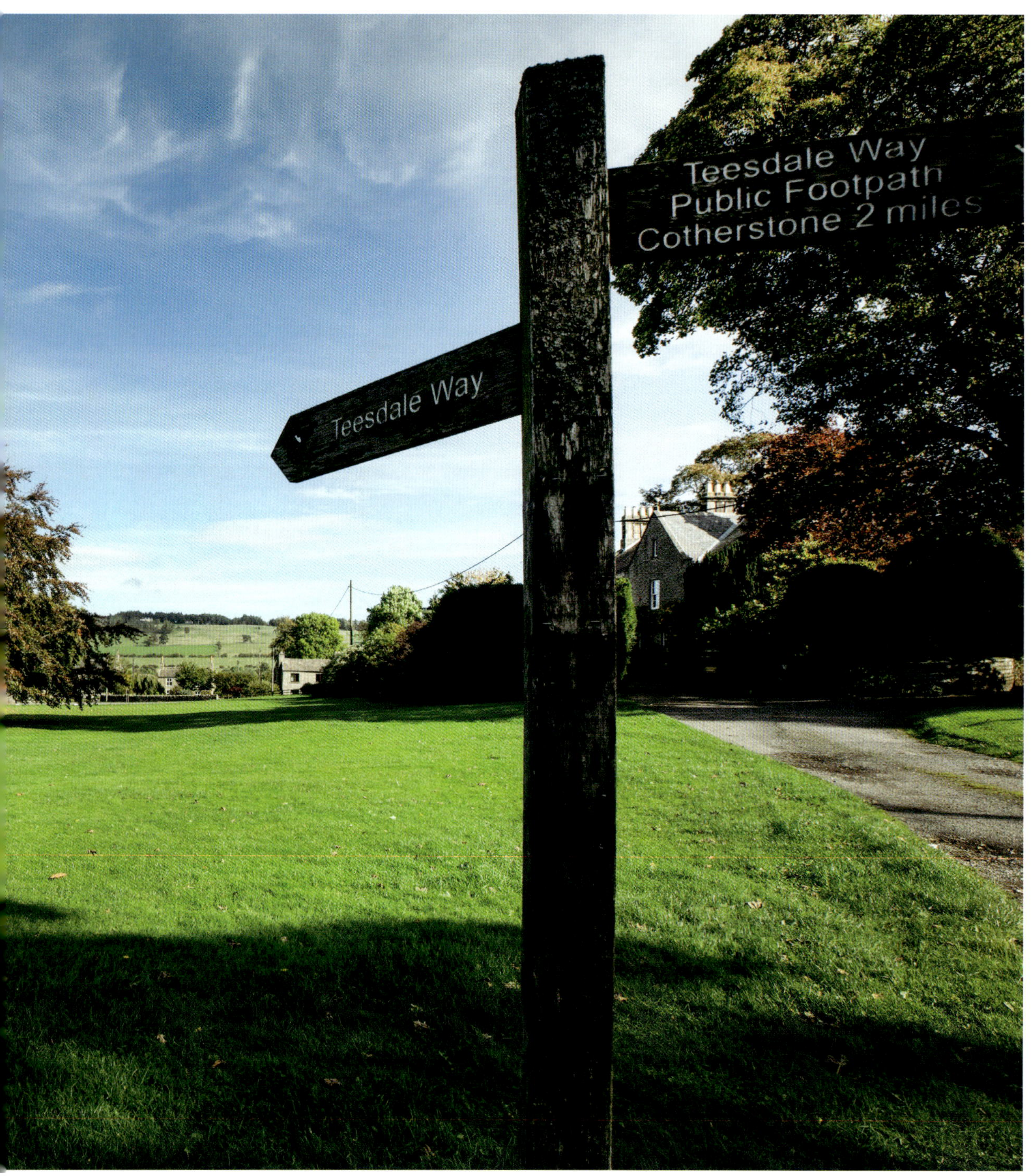

Above: the Teesdale Way crosses the beautiful village green at Romaldkirk.
The Teesdale Way runs 92 miles from Dufton to Redcar on the east coast.
St Romald's Church (right) has some Anglo-Saxon walls

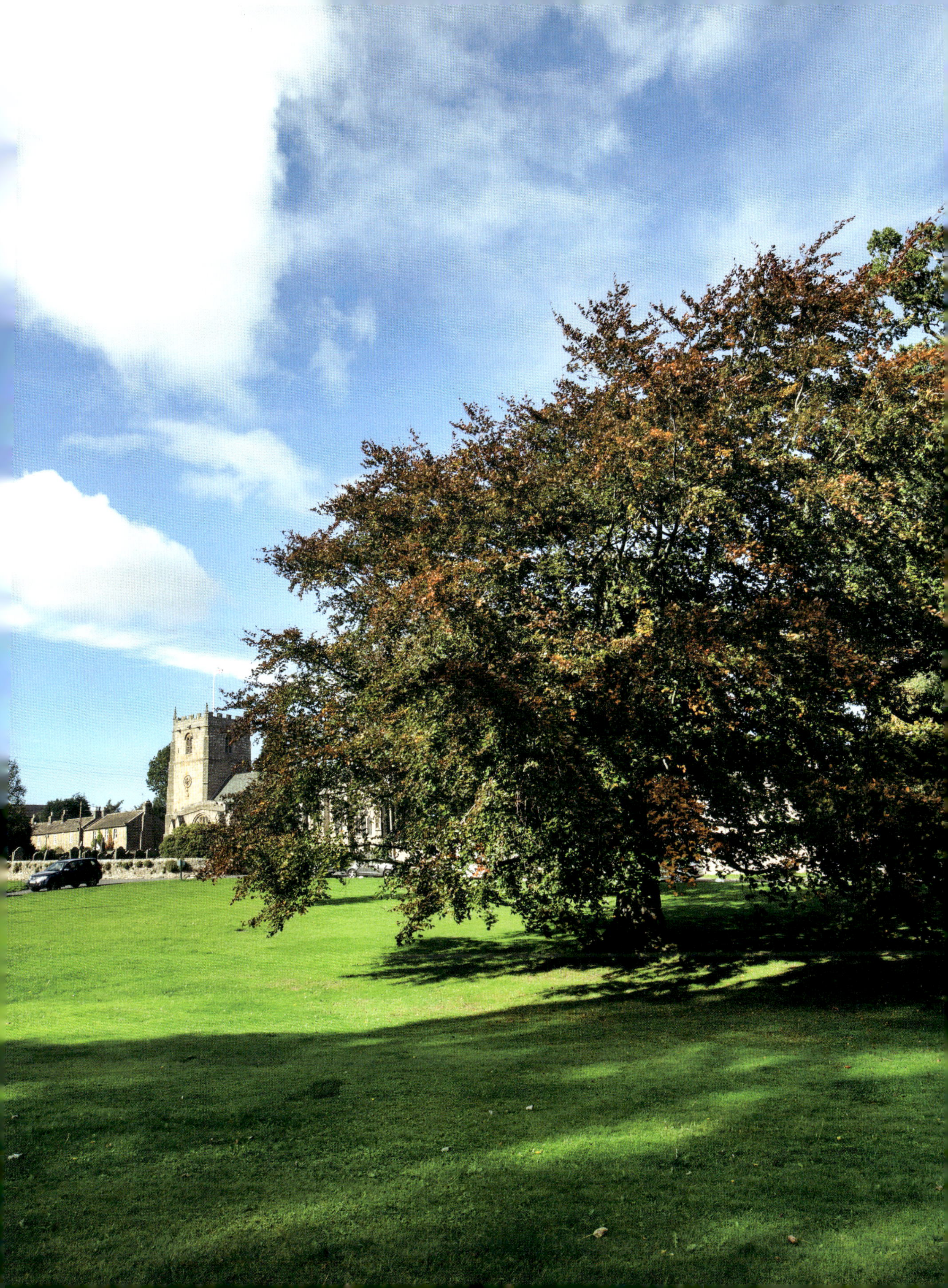

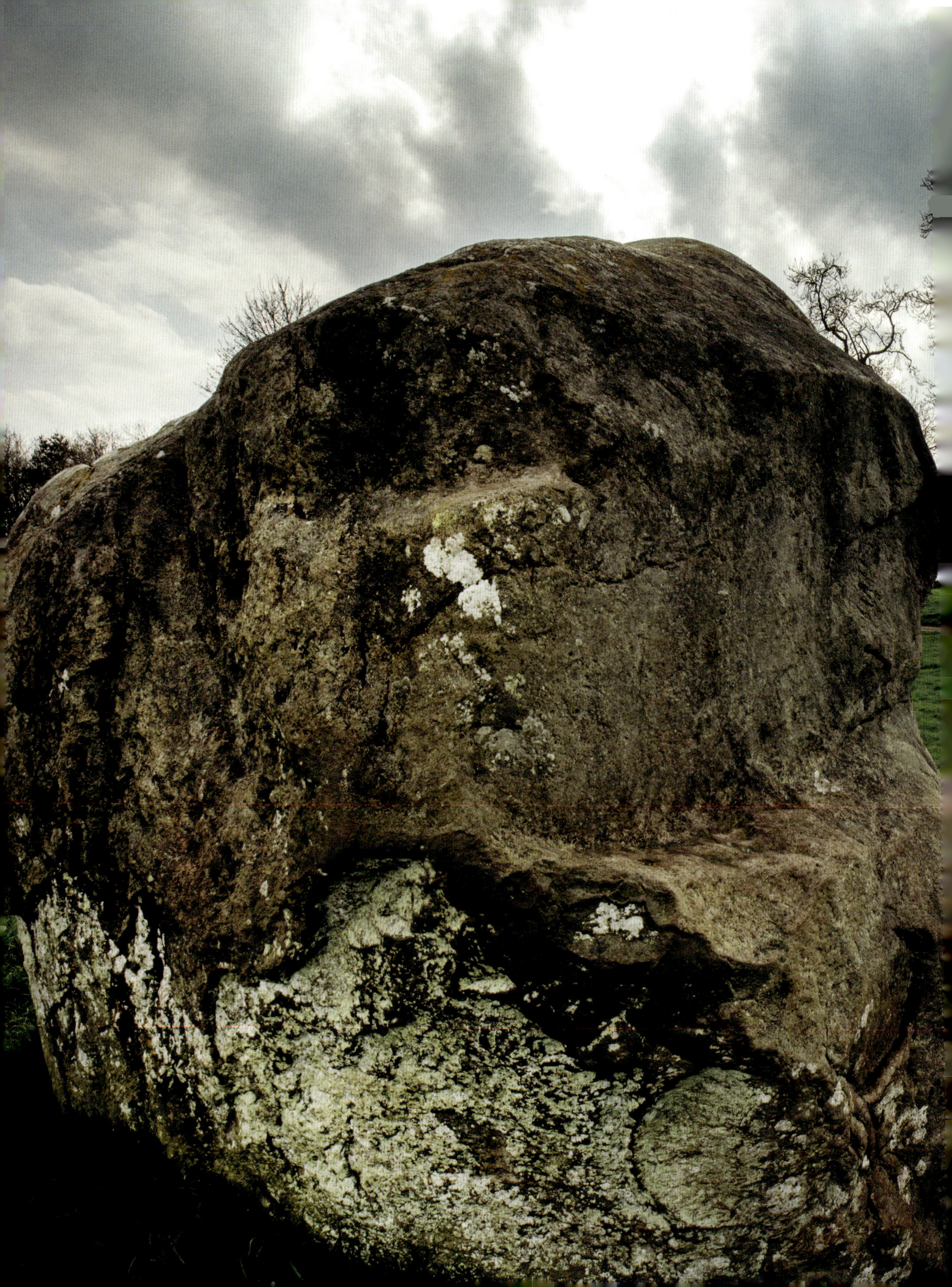

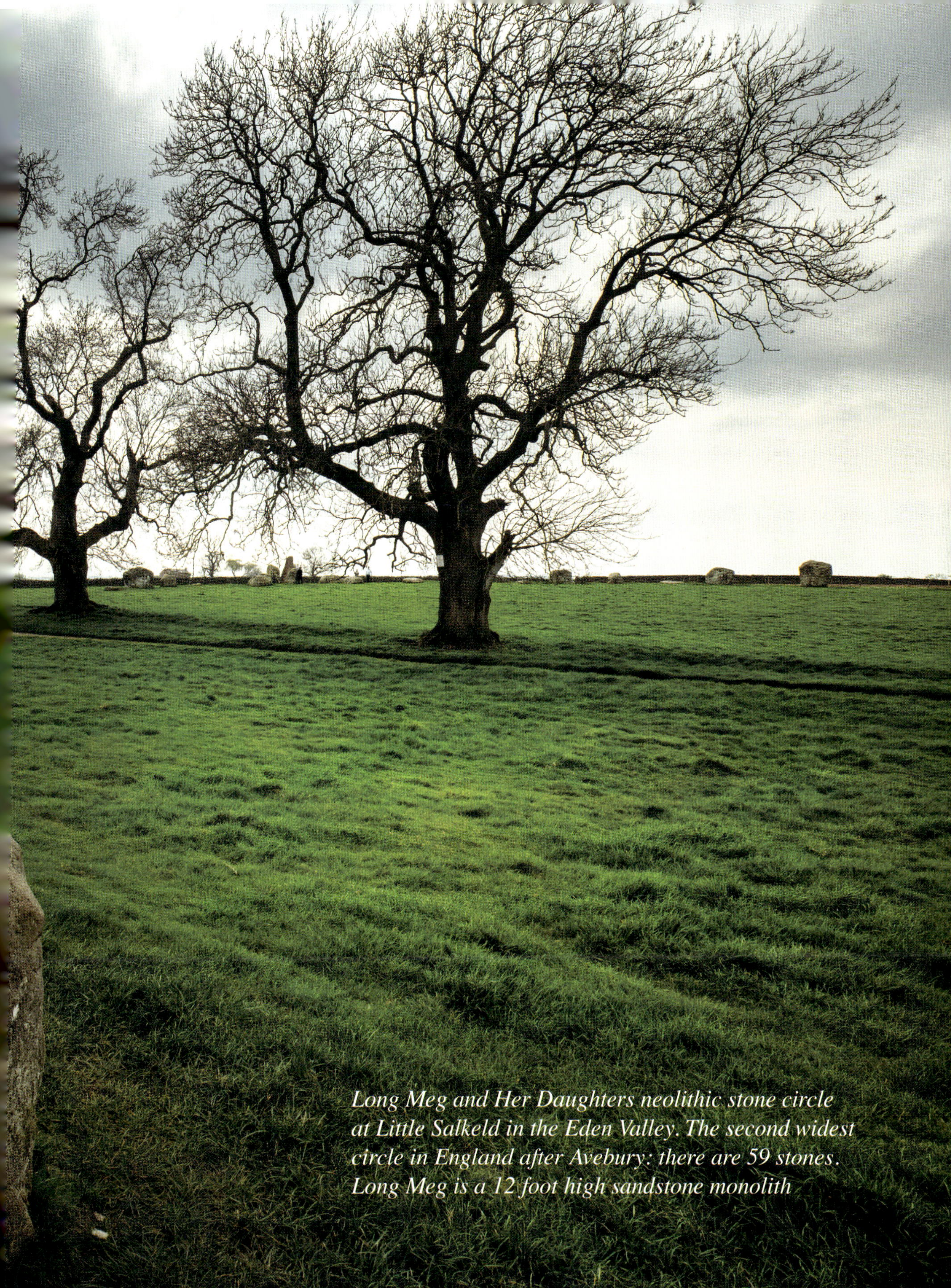

Long Meg and Her Daughters neolithic stone circle
at Little Salkeld in the Eden Valley. The second widest
circle in England after Avebury: there are 59 stones.
Long Meg is a 12 foot high sandstone monolith

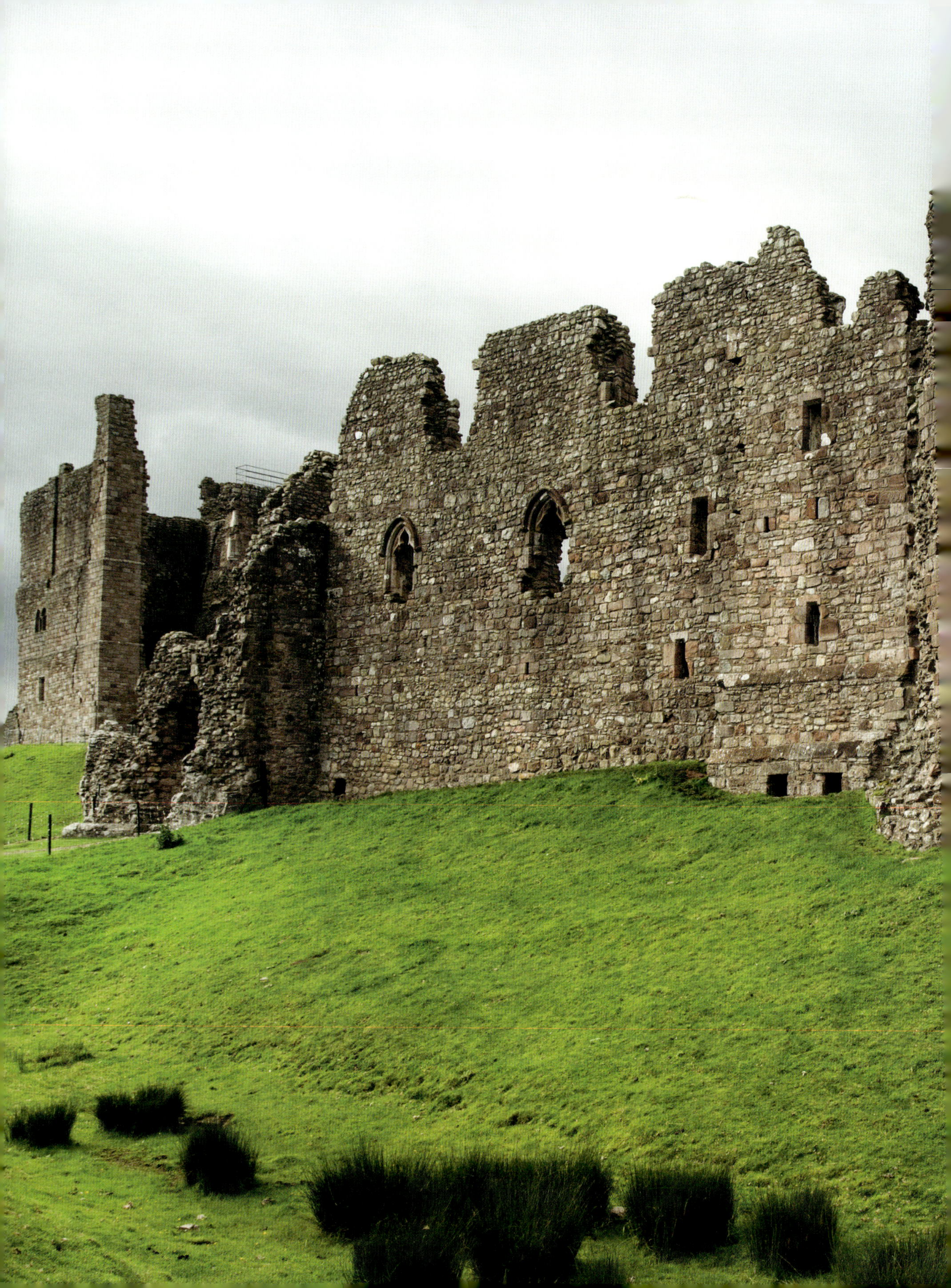

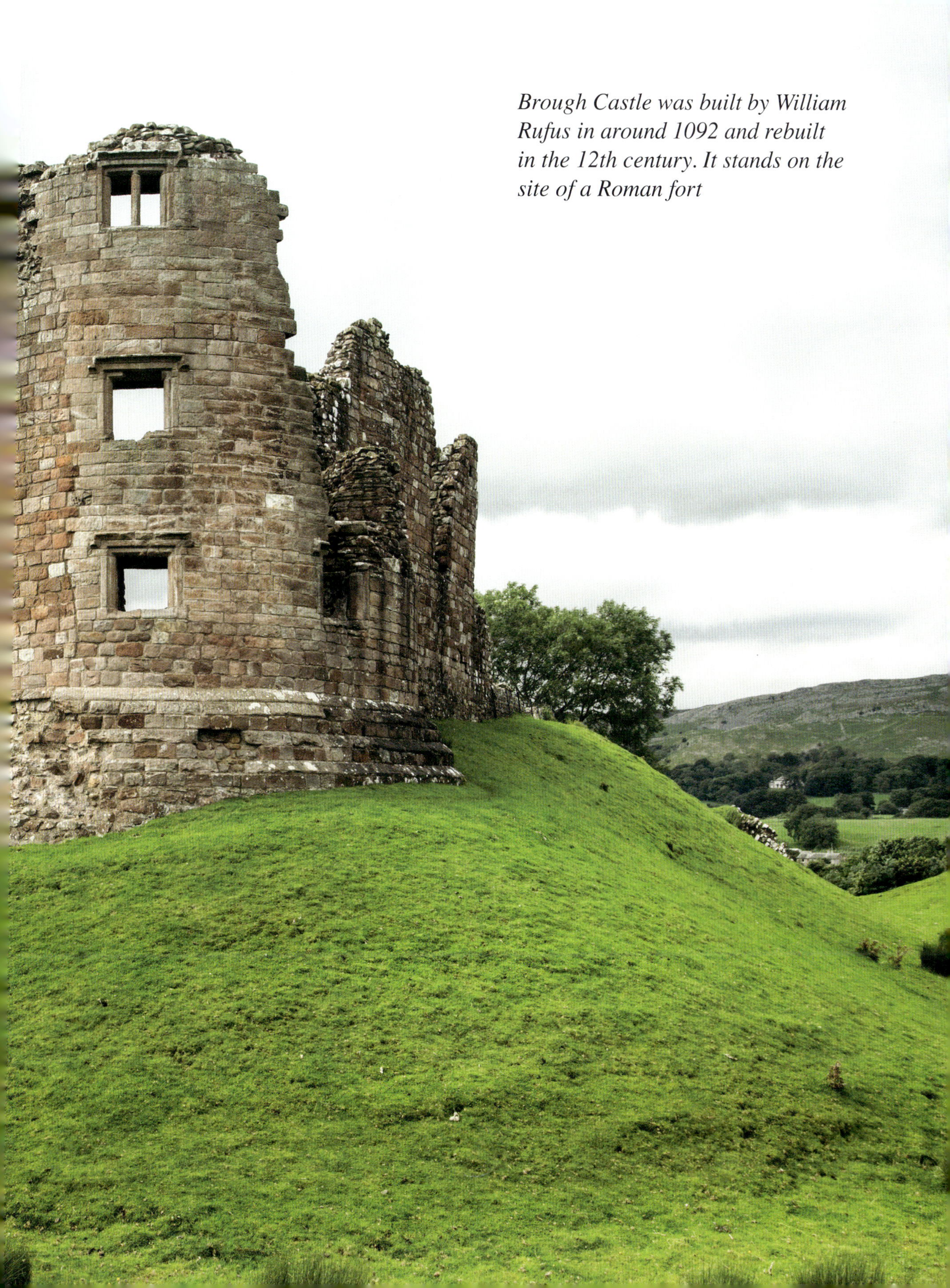

Brough Castle was built by William Rufus in around 1092 and rebuilt in the 12th century. It stands on the site of a Roman fort

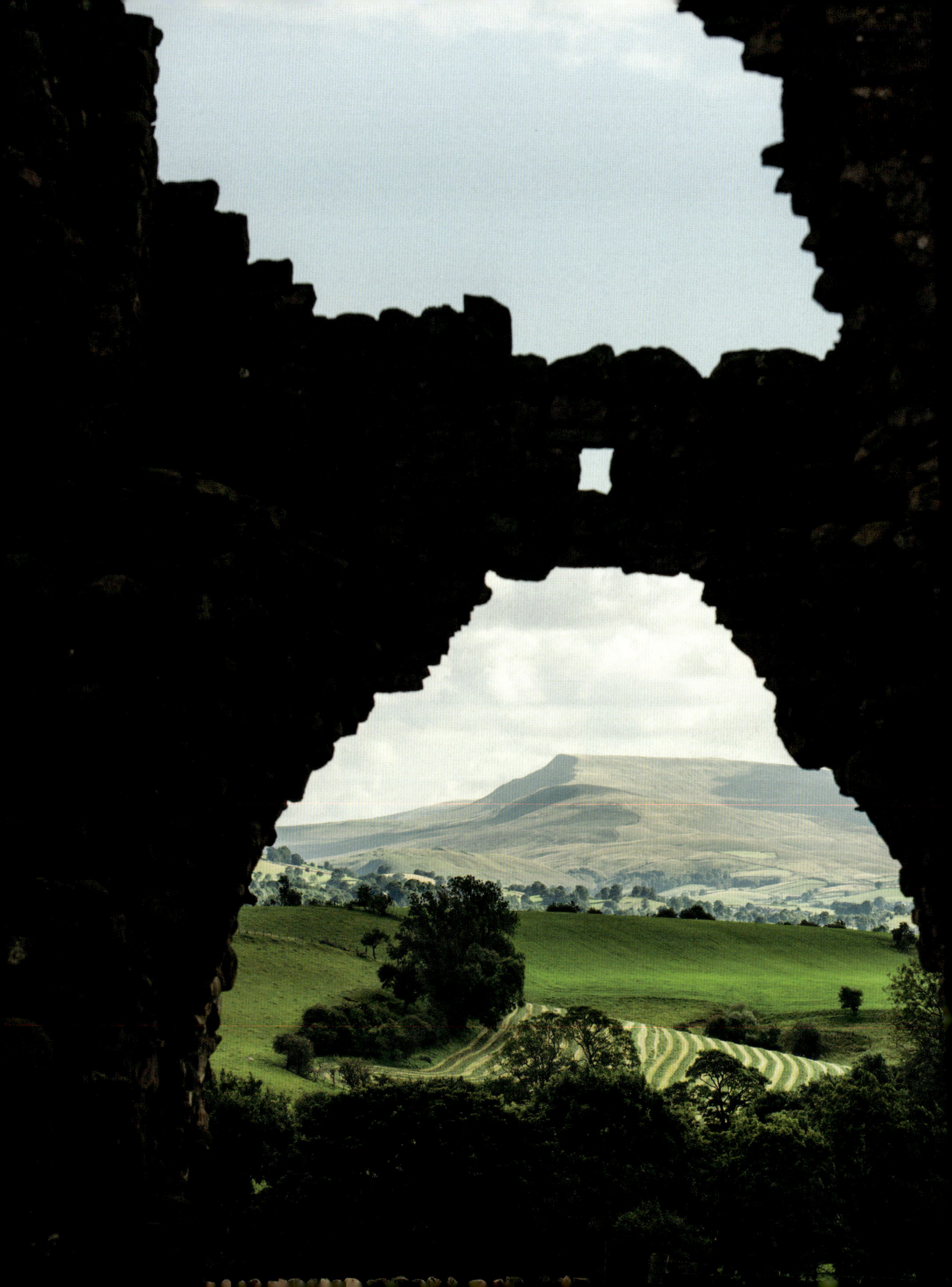

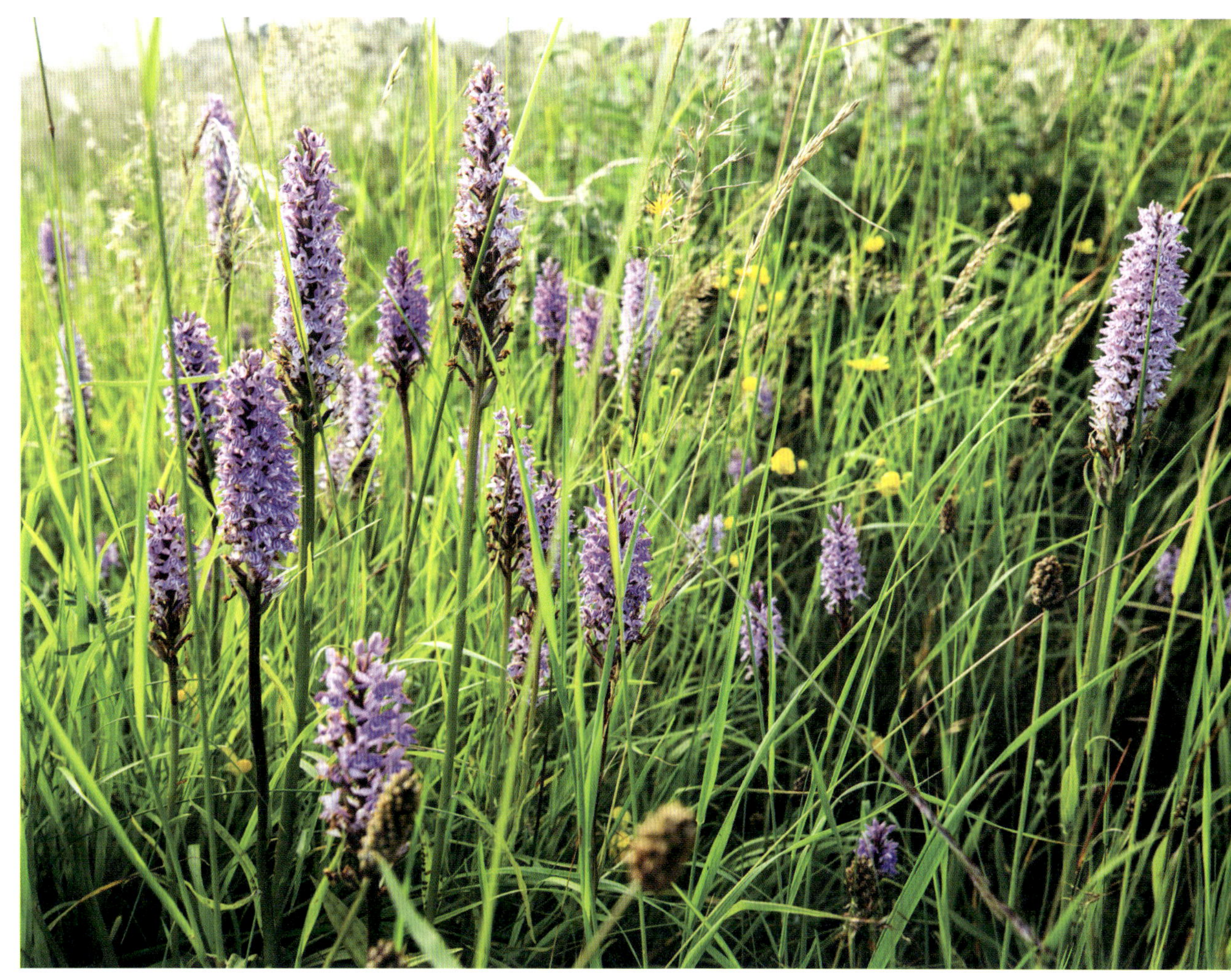

Above: Common Spotted Orchids in a roadside verge at Windmore Green above Brough

Left: A view of Wild Boar Fell in Mallerstang seen through an arch in Brough Castle

Overleaf: The Pennine Way alongside the River Tees at Forest-in-Teesdale. The ruined Wheysike House is across the river

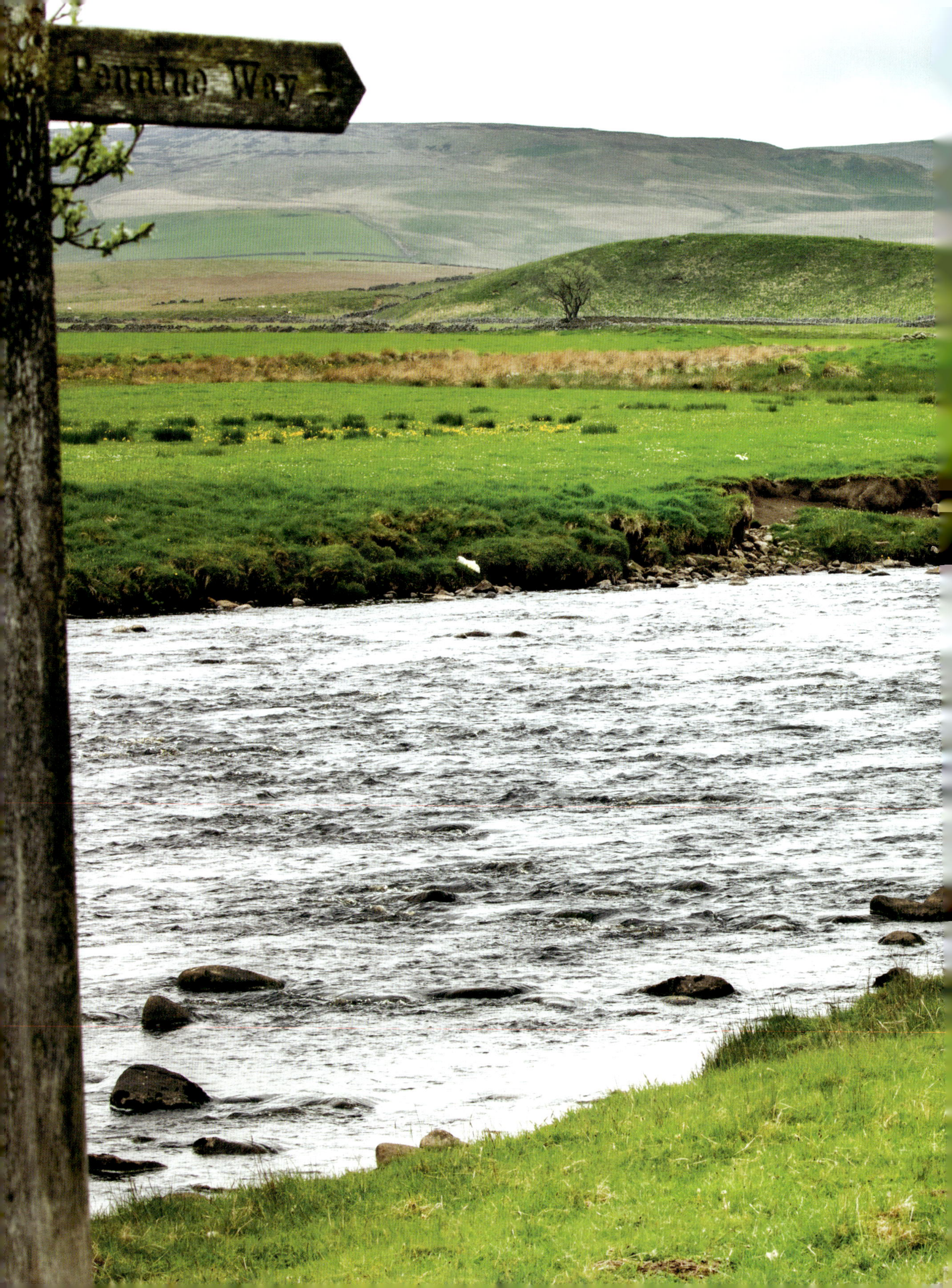
Pennine Way

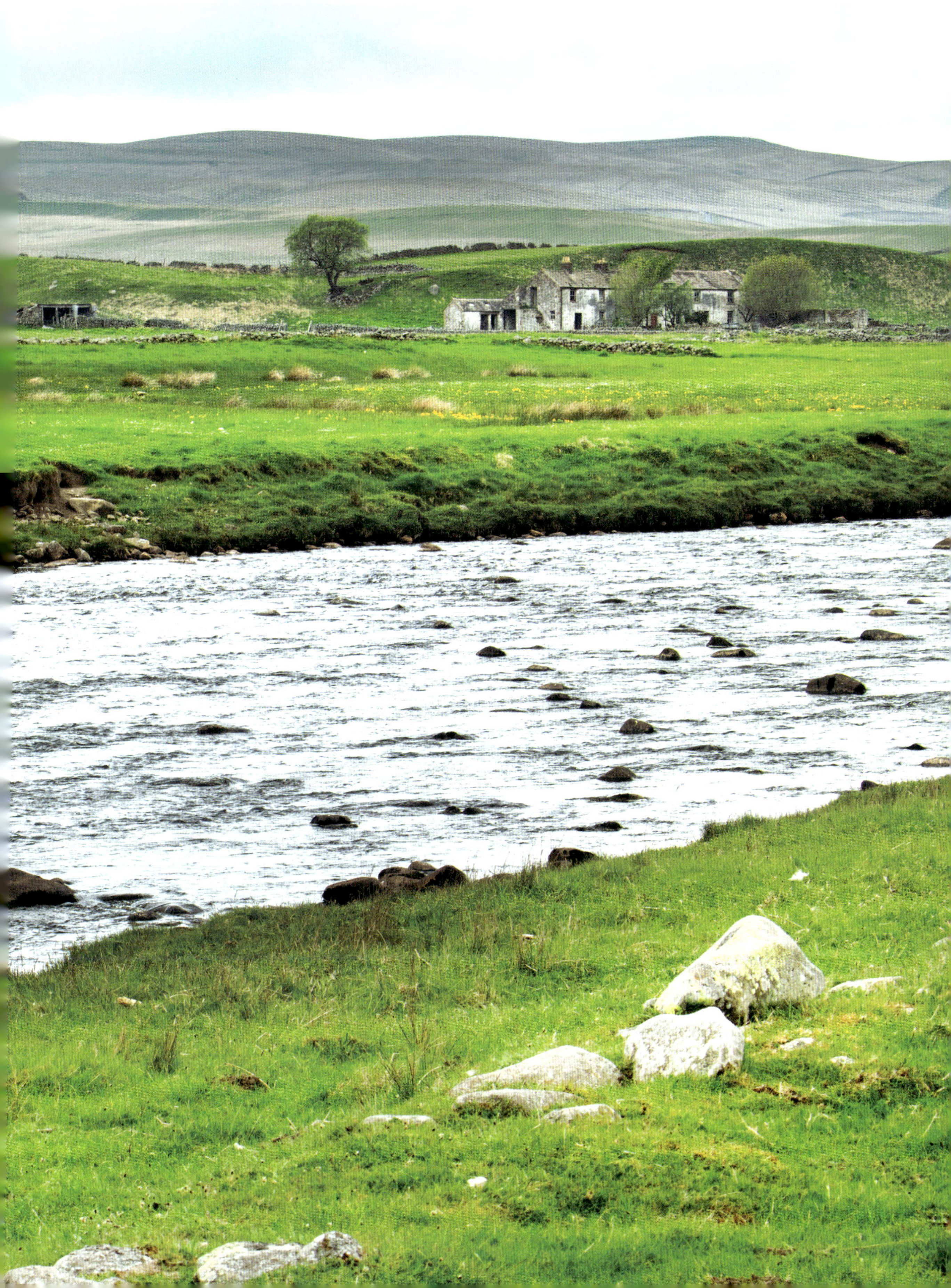

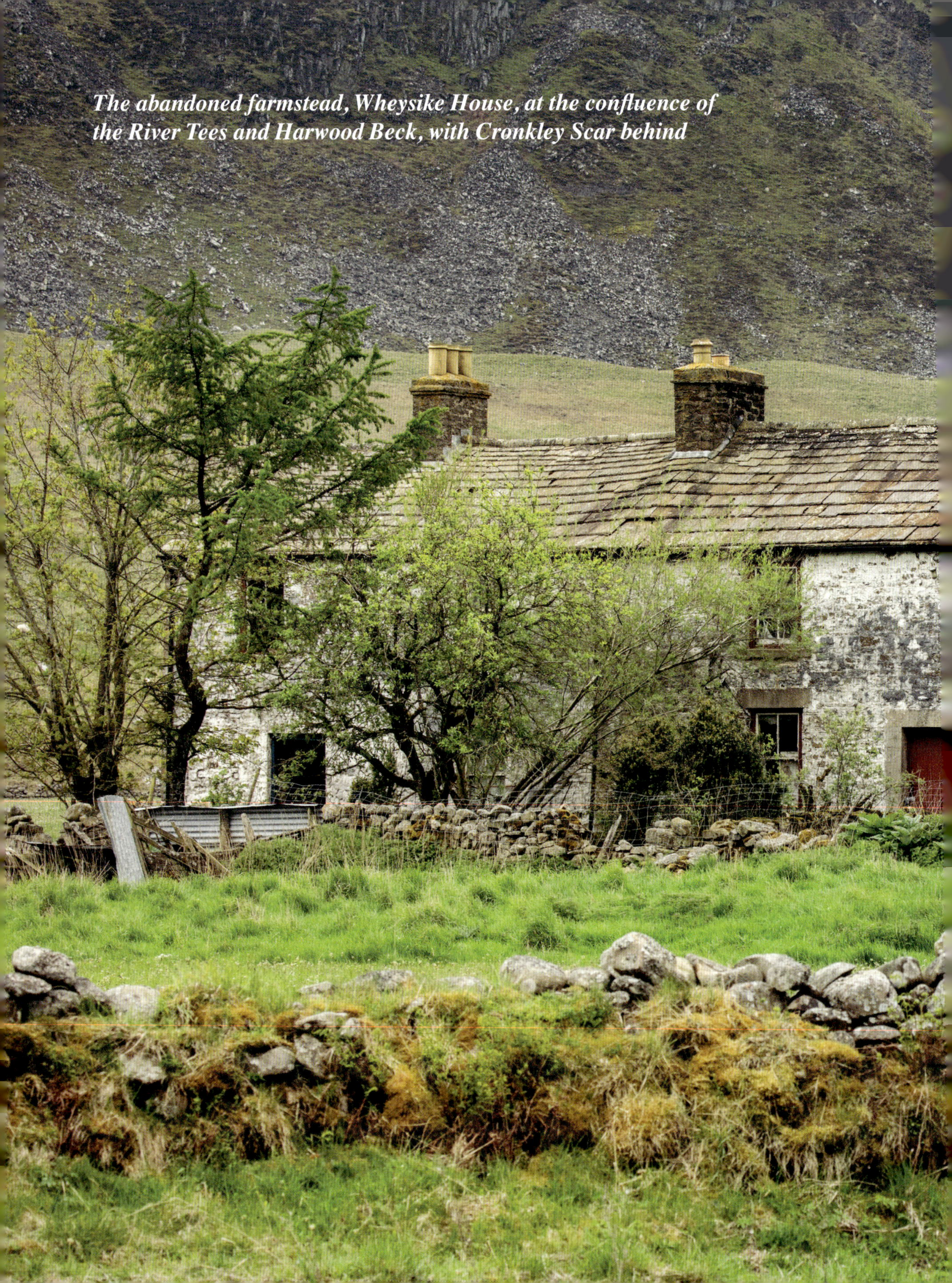

The abandoned farmstead, Wheysike House, at the confluence of the River Tees and Harwood Beck, with Cronkley Scar behind

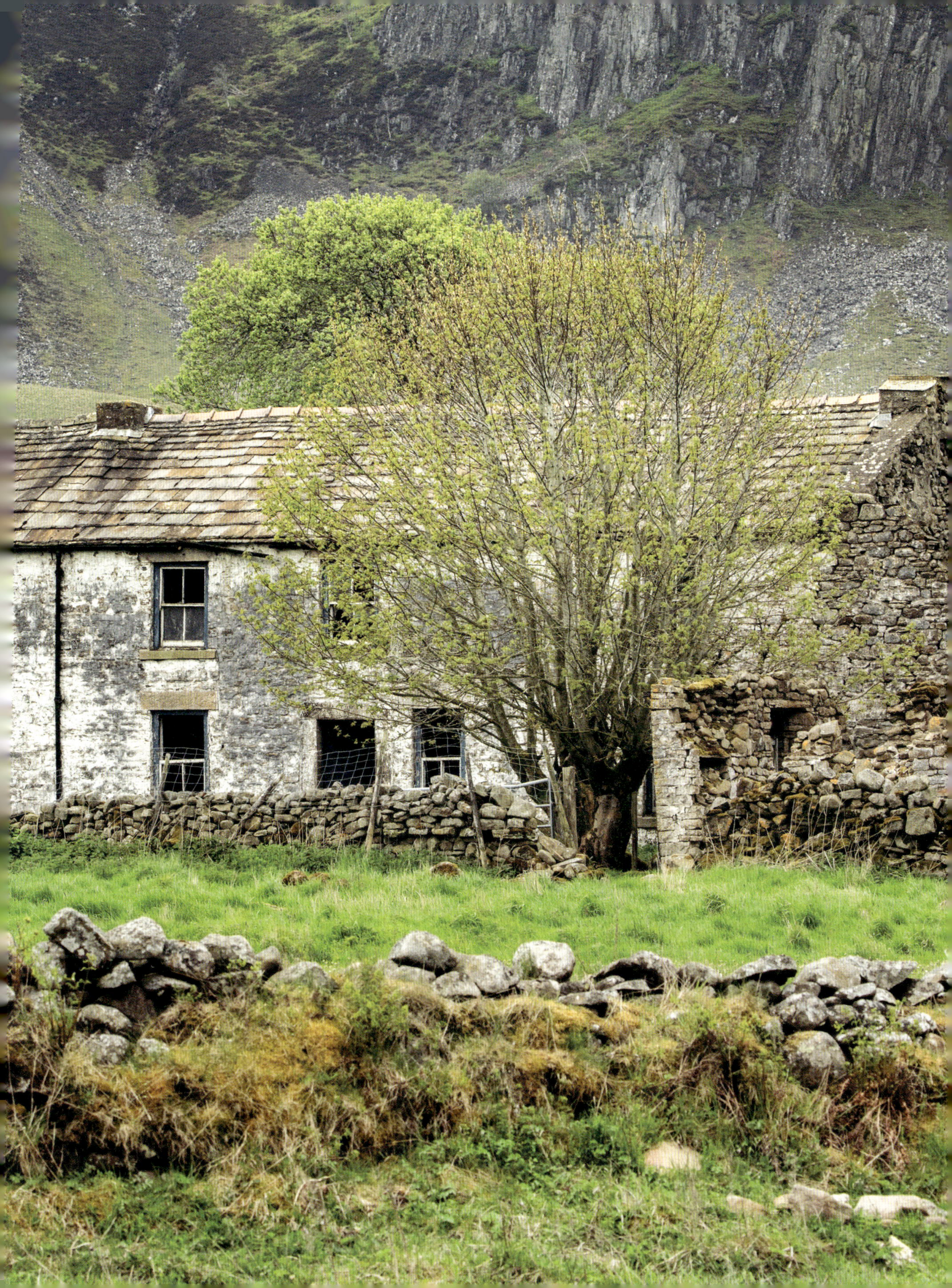

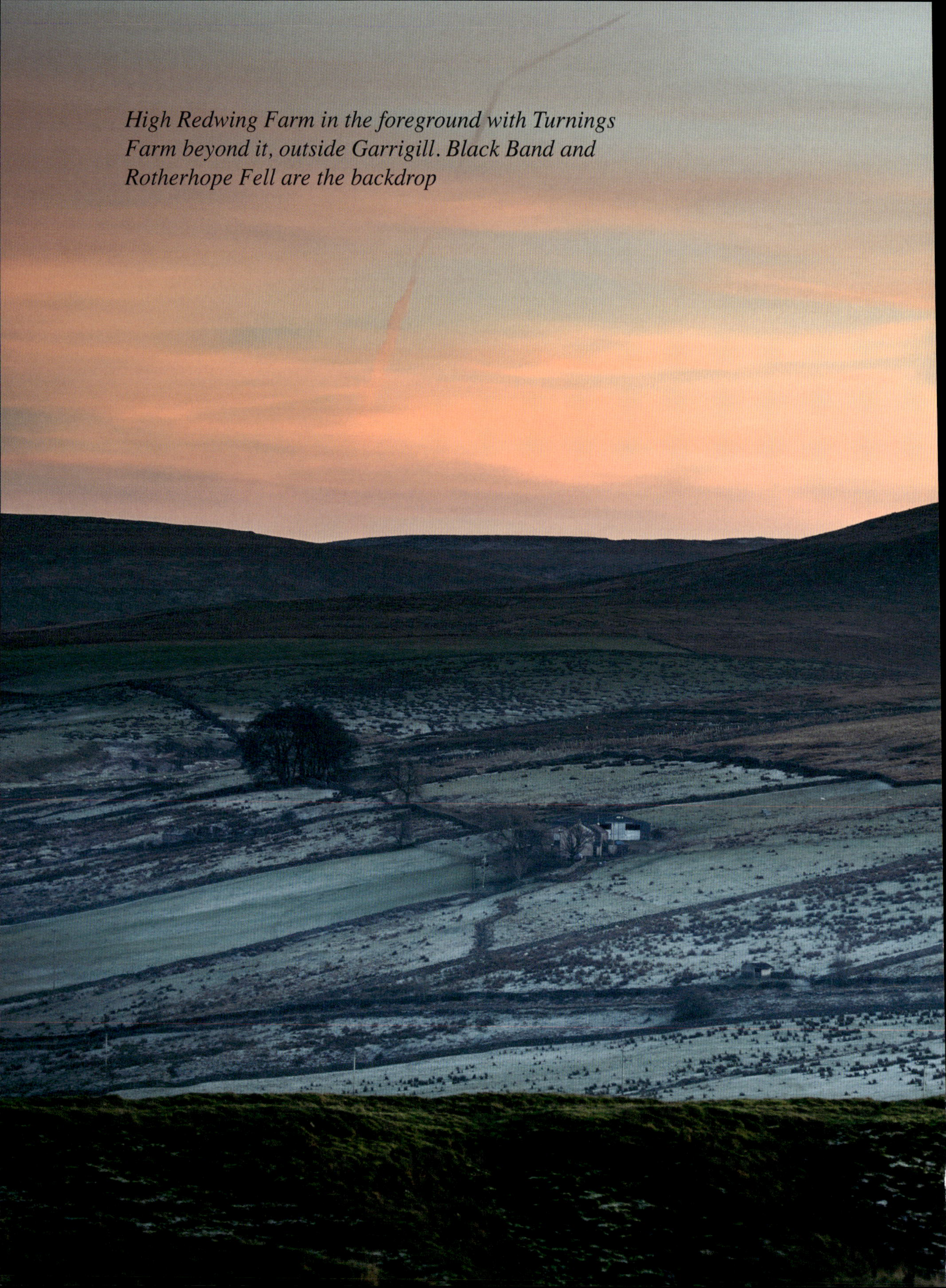

*High Redwing Farm in the foreground with Turnings
Farm beyond it, outside Garrigill. Black Band and
Rotherhope Fell are the backdrop*

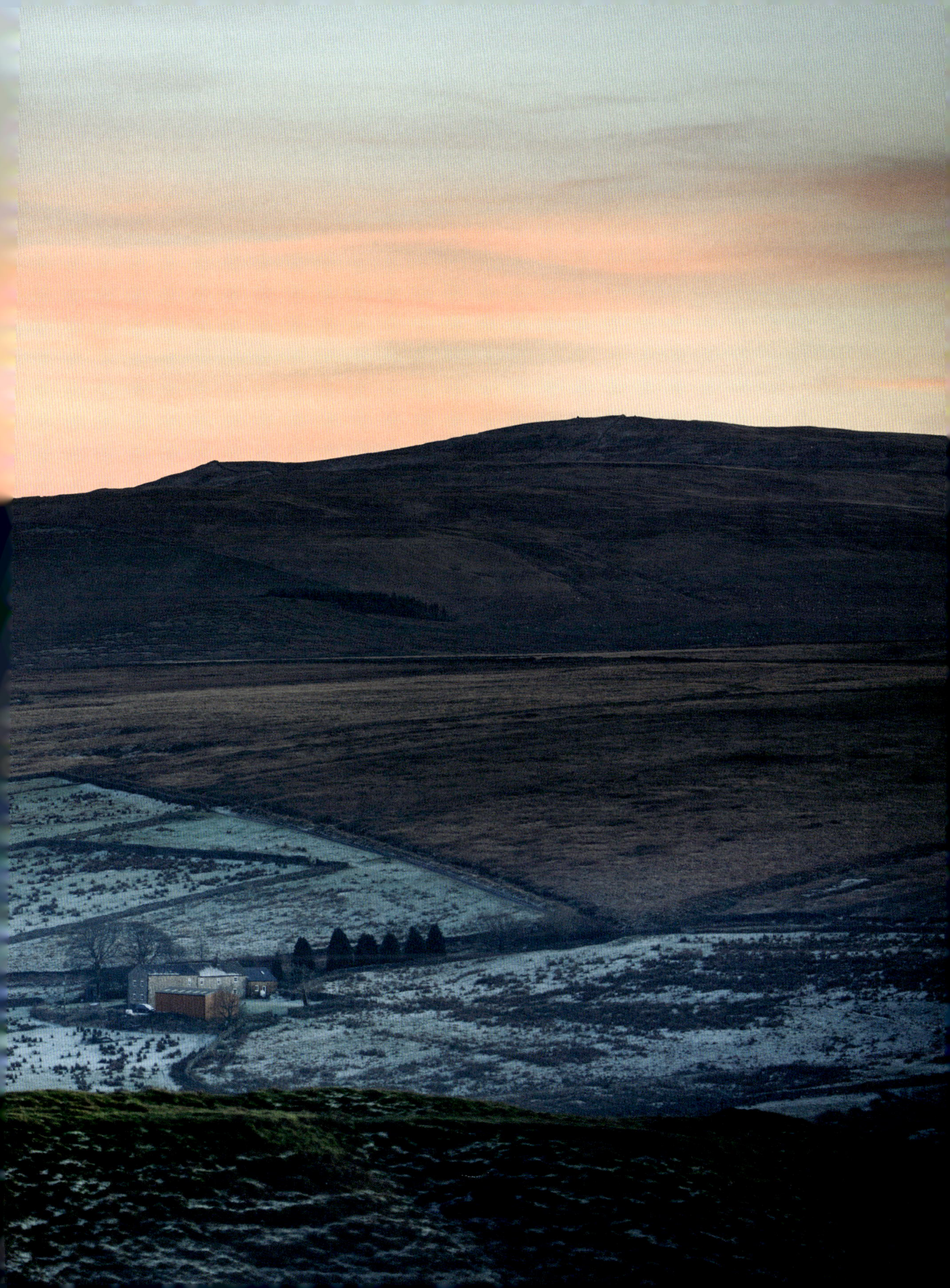

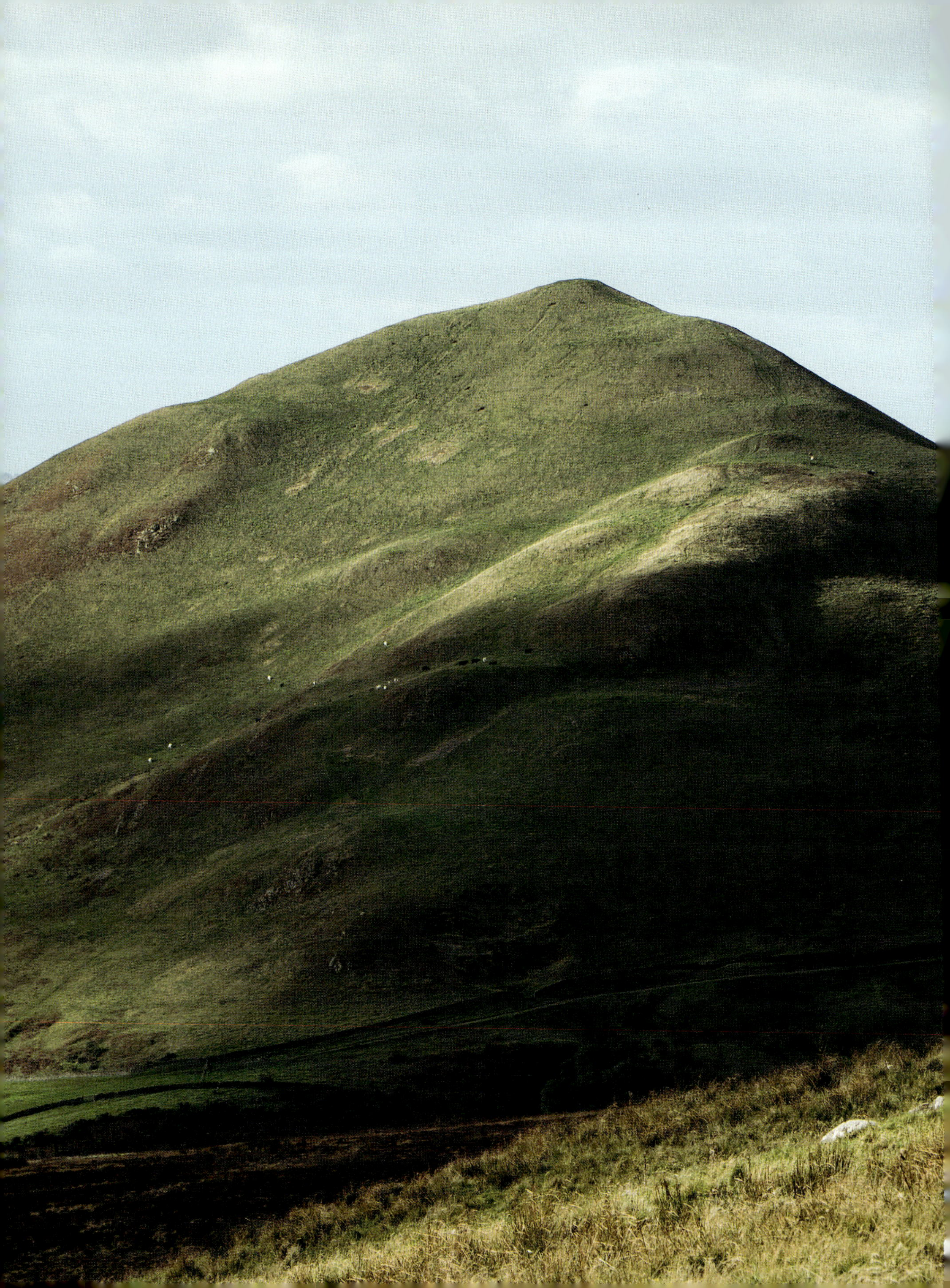

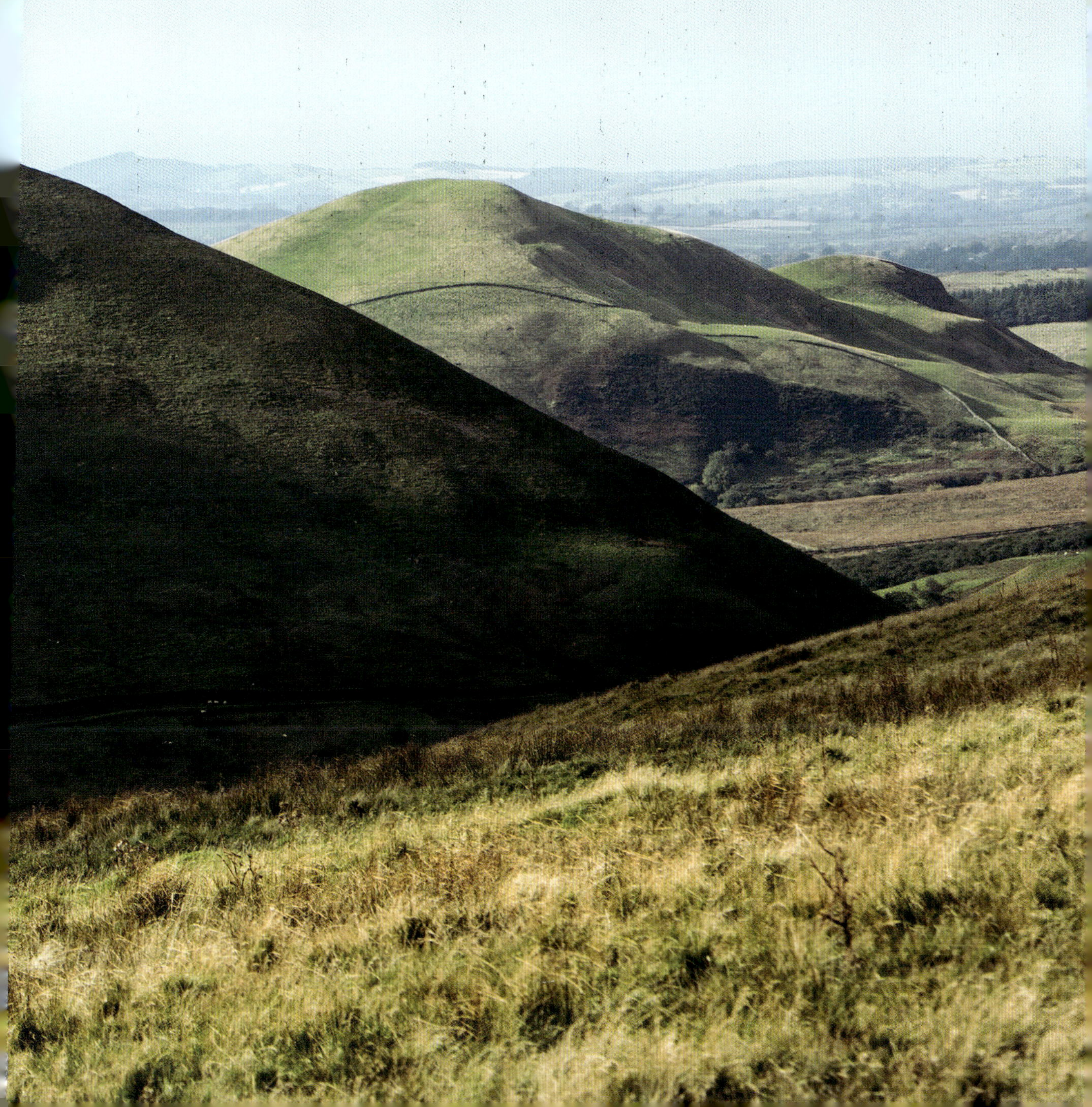

Dufton Pike and Knock Pike seen from the Pennine Way on the route to High Cup. The conical shape of these hills is due to their formation 480 million years ago from volcanic ash and slate, and a fault line separates them from the limestone and shale of the rest of the North Pennines behind; these pikes are about 100 million years younger!

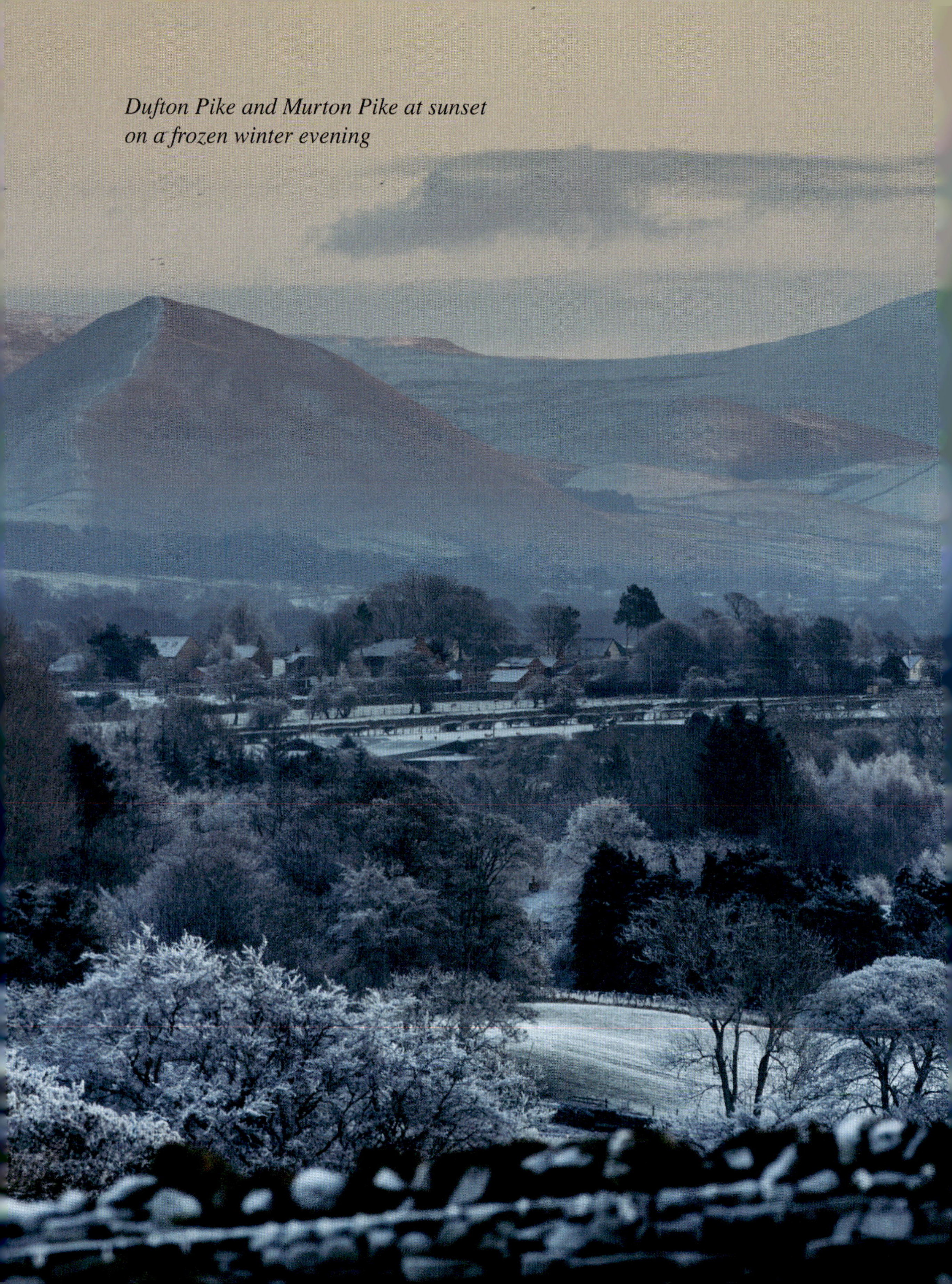

Dufton Pike and Murton Pike at sunset on a frozen winter evening

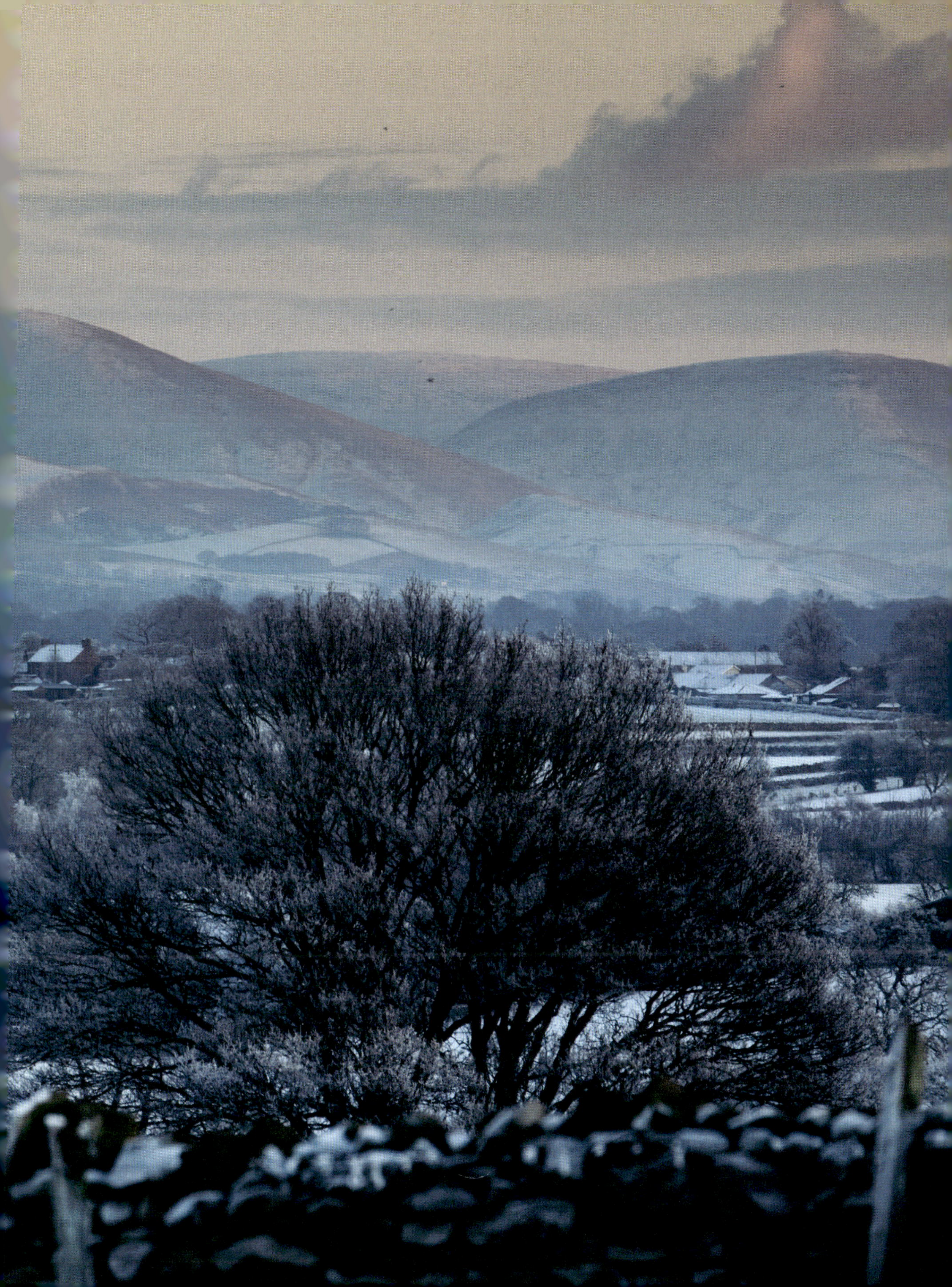

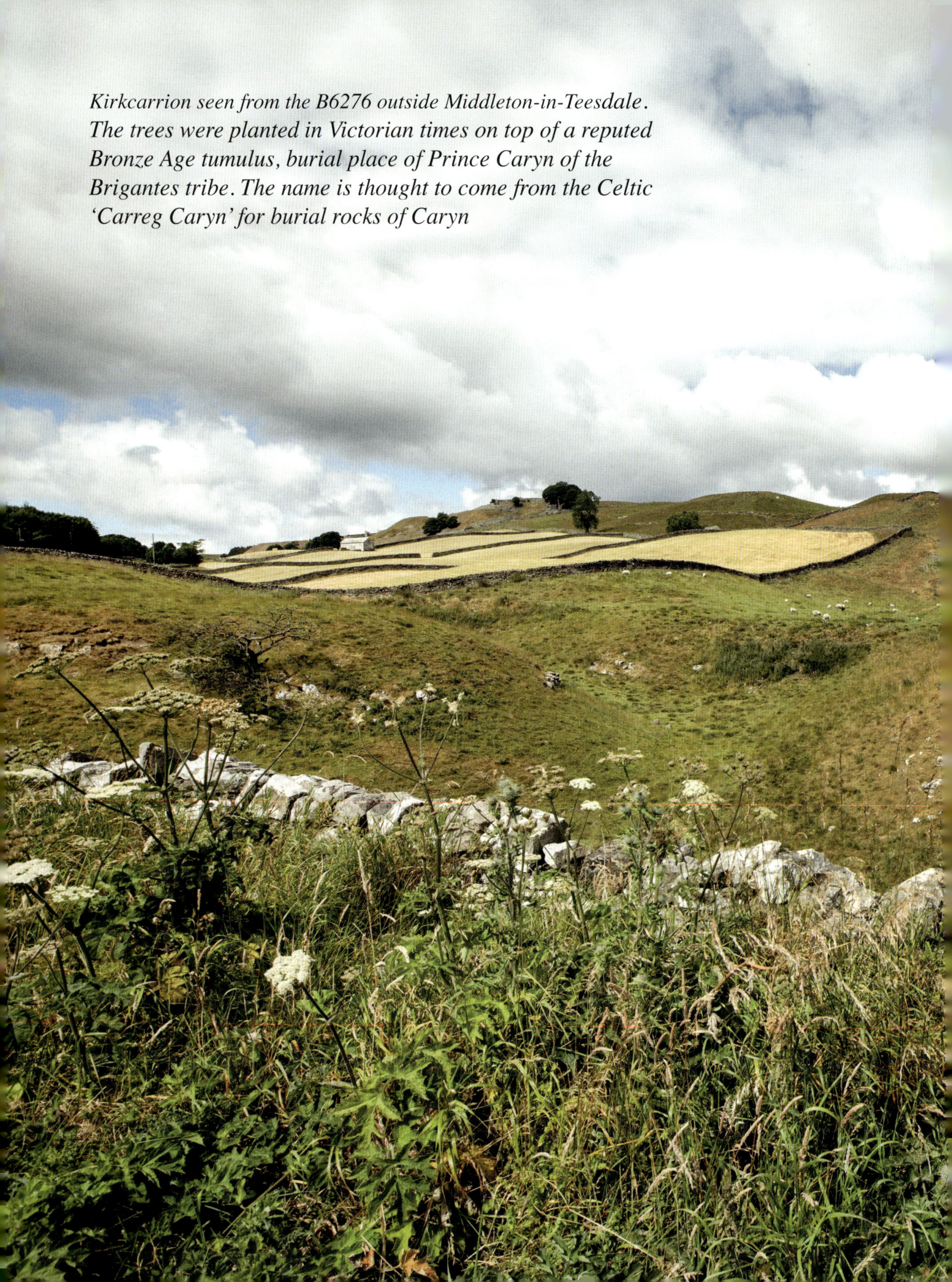

Kirkcarrion seen from the B6276 outside Middleton-in-Teesdale.
The trees were planted in Victorian times on top of a reputed
Bronze Age tumulus, burial place of Prince Caryn of the
Brigantes tribe. The name is thought to come from the Celtic
'Carreg Caryn' for burial rocks of Caryn

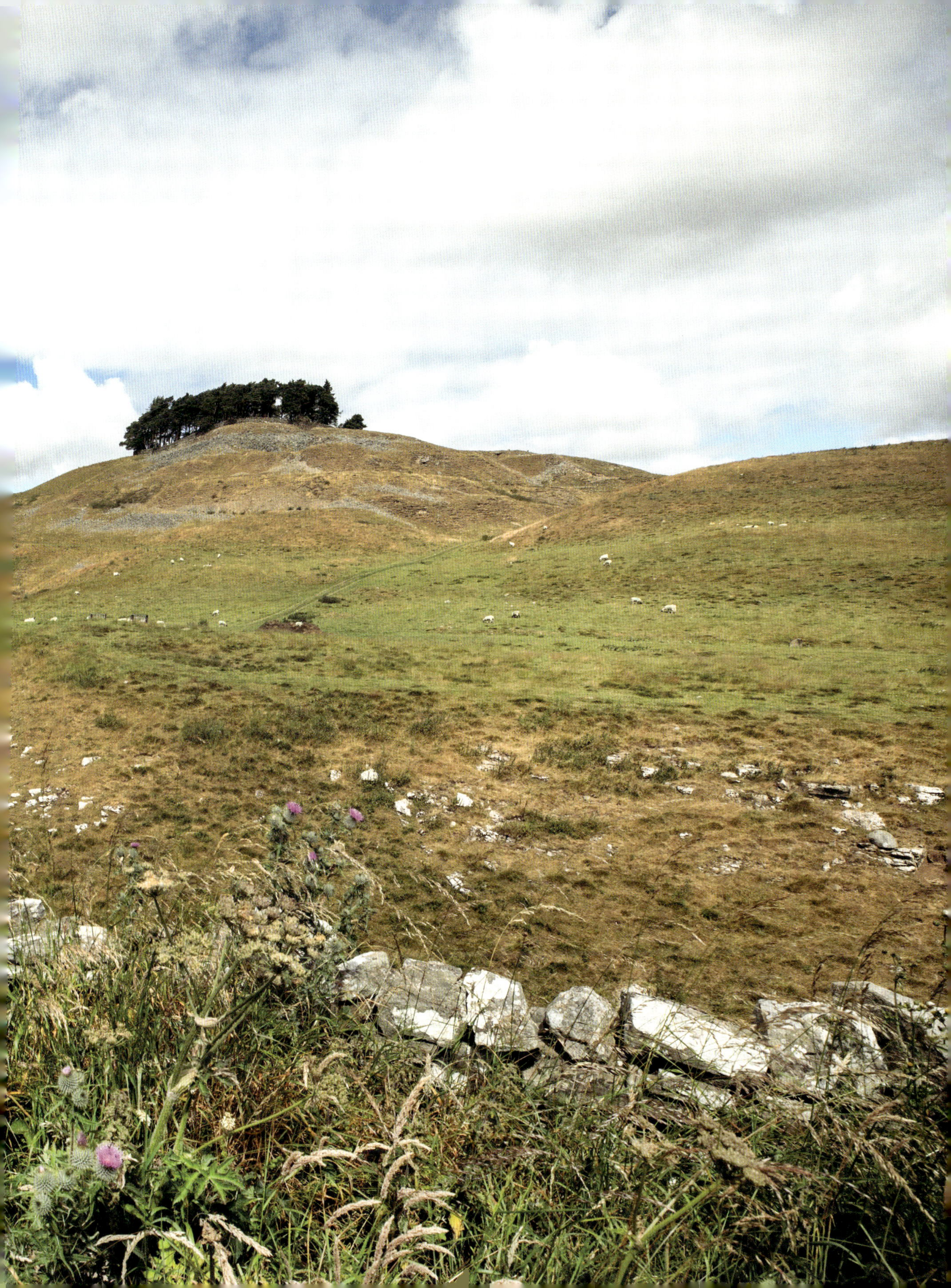

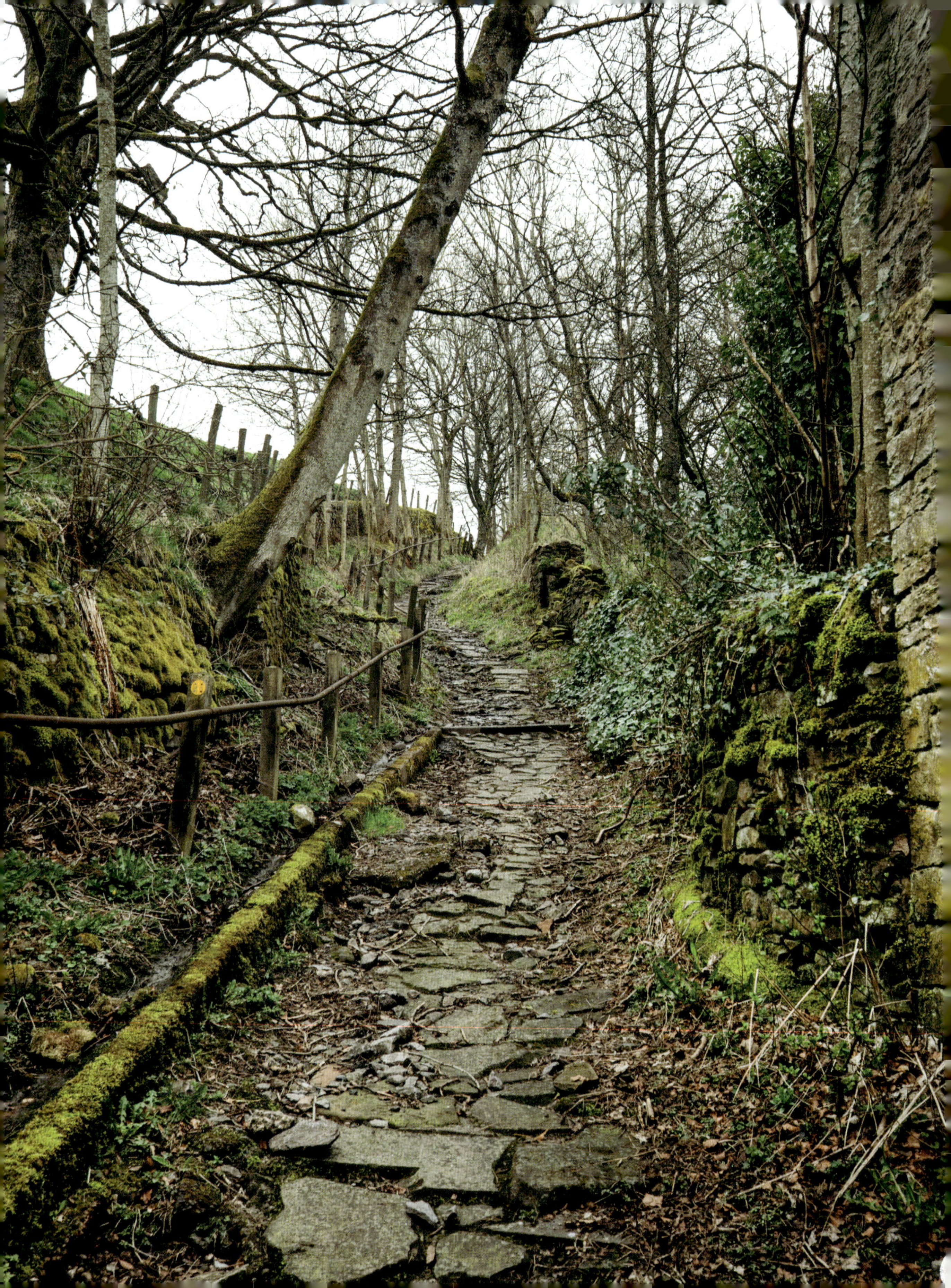

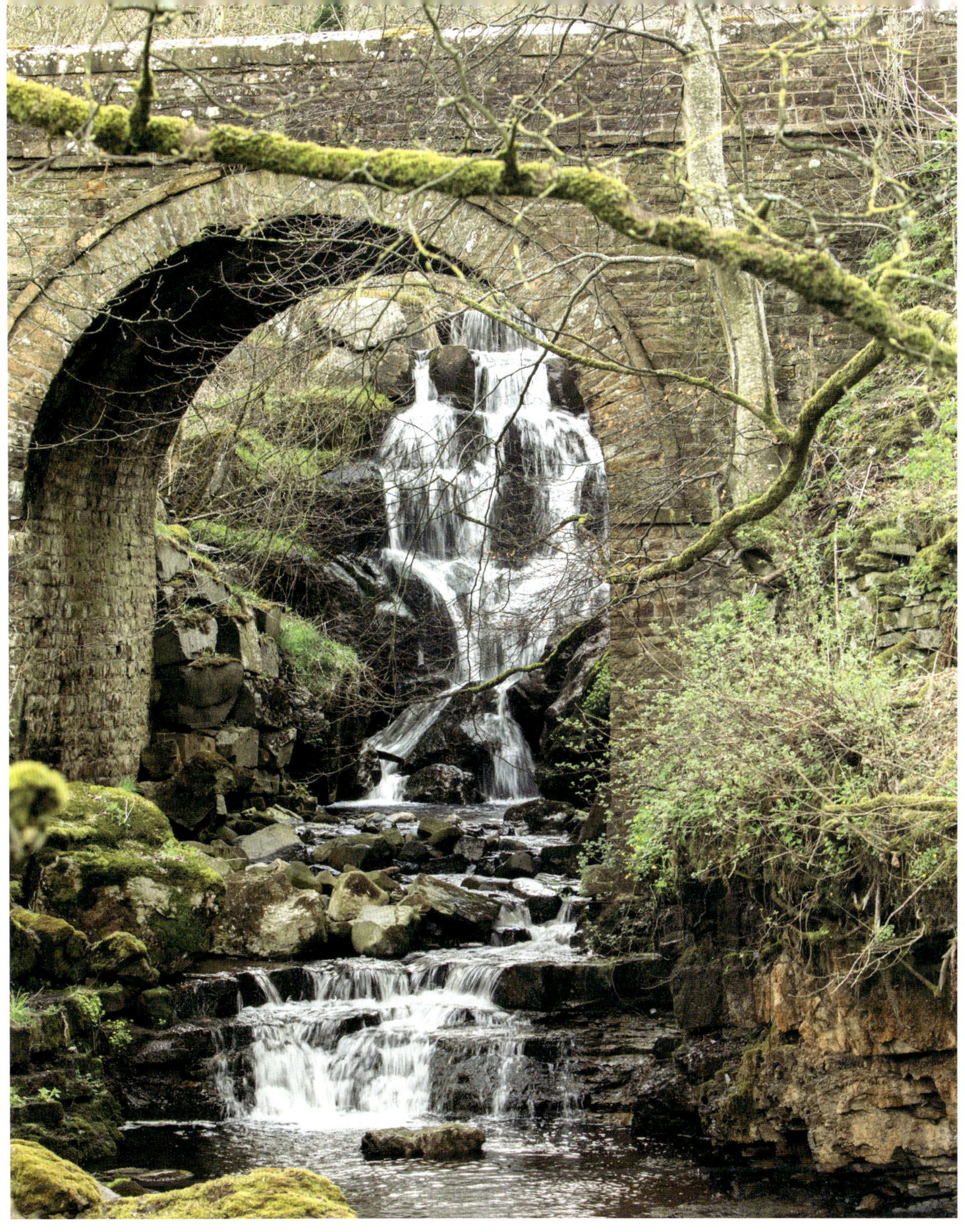

Above: Garrigill Burn beneath Low Houses Bridge at Garrigill

Left: An old packhorse route climbs steeply from Garrigill up to Loaning Head

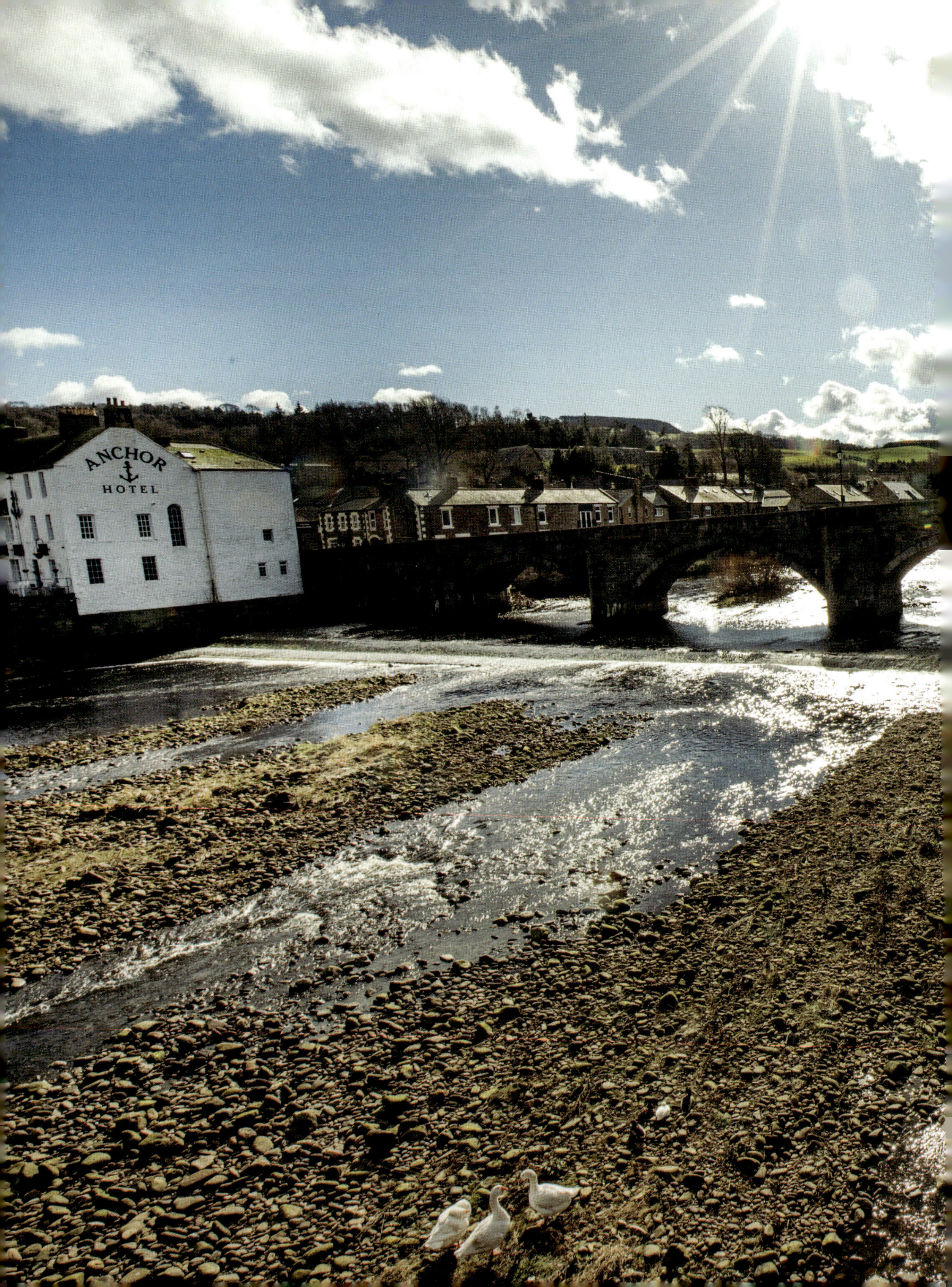

ANCHOR
HOTEL

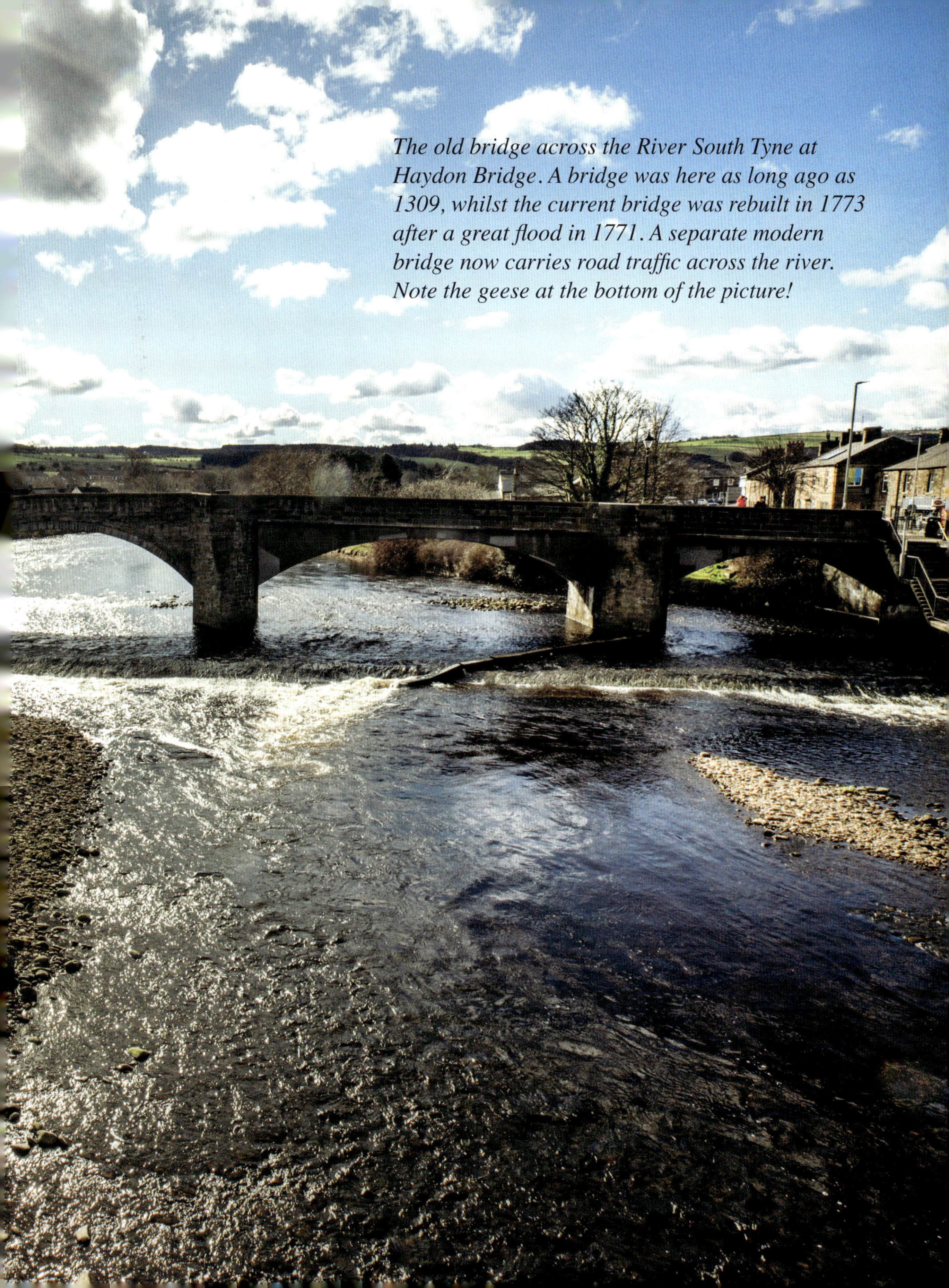

The old bridge across the River South Tyne at
Haydon Bridge. A bridge was here as long ago as
1309, whilst the current bridge was rebuilt in 1773
after a great flood in 1771. A separate modern
bridge now carries road traffic across the river.
Note the geese at the bottom of the picture!

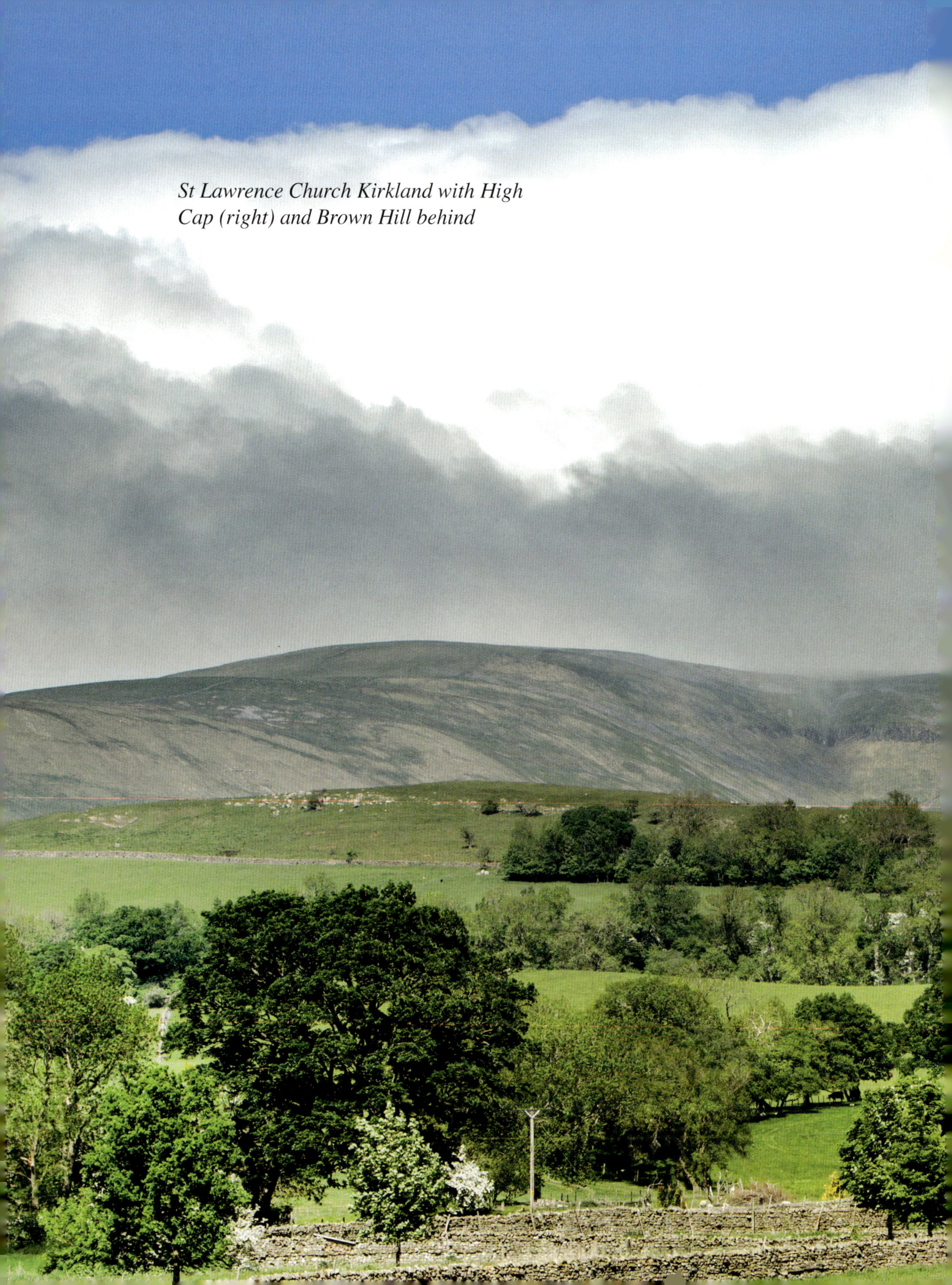

St Lawrence Church Kirkland with High
Cap (right) and Brown Hill behind

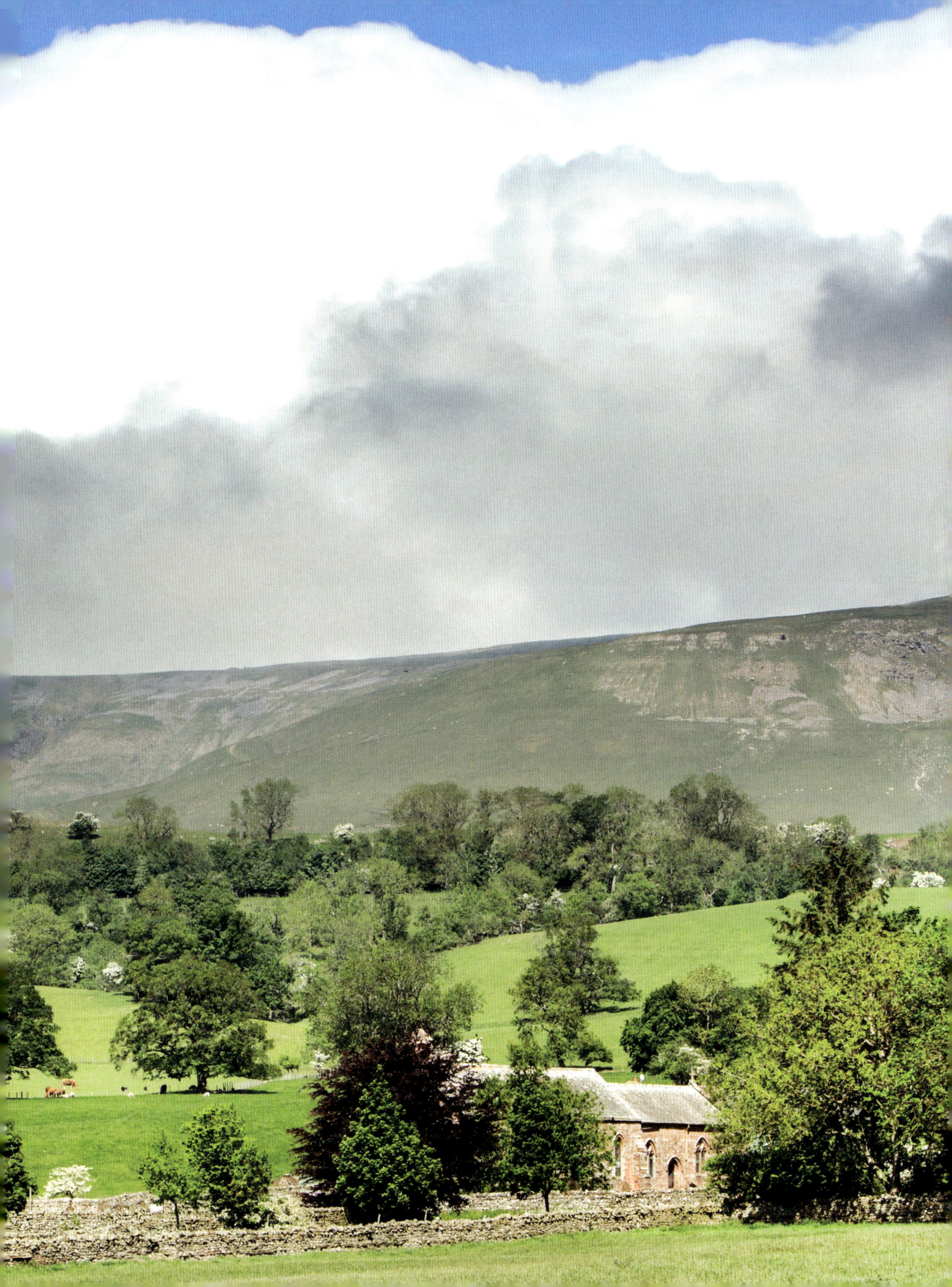

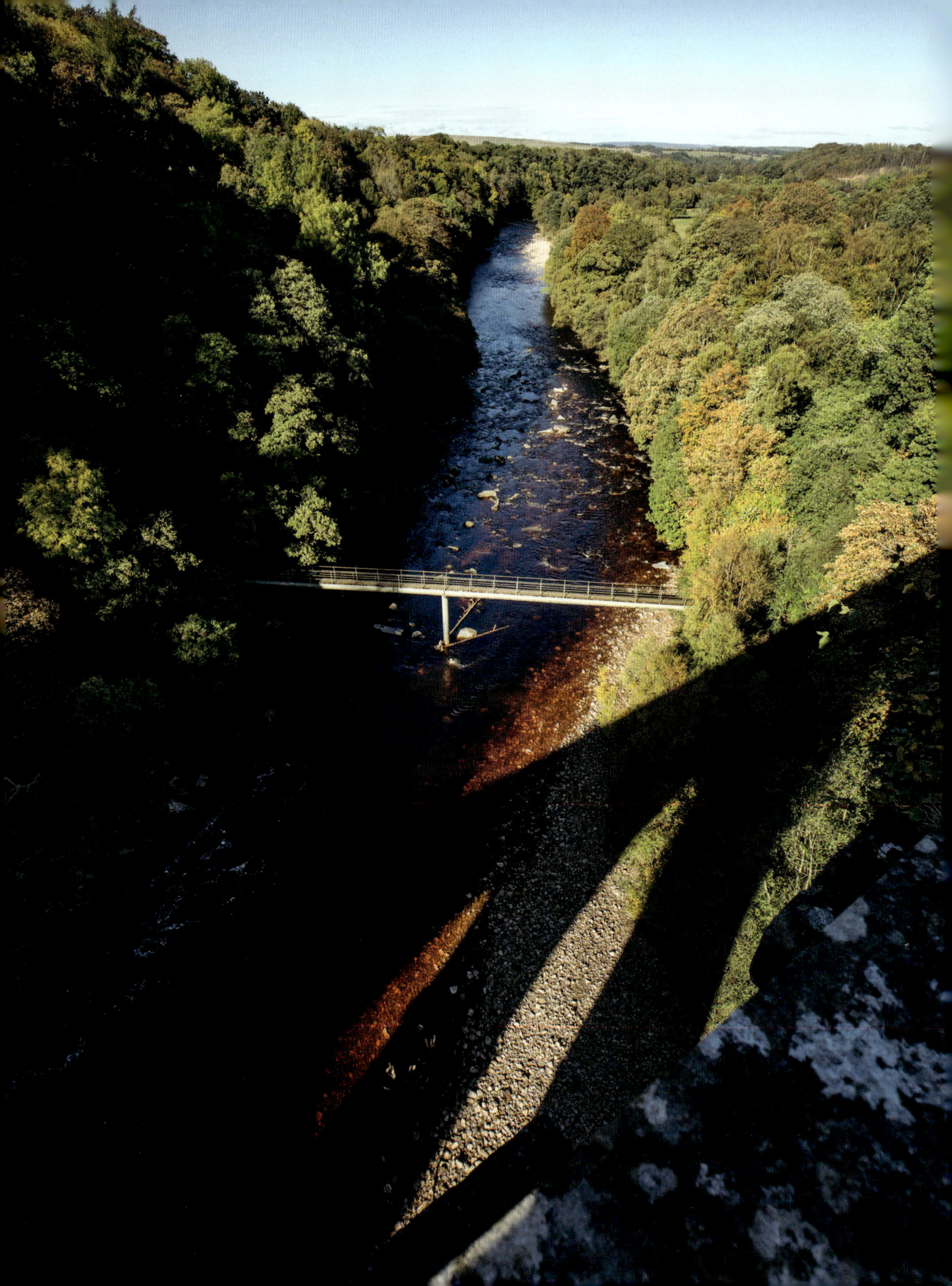

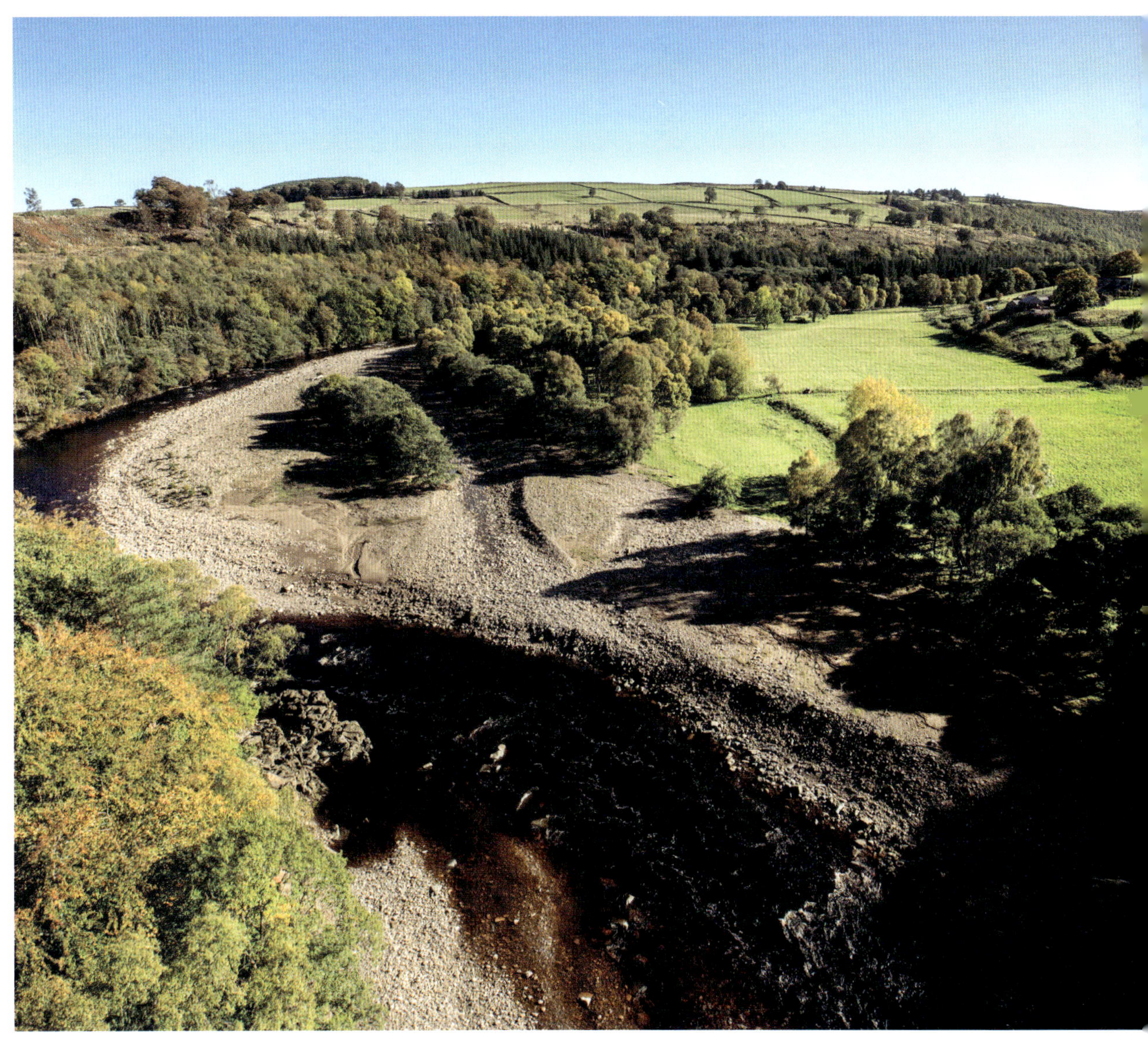

Above: The River South Tyne at Lambley

Left and Overleaf: The shadow of the Grade II listed 19th century Lambley viaduct falls on the River South Tyne below. The viaduct once held the Haltwhistle to Alston railway which hauled coal and lead from mines in Alston and closed in 1976. It is 850 ft long with 9 arches and is 108 ft above the river. The South Tyne Trail now runs along it

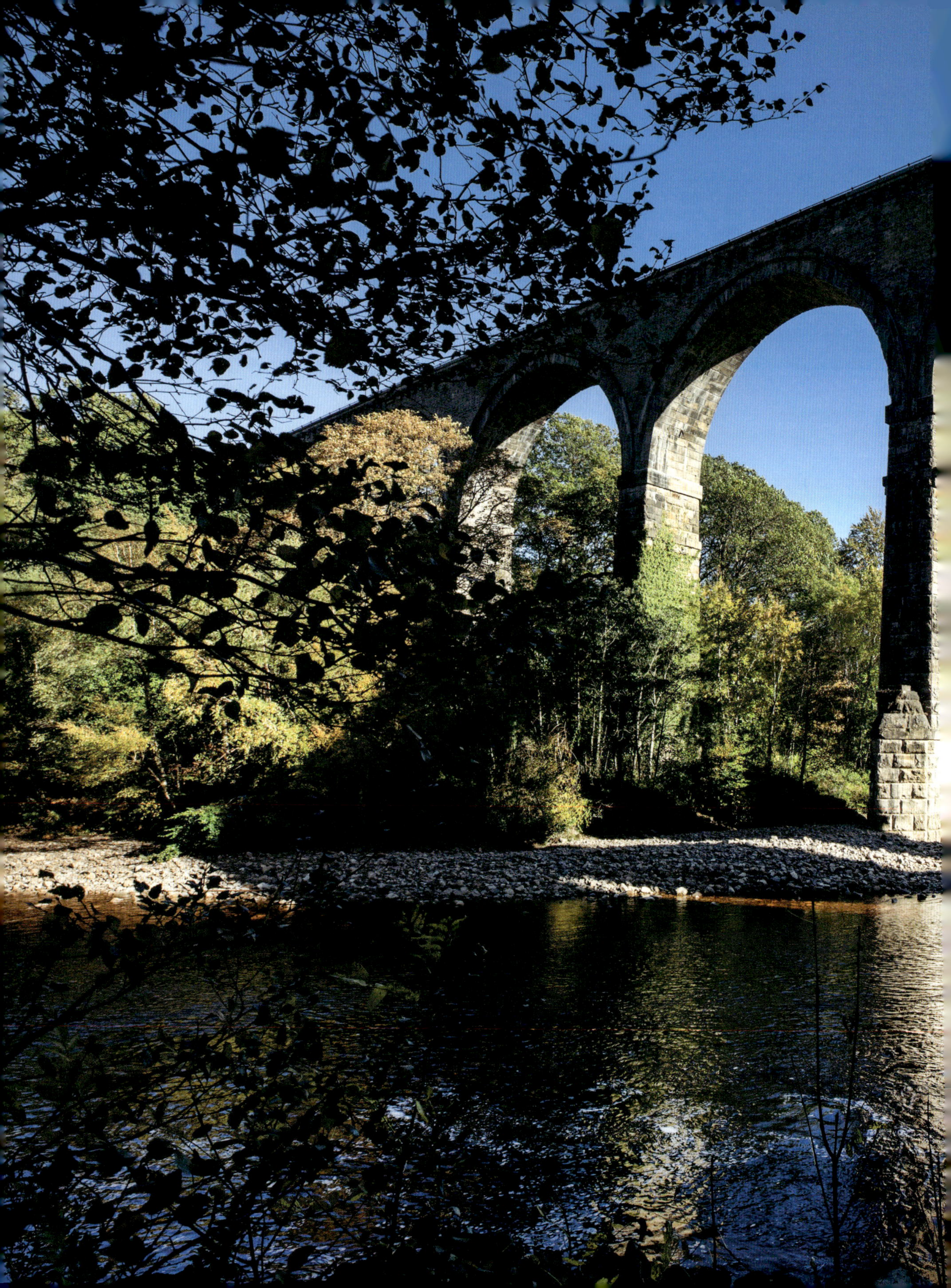

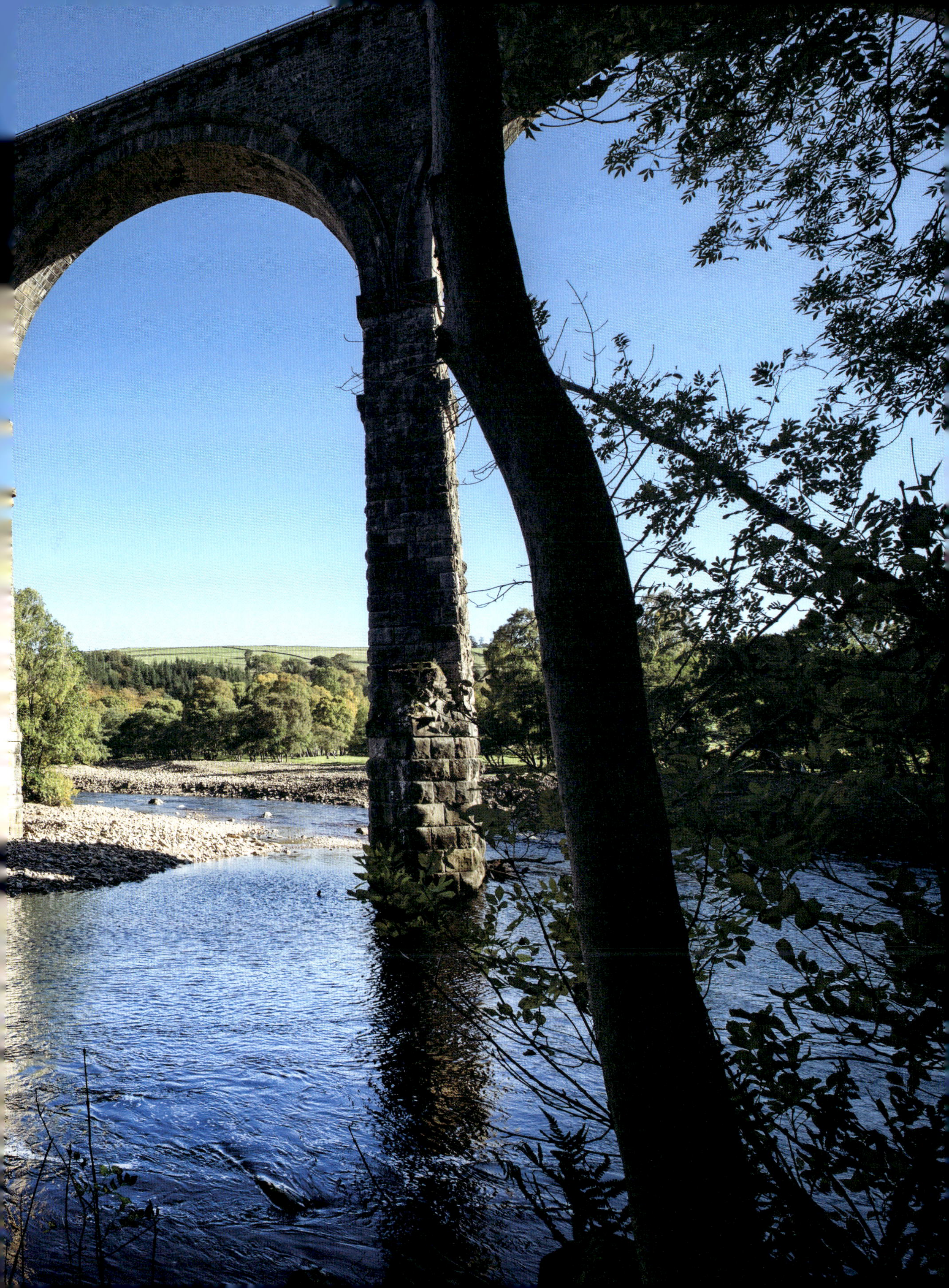

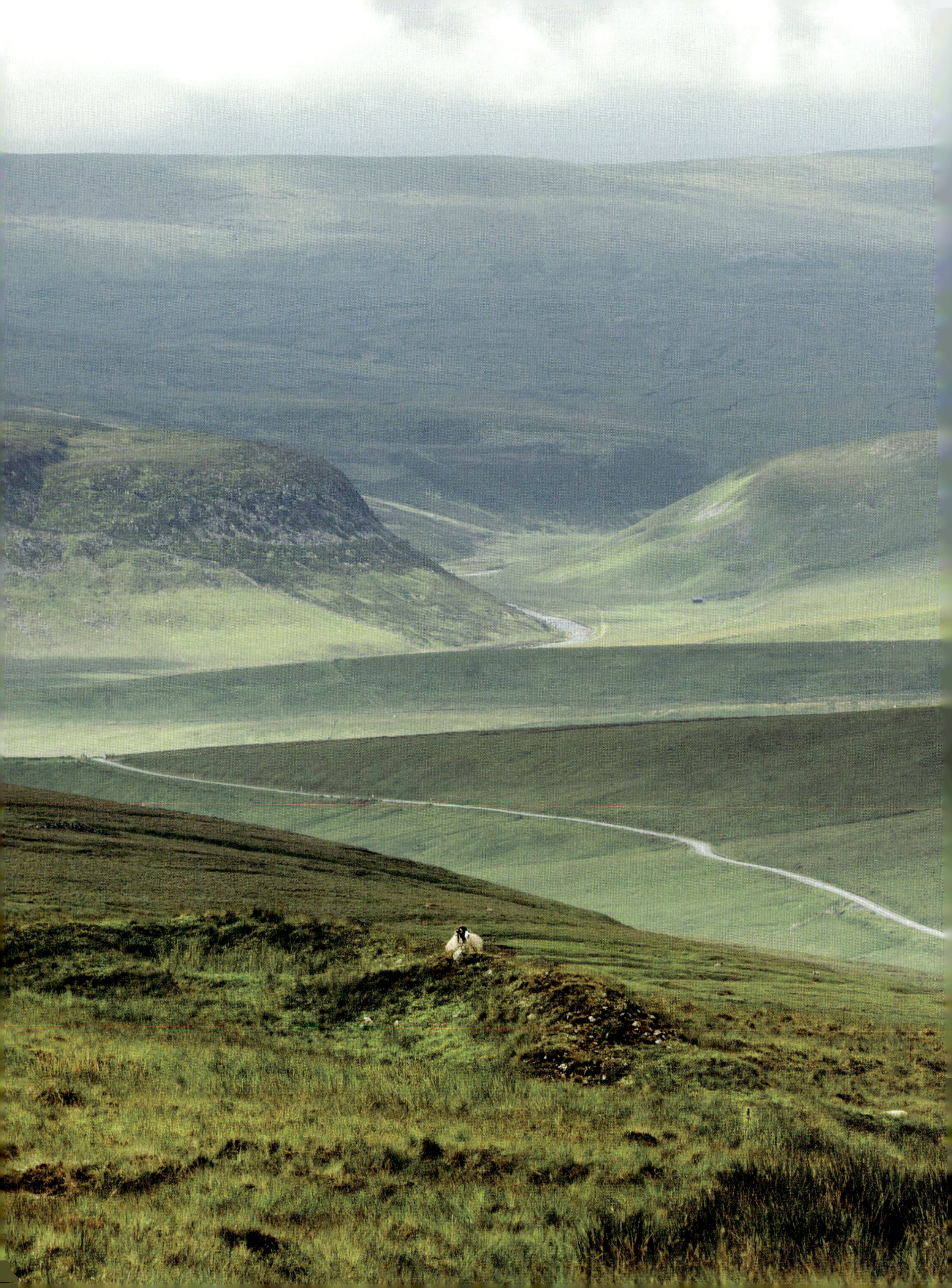

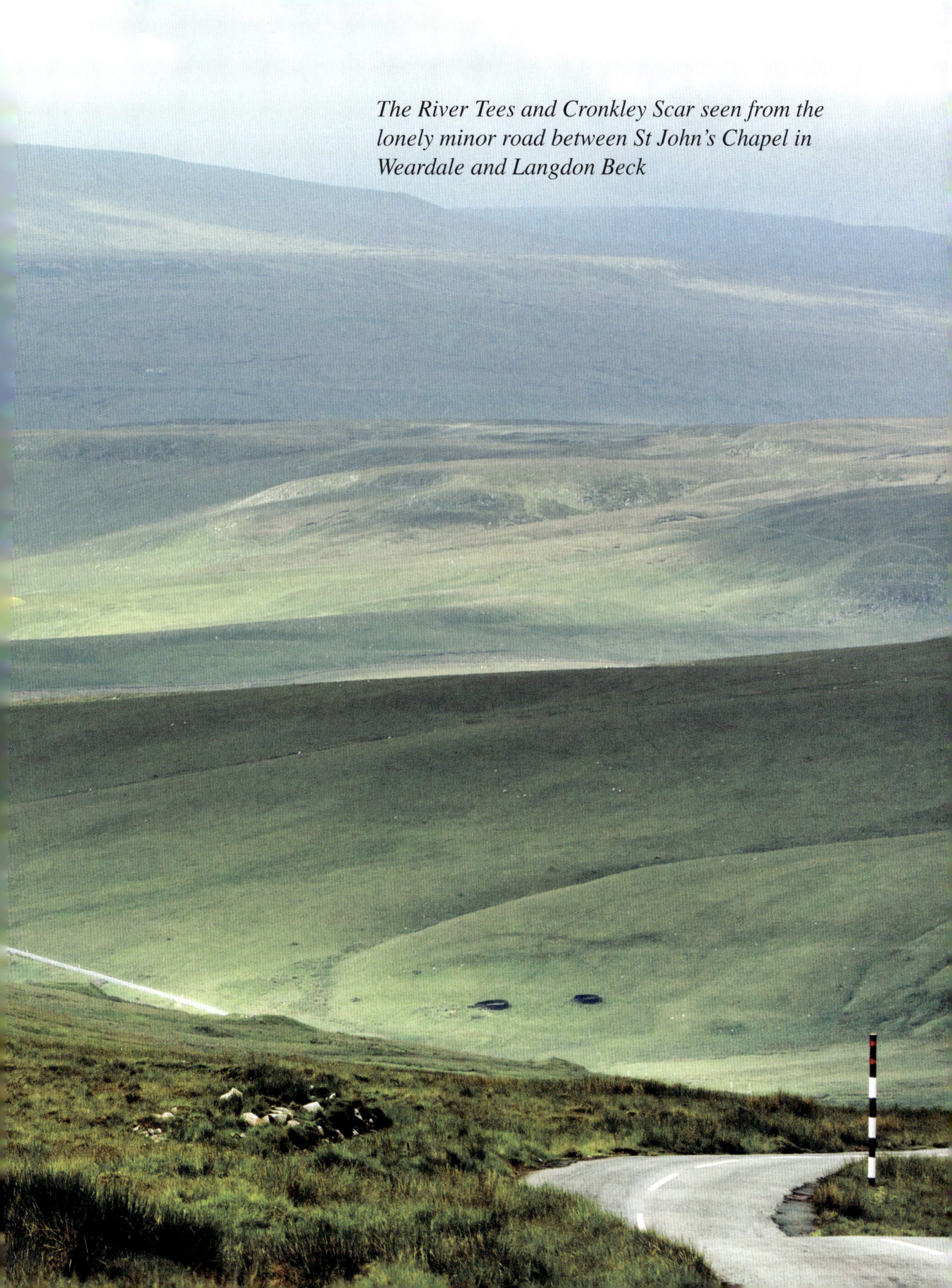

The River Tees and Cronkley Scar seen from the
lonely minor road between St John's Chapel in
Weardale and Langdon Beck

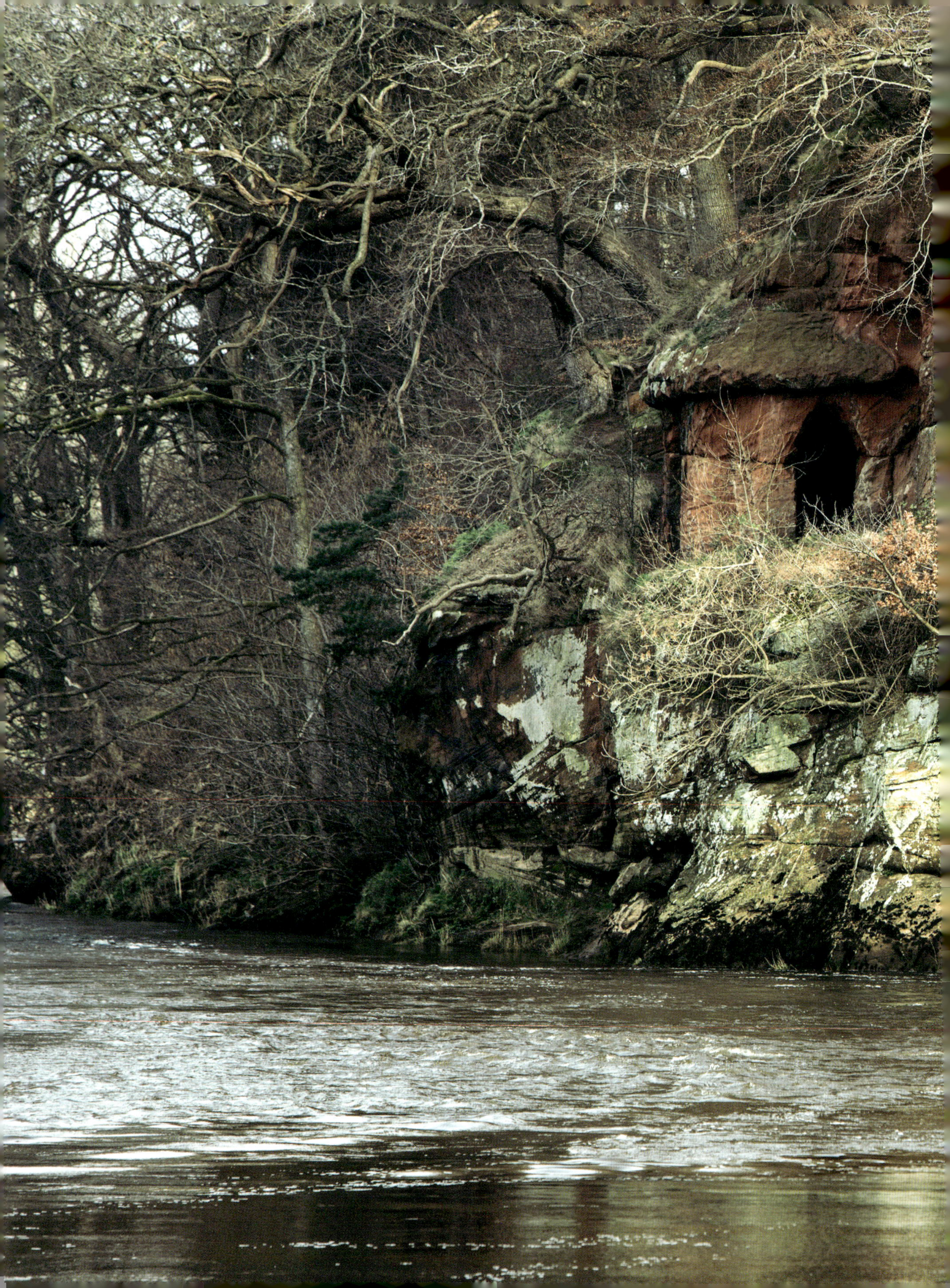

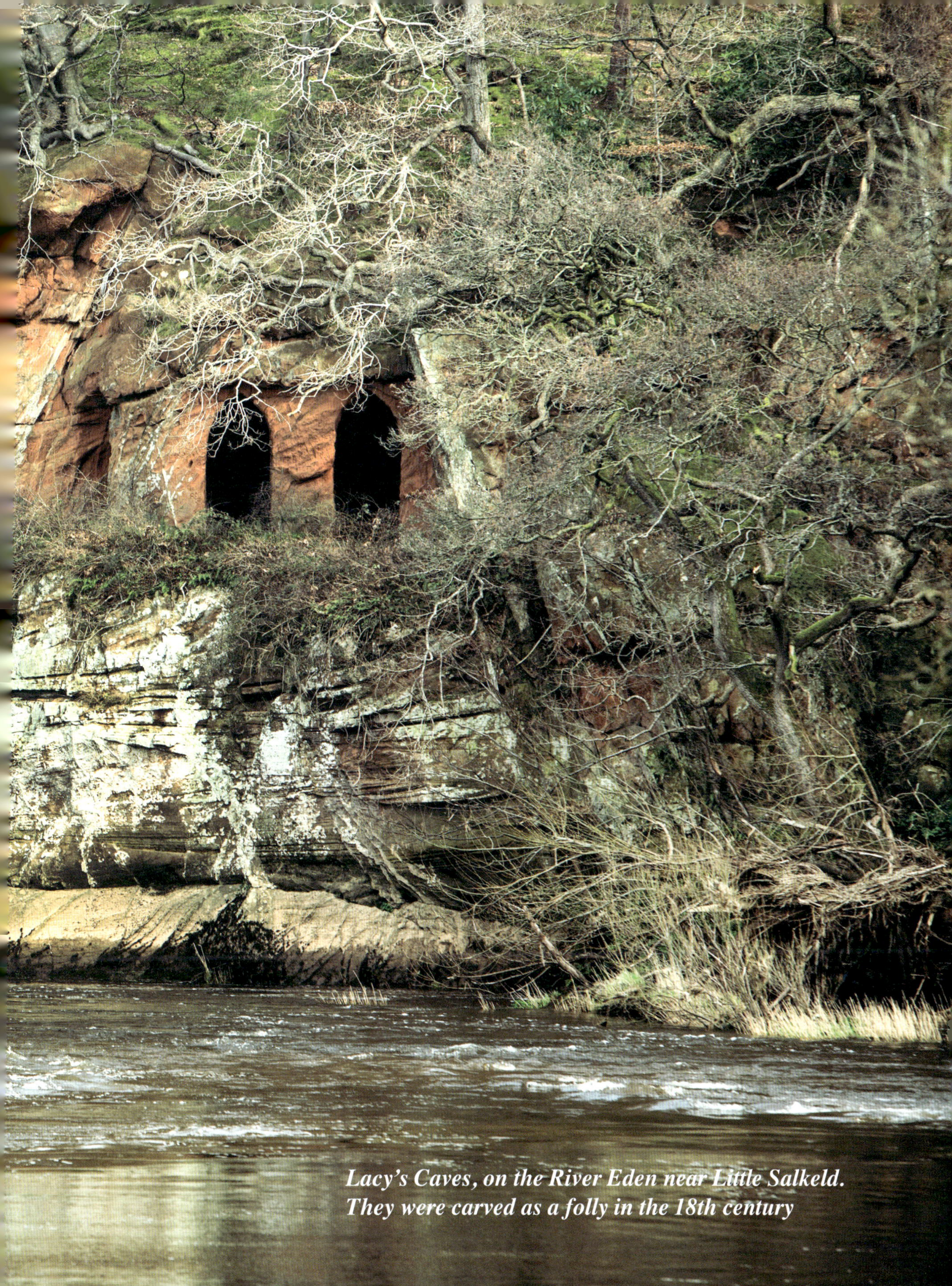

Lacy's Caves, on the River Eden near Little Salkeld.
They were carved as a folly in the 18th century

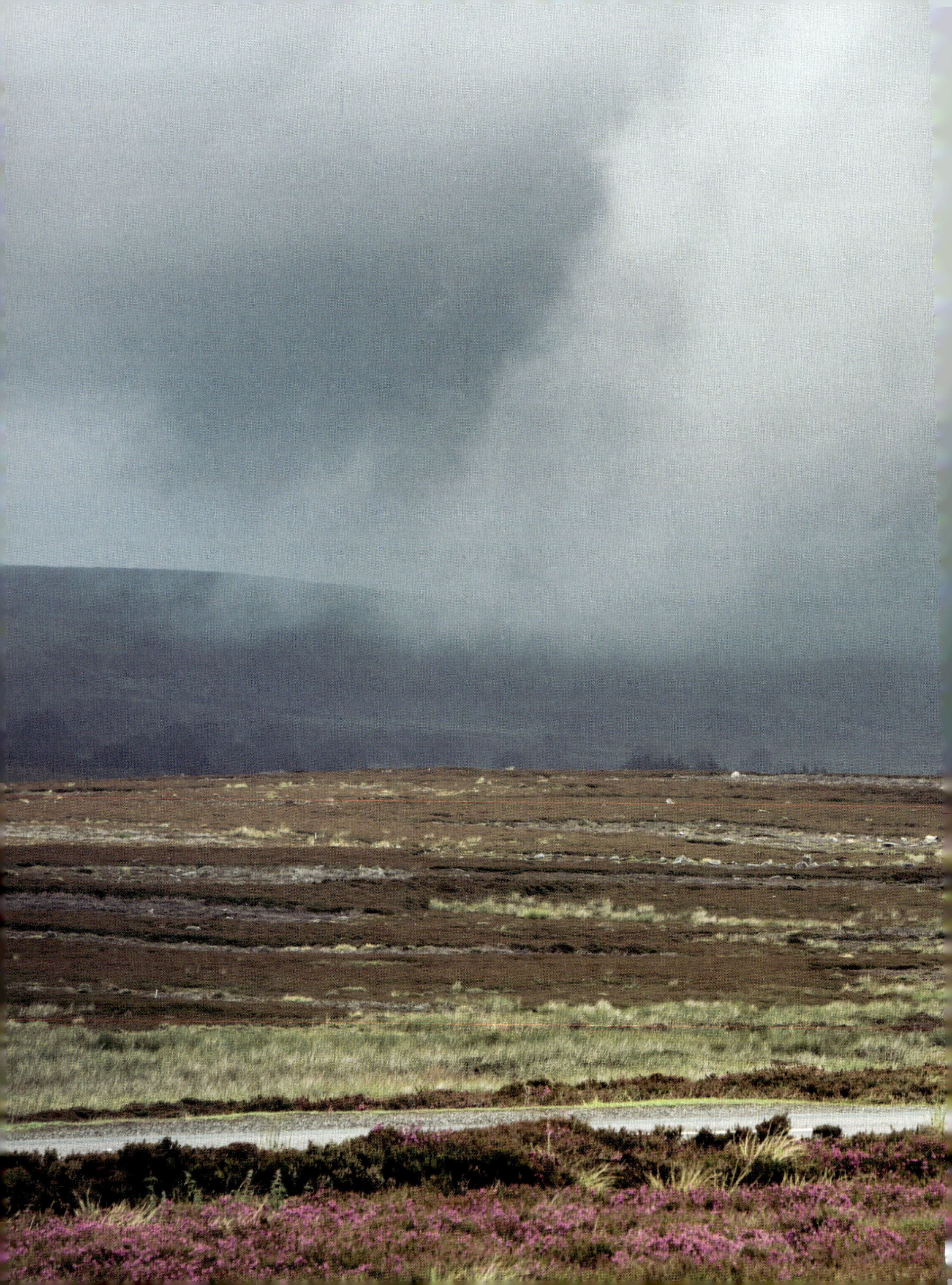

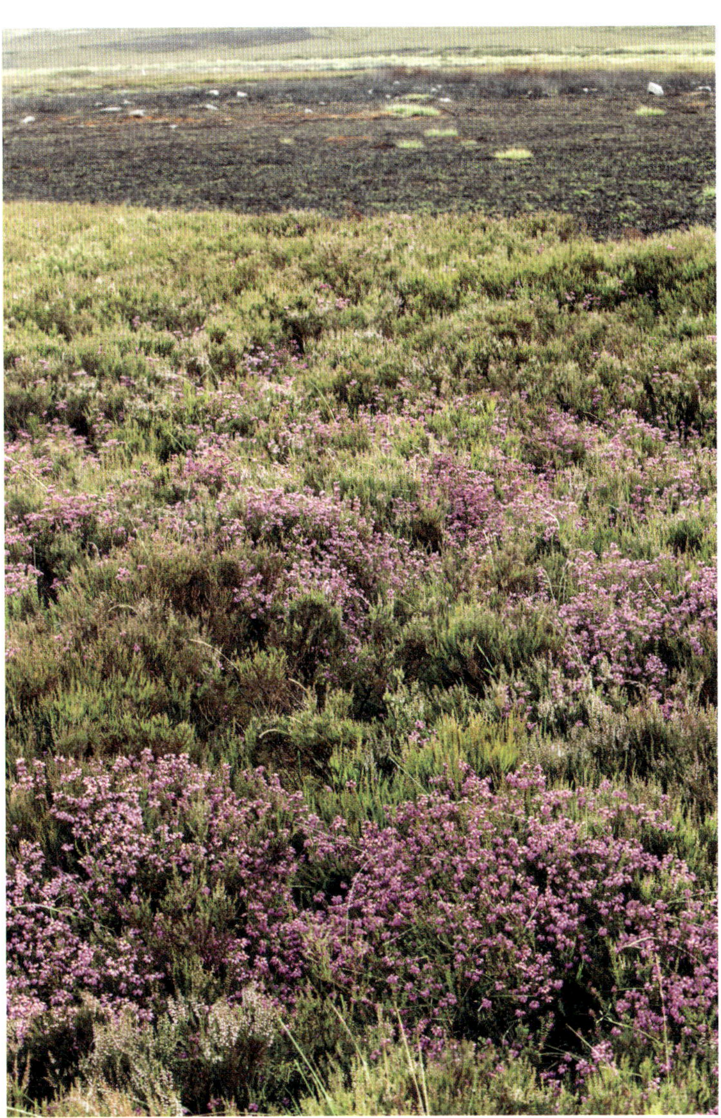

Above: Heather in bloom on Muggleswick Common west of Consett

Left: Low cloud rolls down over Muggleswick Common near Smiddy Shaw Reservoir

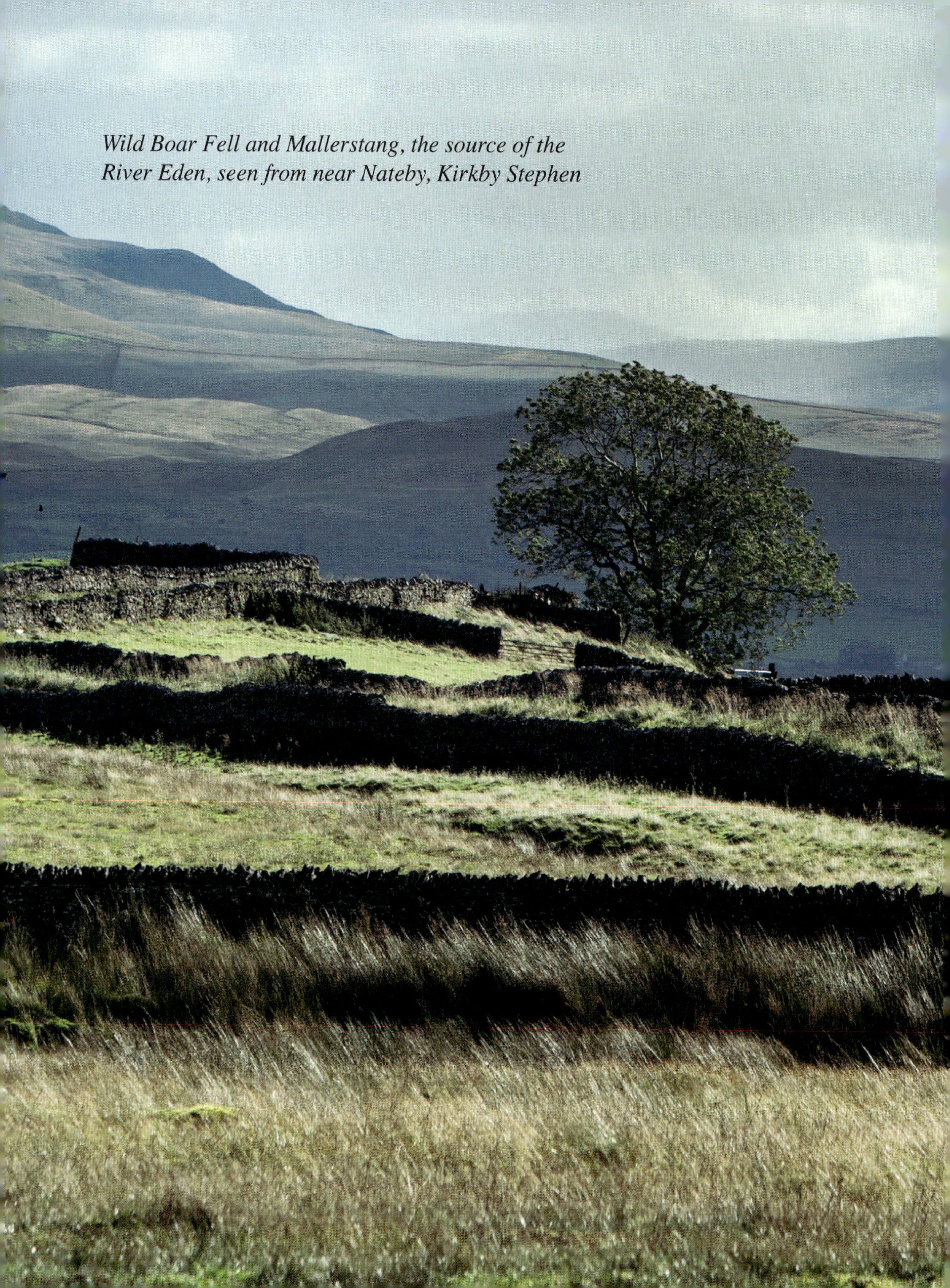

*Wild Boar Fell and Mallerstang, the source of the
River Eden, seen from near Nateby, Kirkby Stephen*

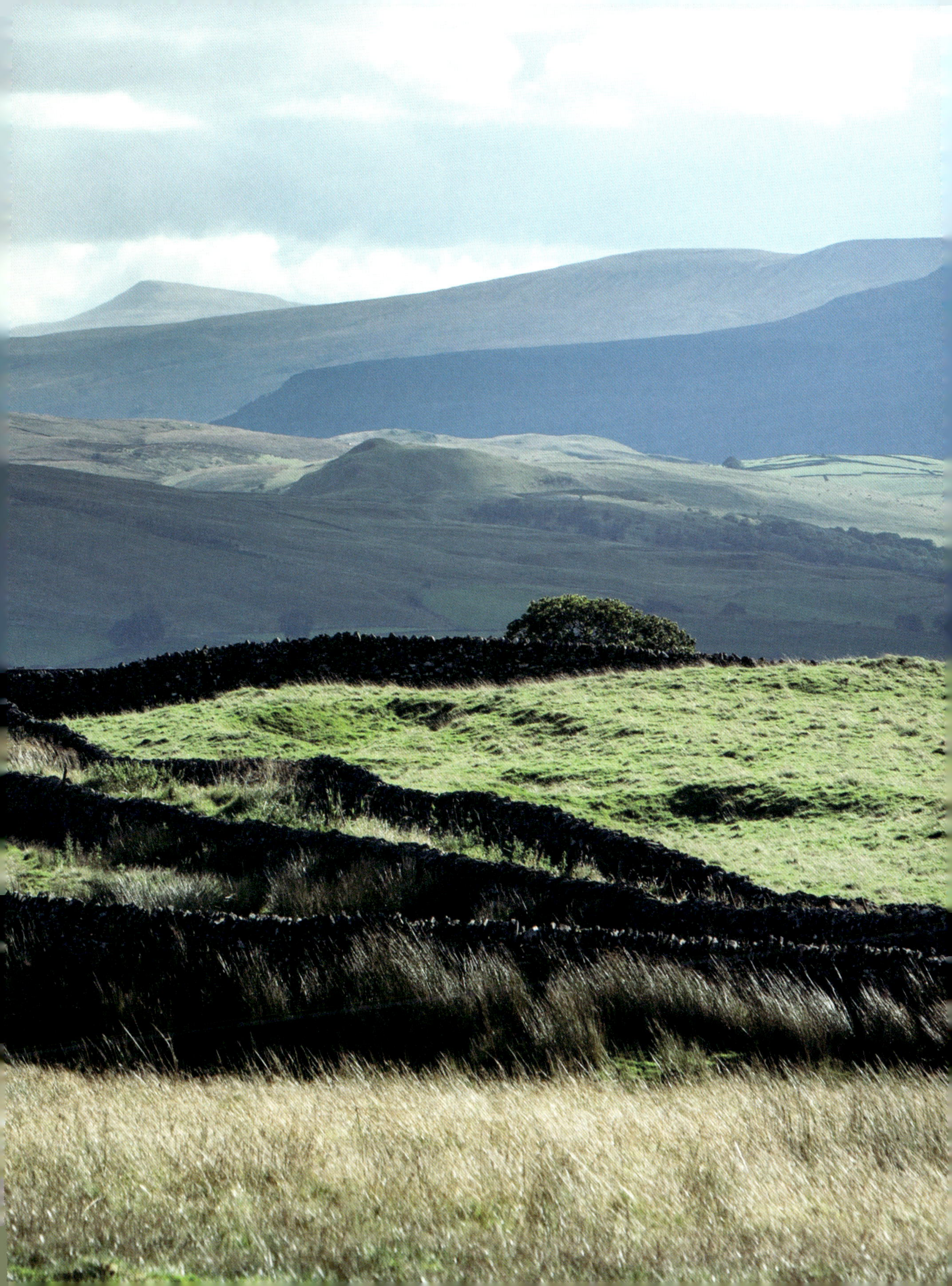

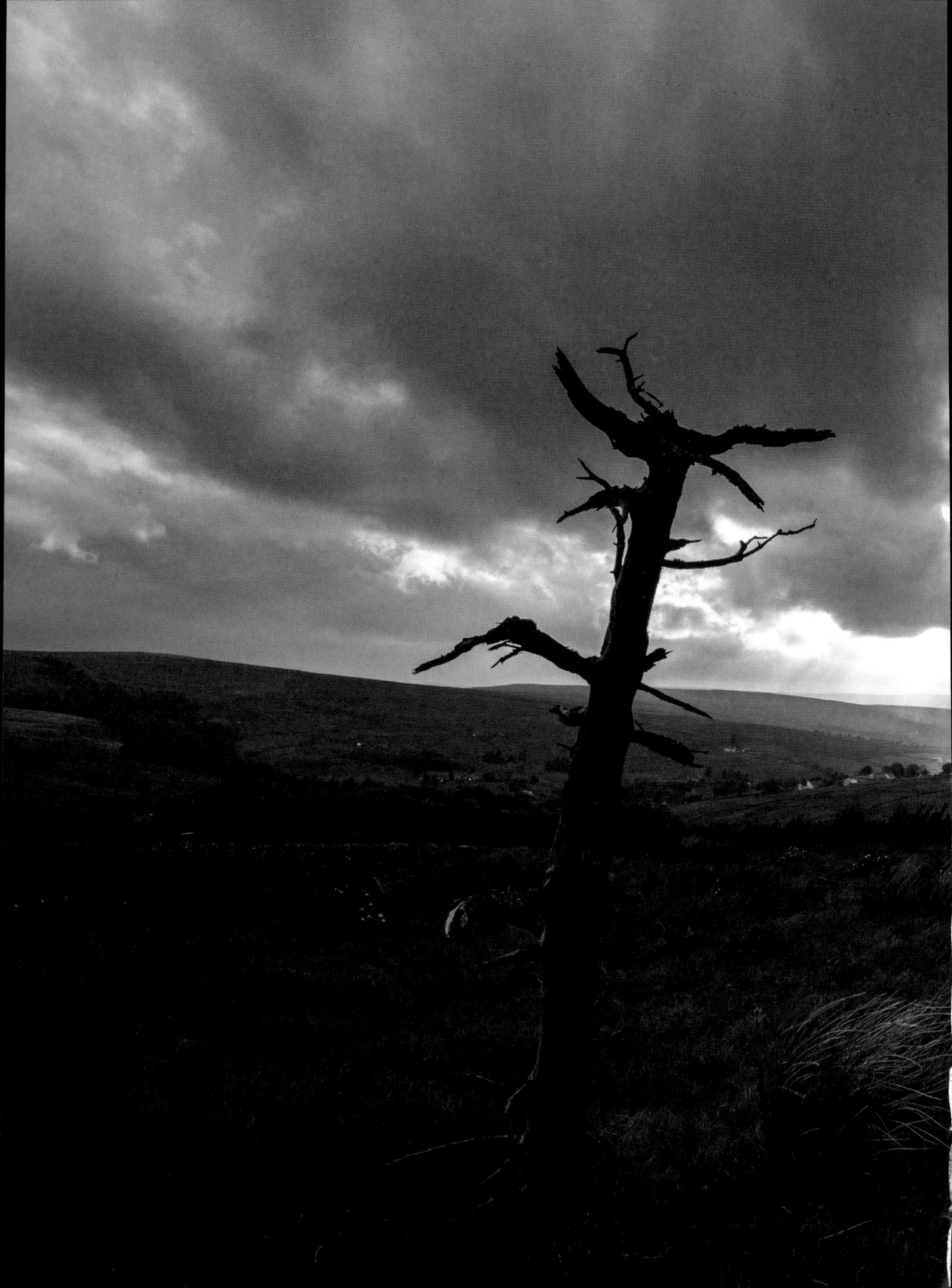

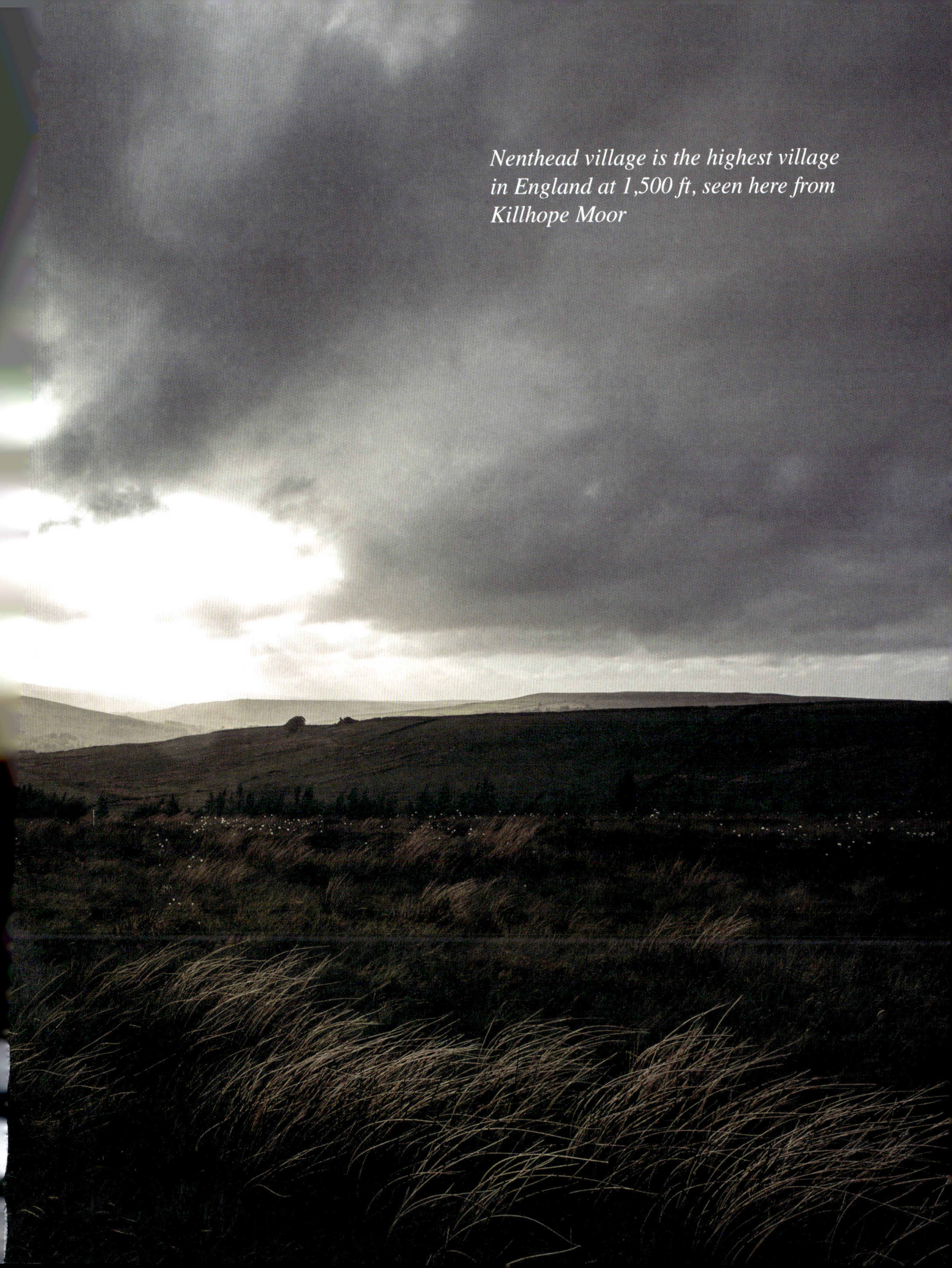
Nenthead village is the highest village
in England at 1,500 ft, seen here from
Killhope Moor

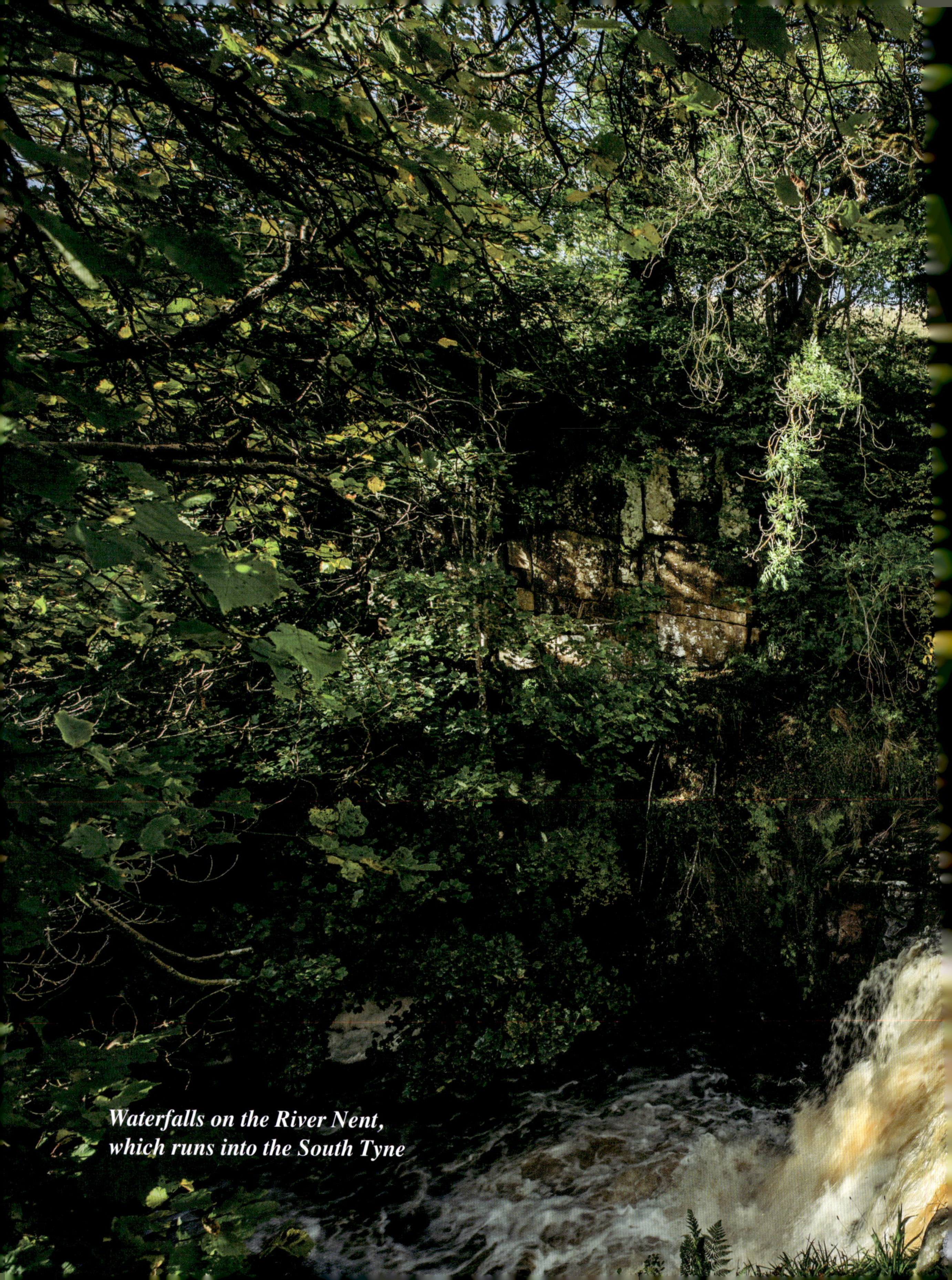

*Waterfalls on the River Nent,
which runs into the South Tyne*

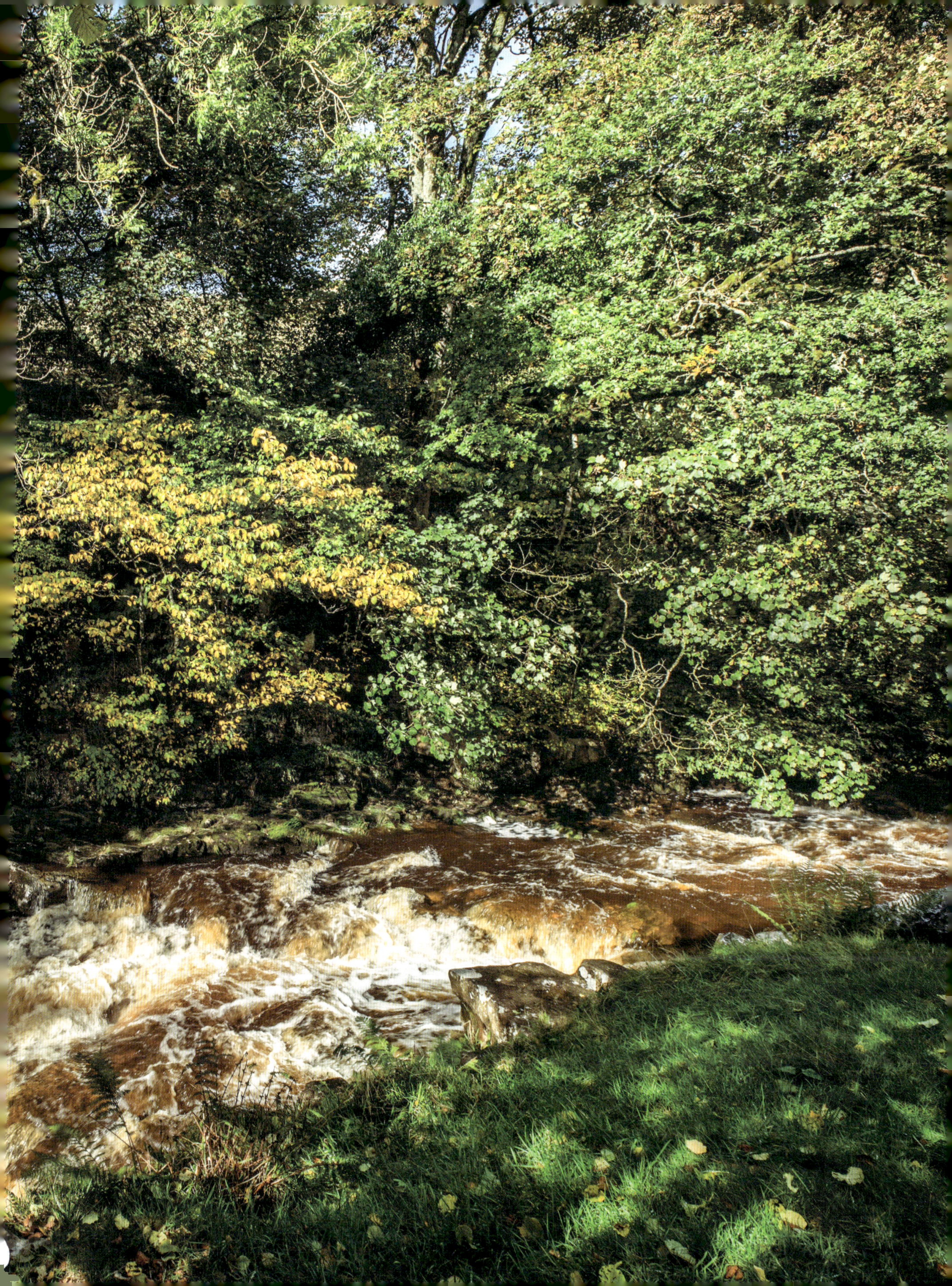

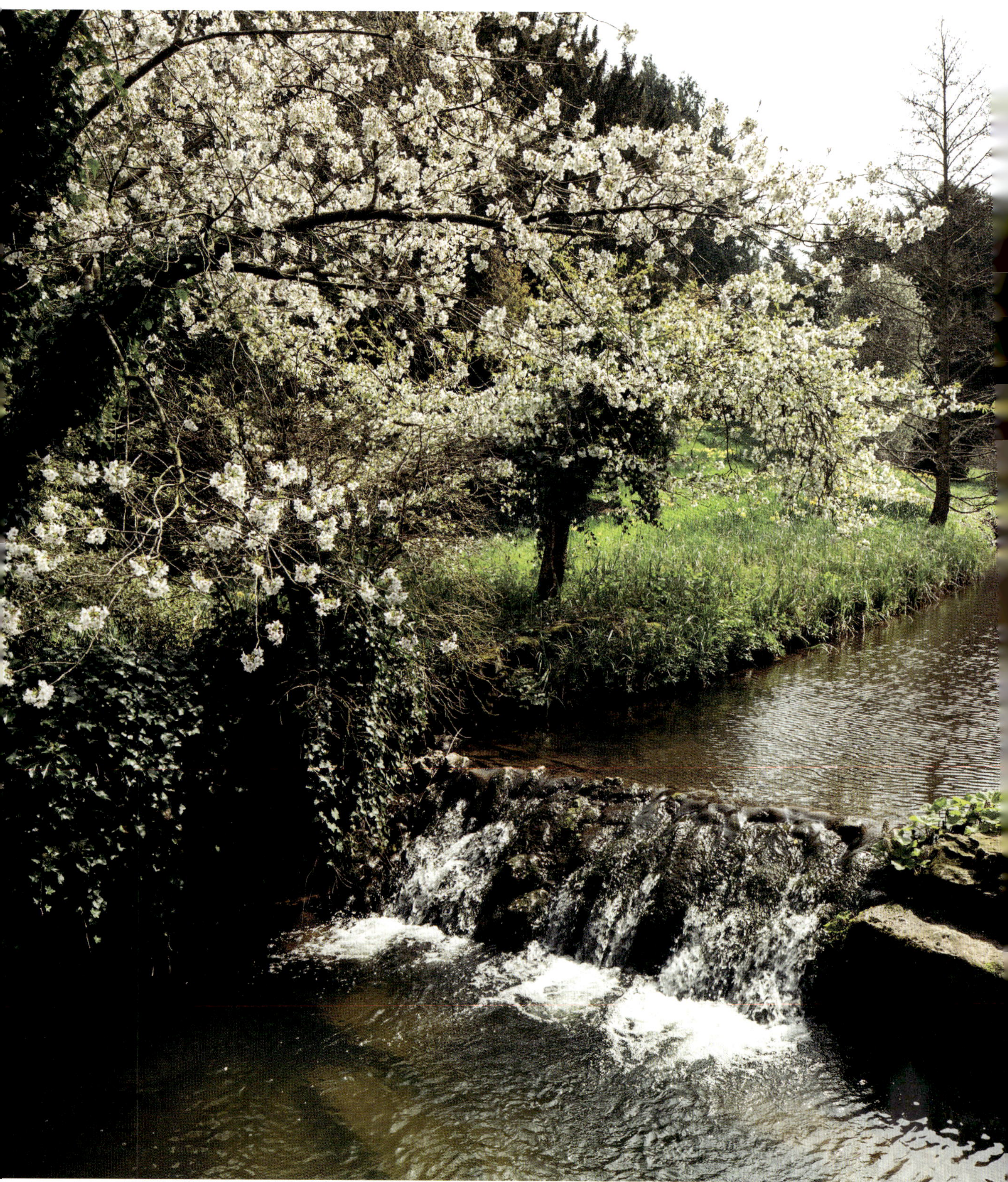

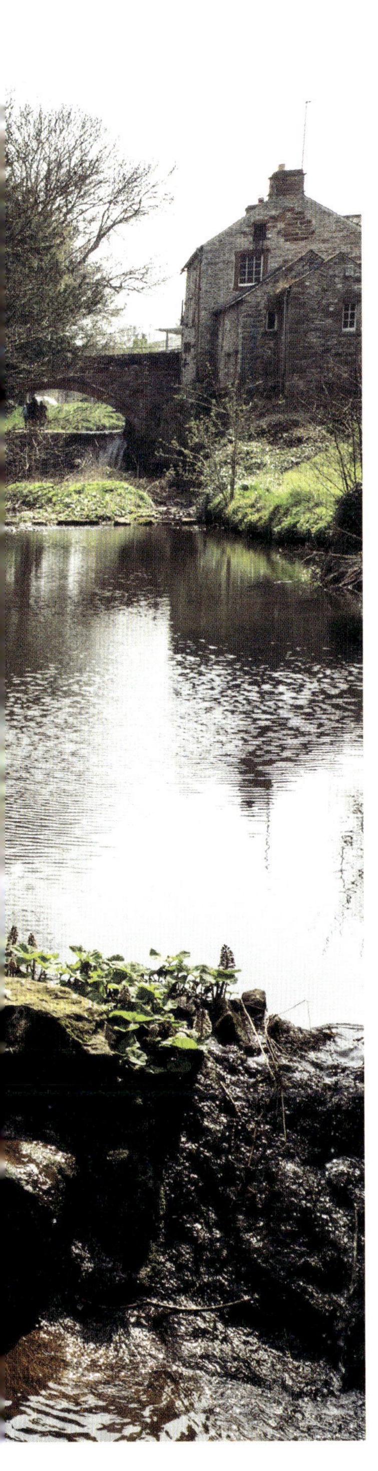

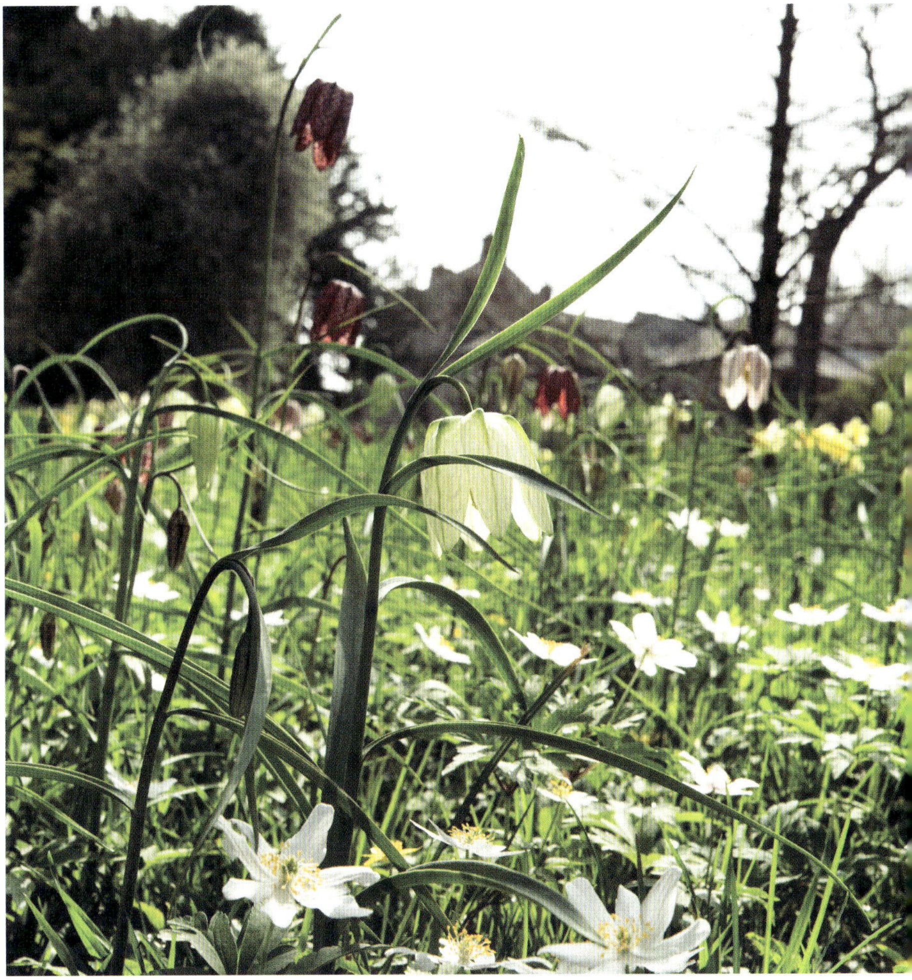

Above and Left: Wild flowers and blossom beside Morland Beck, Eden Valley

Overleaf: A typical North Pennine stone cottage at Ninebanks in Allendale, Northumberland. Ninebanks is hidden away in a deep valley, little visited by tourists. Close by is a Buddhist abbey which speaks volumes about the peace that can be found here

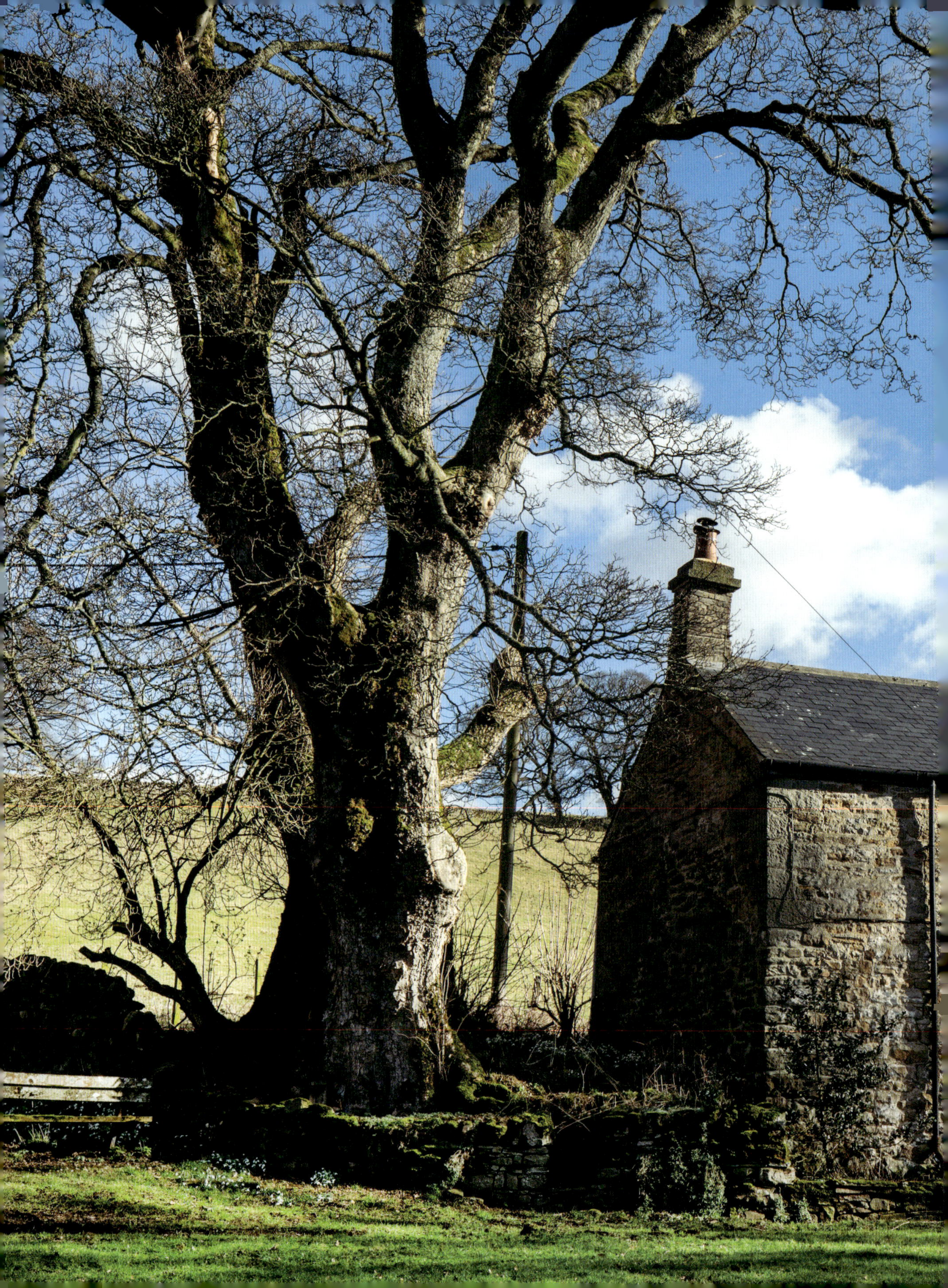

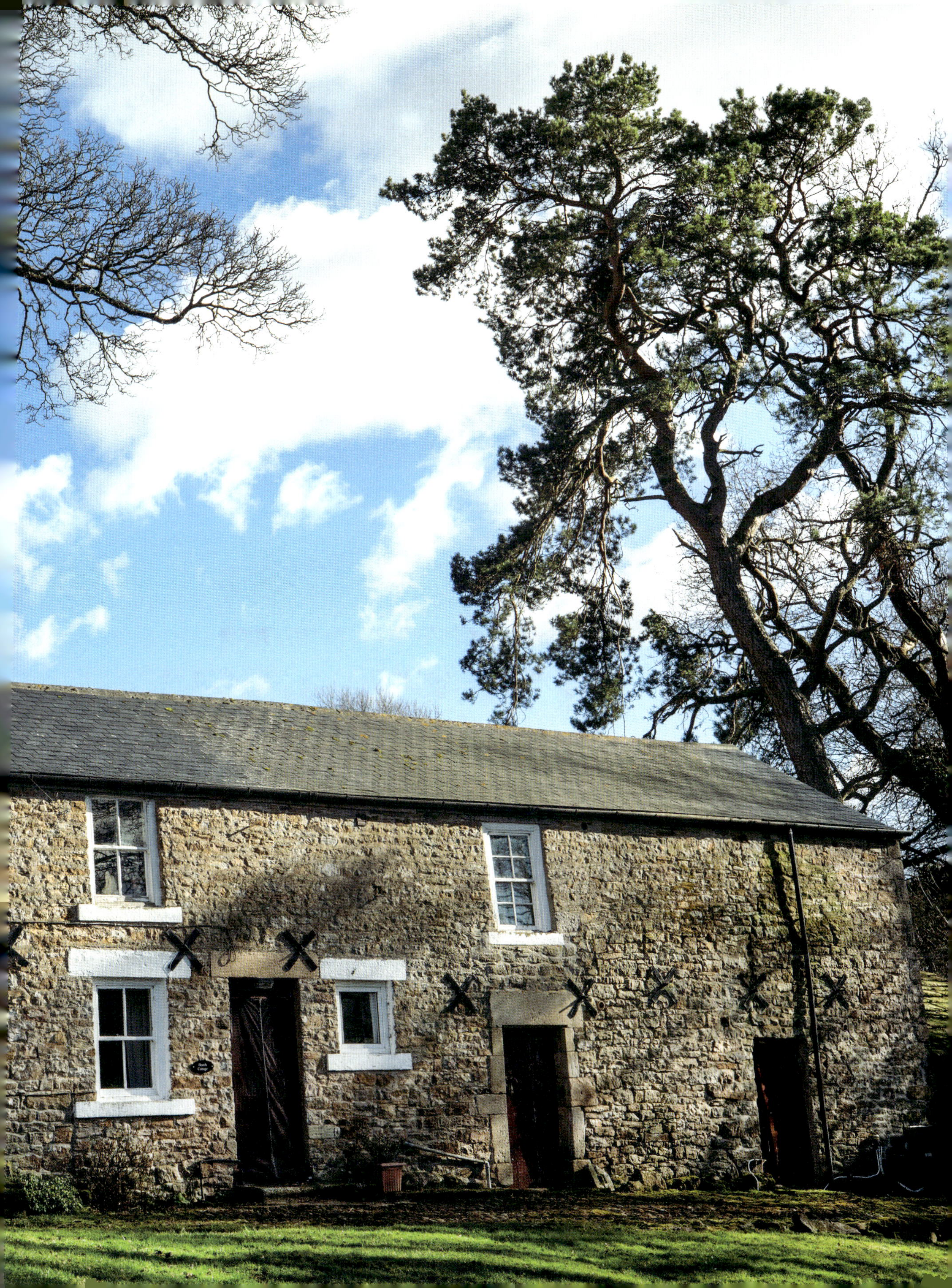

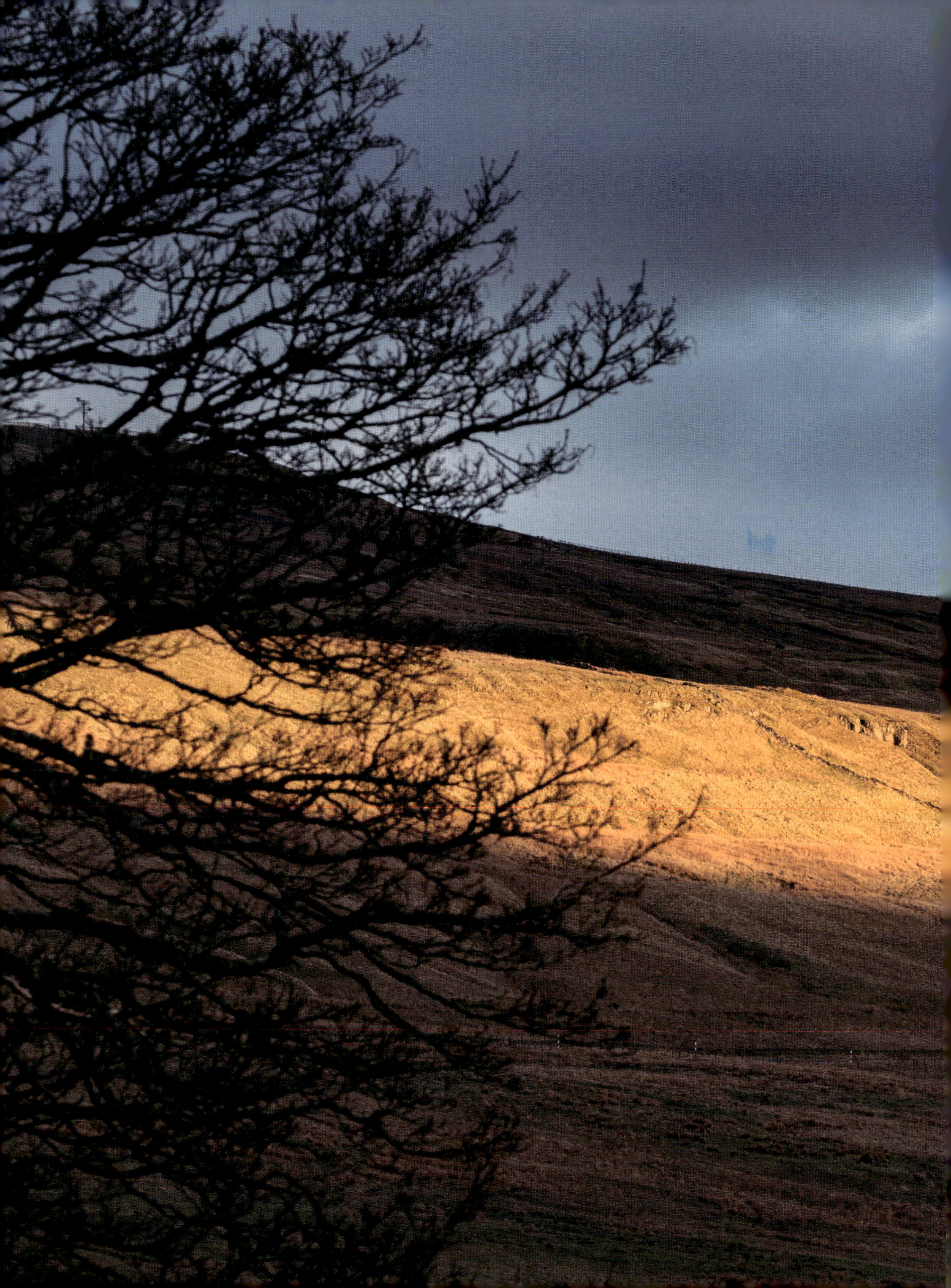

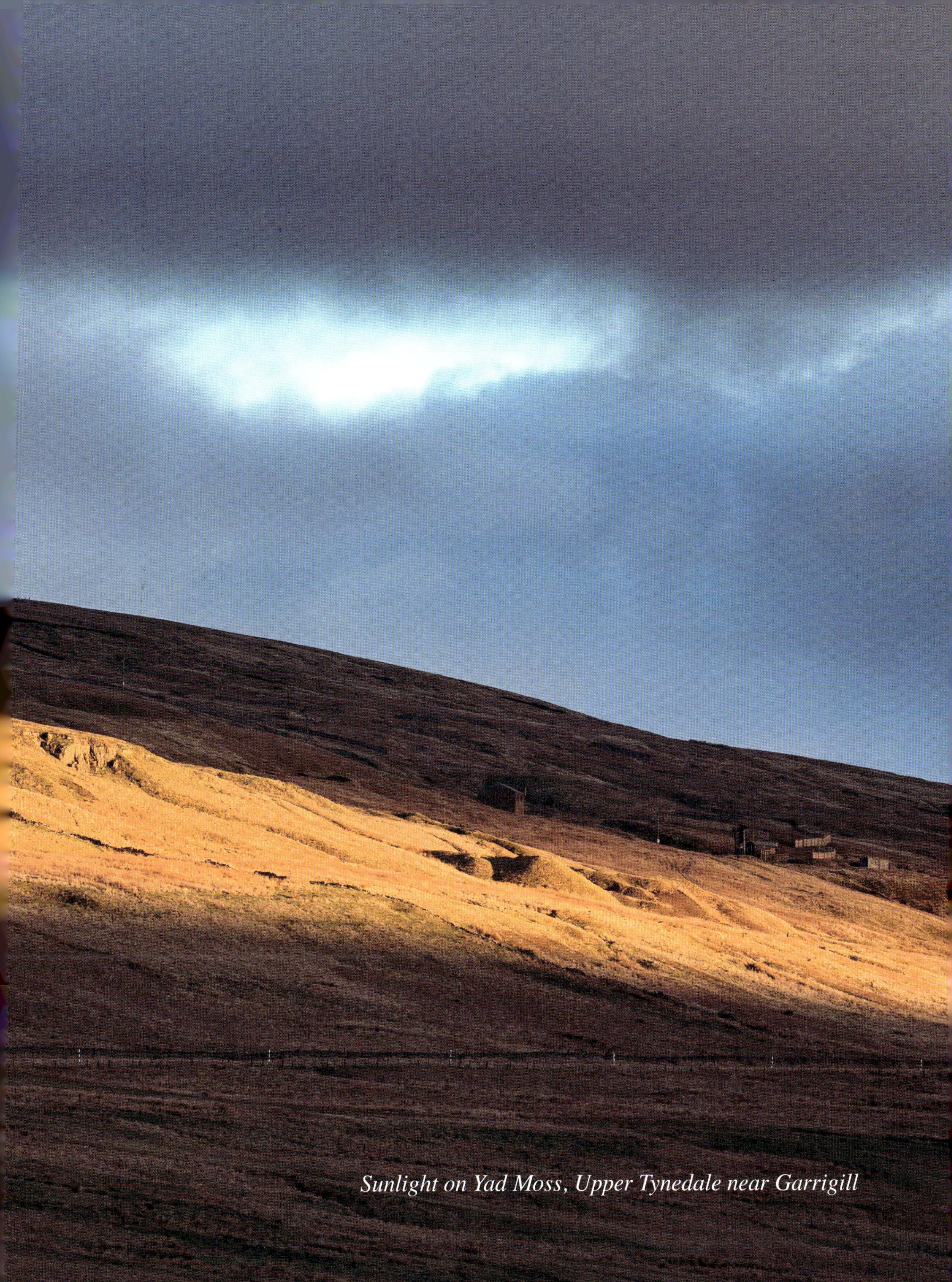

Sunlight on Yad Moss, Upper Tynedale near Garrigill

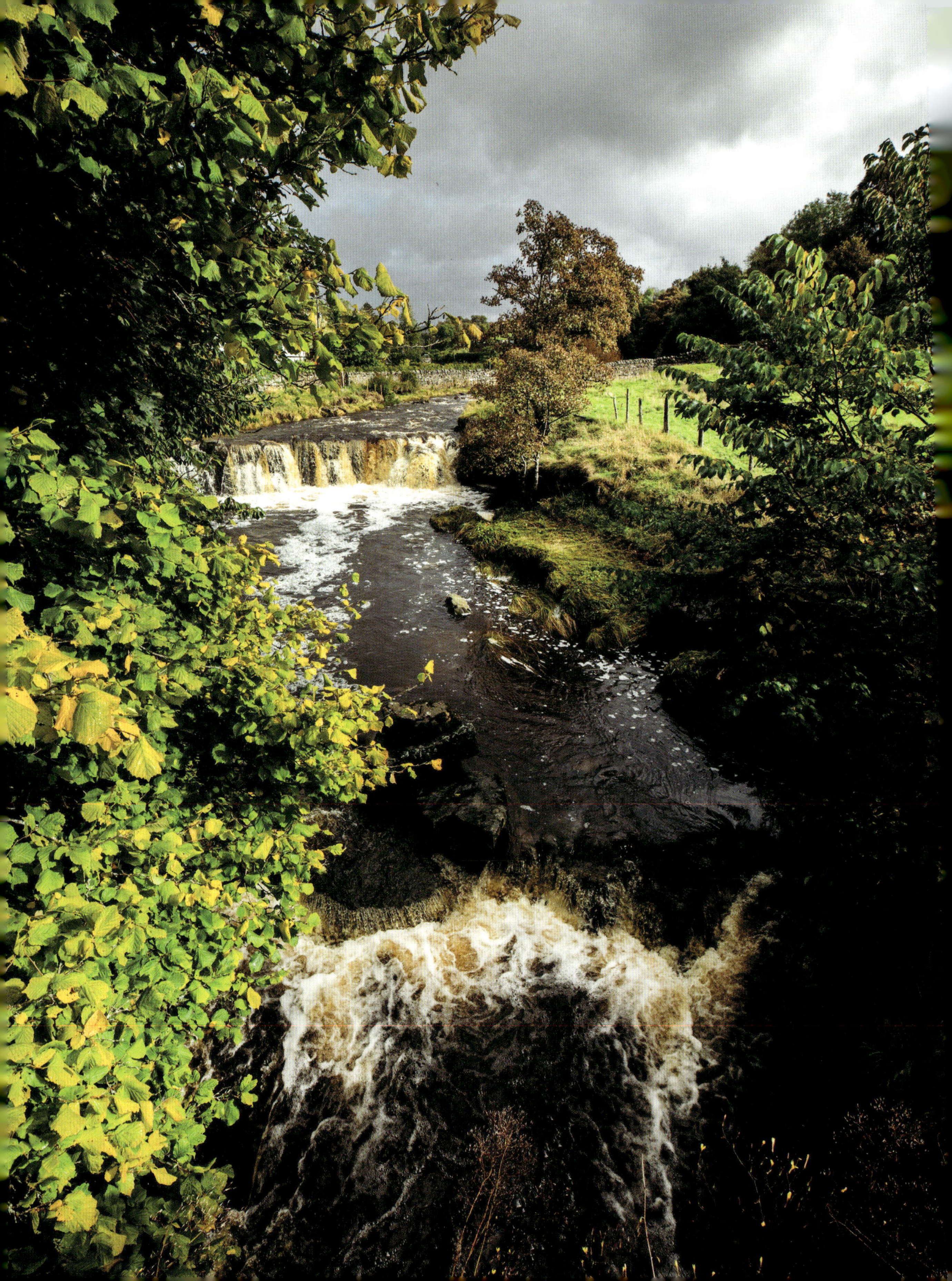

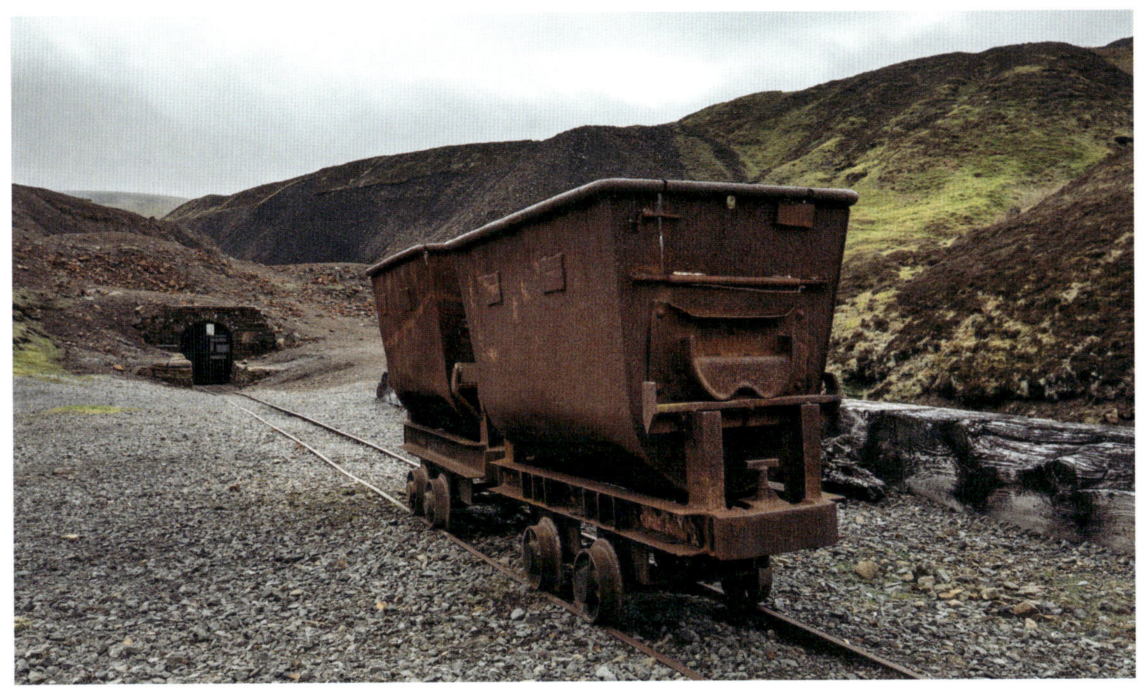

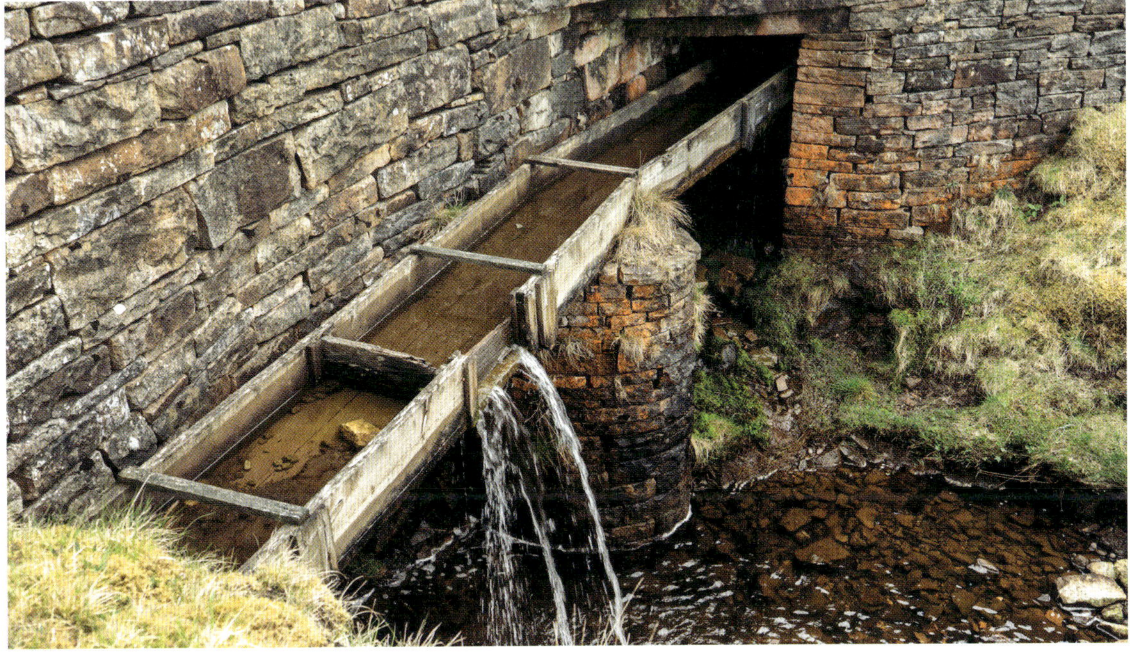

Above: Mining remains at Nenthead Mines

Left: Seven Sisters waterfall on the River Nent

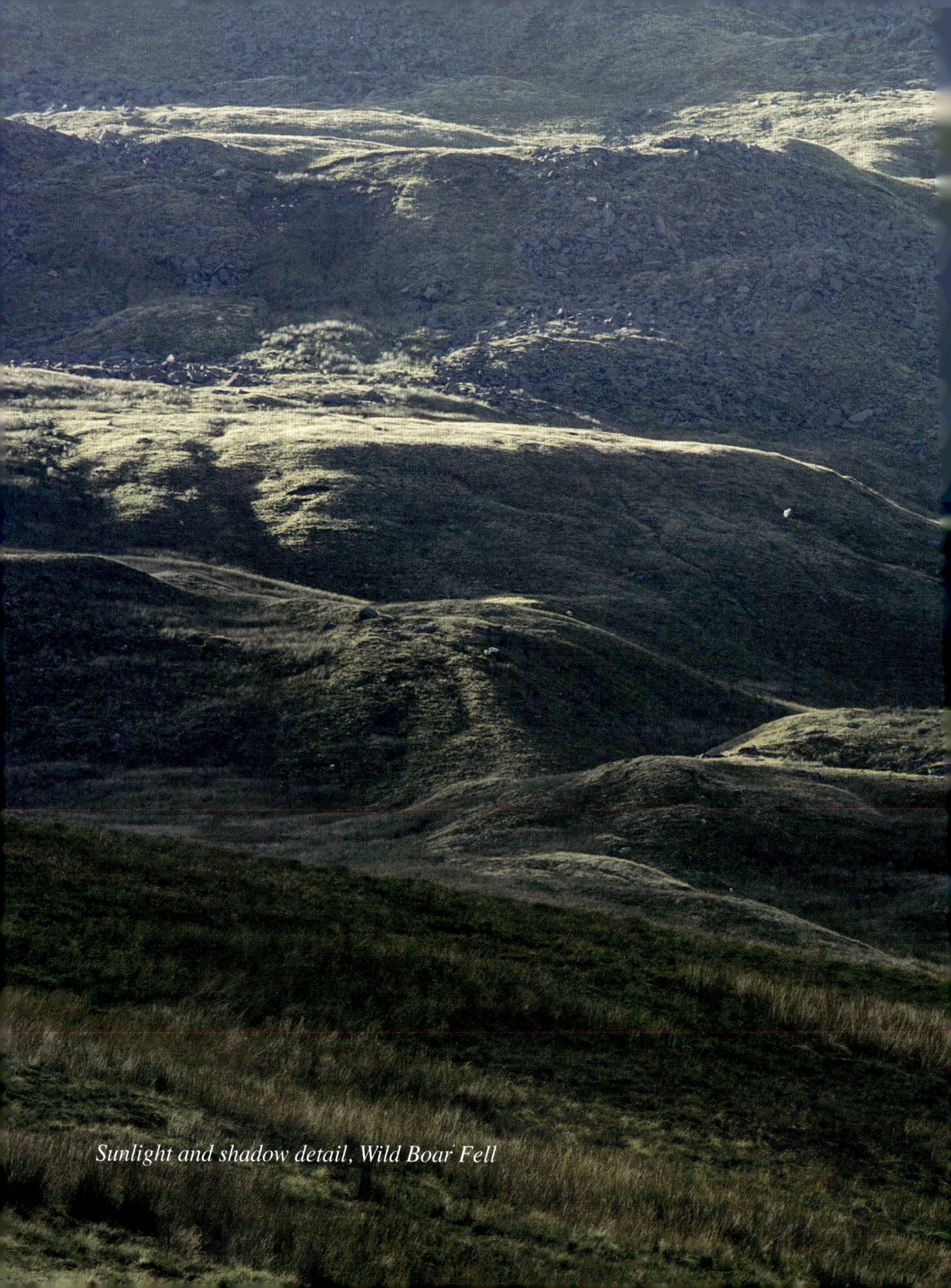

Sunlight and shadow detail, Wild Boar Fell

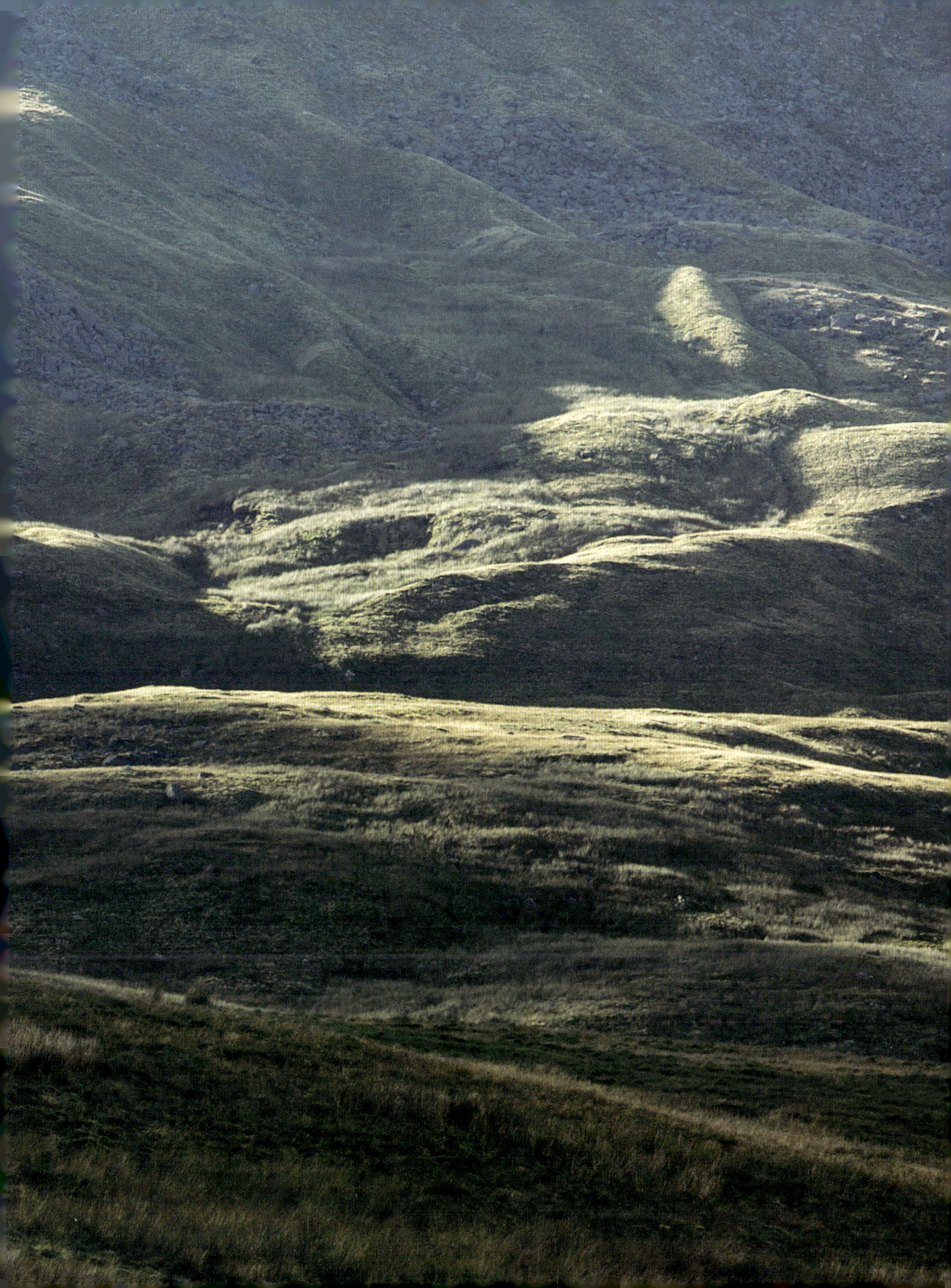

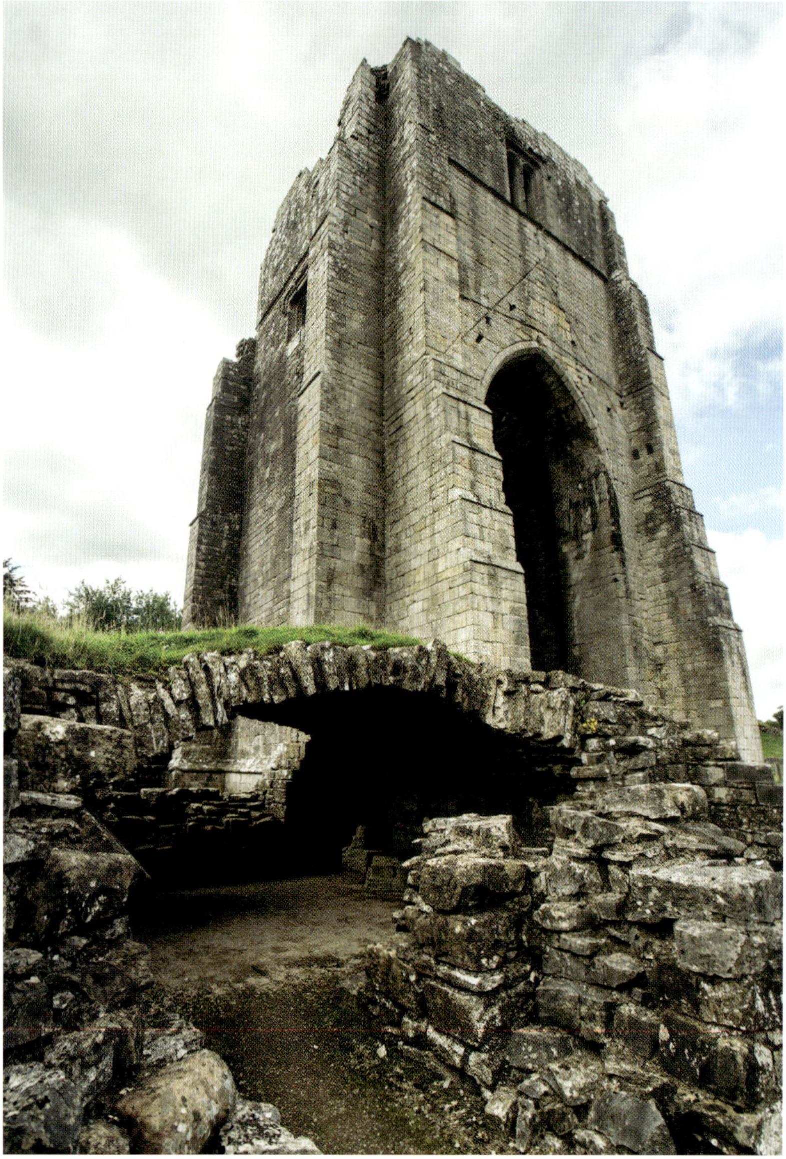

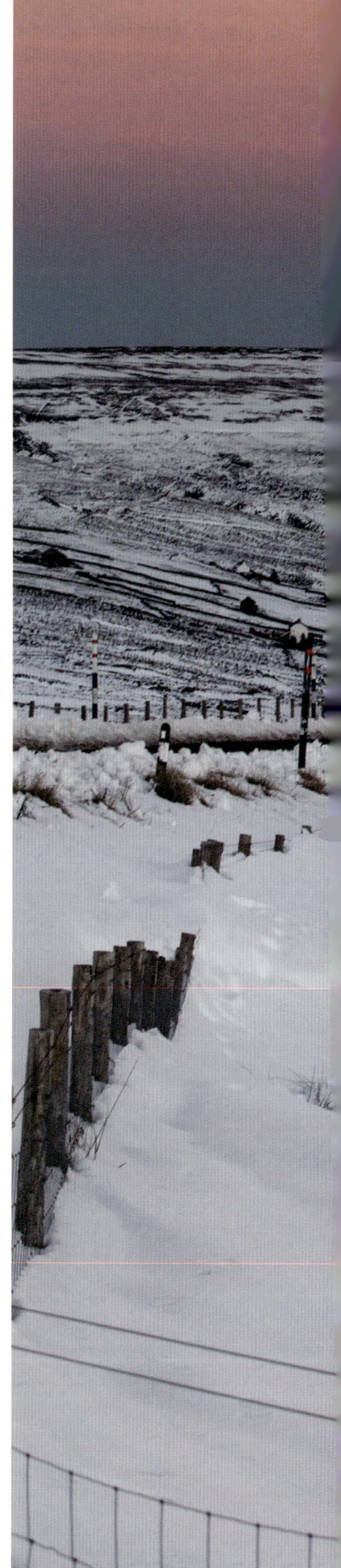

Above: Shap Abbey, dating from 1199, near Shap, Cumbria. When Henry VIII closed the monasteries, parts of the abbey were used as farm buildings

Right: Snowdrifts at Killhope Cross on the road to Weardale from Nenthead. The road reaches 2,057 feet, one of the highest passes in England. Locals often enquire whether Killhope is still open before they travel in snowy conditions

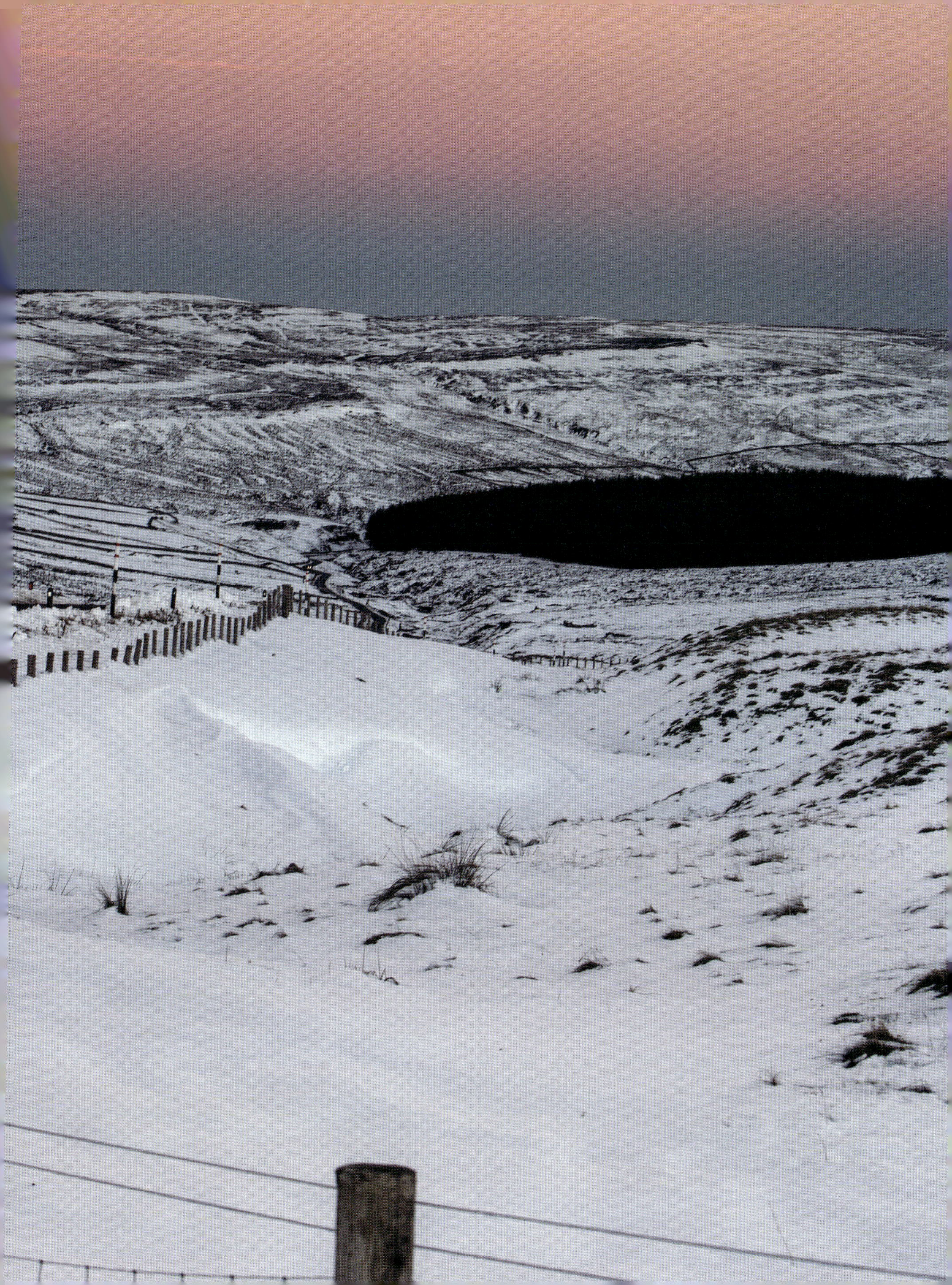

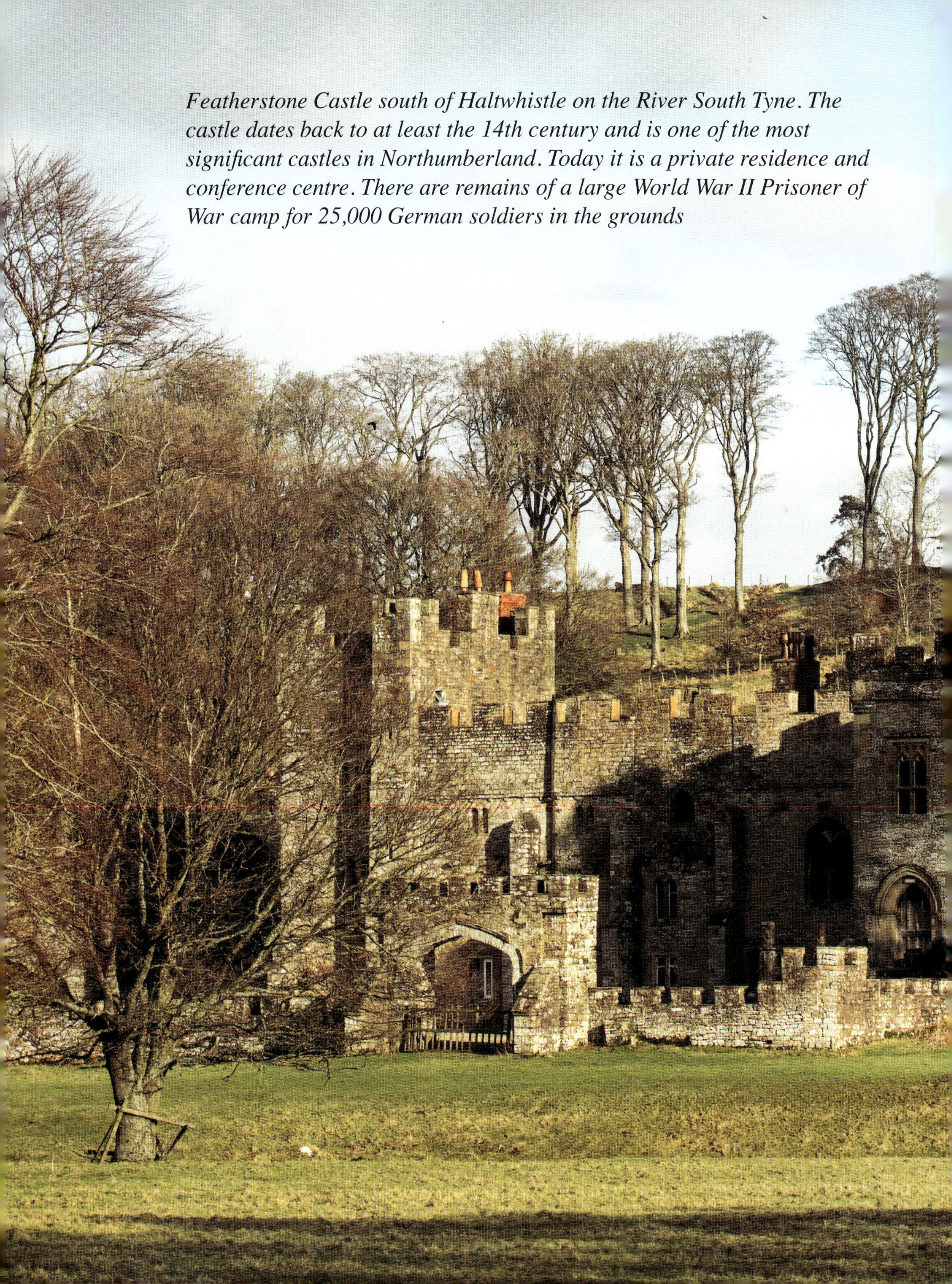

Featherstone Castle south of Haltwhistle on the River South Tyne. The castle dates back to at least the 14th century and is one of the most significant castles in Northumberland. Today it is a private residence and conference centre. There are remains of a large World War II Prisoner of War camp for 25,000 German soldiers in the grounds

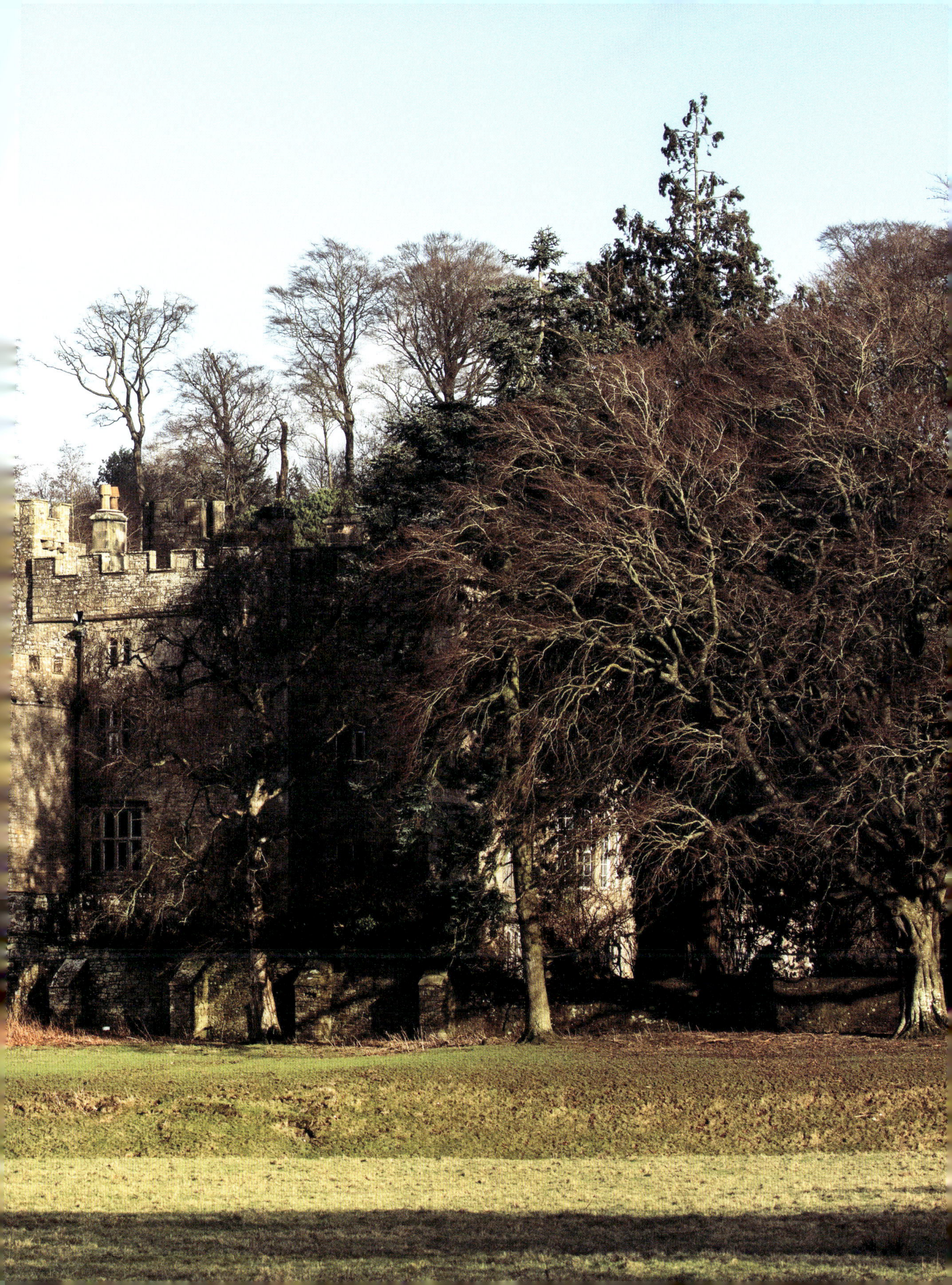

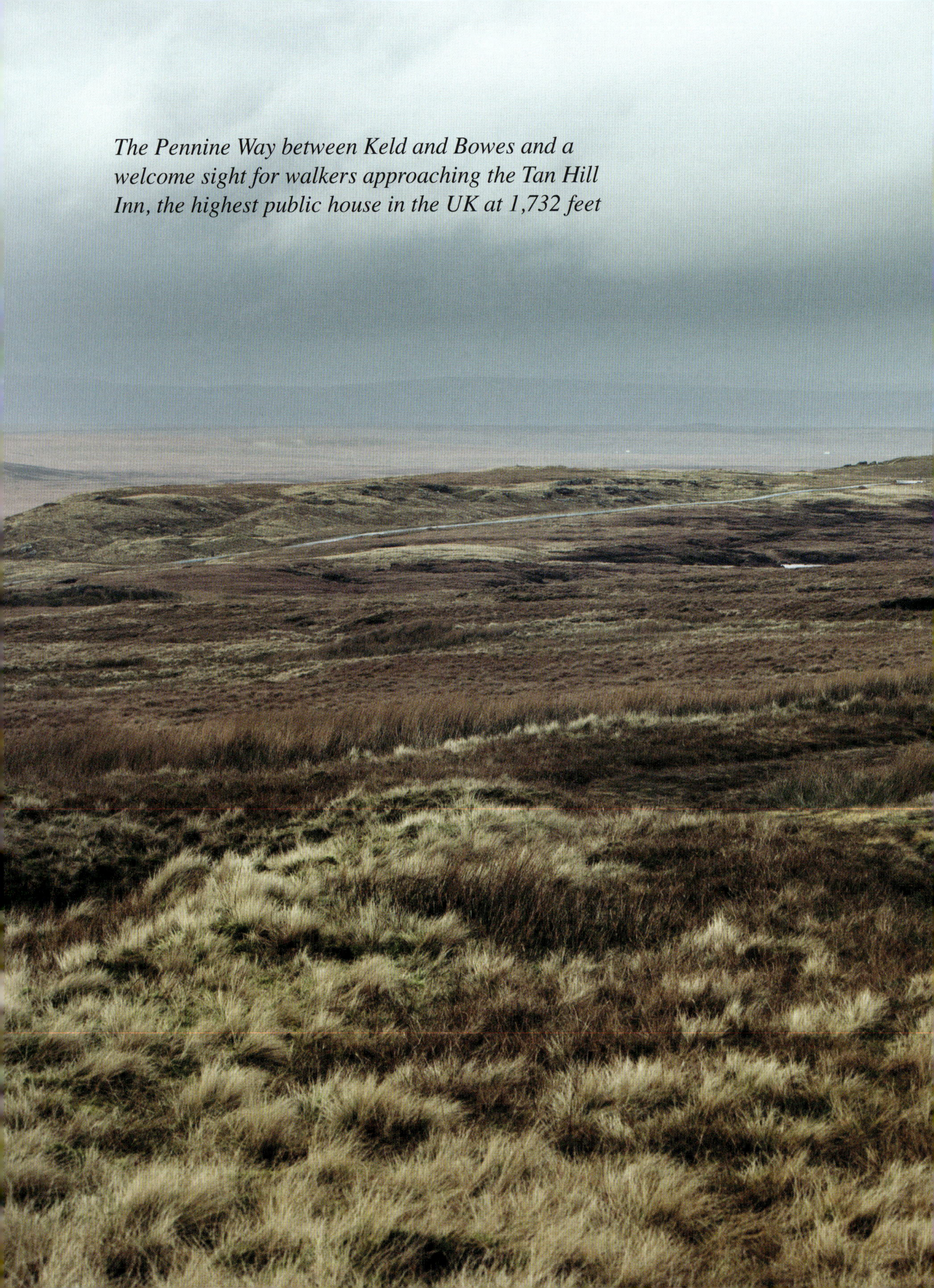

The Pennine Way between Keld and Bowes and a
welcome sight for walkers approaching the Tan Hill
Inn, the highest public house in the UK at 1,732 feet

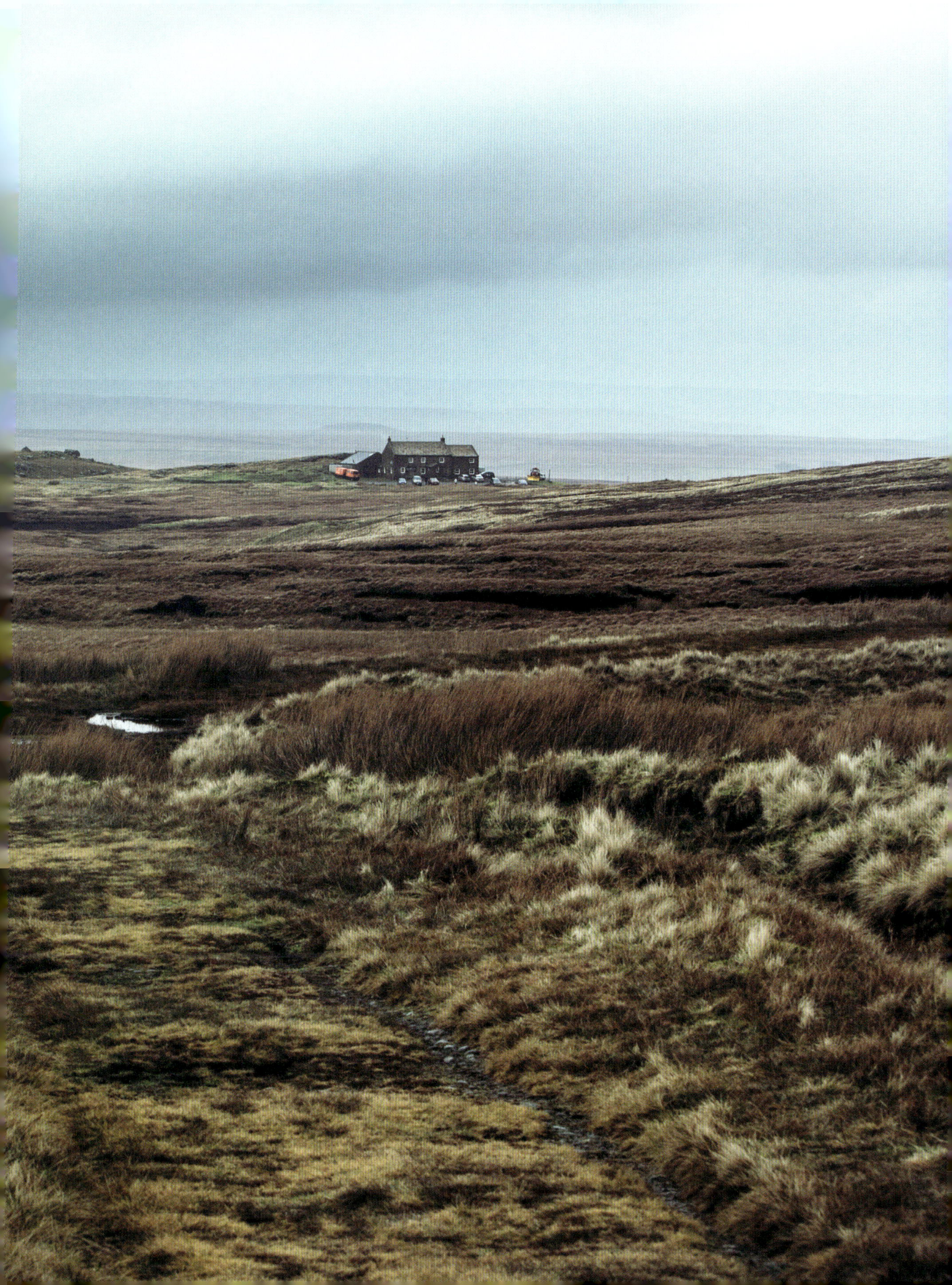

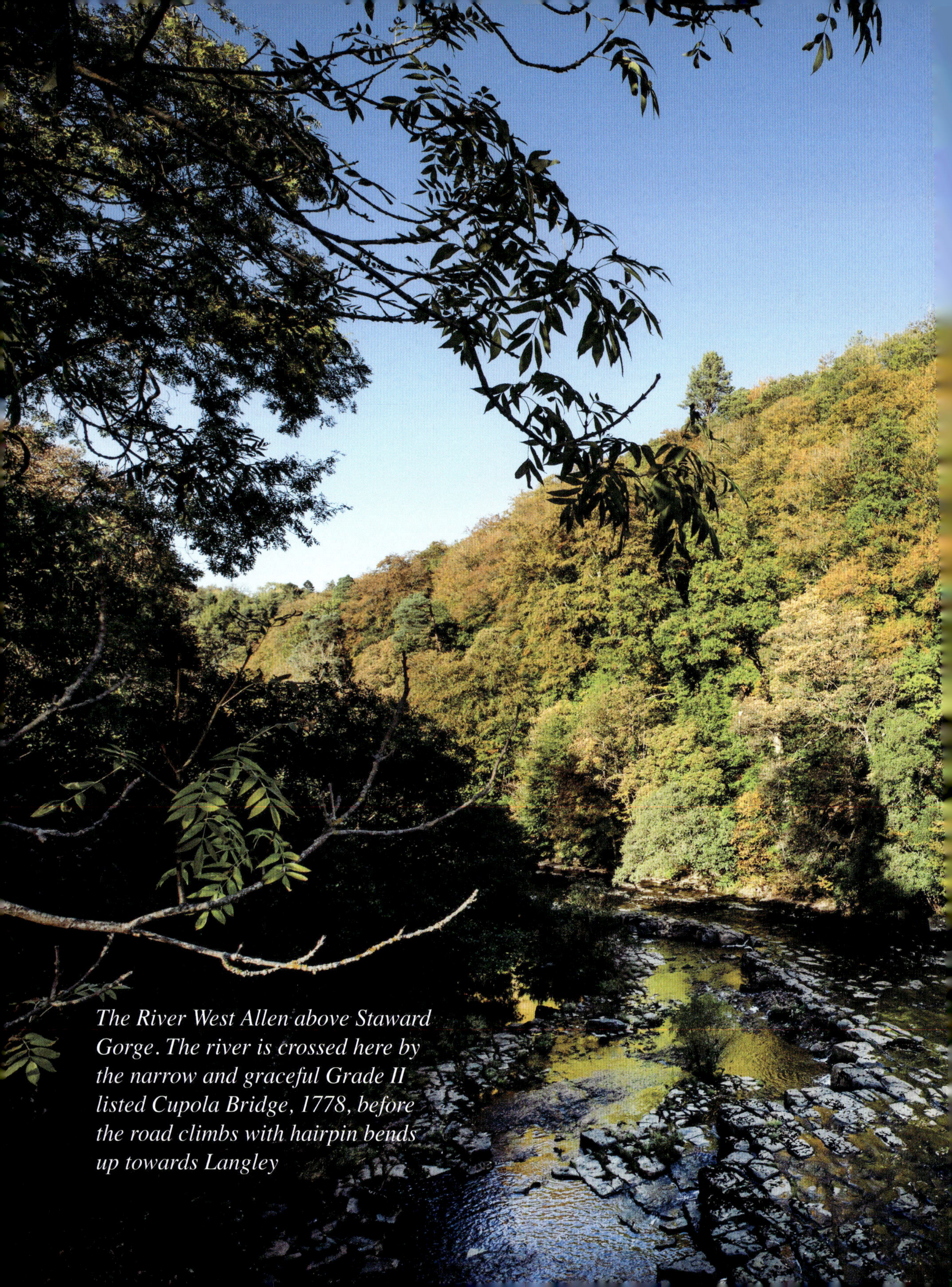

The River West Allen above Staward Gorge. The river is crossed here by the narrow and graceful Grade II listed Cupola Bridge, 1778, before the road climbs with hairpin bends up towards Langley

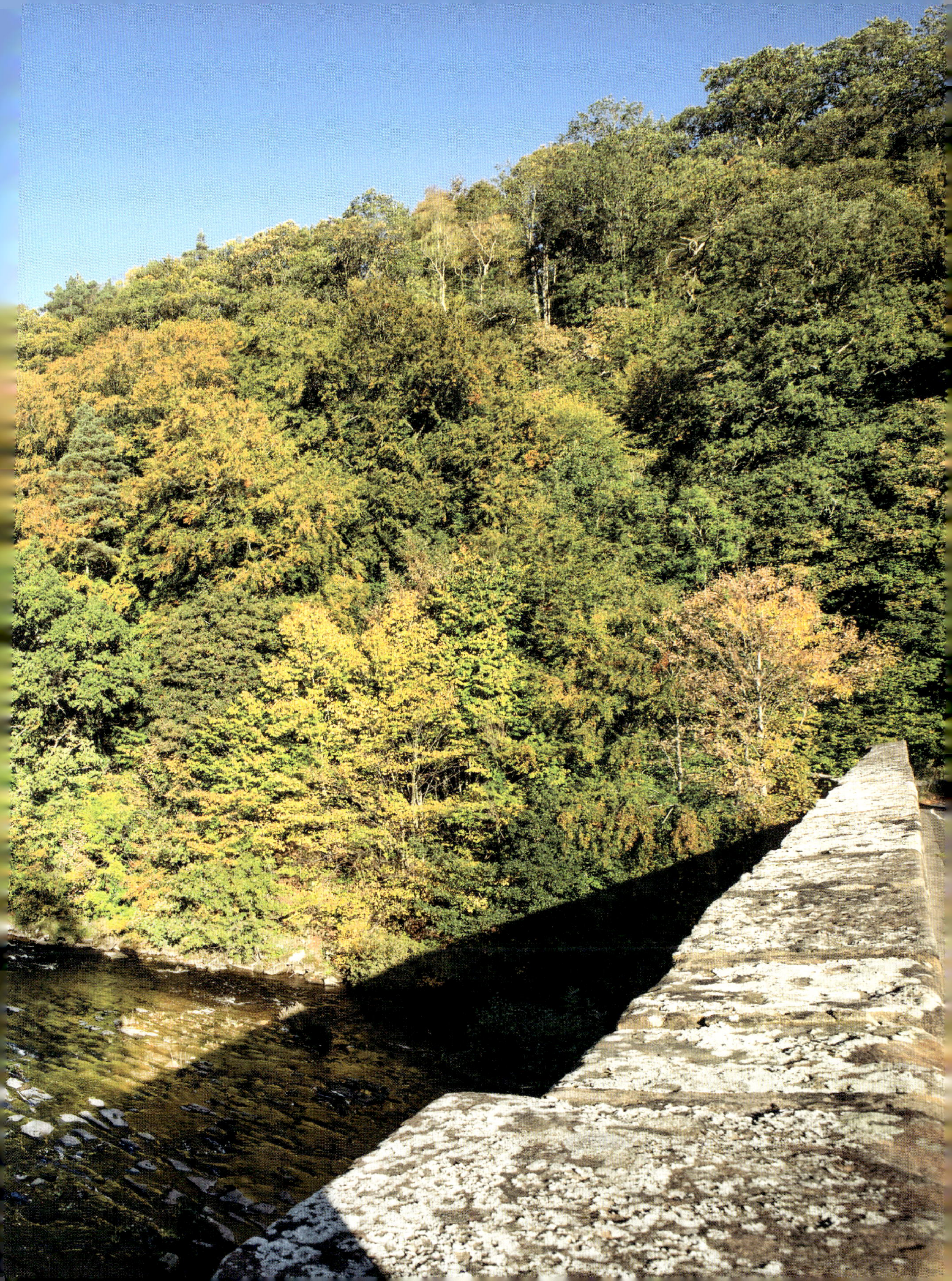

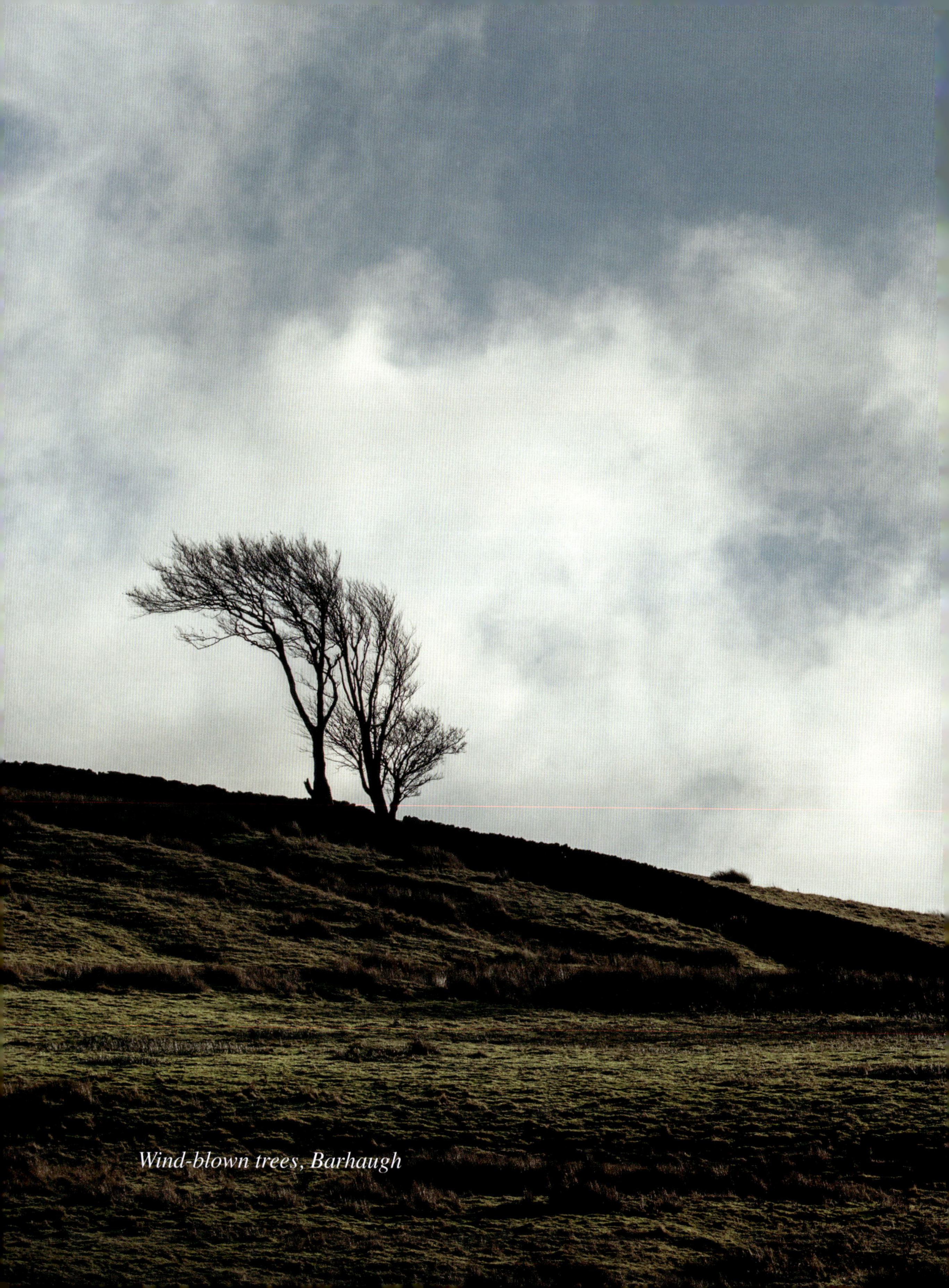

Wind-blown trees, Barhaugh

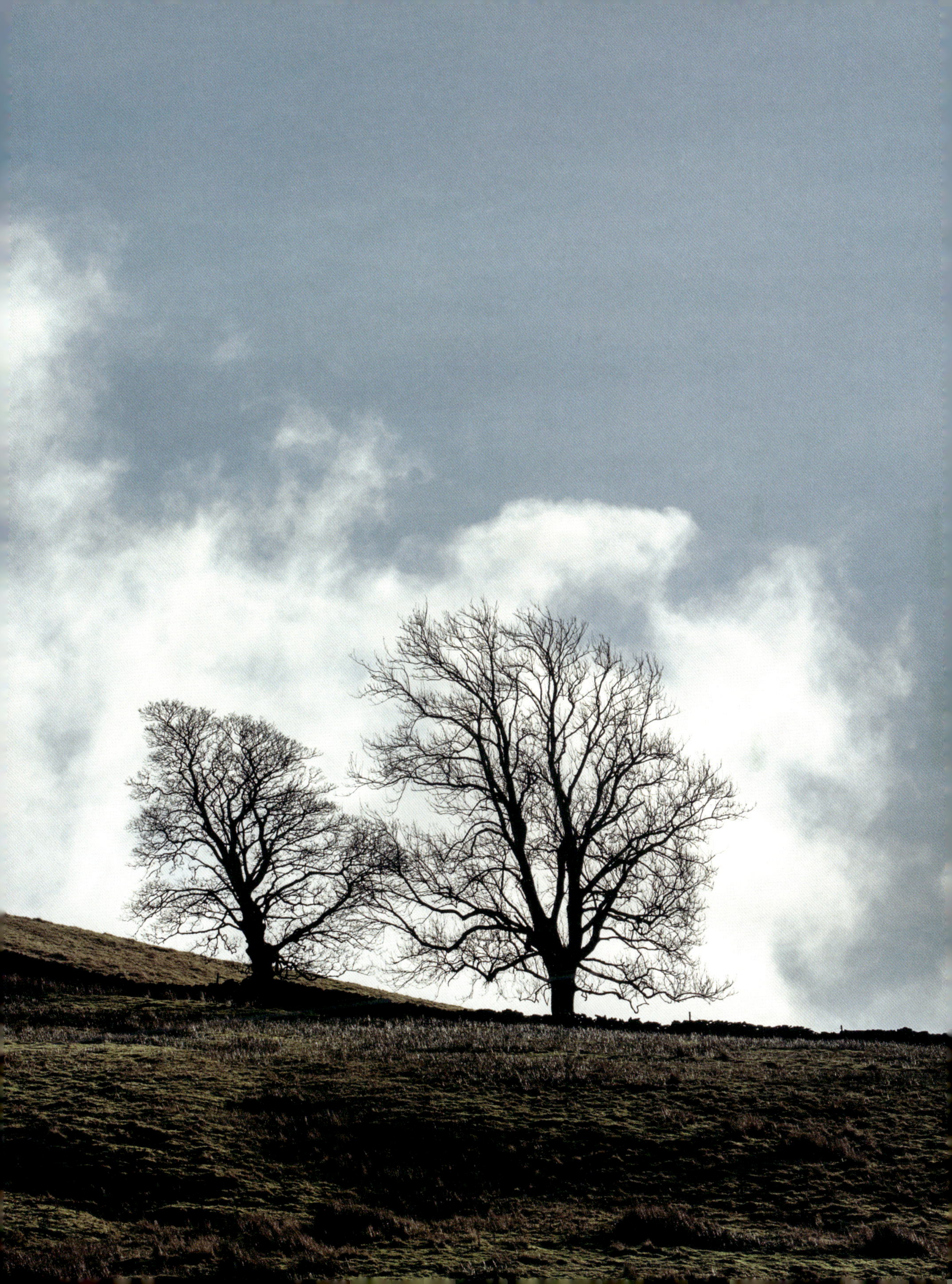

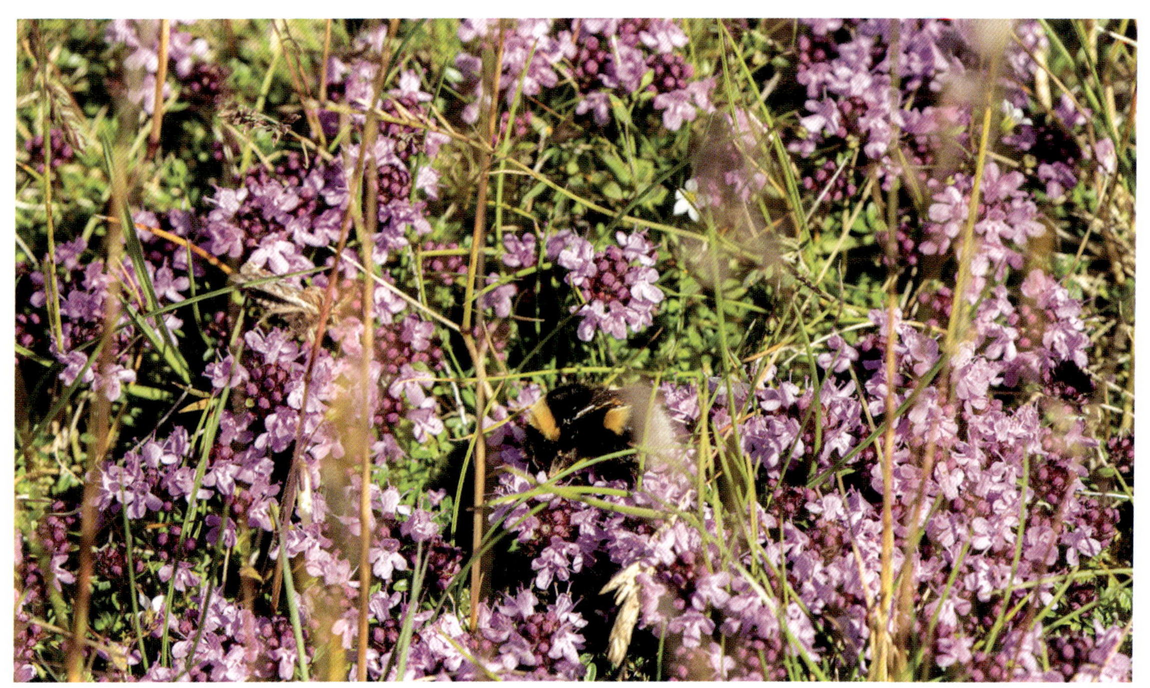

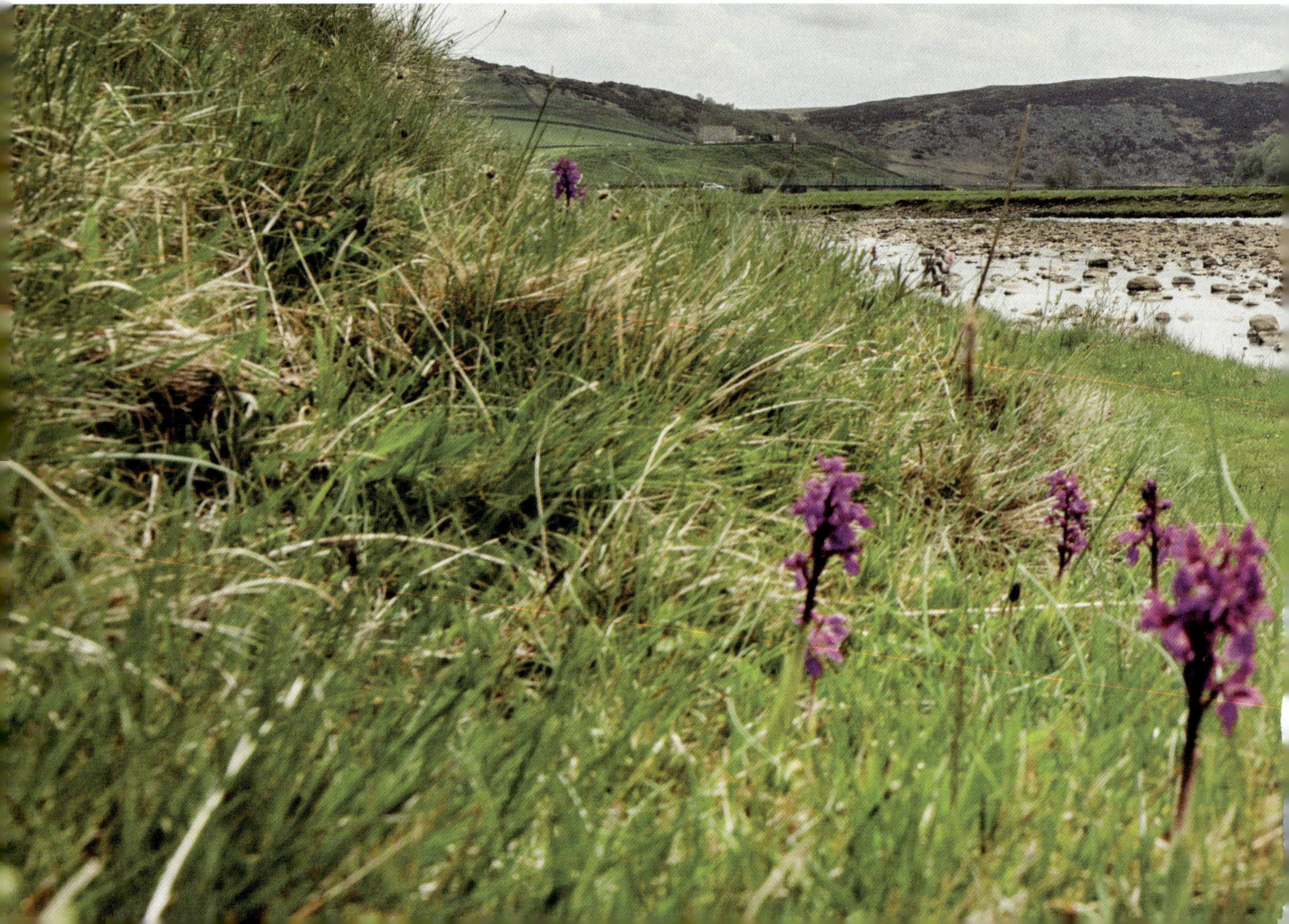

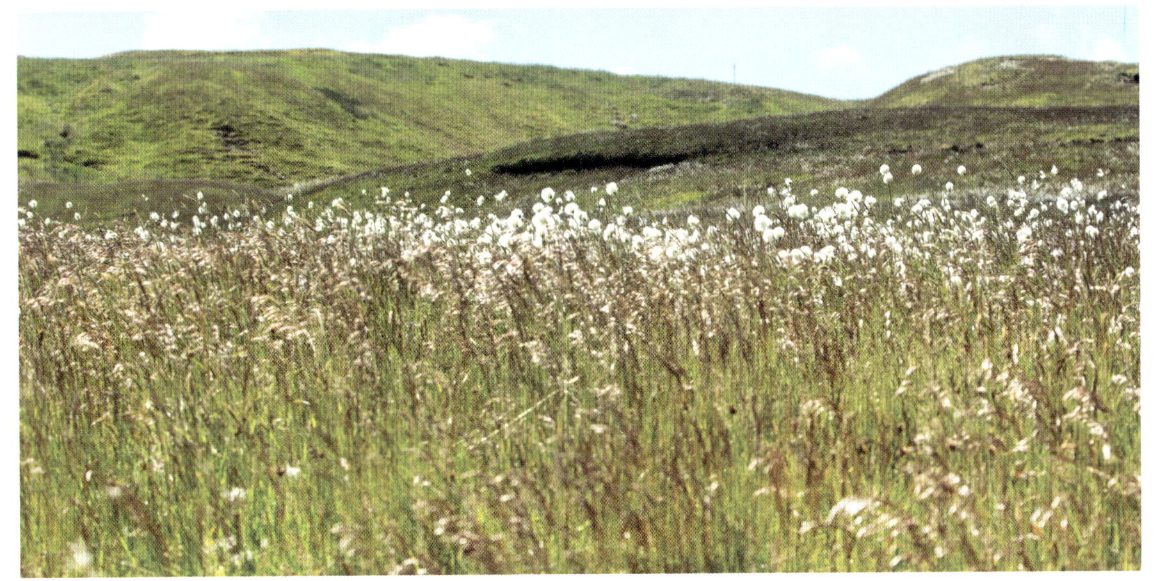

*North Pennine wild flowers: wild thyme, left; cotton grass, above; and below,
orchids on the banks of the River Tees*

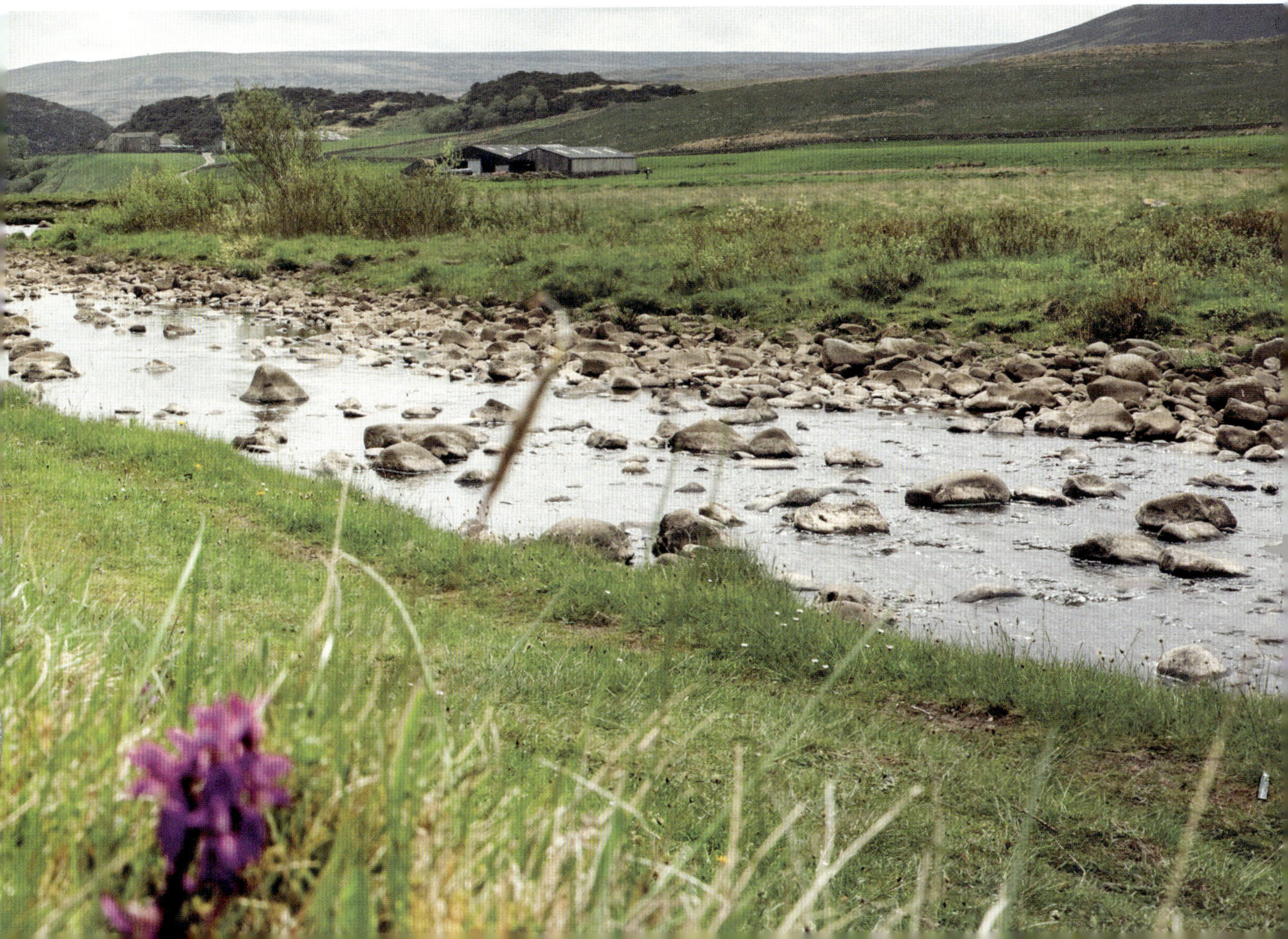

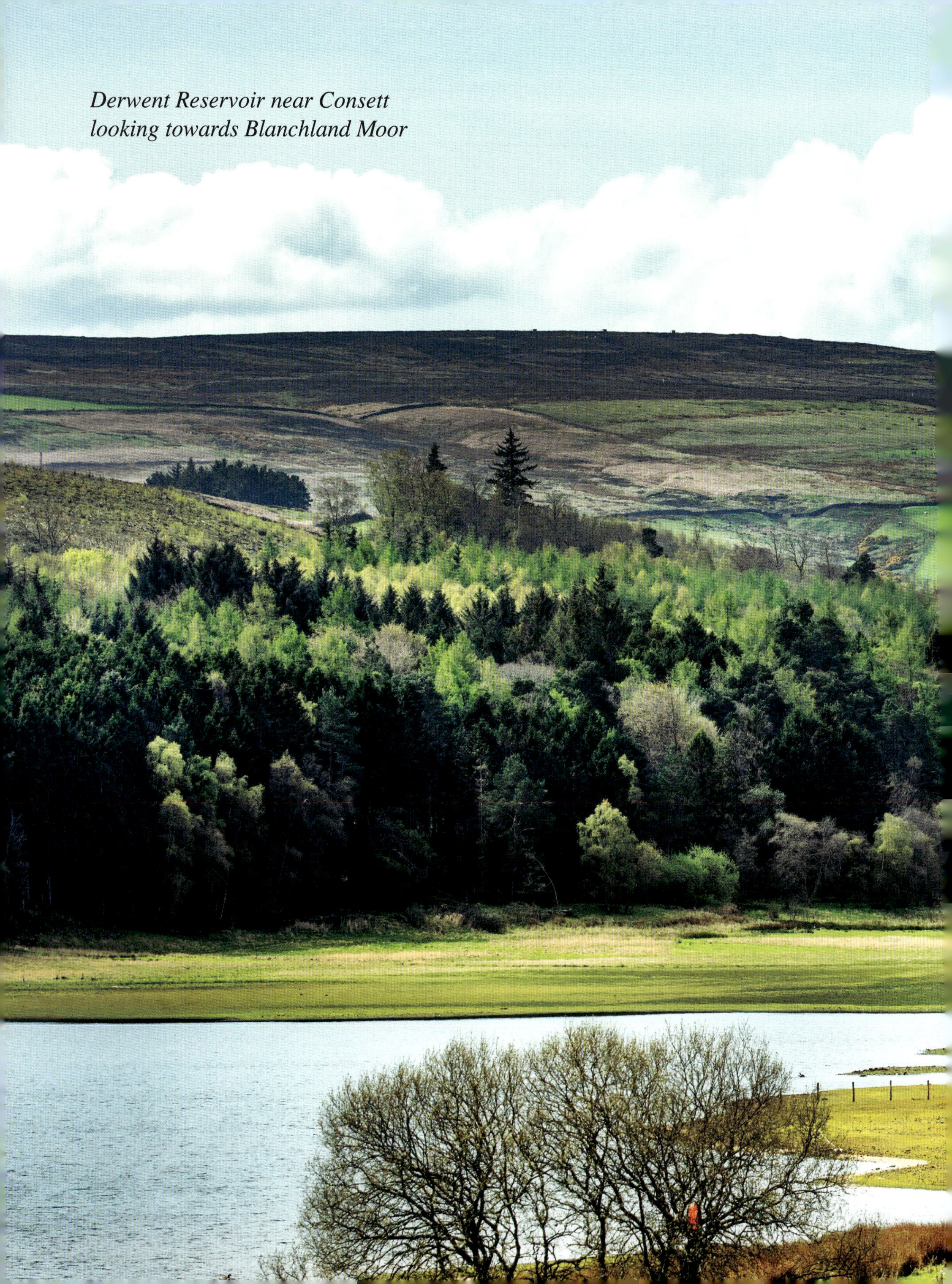

Derwent Reservoir near Consett
looking towards Blanchland Moor

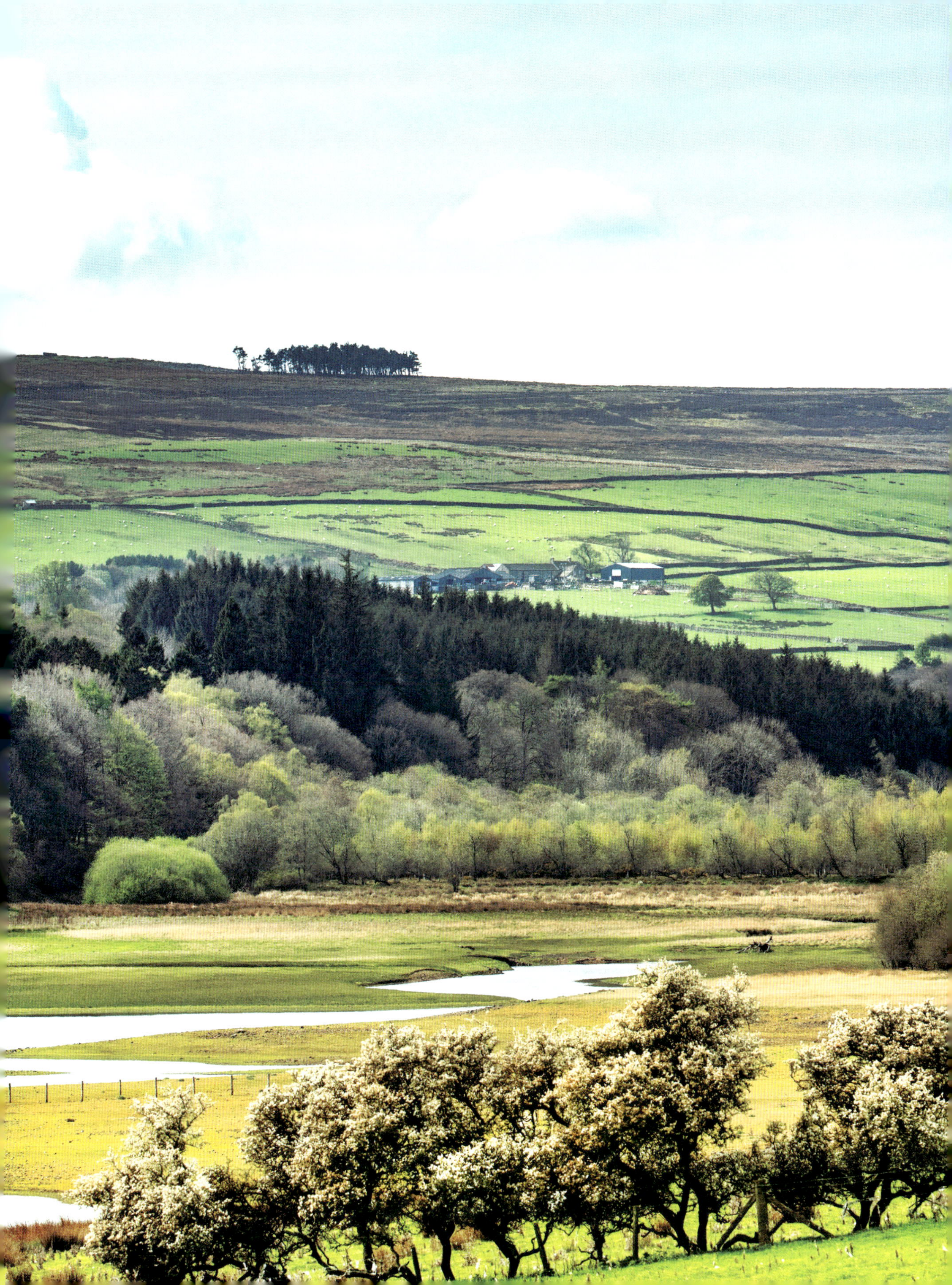

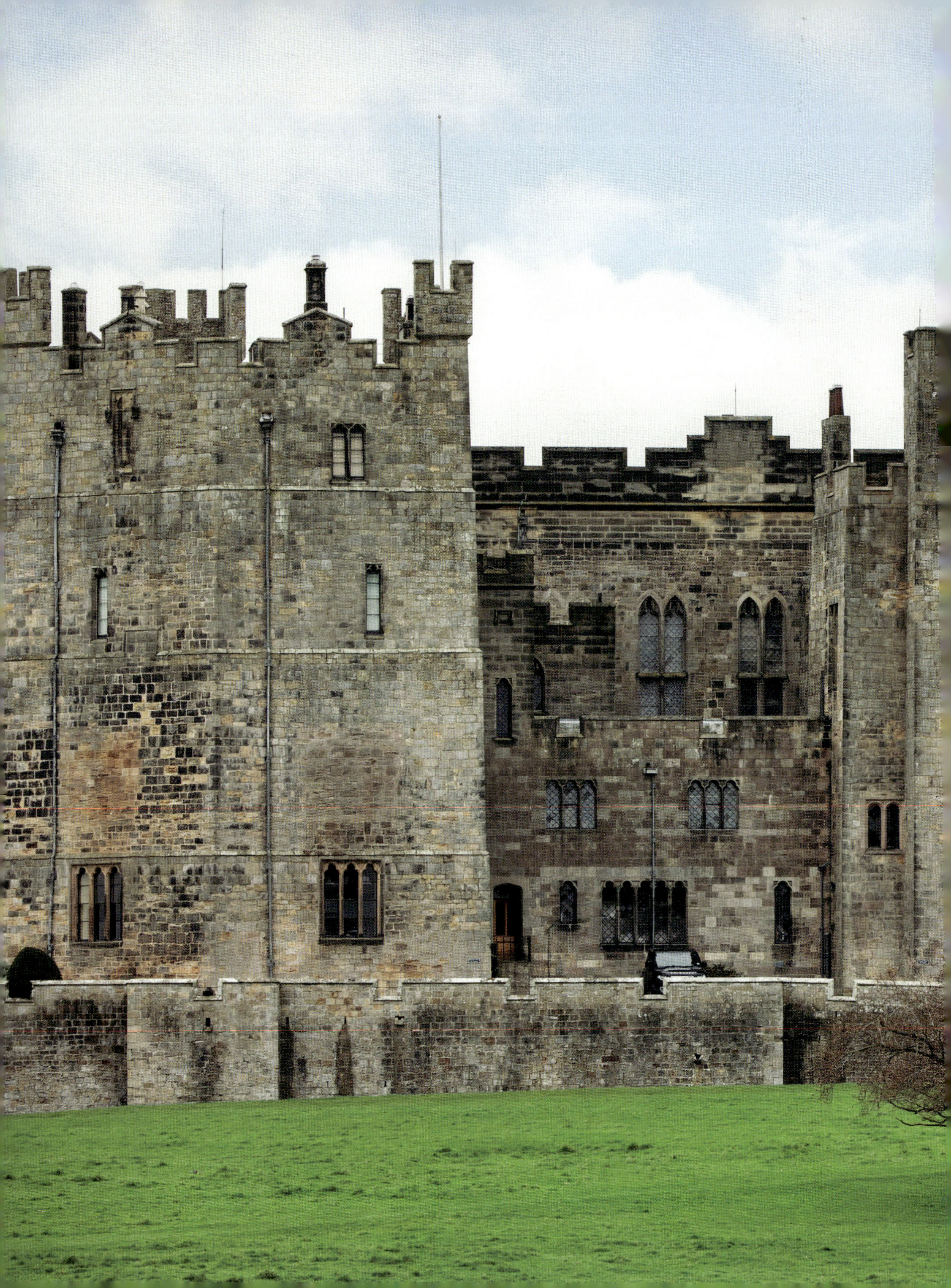

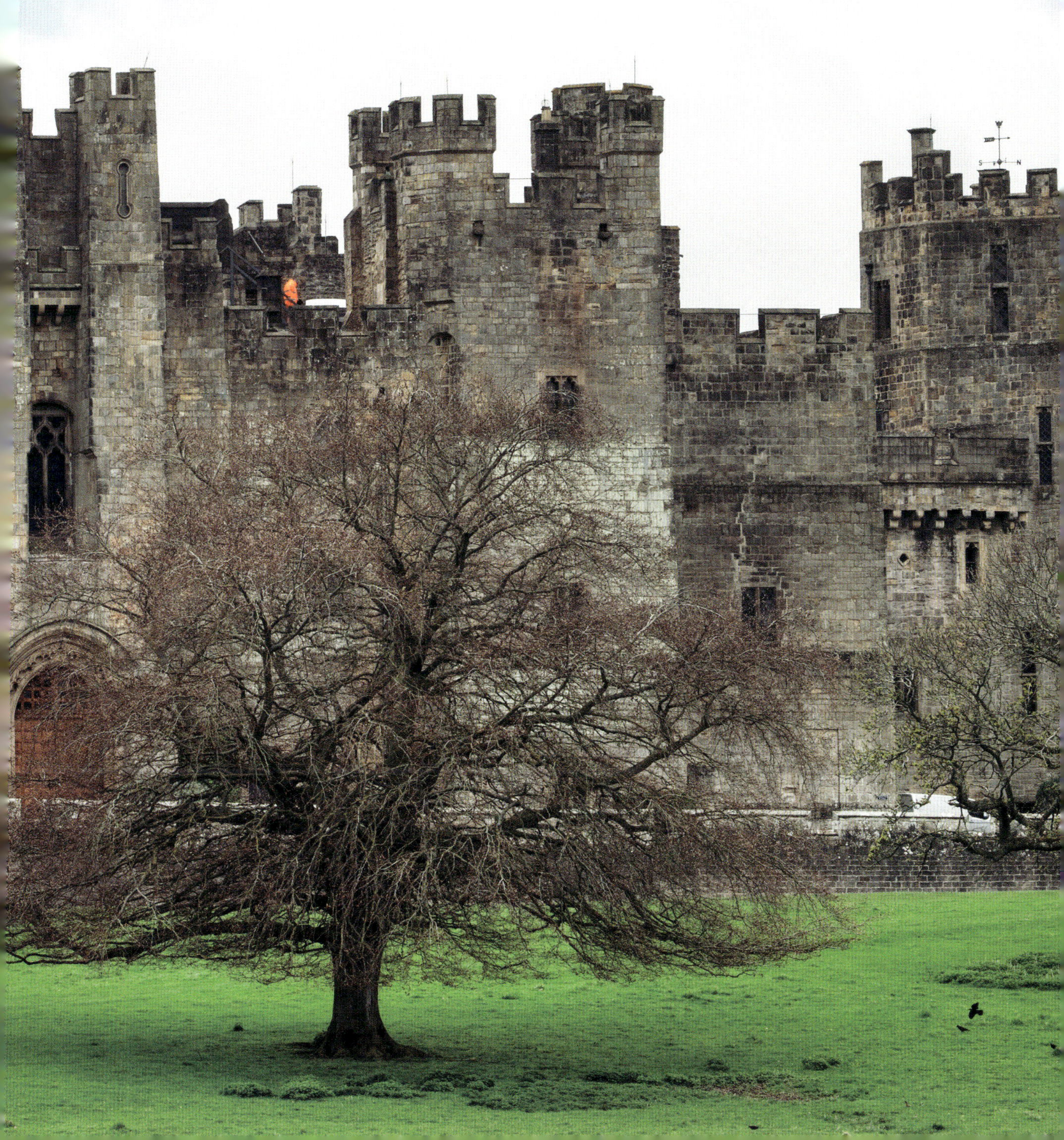

14th century Raby Castle, seat of the Barons Barnard. Raby Estates own much of Upper Teesdale and its estate properties are recognisable by their traditional whitewashed walls

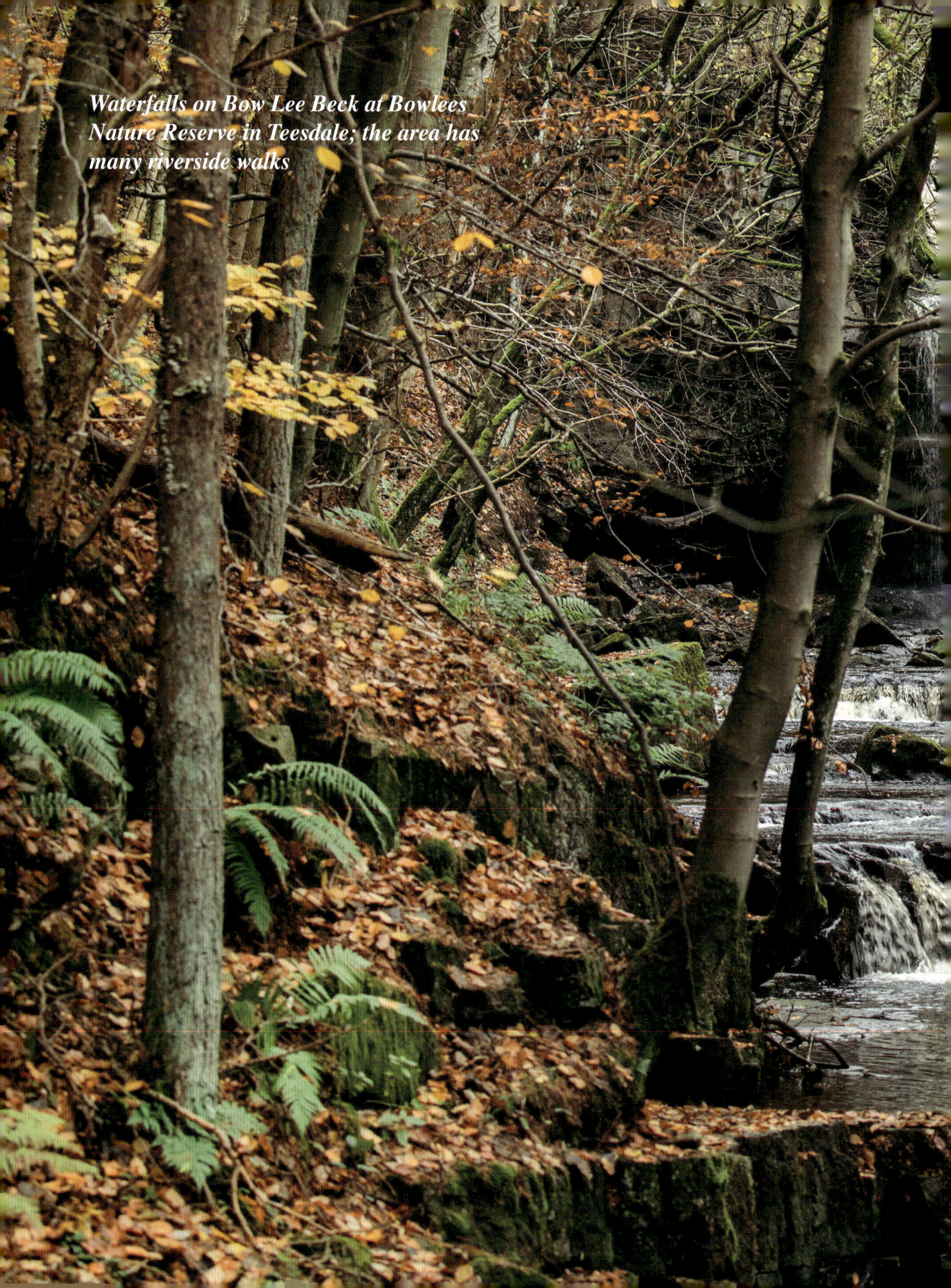

Waterfalls on Bow Lee Beck at Bowlees Nature Reserve in Teesdale; the area has many riverside walks

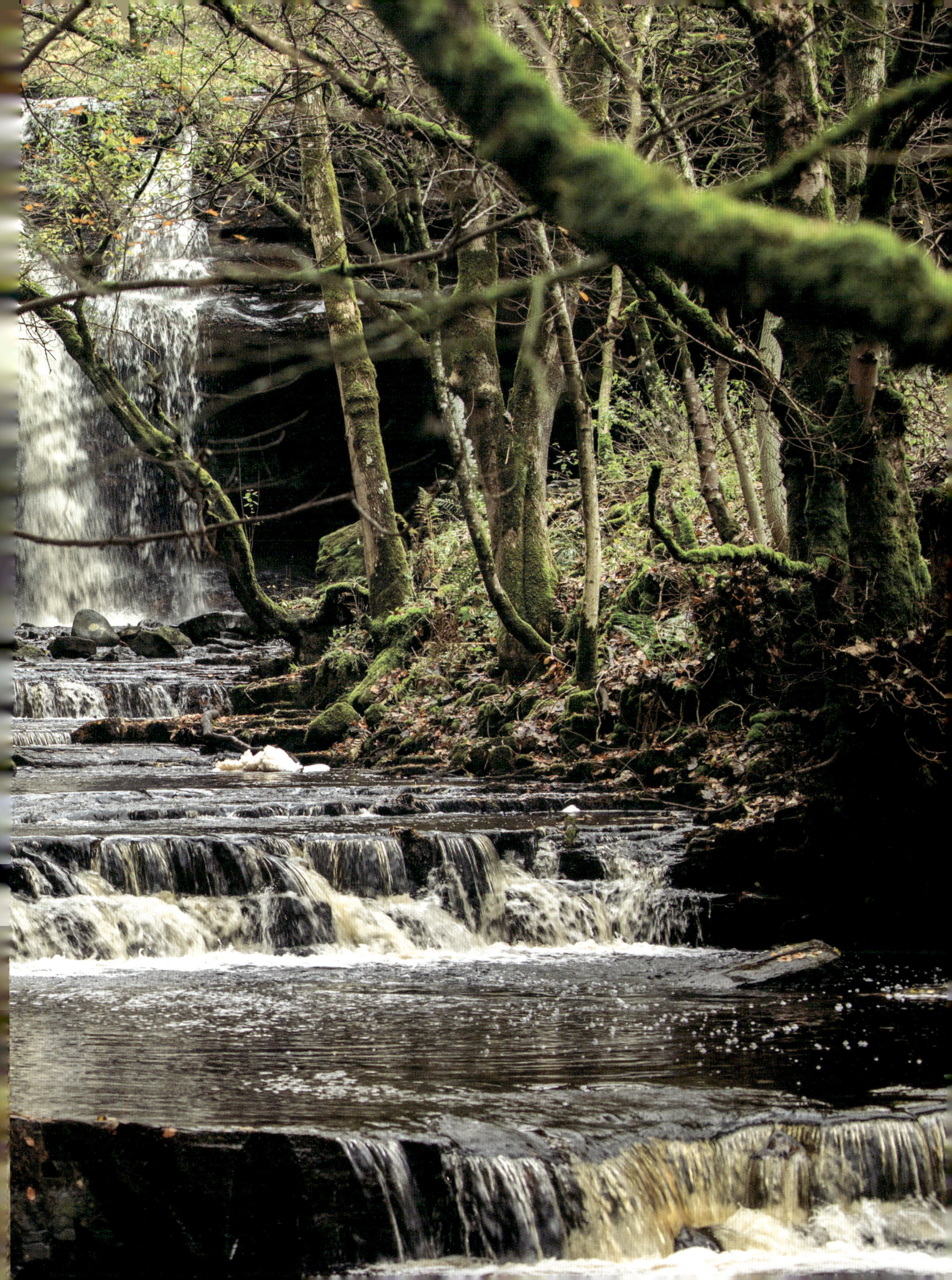

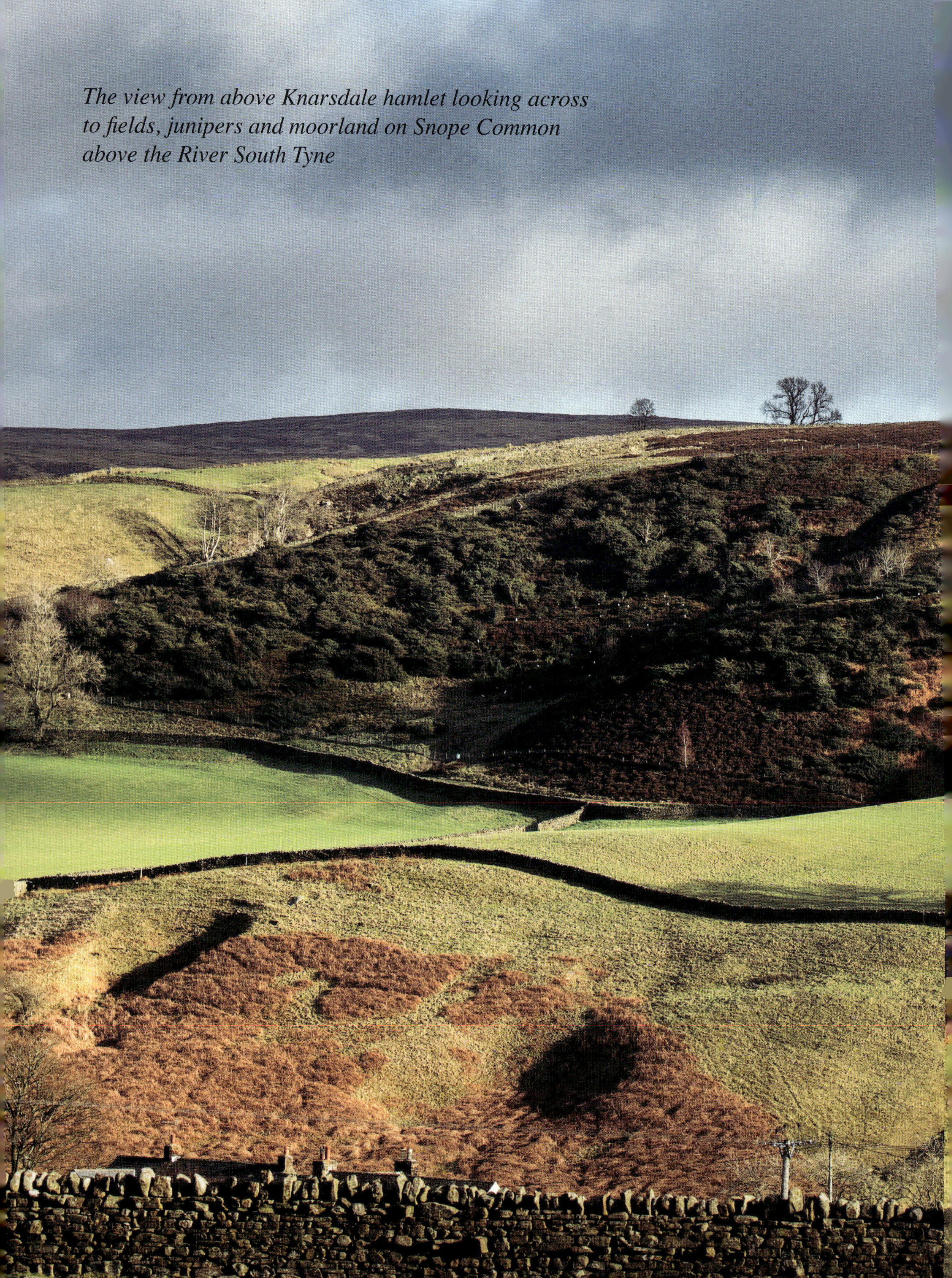

The view from above Knarsdale hamlet looking across to fields, junipers and moorland on Snope Common above the River South Tyne

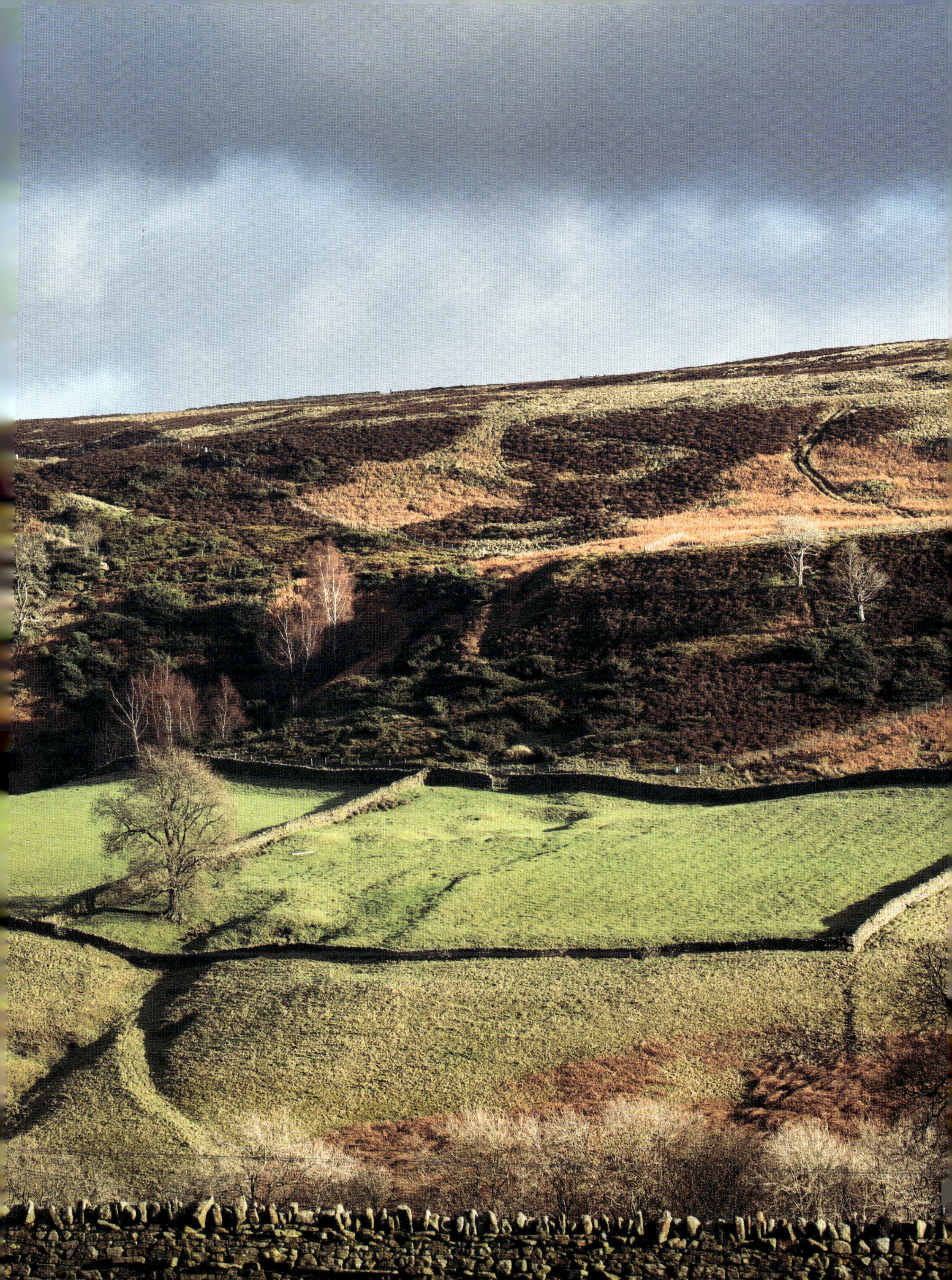

Photographer's Notes

Equipment Used: I use a Canon 5d Mark IV SLR with a 100-400 f4.5L USM prime zoom lens and a 16-35 f2.8L USM lens

Pages

1. I saw this bridge years ago when looking for a house in the North Pennines and always said I would return to photograph it, but I only found it about a month before this book was published!

6. It was a matter of pride to me to walk to the top of Cross Fell for this book. This image was taken just as I set out on the walk, whilst I was still fresh!

8. Another lucky shot taken from Yad Moss when I was on my way home one evening. The colour of the sky and drifting fog in the valley are lovely. It was incredibly cold. I couldn't feel my fingers!

10. We had been for a walk at Talkin Tarn and on our way home caught the sunset over Cross Fell. My poor husband had to sit and wait for me as I took shot after shot with both my lenses. It was icy but very spectacular.

12. I think Low Force is very underrated as it is such a pretty spot and the bonus was watching these brave kayakers go over the falls. Rather them than me! I also love to see High Force from the Pennine Way side of the Tees as you get better views of the falls.

14. It's almost impossible to get an image that does justice to High Cup. From the top or as here on the way up? I like this one because it shows the shape of the valley, the Whin Sill outcrops, and has lovely light with the drifting clouds.

16. The cherry trees alongside the River Eden in Appleby are so beautiful in spring, it's an idyllic scene and a dream for a photographer.

18/20. I find Hadrian's Wall really hard to photograph to successfully capture the height and scale as well as its position in the landscape.

24. I had done very little night photography before and none of fireworks so this was something of an experiment. I wanted to show the town of Alston too. This is the only image in the book taken using a tripod.

26. Alston vies with Buxton as the highest town in England but unlike Buxton it is much smaller and very rural, with masses of character. It isn't an unusual sight to see horses ridden down the part cobbled main street.

36. So many images are just lucky captures. I was driving home after a shoot in Bowes when I decided to take a different road and came into fog starting to cover the sun. I love the starlings and redwings flying above the trees.

38. I couldn't believe the perfection of this reflection. Shortly afterward a dog dived in and ruined it but I must confess I wanted to dive in myself!

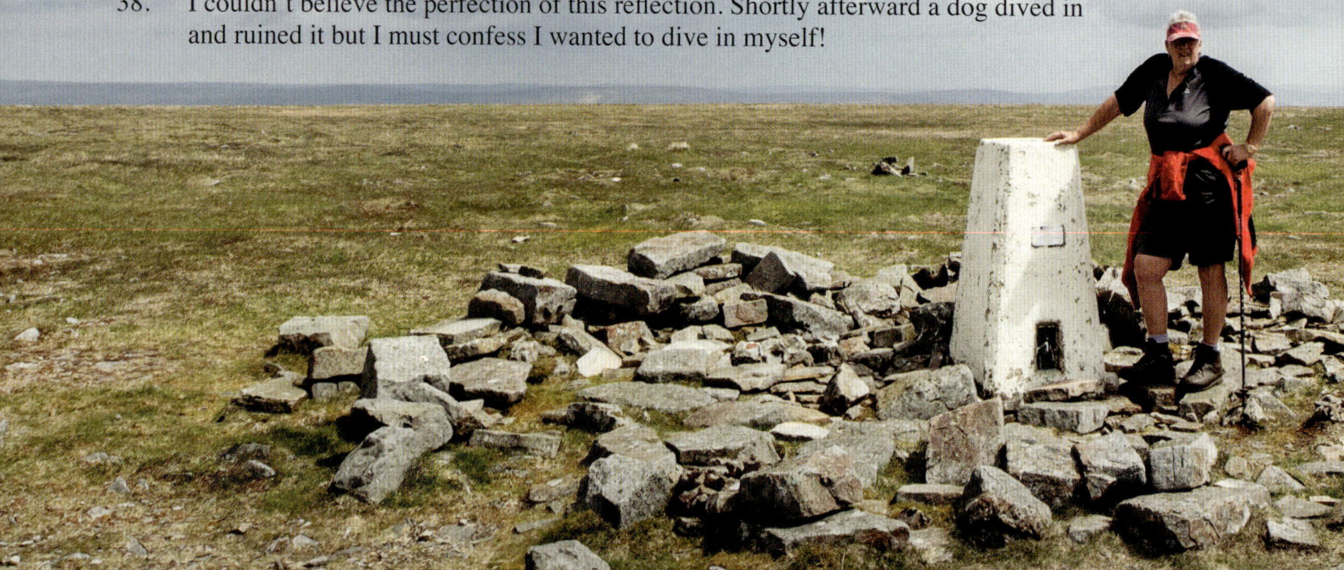

50.   I clambered about on the rocks beside Cauldron Snout, being a bit scared I might slip… but it was the camera I was most worried about.

56.   Blanchland is a 'chocolate box' pretty village, yet on a sunny late spring day there was no one there! Amazing.

60.   Hartside experiences every mood of weather possible. On many occasions the fog in the Eden Valley below makes for great images but the views are spectacular too.

62.   It was a huge surprise to me and to many people that there are several ski runs in the district!

64.   It must have been fate. I took this image three years before we moved into this house. Even then I recognised it was a special place.

66.   I do think Penrith could make more of its castle ruins and history.

68.   I pass this valley each time I travel to Penrith and every time it presents a different mood.

70.   I find it hard to believe looking at the source of the Tyne and the Tees that they become such huge and important rivers downstream, and also that although the sources are so close together they join the North Sea 35 miles apart.

76.   Completing the walk is on my list for this year.

78.   I loved seeing the smoke coming from the cottage chimney. It was about -6 at the time so I wanted to get home and light my own fire.

82.   One of my favourite views as I come over the hill from Tynedale to Teesdale.

98.   You often come across lonely chimneys up on the fells, adding unique character to the landscape.

102.   The road to Geltsdale beyond this point was completely iced up and it was tricky keeping my feet just to get this shot but I love the trees and the invitation to hop over the stile and walk.

112.   The hares were so fast and changed direction without warning making it hard to get a good shot.

114.   This amazing little tree is at the bottom of the road near my house. Wind-bent is an understatement.

116.   Strange how mining remains can look so attractive. The stone walls just frame the humps and bumps.

120.   The atmosphere of this stone circle is remarkable. There is often no one there and the stones stand invincible and silent. It is a magical place.

122.   There is a nice little café with outdoor seating just by the castle walls so this is probably the laziest of all my images as I was sat down with a cappuccino at the time! I did have to move to get the shot of Wild Boar fell and the wayside orchids though.

126.   My editor had mentioned seeing this abandoned house when she visited the area so I wanted to make sure I went there too. It's incredibly atmospheric. It's a beautiful spot but it must have been a hard life here.

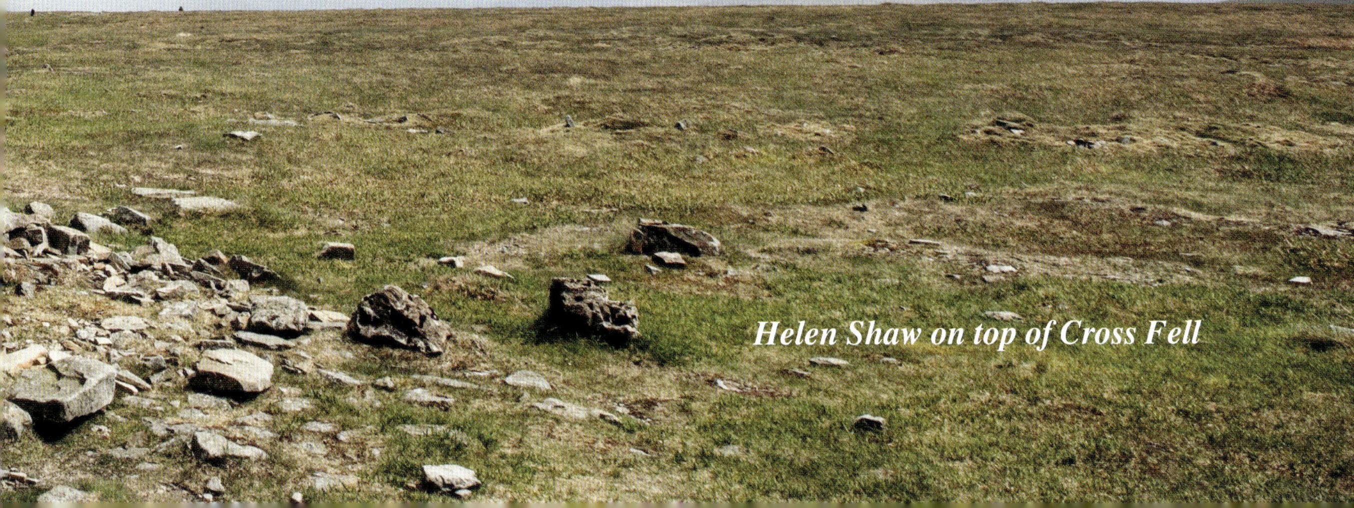

130. A local view near my house. I have to pinch myself sometimes that I live in such a stunning place.

142. I took this image when the Helm Wind was blowing down from Cross Fell. I could barely stand up at times. You can see the helm cloud on the fells above the valley.

148. Don't you just want to get out there and travel that empty road?

150. Imagine these caves lit with candlelight whilst servants brought delicious food and drink and the river babbled away beneath you. Yes it's a folly but what a delightful idea.

152. There are so many moods of weather and such frequent changes in the North Pennines. Here it was pouring with rain in the distance but I was standing in sunlight. I got very wet shortly afterwards.

156. Someone commented that this would be a good cover shot for a murder mystery. To me it is so typical of the wonderfully atmospheric landscapes I live amongst.

158. These falls are found on a perfect little walk up the River Nent from Alston. It's like a little secret glen here.

160. Morland is one of the pretty villages in the Eden Valley and in spring is a total delight.

164. I took this image from my garden. How lucky am I?

166. There is a large scheme to clean the water that emerges from old mines in the Nenthead area. Improving our rivers is vitally important. But to be honest, locals have been swimming in the rivers for years and there is a lot of debate about the scheme.

168. Low sunlight is such a useful tool for a photographer! I love the textures in this shot.

170. As I'm writing these notes there is a blizzard and drifting snow outside my window. It really can snow up here! Fortunately it was a warm summer day when I visited Shap Abbey, but they have some wild weather there too.

178. I absolutely love this image. The bent trees and the clouds drifting below, the sunlight on the fell, I can almost hear the silence of the day I took this picture.

180. The bees were so busy on the wild thyme that I could hear buzzing all around. In summer the cotton grass can make the fells look like it has snowed. And orchids grow casually on riverbanks and verges. Wonderful.

182. Derwent reservoir is quite close to Consett so it is a popular place to visit. On the day I was there plenty of anglers were catching lots of fish.

190. I felt very proud indeed to stand on top of Cross Fell. It's a tough walk from any direction but essential if you live in or visit the North Pennines. Luckily I chose a perfect day. It is well known for 110 inches of rain a year, dense fog, fierce winds and heavy snowfall!

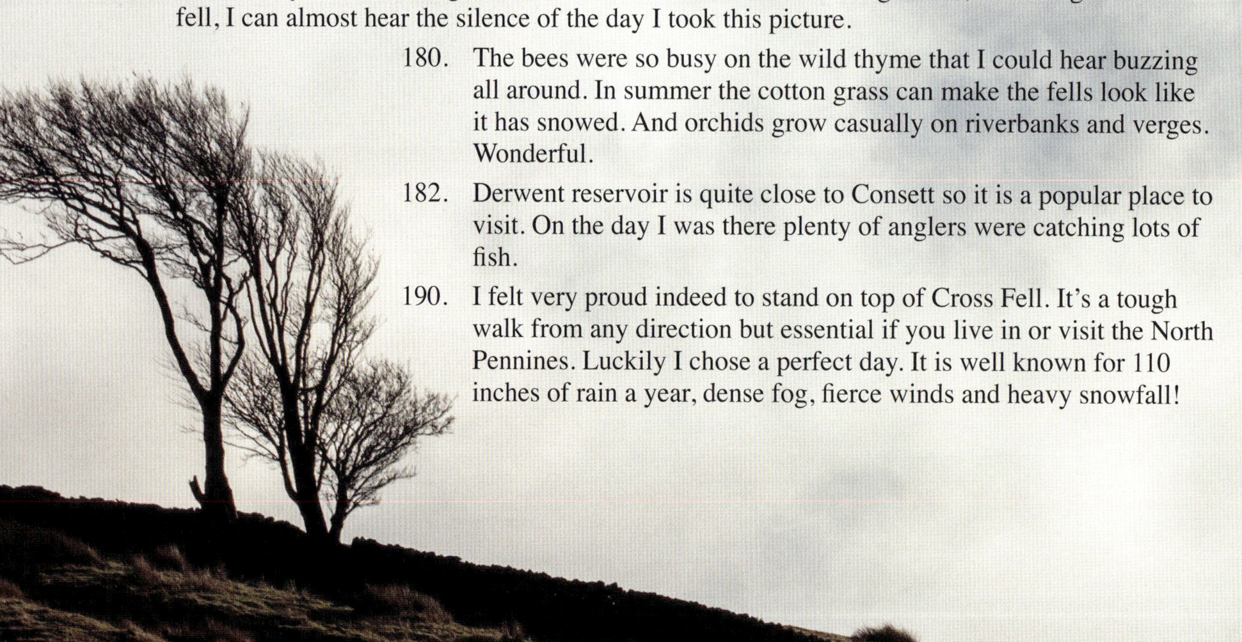